SEEN AND UNSEEN

COMPANIONS
ON MY
APPALACHIAN
JOURNEY

MARGY,

Enjoy!

Paul

PAUL FITZ-PATRICK

Wasteland Press

Shelbyville, KY USA
www.wastelandpress.net

Seen and Unseen Companions On My Appalachian Journey
by Paul Fitz-Patrick

First Printing – July 2013
ISBN: 978-1-60047-884-0
Library of Congress Control Number: 2013943786

Printed in the U.S.A.

0   1   2   3   4   5

CONTENTS

To follow along more accurately with Paul Geary's journey go to www.nps.gov/appa and you'll find the public domain maps which these were borrowed from. Click on the Official Appalachian Trail Brochure Map and it will be easier to follow along with his journey.

CHAPTER ONE

Top Down

Springer Mtn., Georgia - 2160.2 miles. That's what the sign reads on top of Mt. Katahdin, in Maine. It's a long way to hike and it was something Paul Geary always wanted to do, but never had the time to try it before the summer of 1995. However, the summer of 1995 presented Paul with a new set of circumstances because he was without a job and had plenty of time on his hands. Paul wasn't sure what life had in store for him, so he asked his wife and kids if he could take six months off in order to decide what was in their future.

His wife, Laura, was very understanding and she said yes because she knew the previous three years had been a challenge for him. The kids, however, were a bit reluctant to let Dad go.

The Geary family lived in Brandon, Florida, which is a suburb of Tampa. They have three children; the oldest, Theresa, being 13-yrs.-old and the youngest, Steven, being seven. Daniel was their middle child and he was 11.

Daniel was the only one who thought Dad should hike the Appalachian Trail because he knew his Dad loved to hike and camp, plus he realized that Dad needed to do something "awesome." The other two kids also knew their Dad liked to camp because on their semi-annual camping adventures Dad used to sit around the camp fire every night telling backpacking stories from when he was younger. They liked his story of when he and Mom hiked in New Hampshire on Columbus Day weekend in 1979; that adventure got better with every telling of the story. They all eventually supported their Dad and gave in. The deal breaker was when they found out they would all get to start the hike with Dad in Maine.

In early-June of 1995, when school let out in Brandon, everyone was ready to go see Dad off. They flew to Burlington, Vermont and rented a mini-van for the drive to Maine. Dad figured he would drop some stuff off at one place along the Appalachian Trail as they got close to the starting point. After successfully finding a place on a logging road where he could pre-position some supplies they drove to Baxter State Park, which is the northern starting point of the Appalachian Trail or the AT as it is commonly referred to by hikers.

Dad was sure to get the family's reservation early for the Katahdin Stream Campground in Baxter State Park, so that the family could experience the great outdoors. He was fortunate to get a campsite because the campground was so popular; the person who took the reservation information mentioned that there were only five sites left.

Those who felt up to it would hike with Dad to the top of Mt. Katahdin, which is a little over a mile high. On the day of the hike they all wanted to hike up Mt. Katahdin, so Dad was happy they would all have the experience of hiking up the highest mountain in Maine. He left his backpack at the campground, so that he could help if any of the kids fell behind. The hike up and back took eight hours, which included a one hour lunch break at the summit. He wasn't concerned with time that first day because he just wanted to spend time with his family.

Laura made dinner that night in that Paul would have lots of cooking opportunities over the next six months. The kids slept well that night because they were exhausted from the trek up Mt. Katahdin.

He had copied down a prayer from a book of prayers in the church library and he brought it along because it seemed fitting for such a journey. He planned to read it frequently on his trek, so he read it out loud before going to sleep on that first night of his Appalachian adventure:

"Lord Jesus Christ be my companion, guide and protector during my journey. Keep me safe from all danger, misfortune and temptation. During my journey surround me with Your holy angels and keep me safe from seen and unseen dangers. Grant that I may carry out my plans and fulfill Your will. Help me to see the beauty of creation and to comprehend the wonder of Your truth in all things. By Your divine power grant me a peaceful and successful journey and safe arrival and please Lord, guard and protect my family while I'm away and be their constant companion in all things. In You I place my hope and trust and it is You I praise, honor and glorify, together with Your Father and Holy Spirit, now and forever. Amen."

The next morning the Geary's would go their separate ways. There were hugs and kisses and even some tears as Laura and the kids returned to Burlington, Vermont to catch their return flight to Tampa. Before returning to Burlington, however, they would make a couple stops in between to visit friends of theirs from past military assignments. The Geary's lived in Northfield, Vt. back in the early to mid-1980s, when Dad taught Air Force ROTC at Norwich University, which is about 12 miles south of Montpelier. Laura and the kids would visit some friends from their Norwich days as they drove back to Burlington, Vermont. Their friends, the Farmer's, were now living in Waterville, Maine which was less than 150 miles south of Baxter State Park.

Paul, on the other hand, would continue his hike through "The Wilderness," which was the next 100 miles of his Appalachian adventure. People who hiked "The Wilderness" generally recommend bringing 10 days' worth of supplies for that portion of the hike. However, he didn't want to carry all that weight and that's why he pre-positioned some things about halfway into the wilderness hidden alongside a logging road. He hoped his supplies would be undisturbed.

If all went right Paul would see his wife and kids just prior to Christmas, which was more than six months away. He planned to average 12 miles a day. Some days he would cover more ground and some days he would cover less. The Presidential Range in the White Mountains of New Hampshire would fall in the latter category. He hiked "The Whites" many times before, but never alone. He wasn't trying to break any records; he just wanted to challenge himself and commune with nature and God for several months.

Paul's plan was to use shelters built by the Appalachian Mountain Club (AMC) whenever possible; AMC shelters, for the most part, are about a day's hike a part. If he couldn't find space in a lean-to, which was very possible during the summer months, he would use his backpacking tent.

Leaving from Mt. Katahdin in late June has its advantages. Black Fly season is over and the days are long with lots of sunlight.

Paul remembered how Black Flies could make your life miserable. One such time was when he went backpacking in the Presidential Range in early June, the Black Flies bit right through his clothing. He remembered trying to eat with a mosquito net on his head, but he found it took his appetite away. Black Flies, on the other hand, generally don't bother you when it's raining, so he was happy to see it rain and there was lots of rain on that particular backpacking trip, which was just prior to his entering the Air Force in 1976.

Paul had originally planned to go backpacking in Wyoming that summer with a classmate of his father's. However, the Air Force moved his report date up about a month, so they both agreed on the Presidential Range in New Hampshire's White Mountains instead of the Wind River Wilderness area that is southeast of Yellowstone. That trip in early June of 1976 was the first time Paul stayed in an AMC hut. It was a five day hike and they stayed two nights in huts and his tent for the other three nights.

Long days and more sunlight meant you could cover more miles if you fell behind. If it's hot during the day and you don't feel like hiking, you can rest and continue hiking in the early evening before the sun goes down. All in all Paul figured it would be a grueling hike. It had been many years since his last backpacking trips and probably 20 years since his last six-day hike. That six-day hike was his longest and now he was going to try a 2,160 mile hike in about 180 days. The hardest part would be the time spent away from the family. Theresa was going into 8th grade, Dan the 6th, and Steven would be starting the 2nd grade in the fall. Laura, a registered nurse, had a job close to home, so if she had to be there for the kids, she could be.

Having hiked up Mt. Katahdin the day before with the kids, Paul's starting point on the second day was the Katahdin Stream Campground. When the family left, he started hiking at about 11:00 a.m. and he was sure he could make it to the Abol Bridge by about 4:00. The Abol Bridge is where a lot of the professional photos of Mt. Katahdin are taken for postcards and coffee table books. More importantly the bridge provides a safe way for hikers to get over the Penobscot River.

Since Paul didn't reach the bridge until 6:00 p.m., he decided to stay there for the night. The small store at the north end of the bridge had some goodies to eat and a tent site to rent. He hoped he planned his expenses right for the six month adventure. He sold his unused leave in order to finance the trip. Laura would let him know when he got low on funds and whether he should stop; he didn't want to be any more of a burden to Laura and the kids than he already was. Paul marveled at the view of Mt. Katahdin as he ate his dinner there near the Abol Bridge. It was no wonder photographers chose that location for their photo shoots. The scene was magnificent.

Day three started out with Paul entering into what is officially called "The Wilderness." It is some of the remotest parts on the AT. If you look at a road map there are no roads between Baxter State Park and Monson. Paul was fortunate, however, to find an old logging road, so that he could pre-position his supplies. He wondered if he would make it through the 100 miles. That's what he asked himself.

Or, would he just give up and go home? If he made it half way in, he would have just as far to get back out. He began to wonder what the record was for the shortest trip on the AT.

Paul remembered reading about someone who started out in Georgia, on Springer Mountain, and they gave up when they got to the Chattahoochee River, which was about 50 miles from where they started. He hoped he did better, but he knew for sure that he wanted to make it at least to Pine Grove Furnace, Pennsylvania, which was the official half-way point on the trail.

Continuing on, he made it to Rainbow Ledges from where there is an impressive view of Mt. Katahdin. He couldn't believe he'd only gone 10 miles from Abol Bridge because it felt like he had hiked 20 miles. It was only 5:00 p.m., so he decided to go the extra four miles to the Rainbow Stream Lean-to. Getting there late, he set up his tent, filled his water bottles, ate trail mix, slathered on insect repellant and went to bed. That ended his third day. (30 FK)

It was raining lightly on the fourth day, so Paul skipped his morning coffee and ate a Pop tart along the trail. Never a fan of Pop Tarts, it didn't taste bad after three days of hiking. Some hikers go cold their entire trip. In other words, they rarely use their stoves. They eat cold food and whatever anyone offers them along the way. Paul had planned to try that as much as possible, but he didn't think he would have to resort to that already on his fourth day. In order to conserve weight he brought a stove that used solid fuel tablets. The problem with it is that you can just about get water to boil with the solid fuel tablets and then just as the water boils the fuel is done. It does save weight, but he loved hot coffee in the morning. He was also concerned that if he couldn't boil water then he couldn't make his water safe to drink.

Paul started out the day at 6:00 o'clock and he decided to make it to the Nahmakanta Stream Campsite which is listed at 44 miles from the top of Mt. Katahdin. Hiking could be pure drudgery and the thrill of it runs out after a while, but he didn't think it would get that way in the first week. It was fun as a 21-year old when he was hiking with his friend Stacy, and definitely more fun when he hiked with his wife. Hikers passed their time in various ways, but he passed the time reciting the rosary, other prayers, and singing, but he only sang when he was sure no one could hear him.

Of course he could say an entire rosary which was fifteen decades, but he generally broke it up. He remembered back to when he first got stationed at MacDill AFB and a friend of his, by the name of Glen, who wasn't very religious, walked in on him one day as he was eating lunch and saying the rosary. He asked Paul to explain it to him because he found it interesting.

Paul explained the rosary as best he could to Glenn. He explained that the rosary has Jesus as the center and that you are praying both with and through Mary to Jesus. He explained to Glen that the rosary was divided into three parts, each focusing on the life of Jesus.

There are the Joyful Mysteries which center on God becoming man in the person of Jesus. It starts with the Angel Gabriel telling Mary that she will conceive the son of God, and that particular decade is known as *The Annunciation*, followed by Mary visiting her cousin Elizabeth known as *The Visitation*. And then there is the birth of Jesus, known as *The Nativity*. The Nativity is then followed by *The Presentation* at the Temple and lastly, *The Finding of Jesus in the Temple* when Jesus was 12. Paul went on to explain that each decade of the Joyful Mysteries began with an Our Father, followed by ten Hail Mary's, and then one Glory Be. Then he also went on to explain the Sorrowful and the Glorious Mysteries to Glen.

The "Sorrowful Mysteries" Paul said are about Jesus' Passion, in other words His death. They start with *The Agony in the Garden*, which was when Jesus prayed in the Garden of Gethsemane before he was handed over to the authorities, followed by *The Scourging*, *The Crowning with Thorns*, *The Carrying of the Cross*, and finally *The Crucifixion* on Cavalry. The "Glorious Mysteries" which Paul went on to explain further were basically the events which happened when Jesus arose on the third day. The Glorious Mysteries are broken up into the following five: *The Resurrection*, *The Ascension*, *The Descent of the Holy Spirit*, *The Assumption of Mary into Heaven*, and *The Coronation of Mary.*

'That's a lot of prayers," Glen said to Paul. Paul thinks he responded he responded to Glenn "well if you don't think you can finish those all in one setting they recommend you break them up as follows. You can say the Joyful Mysteries on Monday and Thursday, the Sorrowful Mysteries on Tuesday and Friday, and the Glorious Mysteries on Wednesday, Saturday and Sunday."

"That's confusing" Glen said to Paul, and Paul said, "It's not that hard when you think about it. All Christians should know the Our Father because Jesus taught that to His Apostles. The Hail Mary, which is based on Luke's Gospel, is very easy once you learn it."

"And how about the Glory Be?" Glen said.

"The Glory Be, as I see it, is a petition to God and it goes like this 'Glory be to the Father, and to the Son, and to the Holy Spirit, as it was in the beginning is now and ever shall be, world without end. Amen."

'How is that a petition?"

"Now those are my words and I don't know that I'm explaining it right, however, we are asking God to make things right according to His design."

When Paul focused again on the present, and not something that happened a couple years back, he said the "Sorrowful Mysteries." As Paul finished the decade he remembered back to that conversation with Glen and saying, "Oh, there's one more prayer I forgot to tell you about. You end the rosary with the *Hail, Holy Queen* and it goes like this: Hail, Holy Queen, Mother Mercy, our life, our sweetness, and our Hope. To thee do we cry, poor banished children of Eve; to thee do we send up our sighs, mourning and weeping in this valley of tears. Turn then, most gracious advocate, thine eyes of mercy toward us, and after this our exile, show unto us the blessed fruit of thy womb, Jesus. O clement, O loving, O sweet Virgin Mary! Pray for us, O Holy Mother of God that we may be made worthy of the promises of Christ.

Focused again, Paul said the "Sorrowful Mysteries" again, but this time he paid better attention to each part of the Passion of Christ. Doing so, Paul was better able to understand what Jesus went through nearly 2,000 years ago. The Rosary was always reassuring to him with its combination of prayers. Before the hike, he often said a decade of the rosary after climbing into bed at night. If he fell asleep before he finished, he was told that his Guardian Angel would finish the Rosary for him.

Paul wondered how many rosaries he would recite on his six month journey. He wondered how many Apostles Creeds, Our Fathers, Hail Mary's and Glory Be's he would say? He would make a mental note at the end of each day of how many Rosaries he said and would do the math when he got back home to Florida. He brought a pen and a composition journal to jot down notes, but since he couldn't stop to make a note every time he finished a Rosary he would put hash marks to represent how many he thought he completed. When he wasn't saying a Rosary, he looked at the views, and would also have thoughts of his family. One such thought early on was how many of the kids' soccer games he would miss and how many school functions he wouldn't be a part of.

Paul's thoughts frequently turned to food. He remembered back to the first marathon he ran in Chicago in 1977. As he was running along Lake Shore Drive in the first Mayor Daley Marathon, he had a sudden desire for pineapples. Why pineapples? He wasn't sure, but just in case he brought some dehydrated pineapples with him. If his stash was still undisturbed at the Logging Road the next day he'd have his pineapples. If someone did happen upon his stuff then he hoped whoever it was enjoyed the dehydrated pineapples, but didn't take his water.

Paul made it to the Nahmakanta Stream Campsite by 6:00 p.m. and there were only two other hikers there with their dog. He set up his damp tent, so that it could dry out before using it again; it was still wet from when he packed it in the morning. He would let it air dry as much as possible figuring the light breeze out of the west would help it dry out. He reflected back on the day. It was his best hiking day thus far; he had gone 14 miles in 12 hours, which included a one-hour break to readjust his boots and pack. He felt like he could have gone farther, but he didn't want to overdo it. It was far more important to build up his stamina for "The Whites." He had a freeze-dried Turkey Tetrazzini dinner, talked with the other hikers, and marked his Rosaries for the day in his journal. He said 15. Paul smiled to himself thinking it was a good idea to save the math until the end because his mind faded. He did decide however, to mark the mileage at the end of every day by putting the miles used in his Appalachian Guidebook followed by FK to represent the number of miles From Katahdin. So the miles listed at the end of every day reflected the number of miles from the top of Mt. Katahdin. He also decided to use the same road abbreviations from his Appalachian guide, so that meant ME101 translated to Maine Route 101. (44 FK)

In the morning the sound of the other hikers woke him up. One of them had a Sierra Cup tied to his backpack and it clanged with every move he made. The fact that the guy's black Labrador retriever was panting heavily outside Paul's tent didn't help either. He thought about bringing their dog Heidi along for the trip because she loved walks.

Heidi was a mixed breed Terrier, but she looked like a small German Shepherd. Paul wouldn't have felt right taking her away from the kids, but she would have been good company, but not good for getting rides whenever he would have to hitchhike. He wondered how that worked for hikers with their dogs. Wouldn't people be reluctant to pick a hitchhiker up if they had a dog?

Paul made it to the logging road by 8:30 a.m. and his stuff was where he left it. The dark brown trash bag blended in with the surroundings. He was thrilled to drink some fresh water. Or maybe not fresh, but fresher than the stuff he had been drinking for the past two days. Of course he would now have to carry the two one gallon jugs to a place where he could dispose of them properly. He used about a quart of water out of one of the two jugs in order to wash out his Lexan water bottles. Iodine tablets take care of germs and bacteria, but leave a bad taste in your mouth and in your bottle. Since he couldn't waist fuel to boil water, iodine tablets were the logical choice.

They had water purifiers at the backpacking store, but they were a little too heavy and expensive. Hopefully, this would be the only time on his trip that he would have to carry gallon water containers. A gallon of water weighs 8 pounds, so Paul's backpack would be at least 16 pounds heavier after he put his supplies in it.

The dehydrated pineapple was terrific. It wasn't as good as fresh pineapple, but it was an acceptable substitute. It was very sweet. After taking a 45 minute break to replenish his supplies, he continued on. His goal was to get to Cooper Brook Falls Lean-to, which is just less than 60 miles from Mt. Katahdin. It was a pretty hike, but he started to miss his wife and kids. He wondered how their visit went with the Farmers. Fortunately, the Rosary helped him take his mind off them and he thought about the Holy Family instead. On the decade of the Rosary called the *Visitation*, Paul felt insignificant compared to the 14-or 15-year old girl who was pregnant and had to walk 60 miles, by some estimates, to help her cousin Elizabeth, the mother of John the Baptist. His trek didn't seem so difficult when he thought of it in those terms.

At 7:30 p.m., he arrived at the Cooper Brook Falls Lean-to. His guide book talked about a swimming hole in front of the shelter, so Paul decided to brave the cold water for a swim to get off the day's sweat. Two brothers who were camping there for the night kindly offered him some Spam & cheddar cheese on Pita bread and Paul gladly accepted. It reminded him of a day-hike he and Stacy took back in 1975 during their senior year in college. The difference was that on that day the temperature was about 10 degrees with a brisk wind. He had wanted to try out his new backpacking stove for a future winter backpacking trip, so he used that opportunity with Stacy. He and Stacy fried Spam and melted longhorn cheddar cheese over the top and had it on Rye bread. However, the Pita bread seemed more logical than rye bread, so he would have to be sure to mention that in his journal entry that night.

He remembered back to that hike with Stacy and how the SPAM tasted so delicious; of course any warm food would have tasted delicious at that point. Stacy also brought a bottle of his father's red wine to wash it down. That was one for the gourmet magazines Paul mused. Which wine do you serve with Spam?

Paul had not stayed in an AT shelter yet, so this would be his first night in a lean-to. At about 9:00 p.m. more hikers arrived. He was glad he didn't have to set his tent up, but the stench from one of the thru-hikers nearly convinced him to set up the tent before he fell off to sleep and he slept well despite the odor. (60 FK)

Day 6 would be an easy day, or at least that was the plan. Everyone was up early and the first hikers were off by 6:00. They planned to do in two days what took Paul five and that caused Paul to wonder what fun that was. How about stopping to smell the roses? Of course, back in college, Stacy accused him of that very same thing. Since that time he came to appreciate the small things in life. When he was passed over for promotion to Lt. Colonel there was a girl in his class at the Armed Forces Staff College who suffered a miscarriage. When Paul heard that, his problem seemed small in comparison. He wondered if she was ever able to have a child.

He began to think he pushed it too hard the day before because he wasn't ready yet for a sixteen miler. He was tempted to call it a day at the East Branch Lean-to, but he still had several hours of sunlight. He did, however, stop to take a nap and soak his feet in the river. He felt much better after the nap in the lean-to. Sometimes you just need to take it easy. Back when he hiked in the White Mountains with Mr.

Arthur, his father's classmate, Mr. Arthur use to get slower and slower and would say he needed to take a break. Mr. Arthur used to take a salt pill along with his break and it was like magic how he had a burst of energy. Paul felt better and began hiking again. The nap and the foot soak worked wonders.

The vertical climb along the trail was noticeable. When he took his break at the East Branch lean-to it was 1,240 feet above sea level according to his AT guide and the Logan Brook Lean-to was listed at 3,655 feet. He didn't really notice the elevation changes the two days prior, but for some reason it now required more effort and more water. He used the last of the water from what he had pre-positioned, so he would have to get water at the creek near the lean-to. He would now have to go back to using the iodine tablets and have that yucky taste in his mouth.

Paul got to Logan Brook Lean-to by 7:00. He was glad he didn't stop for the night at the previous lean-to because he at least made it further than the guy in Georgia, the one who only lasted 50 miles. There was still space in the lean-to, so he spread out his sleeping pad and sleeping bag in the empty space. There was actually room for two. One of the hikers was boiling water and asked if he wanted some, too. Not eager to resort to the iodine tablets, Paul said he would love some hot water.

The people you meet on the trail are very interesting. There are actually all types, but when it comes down to it, everyone puts one foot in front of the other when they walk. In other words, people are all the same, or as Paul's boss used to say, "Same wine, different label." It's rare for anyone, especially thru-hikers, to still be awake when the sun goes down, but he fell right to sleep. (71 FK)

Day 7 marked the longest backpacking adventure Paul had ever done. The one he and Stacy did on the AT along the Blue Ridge Parkway had been his longest one up until that point. That trip was just six days. So, in itself this was his personal best. Would he call it quits when he got to Monson, Maine, the first city once you leave The Wilderness? Or will he press on? That was the question on his mind when he left the Logan Brook lean-to at about 7:00 a.m. He began to have doubts about whether he was up to it all. What was he thinking when he planned this? Was he just upset with the Air Force or with God? He still had well over 2,000 miles to Springer Mountain Georgia and thinking about it made it hard for him to concentrate on saying the Rosary, so he said the St. Michael prayer in order to get his focus back again:

> *"Saint Michael the Archangel, defend us in battle. Be our protection against the wickedness and snares of the devil. May God rebuke him, we humbly pray; and do Thou, O Prince of the Heavenly Host - by the Divine Power of God - cast into hell, satan and all the evil spirits, who roam throughout the world seeking the ruin of souls. Amen."*

He seemed to be able to concentrate again after saying the St. Michael Prayer. It always seemed to help; it proved to be his "armor" like St. Paul said back in the 1st Century AD.

Paul stopped at about the 77-mile mark because he felt a stinging sensation on his neck just to the right of where his backpack strap crossed his right shoulder. He swatted where the stinging was and when he did that the stinging sensation became worse. It turned out, he had swatted a hornet that was on his neck; since he thought there might be more where that one came from he quickened his pace to a jog until he was sure he was in the clear. He wasn't sure if the stinger was still in his neck or whether hornets even leave their stingers once they've stung. He would ask someone in camp that night to have a look for him.

The descent to the Carl Newall lean-to was a welcome change. He normally didn't like downhills, but it didn't seem as difficult as some of the other downhill's he had done over the years. There was no one staying at the shelter when he got there and he considered staying for the night, but when he looked at his watch it was only 12:10, so he continued on. He did rest for a while at the lean-to and he drank some water and had a handful of trail mix. Paul read the guidebook while he was sitting in the lean-to. He had his back up against the lean-to wall and his legs out in front of him. According to the guidebook it looked like the next few miles had some interesting things to see. He put his backpack on, secured the hip belt and then the shoulder straps and he continued on at 12:35 and only made it about 30 feet when he tripped over a rock sending him head over heels.

Paul laid there for about 10 seconds when he felt another stinging sensation on his neck, so he hurried to his feet and started swatting at something.

CHAPTER TWO

Frankly Speaking

As he stood there for several seconds swatting away he realized he was only swatting at air and there was nothing there. He realized then that the stinging sensation was probably only a pinched nerve in his neck and it must have had to do with the way he fell. He was glad no one happened along to see him swatting at the air, because they would have thought there was something wrong with him.

It had been a gradual downhill hike ever since Paul left the Logan Brook Lean-to. He passed through two areas that didn't allow camping on the trail. The first was called the Gulf Hagas Trail and was listed as being 82 miles from the top of Mt. Katahdin. The guidebook said that some people call it the "Grand Canyon of the East." It was beautiful, but not like the "real" Grand Canyon in Arizona. After visiting the real Grand Canyon some years before, Paul thought you would have to have a vivid imagination to compare it to the real Grand Canyon in Arizona. The second protected area he passed through was about 84 miles from Mt. Katahdin and it was a nature conservancy called "The Hermitage." According to his guidebook the area's White Pines provided a lot of the masts for ships back in the days of the American Revolution.

As he stood looking at the trees a hiker caught up to him; he was a boy who appeared to be in his early 20's. He stopped alongside Paul and said, "Can you imagine one of those as a mast for a ship?"

Paul replied, "Yeah, but I just can't imagine getting it from here to the coast. How could they move something that big, especially back then?"

"Well," said the hiker, "the Penobscot River isn't far from here as the crow flies; so they probably took the logs to the Pleasant River and floated them down to the Penobscot River and then on to where they were building the ships along the Atlantic coast. That's my guess," said the hiker.

He nodded but didn't say anything. He just took in the grandeur of the moment. Then he heard the other hiker say, "It smells good here doesn't it?"

"Yeah, it does. I love the smell of pine trees." He wondered why the kid didn't seem to be in any hurry like most kids were and why he didn't have much gear with him. "Where are you headed?" Paul asked.

"I'm headed south. Would you like a hiking companion for a while?"

"Sure, Paul said," wondering who this guy was and why he was so friendly. Before he could introduce himself the boy put out his right hand.

"My name is Frank and I'm from Plattsburg, New York."

"Nice to meet you Frank, I'm Paul and I currently live in the Tampa, Florida area. Where are you headed?"

"I'm just going as far as Monson. Where are you going?"

"Well, when I started this adventure I thought I'd go all the way to Georgia, but now I'm having doubts as to whether I can do it. My mind thinks I'm still 19 or 20, but my body is telling me I'm 42, so I'll see how I feel when I get to Monson."

"Well, maybe something will happen between here and there that will make you decide to go all the way."

What did he mean by that? He wondered. "Frank, what do you think will happen between here and Monson?"

"Paul, I believe, no I know, that something miraculous will happen."

"What do you mean?" Paul replied.

"Well, let me start by saying that anything is possible with God. By the way, hornets don't leave their stingers in you. Let me have a look at the sting, turn around." Turning around with his back towards Frank, Frank patted Paul on his right shoulder and said, "It looks OK."

"Did you see me get stung?" Paul asked, wondering how Frank knew what he was thinking.

"No, like I said anything is possible with God. God has blessed me with the chance to walk and talk with you for a while."

"What do you mean?" Paul asked, feeling uneasy from all Frank's questions and comments.

"Let me explain as best I can. I'm not really from Plattsburg, New York. Well, I would have been if I was allowed to be born; that is where I would have lived. You see, my mother decided to have an abortion when she was 10 weeks pregnant."

Paul thought that this must be some kind of a practical joke, but who would plan such a thing? Frank continued talking before he could think of anything to say in response.

"You see God let me be here with you to help you. You were wondering what God's plan is for you, so he sent me along to ease your anxiety."

"What anxiety? Paul asked.

"You have anxiety over having to get out of the Air Force because you were passed over for promotion. Plus, you have anxiety over how you will provide for your wife and kids."

Paul couldn't believe what he was hearing. Everything Frank said was true. "Well, if what you say is true, what is God's plan for me?"

"Paul, you will have to figure that out for yourself. You see, God has let me visit you to reaffirm that He knew you in your mother's womb. He knew me, too, when I was in my mother's womb, but He didn't interfere with her free will. I can tell you what God's plan was for me. Do you want to know?"

"I'd love to know," Paul said.

"God had a simple plan for me. I was to be riding on a school bus one day when the driver had a heart attack. Since I would have been sitting in the row behind the driver because he was keeping an eye on me, I would have taken over the wheel and the effects of the crash wouldn't have been so bad. However, seven children died on that bus. One of the girls would have grown up to be an anesthesiologist and one of the boys would have grown up to be a priest."

Paul reflected on that a while and then he said, "God's plan for you was very simple."

"Paul, don't overlook the simple things in life. God's plan is perfect. Actually, I would have grown up to be a New York State Trooper. I would have turned my life around because of what I did that day and the admiration I would have received for my actions when the driver had his heart attack."

"I'm sorry Frank; my comment didn't come out quite right. Can I ask you a question?"

"Yes, go ahead." Frank said.

"Why did God send you in particular to help me? Can you answer that?"

"Maybe I can. Think back to 1983 when you were on your first field trip to Plattsburg Air Force Base with your ROTC students. When you got off the Grand Isle Ferry from Vermont, several ambulances passed you by and you said a simple prayer to God. You said "Dear God help whoever it is that those ambulances are for and guide the medical staff responsible for their care. God heard your prayers. He also hears the Rosaries and prayers you've been saying."

"Frank, is there anything I should know?"

"Paul you already know it. God's plan is perfect and if people would only follow His commandments, live the Beatitudes, and honor His Son and Spirit, and then everything will be okay."

"It's easier said than done in this busy world," Paul said. "Frank, you know I believe what you told me, but something doesn't compute. That accident was back in 1983, only 12 years ago. Why is it you look at least 20 years old?"

"Paul, remember, anything is possible for God. He must have thought I needed to look this age. Now if you don't mind, God is letting me go to where I would have grown up. I want to go see Plattsburg and Lake Champlain now."

"Frank, I thought you said you were going to Monson."

"I was prepared to go there if you wanted me to go, but I thought you might want some time to reflect on what I've shared with you."

"Frank, here's the thing. You always dream of something like this; being able to talk to God, or at least knowing what God's plan is for you, but I can't think of what I want to ask."

"Then take your time and when you can think of those things or questions you can ask God in prayer. And if it is God's will, He will help you."

"So is that it? Will I ever get to see you again?"

"Paul, you'll see me again if it's God's plan. Remember Paul that God's ways are not your ways."

Sticking out his hand, Paul shook hands with Frank. Frank turned around and started walking back in the direction they had just come from.

Paul had lost all track of time and wasn't sure where he was. He had climbed in elevation while he was talking to Frank, and that he was sure of because he was sweating more and was also a little bit out of breath. He stopped and sat down on the front of a large boulder so he didn't have to take off his backpack. His sleeping bag rested on the granite rock and it felt good to take the weight off his knees. He then took out his journal and jotted down some notes. Paul was thirsty, so he took out his Lexan water bottle for some water. There was something different about his water bottle. It was full. It should have been half full because he remembered drinking some and pouring some over his neck after he got stung. That's curious, Paul thought to himself. How can that be?

Despite being out of breath he felt good; his legs weren't tired, so he decided to continue on to the Chairback Gap Lean-to which was about three miles further. The one good thing about Frank's visit was that he felt reinvigorated, both physically and spiritually. Paul wondered if he will have any other visitors sent from God. He still had time to fit in a Rosary, especially since God liked them.

It was 6:45 p.m. when Paul walked up to the lean-to, but there were no spaces left, so he found a place for his tent. After he set up the tent he decided on dinner. Looking into his backpack, there were three entrees left, a Chili Mac, a Beef Stew and another Turkey Tetrazzini. He decided on Chili Mac. After finishing, the not fully re-hydrated Chili Mac, he decided to buy a different stove in Monson. Paul couldn't get the water hot enough, so his food wasn't fully re-hydrating and to make matters worse he felt like he chipped a tooth on one of the macaroni, but when he checked he couldn't feel anything out of place.

Paul wondered how people could do the whole AT with a solid fuel stove or no stove at all for that matter. He decided to buy a white gas stove in Monson. He remembered the stove he had when he first went backpacking with Stacy. It was called a Phoebus and it was a monster of a stove invented for mountain climbers in cold conditions. He wouldn't need one quite that powerful for the rest of his trip, but he would see what was available in Monson.

As darkness approached he got into his tent and reflected back on the day. It was hard not to be in awe of what he witnessed, but Paul still wasn't sure it wasn't somebody's idea of a practical joke. However, how could you explain the water bottles? He completely drank one of his water bottles and half of the other one and then he put them both back in his pack until he passed a water source. When he went back into his backpack to get the water bottles to fill them, the bottles were completely full. That was miraculous. Paul wondered how long they would continue to do that. He wondered what Frank did to make that happen? One thing was for sure, it would be great if he never had to use the iodine tablets again.

Paul drifted off to sleep, but not before thanking God for sending Frank. He also thanked God for his full water bottles. (88 FK)

The activity around the shelter began at about 5:30 a.m. The hikers in the shelter were laughing about something. There was one other tent besides Paul's and it belonged to a young couple. At least that's who he saw outside the other tent as he was zipping his up for the night. He made warm coffee as best he could along with warm oatmeal. Never a fan of oatmeal at home, it always hit the spot on the trail, even warm oatmeal as opposed to hot oatmeal was somewhat satisfying. He decided to save his last Pop Tart for a mid-morning snack.

It started to rain once Paul packed everything and he was thankful for that. It's no fun rolling up a wet tent, not to mention the extra weight you have to carry. He remembered the time he went family camping when he taught at Norwich University. Their brand new 10' x 12' canvas tent got soaked the last day of their long weekend getaway. It must have weighed 75 pounds, but since they were car camping he just threw it into the back of their min-van and tried to dry it out once they got home. However, it rained for a solid week after they got back to Vermont, so it was impossible to dry it out in their basement.

The tent was still damp when they returned it to the store and fortunately there were no questions asked. In its place they bought a big nylon dome tent that one of the boys thought looked like Darth Vader's helmet. They still use Darth Vader's helmet for family campouts.

Paul started hiking at about 6:30 a.m. and he was concerned the rain could cause problems. He was planning to go most of the way to Monson, but decided he would be cautious because the guidebook mentioned how treacherous the footing could be for the next seven or so miles if it rained. It was a bit tricky, particularly going downhill and it was almost as if someone sprayed something on the rocks and tree roots to make them more slippery. He didn't mind all the up hills as much as he did the down hills. He figured that all his years of jogging had taken its toll on his knees. He remembered again the Chicago Marathon and how he put mole skin on the bottom of his feet and the tips of his toes for cushioning. When he completed the marathon he couldn't get the mole skin off. He had to soak them in the hotel tub for 30 minutes in order to get the moleskin off his feet.

The combination of the up hills and the treacherous footing made it a low mileage day. However, it was a good Rosary day. In fact, this might be Paul's best Rosary day. When the rain let up a bit he munched on his Pop Tart and gulped his nice clean water. Paul liked hiking in the rain because it kept him cooler. He didn't wear his rain gear because it was pointless since you could get just as wet from perspiration if you left your jacket on. Then when you stop hiking for the day you wouldn't have a jacket to keep you dry.

Paul noticed he was now thinking ahead instead of thinking about finishing in Monson and that was a good sign. It must be due to Frank's visit the day before and the fact he knew God is with him on his journey. Checking his watch it was almost 1:45, about seven hours since he started. He had plenty of sunlight left and the rain slowed to a mist. Therefore, instead of stopping for the day at the Cloud Pond Lean-to he continued on to the Wilson Valley Lean-to, which was still nine miles away. There was just one more uphill and then a short downhill portion, which was followed by relatively flat area for the last five miles. It stopped raining, so he decided to go faster when he reached the flatter terrain.

There weren't many hikers on the trail, so when he got to Slugundy Gorge he decided to go for a swim in the watering hole. Paul saw a description of it in his guidebook and it looked like a nice place to stop. The water was a bit cold, probably from the rain, but it felt good to change out of his wet clothes. He rinsed out his shorts, T-Shirt and socks and put on a new set of everything. He tied his wet clothes to the back of his backpack and then checked on his water bottles. They were still full, so he took a generous gulp or two to wash down his trail mix which consisted of peanuts, M&M's, and raisins. Paul continued on, hoping the rest break would revitalize his legs. It did.

There were three other hikers when Paul got to the Wilson Valley Lean-to at 7:30. Two were using their tent, so he could have a place to stay in the lean-to. It would be a Turkey Tetrazzini night. The lone guy in the lean-to offered the use of his stove and he mentioned he was going back to Monson the next day. He said he was just out for a two-day hike. Paul wondered if this was another visitor sent by God and he kept waiting for him to interject some tidbit of information into their conversation that only God would know, but he never did. As soon as Paul finished dinner the lone guest put away his stove and went to bed. So much for another heavenly companion, he thought to himself.

Paul added a few notes to his journal and said another rosary. Since he didn't bring rosary beads he kept track in his head and then he would put hash marks in his journal to represent a Rosary said. Some people find the repetition of the prayers, especially the Hail Mary's, monotonous, but Paul found them soothing. He started saying the Rosary again when he was passed over for promotion. It was always a part of his afternoon drive home. He didn't pray it in the morning because he listened instead to the Catholic Radio Station in Tampa. The radio station was called WBVM and BVM stood for the Blessed Virgin Mary. He fondly remembers listening to WBVM every morning on his way in to MacDill AFB. *Living His Life Abundantly* came on the radio at about 6:30 a.m.

He credits that radio show for starting him on his journey back to God. The host, Johnette Benkovic, was always very upbeat and Paul couldn't ever remember hearing a Catholic talk so strongly about their relationship with Jesus. In fact, the name of her show was based on John's Gospel Chapter 10 verse 10, "…I came so that they might have life and have it more abundantly." Listening to that show on the way to work "charged his battery" and got him through the day.

His lone roommate was snoring, so he put in his ear plugs and rolled over saying his nightly prayers. His Guardian Angel finished his Rosary for him because he fell asleep. (104 FK)

Paul was awakened when he heard his roommate's boots walking across the wooden planks in the lean-to. It was 6:00 a.m. and the day Paul would be able to talk with Laura and the kids. Of course, he still had to get to Monson and a pay phone.

His roommate offered the use of his stove again, so he accepted. Paul came to find out the lone roommate's name was Arty and he was from Portland Maine. He came up for two days since he had to work on the 4th of July, which was exactly a week away. He said the place would be crawling with hikers and campers that next week, so when his boss asked for volunteers to work on the 4th of July he accepted, providing he could get these days off. Arty packed up his gear after Paul was done with breakfast and then he headed out. He left 30 minutes after Arty and it was just a little over 10 miles to Monson.

Not long after starting out Paul came to Big Wilson Stream, which he had to ford. Before he crossed the stream he watched the water as it passed by. When he was certain that he wouldn't get pulled by the current he crossed the stream after he took his boots and socks off. Despite the rain the day before Paul crossed Big Wilson Stream with ease.

Next was Little Wilson Falls, which according to his guide book had one of the highest waterfalls on the AT. Instead of taking a break at the falls, Paul decided to continue on without a break. He'd rather get to Monson so he could call his wife, re-supply, and buy a backpacking stove.

The last two miles to Route 15 were downhill, so it was quick going. Once he got to Route 15 it was about four miles into town. Paul tried hitchhiking into town.

It had been years since Paul hitchhiked. He and Laura had hitchhiked in order to get back to North Conway after their harrowing backpacking experience in October 1979. Paul thought, however, that they must be more accustomed to hitchhikers in the area. He started walking towards Monson because he knew he would be less likely to pick up a hitchhiker if they were just standing there and not making any effort. After about 20 minutes an El Camino picked him up. It was just like his neighbors El Camino in Brandon, except for the color.

The owner of the El Camino, whose name was Pete, said he was just checking his place on Moosehead Lake. He was checking it for all the visitors he'd be having for the 4th of July weekend. Pete was from Old Town, where they made the canoes. In fact, he worked in the Old Town canoe factory. Paul shared a story with Pete from when he and three high school buddies visited the canoe factory in Old Town back in the summer of 1972. He and his three friends were camping at a place close to Old Town, so they went for a factory tour. When they showed up at the factory and said they wanted a tour, some guy gave them a brochure and said, "Feel free to look around, but be very careful."

Pete was nice enough to drop Paul off right at the Pie Lady's. The sign said to leave your backpack outside, so Paul did as the sign requested. Fortunately, there were no other backpacks, so he figured he would be able to get a bunk. As he entered the lobby a bell over the door announced his entry. Someone came right out of the kitchen and walked to the rear of the check-in counter.

"Hi young man, do you have a reservation?" she asked.

Paul said he didn't have a reservation, but hoped she had a private room for the night. He said he also needed to pick up a package that he had mailed to himself and when he told her his name, she said there were two packages for him. He wondered what the second package was.

The owner wanted to take care of the room first and then she'd get Paul his packages. They did have a private room, which included a shower and a towel. The woman's name was Sydney and said it wasn't busy, but she said the coming weekend would be very busy. So, she gave him the package he had mailed to himself. It had several freeze dried meals, a small tube of toothpaste, a new toothbrush and biodegradable soap. Sydney said that another hiker left a package for Paul, so she went and got that as well. When he opened the box there was a Svea 123 backpacking stove, an empty fuel bottle, and several packets of freeze dried coffee. There was a note attached to the stove that read, "Enjoy the <u>hot</u> coffee." The note was signed, "Frank."

"Sydney, can you tell me when Frank left this?"

'Two days ago."

So, Frank was who he said he was Paul thought to himself. The water bottles filling on their own should have been sign enough. Did he mention Stacy's Svea 123 to Frank? He may have mentioned wanting to buy a different stove because he was unable to boil water, but Paul didn't even think they made the Svea stove anymore.

Stacy had a Svea 123 for years and years and to the best of Paul's knowledge he still did. Stacy's stove was nice and compact and because of that they took it on their six day backpacking adventure along in the Shenandoah's instead of his monstrous Phoebus. That was still one of the most memorable hikes he and Stacy ever went on.

"Excuse me Sydney, where is the closest pay phone?"

"The only reliable one is in front of the General Store. Will you be eating dinner here?"

"Yes I will."

After checking into his room and getting his backpack unpacked, Paul went to the pay phone at the General Store. Using his pre-paid AT&T card he placed the call to Laura's work. When she answered and said, "This is Laura." he didn't know where to begin. "Hi, honey, this is Paul." He could hear the excitement in her voice. He filled her in on his hike, but didn't mention Frank. She said the kids were great, but missed him a lot. She wanted to know if he'd be calling back tonight. Paul knew they were at Vacation Bible School this week, so that's why he didn't call home first.

"Yes, honey, of course. Just couldn't wait until tonight to tell you I love you."

After the phone call Paul checked out the General Store. He looked to see what he wanted to buy for the next leg of the trip, but while he was there he saw one of his favorite candy bars, which was a Mallo Cup, so he bought two and went back to the Pie Lady's. He planned to go back to the General Store later to get the supplies he would need for the next part of his hike.

Next, he picked up his laundry and went to the Laundromat. There was no one else doing laundry so it was quick. He didn't bother with whites and colors he just threw everything in together and then went back to the General Store and got supplies for his next couple of days. He would be crossing US201 in about three days where he could get supplies, but his next mail drop was at ME 27, which was over 70 miles from Monson. Satisfied he got everything he needed for the next three days Paul returned to the Pie Lady's.

Dinner was great that night, it was especially heavy on veggies and fruit which was exactly what Paul had missed from his diet the previous week. After dinner he went to call Laura and the kids and they were all very excited to talk. He said he'd call in another three days if he could, but for sure when he got to Stratton, Maine.

The kids had a big map tacked to the wall in the dining room and they were keeping track of his location as best they could. Laura turned the map into a learning experience, having them not only place a sticker where they thought Daddy would be, but they had to explain why they thought that.

When he got back to his room he showered again and shaved off the 10 days of growth. There's nothing like a shave and good hot shower to make everything seem better. Some hikers don't shave the entire time they're on the trail, but he never liked the bearded look on himself. He set the alarm for 5:15 a.m. and went to sleep. The bed was nice compared to the one inch thick sleeping pad he had been sleeping on the previous nights. Paul did buy another half inch pad to make sleeping on the trail less painful. His hips were sore from sleeping on his sides. Most thru-hikers get rid of weight as they go, but he had actually picked up a couple extra pounds with the stove, fuel bottle, and foam pad.

When the alarm went off the next morning he felt refreshed. The aromas coming from the kitchen were great. The smell of fresh brewed coffee was particularly good and he had three cups. Paul had a bowl of yogurt with granola and blueberries and he bought a sandwich and some fruit from the Pie Lady, so he wouldn't have to waste time for lunch. He arranged a ride to the trail head at 7:00 a.m., so that gave him just 20 minutes to pack and freshen up. Paul was the only south bounder on the shuttle, but there were three north bounders.

It was cooler than the day before, so the hike was nice, that is until he reached the East Branch of the Piscataquis River. He had to ford the river, so he took his boots off and tied them to the top of his backpack. The water was about knee deep, so he picked up a stick he saw lying alongside the river bank. It may have belonged to one of the north bounders from the day before, but regardless of who's it was he was thankful to have it. Having lost track of the time, he realized it was about lunch time, so he sat on a boulder once he crossed the river and ate his sandwich while he let his feet air-dry.

As he put his boots back on he remembered when he and Stacy had gone backpacking in the Bridger Teton Wilderness area in Wyoming back in 1977. Stacy and he had to ford a stream, so they took their boots off and tried to toss them across. One of Paul's boots missed the bank and went into the stream, but fortunately it got caught on a stick a short way down the stream. That's why he tied his boots to the back of his pack this time instead of throwing them; the river in Maine was much wider than the stream in Wyoming.

Continuing on, he made it to the Horseshoe Canyon Lean-to by 1:45. He considered staying there for the night because it was so pretty, but he decided he had too much daylight to waste. About three miles after the lean-to, he came to the West Branch of Piscataquis River. The trail bordered the river for a couple miles and it was very beautiful.

Whereas the trail had been more or less flat since Monson, with few changes in elevation, he now began a steady uphill climb. He stopped to drink some water several times and took a generous handful of trail mix each time. It was nearly 7:30 p.m. when he made it to the Moxie Bald Lean-to, approximately 132 miles from Katahdin. It was his longest single day hike since he started; he had hiked approximately 18 miles since he left Monson.

He was too late to get space in the lean-to, so he pitched his tent and went about preparing dinner. He filled his stove, compliments of Frank, and fired it up and the sound the stove made was very familiar; it sounded like Stacy's did. It was nice to have boiling water within just a number of minutes and it was also great to eat fully re-hydrated food for a change.

Paul finished off his Chili Mac and thought about all the backpacking stoves he had had over the years. His first stove was the Phoebus, which was a birthday gift from his brother Bill. That stove was lost or stolen. He replaced that with the Coleman Peak One, which he bought in 1979 for his and Laura's backpacking trip on Columbus Day weekend. They still have that one in their garage in Brandon, but it was too heavy to bring along. Then when he went to Italy in 1980 he inherited one from his brother Dave; it was a butane stove. It was very nice because it didn't require priming and it produced heat immediately. However, Paul wasn't sure if he could get the blue butane cylinders on this trek. Lastly, he bought a two burner Coleman propane stove for family campouts. It worked very well and had lots of uses, one of which wasn't backpacking. It was nearly the size of his back pack and probably weighed 10-12 lbs. not including the propane cylinders.

After cleaning up after dinner, he jotted down some notes in his journal, along with his rosary count for the day. He looked at his map and guidebook to see what he could expect the next day. It was approximately 19 miles to Caratunk, Maine. After today he didn't think he could do it, especially with the rugged terrain. He planned to go to the lean-to after Pleasant Pond, which was a distance of about 13 miles. Then the next day, which would be Friday, he would stop in Caratunk to replenish his supplies, but not spend the night. Paul slipped into his small tent at about 9:00 and went to sleep. (132 FK)

The other thru hikers, who were all north bounders, were up early. They were all anxious to get to Monson and re-supply before they entered the 100 Mile Wilderness. He talked to two of them when they walked by his tent. They shared that they were both college students who took the spring semester off, so they could hike the AT. Paul didn't know very much about the Appalachian Trail when he was in college. He discovered it after graduating from college in 1975 and even if he had heard about it, he wouldn't have been able to take a semester off. He did, however, want to do a semester or full year in Spain, but he couldn't since he was in the two-year AFROTC program which made no allowances for time off to study abroad.

Paul started out from Moxie Bald Lean-to at about 6:30 a.m. The hike was very steep going up Moxie Bald Mountain and there was a 1,400 foot increase in elevation in the space of about two miles. There was a good view to the north and the south, but his attention turned to his family. He wondered what the kids were doing in Vacation Bible School. Theresa was a teacher's helper because she loved that kind of stuff. The boys, Daniel and Steven, would both be OK as long as there was some kind of outdoor activity. He also wondered how Laura was holding up.

From the top of Moxie Bald Mountain it would be about the same distance down as it was going up. That would be a frequent occurrence when he got to the White Mountains of New Hampshire. He remembered when his father's classmate and he went hiking in June 1976; they ran into two German hikers who were hiking the Presidential Range. Mr. Arthur asked the German's why they chose New Hampshire instead of the Rockies and one of them replied, "Because it's more challenging."

Paul stopped for a break and drank some water at the Bald Mountain Brook Lean-to. It had only been four miles since he started out, but it felt like ten. He still had about nine miles before he could call it a day. There was another hiker there also taking a break, but he was headed north. He was headed to Mt. Katahdin, but he wasn't hiking the entire AT. He was what they refer to as a Section hiker, a person hiking the AT one section at a time. Josh was a computer programmer from Connecticut who saved up all his overtime, so he could have a month's vacation every year in order to hike. He said it worked out to be a good annual weight loss program for him. This was Josh's second section; he had done Vermont and New Hampshire the summer before.

After a 30-minute break they were both ready to start hiking again. Josh went north and Paul continued south. The next three miles were mostly downhill and he was making good time. He needed the extra time because it was a demanding five or so miles up to Pleasant Pond Mountain. He stopped several times along the way for trail mix and water. Paul was thankful he didn't have to waste time filling his water bottles and knew that it kept him from dehydrating. He wondered how much time he would save over the course of the next five-and-a-half months by not filling the water bottles.

It was almost 5:15 when he got into camp and he was there early enough to get a space in the lean-to, but he decided to use his tent instead. A tent does have certain advantages. It is private, so you don't have to contend with snoring and anyone else's body odor. The drawback of a tent is that it adds weight to your load. Paul's tent weighed about 3.4 lbs. The other drawback of a tent is when it gets wet, because you'll end up carrying some of the rain water no matter how much you shake it out.

Paul decided on Chicken A La King for dinner, it was one of his favorites. After dinner he wrote in his journal and spoke with some of the other hikers. Two were headed south and four were headed north. One of the conversations was on religion and God. Someone was talking about miracles and if they really happened. Paul shared two stories on miracles with the group. The first story happened when their mother took both he and his brother Dave to Italy as a graduation present. He had just graduated from high school and David from college. While they were in Italy they went to Naples with a priest by the name of Father Crippa who worked in the Vatican.

Father Crippa took them to an old church in Naples, whose name Paul couldn't recall. The nun who answered the door didn't want to let them in, so Father Crippa showed his Vatican ID. Reluctantly the nun let them in and Father Crippa explained why they were there.

Father Crippa told them about a young nun, by the name of Patricia, who worked in that parish many years before. She died at a young age and left her family's wealth for the good of the local community. As a way to show their thanks for what Patricia did, the people of the parish put her in a casket with a crystal top. Her body lay uncorrupt for years and they said that when you looked into her casket it looked as if a young girl was sleeping.

As the story goes, years later someone broke into the church one night and broke the crystal top of her casket. The robber reached into Patricia's mouth to take one of her teeth and when he did that blood started gushing out of her mouth. The robber screamed and then he fainted falling to the floor. Two nuns who were getting ready for Mass the next morning came in to see what all the commotion was about and they saw the robber laying on the floor with broken glass all around. When they looked into the casket, blood was flowing from Patricia's mouth. The nuns took two empty cruets, the little bottles that hold the wine and water, and they captured Patricia's blood in them.

At about the time Father Crippa finished the story the little old nun came back into the room carrying something. It was a metal stand with a glass bottle in the middle. The little glass bottle was one of the cruets which the nuns used to capture Patricia's blood. It was dried blood. Father Crippa asked everyone to join him in some Hail Mary's, so they did.

As they prayed, the brown solidified blood changed into a blood red liquid. Then you could see bubbles in it. Some say it was boiling blood, but Paul could only say that it was bubbling. When they stopped praying the blood returned to a solidified state.

Paul went on to explain that when he was stationed in Naples several years later he asked his Italian secretary if she knew where that church was. She didn't know where it was, but she had heard about St. Patricia's boiling blood. She looked into it at his request and she discovered that the church had been closed because the building was unsafe. No one knew where they moved Patricia's blood.

One of the thru hikers said he heard about some Saint's blood that boils every September and wondered if that was the same Saint. Paul told the hiker that there was yet another saint whose blood boils, by the name of Gennaro and he went on to explain that St. Gennaro's blood boils on his feast day near the end of September. If St. Gennaro's blood doesn't boil, it's believed that some tragedy would befall Naples. Everyone enjoyed Paul's story, so they asked him to tell his other miracle story.

He was a little reluctant at first, but he did. He told them how he was at an Air Force school back in 1980 in Montgomery, Alabama and he explained how he used to do a lot of running at that time. Because of the running he developed a pain in his left hip and when the pain got bad enough he thought he should get it checked out at the base hospital. They X-Rayed his hip and told him there was a spot on his hip bone.

Paul said the doctor said to him "now I don't want to worry you, but this type of spot looks a lot like what we would see when someone has bone cancer."

Paul explained how they had to schedule him for a more specialized X-Ray that would verify if he had bone cancer. For the special X-Ray they injected a radioactive Isotope into his hip, but it took the better part of a week before he could have that done. Regardless of what the doctor said, Paul did worry; how could you not? He called his wife and she in turn called her mother who belonged to a prayer group at her church in Pennsylvania. They included him in their prayer chain.

The result of the radioactive X-Ray was that there was no bone cancer, so the doctor re-X-Rayed him. There was nothing on that X-Ray either. The spot was gone. "Now was that a miracle?" He asked. "I believe it was."

The mood was good after he told his stories and the night ended on a high note. There was at least one agnostic in the group and he found it hard to believe. However, he didn't rain on anyone's parade; he just sat there, smiled and at times would say "that's interesting." Everyone turned in at about 10:45 and Paul slipped into his tent after adding that experience to his journal. (145 FK)

In the morning everyone went about their business, whether it was fixing breakfast, repacking backpacks, or as in Paul's case rolling up a tent. One of the guys staying in the lean-to came over and asked him if he had ever heard of Padre Pio. Paul said that he had heard of Padre Pio and he shared a quick story with the other hiker. The other hiker left after he shared the Padre Pio story and he left about fifteen minutes later.

It was about six miles to US201 and then a short distance to Caratunk, Maine. Paul would get some supplies for at least two days and call Laura at work. Today would be the last day of VBS for his kids, so he could talk to them when he gets to Stratton, ME. The hike to US201 wasn't as easy as he was expecting, he still had one elevation climb of 1,000 feet. Then it was downhill nearly 2,000 feet. He thought about the guy's question from earlier that morning regarding Padre Pio.

His first recollection of Padre Pio was from his mother-in-law. She had shared a story with him shortly after Paul married Laura. It was an incredible story. As best as he could recollect the story went like this. A girl who Laura's mom worked with had a little sister who was one of the miracles they were using for the cause of Padre Pio's canonization. The girl had been born without some vital organ; Paul thought it was a bladder. She was never able to leave the hospital, so one of the mother's friends brought one of Padre Pio's gloves to the hospital so they could ask for Padre Pio's intercession. The mother somehow got the idea that she should go to Italy with her new born daughter to see Padre Pio and get his blessing.

Against the doctor's wishes the mother took her daughter to Italy and once she was in San Giovanni Rotunda, the Italian town where Padre Pio was living, she took her daughter to two audiences with Padre Pio. On both occasions Padre Pio laid his hands on the girl's head and gave a blessing. When the mother returned to the States, she went back to the hospital to have her daughter checked out. The doctors couldn't believe it; X-Rays showed the baby girl had a bladder growing in her. Because of that miracle Padre Pio was being recommended for the cause of beatification, a step towards canonization and being recognized as a Saint by the Roman Catholic Church. That wasn't the story Paul shared with the thru hiker, though. He shared another one that seemed more unbelievable and more miraculous.

Back in WW II when the Allies were trying to drive the Germans out of Italy, an American bomber was going to fly a mission over Northern Italy. For some reason the plane couldn't complete its mission, but it had already armed its bombs. Since the bomber couldn't land with live bombs the pilot was going to drop the bombs over the Adriatic Sea. When he went to release the bombs he saw a face in the clouds and the face said "don't drop your bombs on my people." The pilot, thinking he was hallucinating, went to release the bombs again and again the face spoke to him, saying, "don't drop your bombs on my people; drop them over the sea."

In that there was cloud cover and the pilot couldn't see the ground he checked with his navigator to see if they could possibly be over land. The navigator said that they were; they were over that part of the leg of Italy which looked like a tumor sticking out below the back of the knee. The navigator said there could be a town below which was called San Giovanni Rotundo. The navigator told the pilot they'd be over the Adriatic Sea again in five minutes or so. The pilot waited five minutes and went to release the bombs again, this time he didn't see the face or hear a verbal command.

The pilot never mentioned that to anyone because he thought they would have taken him off flying status. Years later the pilot read an article in *Readers Digest* about a Capuchin Priest who had the gift of bi-location. Bi-location meant he could be in two places at once. When he saw a picture of Padre Pio years later, he realized that it was him whose face he saw in the clouds and the one who commanded him not to drop his bombs. The hiker seemed impressed with that story and he said he would research it once he finished the AT. Paul refocused his attention to the last few yards of the trail before he got to US201.

Getting to US 201 at 12:00ish gave him time to re-supply and call Laura. Even though it was only a half mile to town, he decided to hitch hike. Someone picked him up immediately. It was a short ride to town and not long enough to even find out about the driver.

The driver dropped him off at the Post Office where there was a pay phone and Paul called Laura. She mentioned the kids were home today because the air conditioner was out in the parish center. He called them next and the kids were excited. Steven wanted to tell Dad about a new trick Heidi learned, Daniel told him about his scout trip planned for the coming weekend, and Theresa filled him in on VBS. Before hanging up Paul said he'd call on Sunday the 2nd of July if he made it to Stratton, but Monday for sure.

After hanging up, Paul went to get some supplies for the next couple of days of his journey. The store had a limited selection of freeze-dried foods, so he bought a sandwich for lunch and some canned fruit to have with his dinner. He picked up a couple other things in case he ran out food. His next mail drop would be in Stratton which was three to four days away. From Caratunk Paul would have to cross the Kennebec River by the ferry, which was back at the trail head. Paul stuck out his thumb and got a ride after 10 minutes.

He waited about 20 minutes for the ferry, which was free for hikers during the summer. According to his guide book, a hiker drowned in 1985 while trying to ford the river, so that was one of the reasons they put the ferry in. As Paul road the ferry across the Kennebec River he was thankful there was a ferry. He couldn't imagine fording the river especially after a couple days of rain. He planned to make it to the

Pierce Pond Lean-to, which was about four miles from the river. It was already 2:45 by the time he got across the river.

Getting into the camp there were several people there, obviously planning to party. Since Pierce Pond Lean-to was only four miles from the river and had a pleasant view, there were a lot of people there for the long holiday weekend. Since the 4th of July was on a Tuesday, most people would take Monday off to make it a four-day weekend. Paul got a tent site on the other side of the pond, across from the lean-to. There were loads of people there and the booze was flowing freely. It looked like this would be another night he would have to use ear plugs. The good thing, however, was that people might offer him food and a beer.

They were a noisy bunch of people, but well behaved. There were only two other hikers using a tent on his side of the pond and they were headed north. They started from Georgia in January and they shared some do's and don'ts with Paul and in turn he passed on information regarding travel northward. When he asked them what the most beautiful part of their hike was, one said the Blue Ridge & Shenandoah's of Virginia, and the other said the White Mountains of New Hampshire.

All the other campers were gathered around the lean-to, so the trio joined in on the party. It turned out the people having the party had all gone to college together in Waterville, Maine, and this had been an annual tradition of theirs since college. No matter where they were living in the United States, they'd all get together there on the 4th of July, or the closest weekend.

The partiers did give them food and beer as they hoped, so there was no need to fire up the stove to cook dinner. The party food was definitely better than anything they had in their backpacks and he was grateful the people offered them all food. Paul and the two other thru hikers slipped away at about 10:15 and Paul wrote in his journal while the other two guys called it a night. (155 FK)

Paul woke up with Charlie Horses during the night and he wished he had some bananas. As he sat there massaging his calves he realized that he shouldn't have had the beer because it added to his dehydration. He made a mental note to not accept any more beer while on the trail. When morning came he was very tired and it was hard to get motivated. He looked at his watch and it was already 7:30 a.m.; he obviously fell back to sleep after he worked the Charlie Horses out. Paul crawled out of the tent and his legs were sore. The other two guys had already left, so Paul walked around a bit and then decided to have breakfast. There was no sign of life at the lean-to because they were all still sleeping. He would have gladly accepted food, preferably bacon and eggs, but since that wasn't likely to happen he fired up his stove and had coffee and oatmeal.

It was 9:00 by the time Paul felt comfortable walking with his backpack on, but his legs still felt weak. There was still no one up at the lean-to when he left; he didn't envy them their hangovers when they got up. It was slow hiking at first, so Paul forced water. It was amazing to drink almost a full liter and put the bottle back in his pack only to have it full again when he took it out the next time. Anything is possible for God, he thought.

He decided to stop for an early lunch and since he never prepared a meal the night before he would have his freeze-dried dinner from the night before. He thought some sweet and sour chicken might lift his energy not to mention his spirits. Soon after the water came to a boil Paul sensed someone walking towards him. He couldn't hear anybody, but he knew someone was there. When he turned around there was a young African-American girl walking up behind him. "Hello," Paul said.

"Hello Paul. I'm Sylvia and the Lord thought you could use some company right about now."

She was right, he was thinking. He was on a high note yesterday, but today seemed to be a struggle for him, especially physically.

"Would you like some Sweet & Sour Chicken?" Paul asked.

"I'd love some, but I'll wait until I get to Dover."

"Dover where?" Paul asked.

"Dover, Delaware. That's where I'm headed."

It was an odd response, so Paul figured she was a heavenly companion like Frank. He didn't ask her outright but he responded. "Dover, I spent a summer there several years ago and I liked it."

"I've never actually been to Dover," Sylvia said; "but I've heard it's a nice place."

"Sylvia, can I ask you a question?"

"Yes. As long as it isn't what God's plan is for you."

"No, though I am curious about that, too. Frank said I would find out God's plan for me when it's time. So, my question to you is what was God's plan for you before you were aborted?"

"God's plan for me was very simple. I was going to baby-sit for someone in Dover and during the course of that evening the baby choked and died. If I had been there, he would not have choked because would have known how to clear the airway because they taught us that in Girl Scouts. The baby who choked would have grown up to be a pediatric physician. In fact, he would have brought a lot of healthy babies into this world in a part of Dover that is economically depressed. He would have saved lives instead of taking them."

"When I said to Frank that God's plan for him seemed very simple, he didn't tell me the whole story. Did you leave anything out about yourself?'

"I would have been a nurse in a neonatal ICU. You see, God's plan is perfect if you trust in him. My mother didn't trust in God, instead she listened to the people who were pressuring her to have an abortion. I also would have saved many babies that were born too early."

Paul remembered what Frank said about their destinies crossing in up-state New York, so Paul wondered if that was the case for Sylvia and him.

"Did our paths cross somehow Sylvia?"

"Yes, they did. Do you remember when you stepped on a needle in your room at the base and you had to drive yourself to the ER to have it pulled out?"

"Yes." Paul said, he remembered it vividly; he was walking across his room on Dover Air Force Base and he stepped on a sewing needle and it went in eye first. When he felt the pain in his foot he swiped at the pain and he drove the needle further into the bottom of his foot and didn't help his hand any either. In fact, he got blood all over the bed and the carpet.

Sylvia continued, "You had to wait awhile because they had more serious emergencies. One of those was a case of domestic violence; you said a prayer for the teenager whose arm had been broken and from the looks of the marks on her face had obviously been beaten. That was my mother. She was nine weeks pregnant when my grandfather took her to the clinic where I was aborted. I had a beating heart and fingers and toes. In another week I would have sucked my thumb as all babies do in the safety of their mother's womb."

"I'm sorry," Paul said.

Sylvia thanked Paul for all his prayers over the years. They helped her, she said.

"How can a one-time prayer help that much?" he asked.

"Because that one generous intercession continues on through time and is repeated by the Communion of Saints. When you say an intercessory prayer for others it is more special than if it had been for yourself. You could have prayed that the ER staff hurried up, so they would take the needle out of your foot. However, you offered it up for my mother and the others in the ER that had more serious injuries than you."

Paul reflected on the many times over the years he had heard that term, "offer it up," but had no idea of its strength and power. He first heard it in grammar school by the nuns and religion teachers; and it was echoed at home by his mother. His mother was always "offering up" some kind of pain or difficult circumstance for others. His father passed away when he was eight and as difficult as that had to have been for his mother, she would frequently say, "God must have wanted your Father earlier than we would have liked."

"Sylvia, I have a couple other questions for you if you don't mind. Like if someone was to come along right now, would they be able to see you? I sense they can't."

"It depends on whether it is God's plan or not. The Pie Lady could see Frank, couldn't she? I don't think anyone else besides you can see me right now if they were here, if that is what you're wondering."

"Sylvia, how is it that you and Frank came to be as you are? Are you Angels? Can you even answer that?"

"We are created beings like you. We were living beings with fingers, toes and a beating heart. Angels are spirit only. We were living beings enjoying God's gracious act of love. God knew us in our mother's womb. Whenever you pray for souls in purgatory you lift us up. A whole Rosary dedicated to the souls in purgatory does a lot. So, if you want to direct any of the rosaries you say for the souls in purgatory you are doing a great good."

Sylvia reached into her rucksack as she stood up and took out some bananas, and then she said, "Paul these should help your legs. Enjoy your lunch and your hike. It will be a good hike for you. That I'm sure of."

Paul took the bananas and thanked Sylvia; she started walking north on the trail and was soon out of sight. He ate the sweet and sour chicken and two of the three bananas and he saved the third banana for later. A hiker came along shortly after Paul finished his lunch and Paul was curious about something, so he asked the passerby if he had seen a young African-American girl headed north. He said he hadn't. It would have been hard to miss her in her bright yellow outfit, so Paul made a mental note of that to write in his journal come nightfall. Sylvia was unseen by others, but Paul could see her and talk to her.

He continued his journey and decided to call it a day at Little Bigelow Lean-to, which was about 12 miles from the Pierce Pond Lean-to. Oddly enough there was only one other hiker there when he arrived at 6:15. He rolled out his sleeping pads on the lean-to floor and took his sleeping bag out of its stuff sack in order to save his place on the wooden floor. Then he worked on dinner, which consisted of beef stroganoff night. He had never tried a freeze-dried Beef Stroganoff dinner before and it wasn't bad, but it wasn't the best freeze-dried meal either. He enjoyed the Chicken A la King the most, but he would save that for the next night.

No other hikers showed up by 8:30, so Paul was happy about all the space they had in the lean-to. The other hiker preferred to stay to himself, so that gave Paul a chance to write in his journal and go to sleep; he was tired and didn't even finish his prayers. (172 FK)

Paul felt well rested in the morning. It was a Sunday and he would miss Mass again, so he took out his copy of The Spiritual Communion Prayer and said it.

"My Jesus, I believe You are present in the Most Holy Sacrament. I love you above all things, and I desire to receive You into my soul. Since I cannot at this moment receive You sacramentally, come at least spiritually into my heart. I embrace You as if You were already there and unite myself wholly to You. Never permit me to be separated from You. Amen."

After praying he made breakfast, which consisted of his banana and a freeze dried omelet. He put extra spices on the omelet to make it more palatable; it was Paul's first attempt at an omelet on the trail. You had to have a good imagination to believe it was a western omelet even though the label said so. The other hiker was gone about 15 minutes after Paul woke up, prayed, and prepared his omelet. The hiker watched curiously as Paul prayed and blessed himself, but he didn't disturb Paul. Paul packed up his own stuff and was on the trail by 7:00.

He was making good time and made it to Safford Notch by about 9:15. The next three miles were very difficult, with a 2,000 foot climb in elevation. At about the 180th mile from Mt. Katahdin there was a memorial plaque to Mr. Myron Avery who was the first person to hike the Appalachian Trail in sections from 1928-1937. Thanks largely to him we have guidebooks of the trail and shelters along the length of the AT. "Thank you Mr. Avery," he said out loud. There was no one around to hear him talking to himself. Or was there?

The next four miles were mostly downhill and he thought about staying at the Horns Pond Lean-tos, but he decided to press on to the next campsite. He had gone only 10 miles since morning, so he continued on, reaching Cranberry Stream Campsite by 6:00 p.m. There was no one staying at the campsite, so the 20 or so people Paul passed coming down the mountain, were probably headed to the Horns Pond lean-tos in order to celebrate the 4th of July, which was still two days away. Another hiker got to camp at about 7:15, so he went over to chat with him. The other hiker was headed south also and he had come 20 miles since 6:30 a.m. He said the partiers at the Pierce Pond Lean-to were still in good spirits both literally and figuratively. Paul added the day's happenings to his journal as he remembered them. He was unsure about how to write about Sylvia and called it a night at 9:15 p.m. (186 FK)

With no disturbances from other campers, Paul slept well. The other south bounder was already gone when Paul woke at 6:30 a.m. Paul decided to have a small bite to eat along the trail because he was eager to get to Stratton, Maine. Paul had had an idea during the night and he wanted to get to a phone to call Laura as soon as possible to see what she thought.

Since he had lost a day or two already and would probably lose another day after Stratton, he figured he could make up a day or two in the White Mountains of New Hampshire. When he was feeling depressed two days prior and before Sylvia's visit, he planned to by-pass the Presidential Range in New Hampshire altogether. He had hiked that stretch of trail many times before, so he thought he would by- pass them. He wasn't a purist who felt the need to hike every mile of the AT, he did want to feel as if he accomplished something at a time in his life when he needed something grand.

Since a sectional hiker could make the same claim that they hiked the entire Appalachian Trail, he could bypass the Presidential Range and make the same claim. Myron Avery's accomplishment was just as important as the average thru hiker, or probably more so since he was the first person to hike it in its entirety. Then Paul got an idea during the night, possibly from reading the brass plaque dedicated to Mr. Avery, the day before. If he could get bunk space in the Appalachian Mountain Club (AMC) Huts in the White Mountains, he could make up the day or two and still feel as if he had accomplished something. Besides, Paul loved the Presidential Range and the challenges the weather can deal you.

His thought was to have Laura phone ahead to check availability and where something was available, he would ask her to reserve a space for him. Then he would make his way through the White Mountains and he could go without a backpack in order to make up time. He figured the 40 plus lbs. he was carrying had to affect his time and endurance, certainly his balance. If he knows exactly when he would get to the White Mountains then he can take a shuttle to drop off his backpack somewhere and shuttle back again. Then he could begin his traverse across the Presidential Range. That way, he figured, he could just take water and a minimum of clothes.

The AMC huts are great. They serve two meals a day; they give you a bunk, two blankets and a pillow as well. Plus they have a very limited supply of snacks and goodies for sale, so that you could have something for lunch. To cap it all off, the hut workers, or the Croo, as they call them, make your stay a lot of fun. He wasn't sure why they spelled Croo that way, but figured it had to do with something unique to their position. Your day may start out with a song to get you out of bed, followed by an after breakfast skit.

Paul made it to ME27 by 9:15 and it was still five miles to Stratton, so he stuck out his thumb while still walking. He got about 200 yards down the road and a logging truck passed by him, but then it stopped. The driver even backed up some, so that he didn't have to walk the quarter of a mile. Paul hopped up into the truck and wrestled his backpack onto the bench seat between himself and the driver. On the way into Stratton the driver said he was going to pass him by, but then he remembered they were having problems with bears in the area where Paul was hitchhiking. The driver said that he would have felt guilty if he read in the newspaper that a backpacker was eaten alive. They made it to Stratton by 9:45 a.m.

First order of business was to pick up his package at the post office, the one he mailed to himself before he left Brandon. When he came out of the post office a big truck drove by slowly and Paul noticed it was dragging something underneath and it looked like someone's body. Everyone ran to see what it was, thinking the same thing Paul did, that the truck ran over someone and was dragging him or her underneath the truck.

CHAPTER THREE

Banana Bread and Partridge

When everyone, including Paul, got up to the truck they could see their fears were unfounded. It was just a big piece of cardboard that probably dropped off the same logging truck which Paul rode in to town on. The truck driver was just the unlucky one to hit it. When the driver got out of his cab there was a look of panic on his face, but when he saw he didn't hit someone he started laughing. Everyone else started laughing along with the truck driver who pulled the big refrigerator like box from underneath his rig. With that bit of excitement out of the way everyone went about their business on this 3rd of July 1995.

Paul was glad the post office was open, because he knew that many businesses would rather have a three-day weekend. The Stratton Post Office had Paul's package that he sent from Brandon, Florida nearly one month prior. He tore it open and looked through the contents and he found what he was looking for in a plain white envelope, the one marked AT&T phone card. Now he could call Laura because his other phone card was almost out of minutes.

Whereas most people had to work on Monday, July 3rd, Laura had off. She put in for a vacation day well before Paul left on his Appalachian journey, because she wanted to spend time with the children. When Laura picked up the phone she was very excited. She said Steven lost a front tooth the day before and Theresa videotaped his mouth, so that Paul could see it when he got home in December. Theresa and Daniel were fine, too. He asked how she was and he could tell from her pause that she missed him. He wondered if it was a good time to tell her about Frank and Sylvia, which he did.

First he told her what Frank shared him about his ferry ride to Plattsburg, New York, some 12 years before. Frank described the scene in detail, seeing all the ambulances and emergency vehicles pass by Paul's van from Norwich University. Then he told Laura what Sylvia told him about his trip to the Dover AFB hospital in the summer of 1984 and how he saw her mother in the emergency room while he was waiting to have someone pull the needle out of the sole of his foot. He also told Laura about his water bottles, the stove from Frank, and Sylvia giving him bananas for his Charley Horses.

Next, he told her his plan to make up some of his lost time. She said she would call the AMC and then tell him what they had to say when he called back later. After he hung up, Paul went to the store to re-supply and then he went to find a hotel or hostel. He decided on one that could offer him a private bath. He shaved and showered and then went to find a place to eat. He decided on the Stratton Diner, where they could indulge his desire for fruits and salads, not to mention peach pie a la mode. The pie at the diner was as good as the one he had at the Pie Lady's.

He was anxious to call Laura again, so he went back to the same pay phone. Theresa answered the phone and she sounded so happy. "Daddy, "she said, "We thought you would be in Stratton today and we were right." She mentioned that the neighbors invited them over for a picnic the next night, on the 4th of July. "Let me put Dan on," she said. Daniel talked about what they did for the day and where they were going to watch the fireworks the next night. When Steven got on the phone he repeated almost everything Daniel said because he was so excited. Heidi was barking in the background, so Daniel must have been playing with her and getting her to bark, so Paul could hear her.

When Laura got back on the phone she said she called the AMC and it didn't look good. They told her to call back after the 4th because it was "crazy busy." They said they would have a better feel for bunk availability after the holiday.

Laura said she was happy for him and felt better knowing that he was in such good company. She asked Paul what Frank and Sylvia looked like, so he gave her a description of both. After he hung up the phone he went to get some supplies for the next part of his journey. He said he would call the next morning if he could, but if he couldn't he would call from Rangely, Maine.

Paul stocked up on supplies, which included getting Coleman fuel for his stove. Several places offered Coleman fuel by the ounce, so he got eight ounces. His 16 ounce aluminum container was still half full, so he topped it off with eight more ounces, which would probably last him 10 days. After getting gas he decided on a different place for dinner, the one that advertised pot roast and homemade soups on the sign out in front of their establishment.

He was glad he had practically all day in Stratton to rest his legs and muscles and do his laundry. As Paul walked by St. John's Catholic Church he noticed on the sign out front that they were having Mass the next morning at 8:00 a.m.; it was a special 4th of July celebration. So, he returned to his motel, wrote in his journal, set the alarm clock for 6:00 a.m. and went to sleep. (188 FK)

When Paul's alarm went off he was already awake, but it felt good just to lay there on clean sheets. He went to eat at the Stratton Diner and then returned to his room to shower. He checked out by 7:35, which left him time to go to Mass at 8:00. The priest gave a nice homily, but what Paul liked best was being able to receive the Eucharist. As he was leaving the church someone offered him a ride back to the trail head.

It was 9:15 when Paul started hiking and while it would have been nice to get going at 7:00, he was very happy to have been able to go to Mass. He had thought about making it to Rangeley in two days, but with the challenging terrain he decided on three.

It was difficult hiking and slow going, but it was beautiful. Paul rested at "The Spring;" at least that was what his guide book called it. He had gone only six miles and it was already 2:45, but he wanted to go at least another four miles and make it to the other side of the Carrabassett River. He had heard on the weather channel before he left Stratton that it would rain tonight. In all likelihood he would have to find a place off the trail, because the next lean-to was at Spaulding Mountain, some eight miles away.

After he crossed the Carrabassett River he was ready to call it a day, but it was still only 5:30, so he decided to hike another hour-and-a-half unless he saw a well-protected place to pitch the tent. At almost exactly 7:00 p.m. he came across a very nice looking site. It was out of view from the trail and well protected from rain and wind. He could even set his tent up under a rocky ledge that was about seven feet high. If it did rain he would stay dry with the help of the rocky ledge. (197 FK)

He put up his tent under the ledge where the ground was soft like peat moss. He also moved a stump closer to the tent, so he would have a place to sit. As soon as he started cooking dinner it started to rain, but he and the stove were well protected. The rain started out as a light rain and then it rained harder almost in sync with the thunder and lightning. He felt safe and secure from the rain and the lightening and it reminded him of a campout he went on near Front Royal Virginia over Memorial Day Weekend in 1976.

He went with his friend Tony and some guy named Joe, who Paul didn't even know. He was a friend of a friend of Tony's that heard they were camping for the weekend and he also wanted to go and since Joe offered to drive they let him go.

Paul couldn't remember exactly where the site was, but it was on the Appalachian Trail. They got there on a Friday night and it rained continuously until Monday. Fortunately, they also picked out a nice site on the side of the mountain. He remembered that they didn't have a tent, just a huge tarp he had bought from Eddie Bauer's. However, the way they tied the tarp it was similar to a lean-to; they stayed dry and could even have a fire underneath the front of the tarp. They only got wet when they had to pee, or get more beer, which made them pee all the more. It was a lot of fun sitting there on the side of the mountain, telling stories, jokes, laughing and drinking beer. He remembered, however, that they had a problem on Sunday night of their three-day Memorial Day weekend.

Joe was cutting cheese from a Gouda Wheel and he handed a piece to Tony and when Tony reached out for it he said, "You forgot to take some of the wax off." However, it wasn't the red wax that covers a Gouda Wheel, it was blood. Joe had cut off the very tip of his thumb and didn't even realize it. Tony, whose father was a doctor, knew what to do. Since none of them were fit to drive because of their inebriated condition and because it was raining cats and dogs, Tony applied pressure to the tip of Joe's thumb to stop the bleeding. Then he poured some Jim Beam over it in order to sterilize it, while Paul put a butterfly bandage on Joe's thumb. It was fortunate Tony had his father's first aid kit. Joe drank some Jim Beam and took some aspirin for the pain. The aspirin was also good for Joe's hangover the next morning.

What a trip that was. Paul hadn't thought of that in years. He still remembered that he couldn't get the smell of the wood smoke off his tarp. He washed it with a hose several times, but he couldn't get the smell off. He never used the tarp again for camping.

Paul looked at his map to see what he could expect for the next day. Sugarloaf Mountain was the next challenge with an altitude of 4,237 feet, making it the second highest in Maine. The trail doesn't go over the top, but there is a vertical climb of about 1,400 feet to where you go around the summit. He was glad it didn't go over the top, though they say on a clear day you can see both Mt. Katahdin to the north and Mt. Washington to the south. He wondered if you could see any fireworks from the summit tonight. Probably not, due to the rain and cloud cover. He hoped to make it to the Brook at the base of Saddleback Mountain, which is listed at 210 miles from

Mt. Katahdin. That would leave him another 10 miles for Thursday and put him in Rangeley, Maine at a decent time.

He slept well and woke by the alarm on his watch. He looked out of the tent and it was still raining, so Paul was glad the overhang kept his tent dry. He made coffee and oatmeal because there was a bit of a chill in the air. After rolling up his dry tent and putting it in a water-proof bag, he was ready to go by 7:00 a.m. The footing was tricky because of the wet rocks and the tree roots.

Paul stopped to read the Commemorative plaque at about the 200-mile mark. It honored the Civilian Conservation Corps (CCC) workers who built the final section of the AT in 1937. Shortly after that the rain stopped and the sun came out and he could see a rainbow. He thought to himself how beautiful the area was. Where the Mt. Abraham Trail met the AT, he decided to take a lunch break. He thought of Abraham in the Old Testament and remembered the story of when he was visited by the Angels of God. Paul felt equally blessed to have been visited by Frank and Sylvia, though they told him they weren't angels.

He thought to himself that he'd like to take a course on the Old Testament at some point in time because he loves it when the books or events of the Old Testament are revealed in the New Testament. He thought too of his love for music and how many of the church songs are based on Isaiah and the Psalms. Paul loved music and missed his choir back at St. Stephen's in Brandon.

His first choir experience, however, was in the first grade. He was so proud and happy when he made it, because his father and two brothers also sang in the choir.

Paul's best choir experience, as he reflected on it, was when he was stationed in Montgomery, Alabama. Their Church was called St. Bede the Venerable and the director was superb. He remembered how once during lent the director chose a song that fit the occasion of the passion and he still remembers the nun sitting in the front row and how she was in tears because of the way they sang the song. The Lord touched her heart and soul through their singing.

He continued on after eating some peanut butter crackers and raisins and he washed them down with water. Crossing Orbeton Stream wasn't too bad considering the amount of rain they had overnight. He did pick up a stick that was lying next to the stream, so that he would feel more secure as he crossed. There were some hikers swimming in the stream and they invited him to come in. Paul looked at his watch as he put his boots back on and it was already 2:30, he thanked them for their offer, but he continued on. He was doing pretty good considering how slow he started out on the wet rocks and roots that morning. He felt confident he would make it to the Brook at the base of Saddleback Mountain by 6:00 p.m.

At 5:15 he came upon the Poplar Ridge Lean-to and was tempted to stay there for the night, but he continued on. His guidebook didn't list any place to camp at the Brook, but he was going to take a chance. From Poplar Ridge to the Brook there was an elevation gain of 225 foot, but it felt like 500 feet. He made it by 6:15 which wasn't too bad considering how his legs felt. There was no one else there, so he plopped his backpack down against a rock and sat next to it. He was exhausted and felt a little dehydrated, which wasn't a good thing. He didn't look forward to any more Charley Horses.

Paul made a freeze dried Chicken a la King for dinner and it was good; it was still his favorite freeze-dried meal. After dinner he looked at his guidebook and it said he was 105 miles from Mt. Katahdin as the crow flies. However, hiking it on the

AT was a distance of 214 miles. He thought that was disconcerting, but then he remembered something he heard one time that cheered him up. He thought he heard it on WBVM one day on his way to work, so it must have been the *Living His Life Abundantly* program. The quote went something to the effect, "God writes straight with crooked lines," and it seemed very appropriate for his situation.

Some hikers passed by at about 7:30 and they were headed to the Poplar Ridge Lean-to. Paul wrote in his journal and said the Glorious Mysteries before going to sleep. He fell asleep during the 4th decade. (210 FK)

Paul woke up at 5:15 a.m. and decided to get going. He decided to eat while he was hiking on the trail. He had a granola bar and a handful of raisins. As he hiked and ate he couldn't believe how refreshed he felt from the good night's sleep. If he could make it to Saddleback Mountain by 8:30 a.m. it would be mostly downhill to ME4 and Rangeley. If he was lucky to hitch a ride as soon as he got to the road, he could be to town by 1 or 2 p.m. If that was the case, he could pick up his supplies, call home, and go for a swim in Rangeley Lake, something his guidebook recommended.

He made it to Saddleback Mountain by 8:20 a.m. and he looked to see if he could see Mt. Katahdin, but he couldn't because it was hazy. The downhill portion of Saddleback reminded him of a downhill portion in the Presidential Range, but he couldn't remember which one in particular. He would find out in another 10 days or so. Until then, he'd just have to keep wondering.

Arriving at ME4 by 1:30 p.m. he stuck out his thumb for a ride and he didn't have to wait long. The driver, whose name was Ted, dropped Paul off at the Post Office for what would be his next to last mail pick up in Maine. Then he would rely on Laura and the kids to keep him supplied by mail.

From the Post Office he went to the IGA Supermarket to supplement what he didn't send himself in the mail. Additionally, he would pick something up for dinner since the place he was staying at offered kitchen privileges to their guests. He called the number in his guidebook for a ride to the private residence, which advertised being right on the lake and serving breakfast. Once at the B & B Paul went for a swim in the lake. The water was cold, but it felt great. He returned to his room after he swam and he showered.

After showering he called Laura and also talked with the kids. He gave them his best guess for when he would get to New Hampshire and what he needed in his mail package that he would pick up in Gorham, New Hampshire.

Dinner was great and his hosts were very gracious to let him cook. There was only one other hiker staying at the B & B and he was headed northbound to Mt. Katahdin. Paul and he talked quite a bit after dinner. His name was Jeff, he was 33 years old, and he was from near Charlotte, North Carolina. He started hiking last September from Springer Mountain, Georgia, the southern terminus of the AT. He was in "no hurry" as he said, because he had taken a year off to "find" himself. Jeff's previous year had been difficult because he got divorced, lost his job, and his younger brother died. You could tell that Jeff was from the south because he had a pleasant way of saying certain words and phrases like Paul's first boss in the Air Force, who was from Athens, Georgia.

Paul's problems seemed small in comparison to Jeff's, so he just let Jeff do all the talking. When Jeff asked why Paul was hiking the AT, he said it was something he always wanted to do, but never had the time. Jeff and he arranged a ride back to the trailhead in the morning, a complimentary service the owners offered. They both agreed on a 7:00 a.m. departure. Paul used his AT &T phone card and called Laura before going to bed.

Paul told Laura about dinner and the other hiker who was staying there; he told Laura the guy's name was Jeff and he was from North Carolina. Then he mentioned that after talking to Jeff he had a greater appreciation of his own life and the crosses other people have to bear. Paul told Laura how much he loved her. Since the room where Paul and Jeff stayed had room darkening shades they could make the room dark, so even though it was still light outside, both he and Jeff turned in at 8:30 p.m. (220 FK)

Jeff was a nice guy, but he snored. Paul's earplugs helped somewhat, but he didn't have a good night's sleep. When the alarm went off at 5:45 he thought he had just fallen asleep. They had a nice breakfast of eggs, pancakes, and bacon, along with coffee and peaches. They left the B & B at 7:00 as planned and got to the trailhead by 7:15. They said their goodbyes and went their separate directions.

Despite the bad night's sleep Paul was hiking well and he made it to South Pond by 8:00. After South Pond the trail gradually started to climb and he made it to Little Swift River Pond by 10:45, a distance of nearly five miles since he started three-and-a-half hours earlier. The trail flattened out somewhat so he kept up his pace. He took a break for lunch about one hour after that, eating the sandwich he bought from the B & B owner. After he ate the sandwich and the fruit, which were compliments of the B & B owner, he continued on after about a 20 minute rest.

Paul had planned to make it to the Bemis Mountain Lean-to, but when he crossed ME17 he was tempted to call the B & B where he stayed the night before because it really wasn't that far away; but, he continued on. Paul arrived at the Bemis Mountain Lean-to by 6:45 p.m. The lean-to was full with weekend campers because it was only about a four-mile hike from ME17. Paul felt like he had had a good day's hike; he hiked nearly 18 miles, which was surprising considering how he felt when he started out the day. In addition to the full lean-to there were two other tents besides his. He was too tired to talk to the neighbors, so he had Chili Mac for dinner and washed it down with lots of water. He wrote ever so briefly in his journal before he fell asleep. (238 FK)

Paul slept right through the night, which was surprising. He always had to relieve his bladder during the night, but not last night. He reminded himself to force water because he didn't want any Charley Horses from dehydration; he would stop at least once every hour for the sole purpose of drinking water. After all there was no need to ration water since he had an abundance of the crystal clear, life giving liquid. He thanked God for the endless supply of water and thanked God for sending Frank and Sylvia. He wondered what they were up to. Whether Frank ever made it to Plattsburg and whether Sylvia made it to Dover. Paul wondered if he would see either of them again.

It was 6:15 a.m. when Paul got up and moving and none of the other hikers were up. Perhaps they partied too much the night before. However, the more Paul thought about it he didn't see anyone before he fell off to sleep. They were either curiously quiet or he was just so tired he slept through the noise. Paul's curiosity got the better of him and he glanced into the lean-to without being too obvious; all the sleeping bags seemed to have people in them. Everything looked fine. He didn't want to waste time firing up his stove, so he packed up his sleeping bag and tent and started hiking. It was 6:45 when he left the Bemis Mountain Lean-to and he was going to try to have his first 20-mile day. If all went right, he would make it to what is called the East B Hill Road sometime before dusk.

It was a beautiful morning. The temperature was pleasant and Paul was walking at a comfortable pace because it was mostly downhill. He crossed a road named South Arm Road and according to his map it went to Richardson Lakes. He continued on, eating trail mix and sipping on water as he hiked and made it to Sawyer Notch by 12:45, still feeling strong. Right after he was thinking how good he felt, the trail started up and when he reached the Hall Mountain Lean-to there was an interesting sight off to the South East. According to his guidebook it was a once satellite tracking station for NASA which had since been bought by some communications company, perhaps MCI. The interesting sight was a series of big satellite dishes. The landscape was a sea of green and then the large white satellite dishes that seemed odd and out of place in the sea of green.

Seeing the dishes and thinking it was an MCI facility he laughed out loud as he remembered something that happened two or three years prior. One day he got a call at work from Laura and she said MCI called to see if they wanted to get under the MCI family plan. Apparently, one of Laura's sisters had given MCI their name to be part of the family plan. Laura asked what he thought because MCI would be calling back in 10 minutes. Paul said, "Ask them if we can call Djibouti directly." He knew that MCI couldn't call Djibouti directly because MacDill AFB had MCI and they had to go through an AT&T operator.

Paul's job at CENTCOM required him to call the military attaché in Djibouti occasionally. So, when the MCI operator called back Laura asked if they could call Djibouti. The MCI operator said it wasn't possible at that time. However, about one year later the MCI operator called back and said it was now possible to call Djibouti direct, so Laura called Paul at work again to let him know that and what he thought. He told his wife to ask the MCI operator if it would be possible to call Tajikistan direct, because he knew that it wasn't possible. They were persistent and they finally had to tell MCI they liked their long distance carrier and didn't want to join MCI's family plan.

From the Hall Mountain Lean-to it was pretty much downhill all the way to East B Hill Road and his destination for the night. He would try to hitch a ride to Andover, Maine, which was still 8 miles away on East B Hill Rd. Andover, Maine was Paul's last mail pick up in Maine and he probably could have done without it, since it had only been two or three days since his last pickup. However, since there was a package waiting for him in Andover he would take the time to pick it up. Besides, he thought there might be a Catholic Church in Andover that had a Sunday morning Mass. He made it to the East B Hill Rd. by 6:30 p.m. and he started walking towards Andover and sticking his thumb out whenever he heard a car approaching. The second car to pass picked him up.

Andover was a quaint town, but then there were a lot of quaint towns in New England. Paul would actually see more of Andover than he had planned. Since he got there very late and it was a Saturday, he would have to wait until the post office opened on Monday. He found out there was no Catholic Church in Andover when he checked into the B & B. The owner at the B & B said they knew a Catholic Family in town and he was sure they would take him to Mass in Rumford the next morning.

Jim, the owner, called Dan and Sheila McNeil, their Catholic friend, and asked if they would give one of his boarder's a ride to church the next morning. The McNeil's said they would be delighted to give him a ride and said they'd pick Paul up at 8:15 the next morning. After he was checked in, he called Laura next to give her an update and run another one of his ideas by her.

His most recent idea involved Dean & Wendy Farmer who were their neighbors when they lived in Northfield Vt. Dean & Wendy now lived in Waterville Maine, which didn't look that far away on a map. Laura and the kids stopped to visit them after they left Baxter State Park, so Laura had their phone number handy. She said the Farmer's would probably love to see him in that it had been over 10 years since Paul saw them last. After speaking with the kids he hung up and called the Farmer's.

Wendy answered and she was delighted to hear Paul's voice. He told her where he would be the next morning and wondered whether she and Dean would be interested in seeing him. Wendy said they would love to see him and they would drive down. She was familiar with Rumford, but didn't know where the Catholic Church was, so Wendy picked a place to meet where she and Dean stopped whenever they traveled through Rumford. She said they would be there at 11:30 the next morning.

Paul decided laundry could wait until the next day because his body knew he went 19 miles and he couldn't wait to hit the sheets. He wrote in his journal, set the alarm clock on the nightstand, and went to bed. He was lucky enough to have a room by himself, but the owner said not to be surprised if there was someone in the other bed in the morning. Jim said they've had people get there as late as midnight. (257 FK)

It was the smell of bacon that caught Paul's attention first and then he could smell the coffee. It felt good to lie there, but he couldn't resist the smells. He decided to eat breakfast first and then shave and shower. He wanted to look reverent and presentable when he went to church and then had breakfast afterwards with the Farmers. He still had a pair of convertible pants which he hadn't worn since he washed them last. Convertible pants were very functional because you could wear them as long pants when you had to be presentable and you could wear them as shorts when it was hot. He still had a clean blue plaid shirt; it was the only nice shirt he brought with him. He loved it because it never needed ironing, or at least that's what he told himself. Laura always had a different opinion on that matter.

The McNeil's picked Paul up at 8:15 like they said they would. Dan and Sheila introduced themselves as he climbed into the back seat. On the way to Rumford, Paul could tell that they were a nice couple and very devout; they had a Miraculous Medal on the driver-side visor and a Rosary hanging from their rearview mirror. It was about 15 miles to Rumford and just a long enough drive for Paul to realize that Dan would be a good friend and neighbor. Dan asked him if he belonged to the Knights of Columbus and Paul said "no."

Whereas Dan was jovial and outgoing, Sheila was quiet and humble. When they got to the church Dan said Paul could sit with them at Mass if he wanted to. It was a pleasant experience driving with the McNeil's to Rumford, yet another good reason to come back to the town someday.

Everything felt right about going to Mass at St. Athanasius & St. John's; he sensed a presence. Even if there weren't a red flickering candle indicating that Jesus was in the Tabernacle, Paul could still feel a presence. At the Sign of Peace, when

Paul went to shake hands with the people around him, he saw Frank and Sylvia about two pews behind him. Paul was very eager to receive Holy Communion and when he did he felt a surge of joy. After Mass he thanked Dan and Sheila for the ride to Mass and assured them that he would get a ride back to Andover from some friends who he was meeting for lunch. However, Dan & Sheila did offer him a ride to the restaurant and he accepted because he wasn't familiar with Rumford.

It was 11:15 a.m. when Paul spotted Dean and Wendy drive up. They hadn't changed much. Dean still wore a long sleeve blue Oxford shirt and LL Bean Chino Khakis and Wendy was wearing a multi-color one piece dress. Dean had put on a few pounds, but Wendy had lost a few. Paul remembered fondly the times their two families spent together in Northfield, Vermont. Dean was a principal at one of the schools and Wendy was a stay- at-home Mom. Wendy, however, had her Master's Degree in Education and wanted to take some time off with their girls before she returned to teaching. Those were fun years in Northfield, Vt., for both Laura and Paul. Wendy and Laura were like sisters to each other and Dean was like a brother to Paul.

Dean grew up in Vermont and he was from a farming family, but Dean didn't care for farming and decided to get an education. He loved History, so he got his BA at some college south of Rutland, Vermont and his MA somewhere else. For his doctorate he went to the University of North Carolina, Chapel Hill and that's where he met Wendy. At the time Wendy's family was living in the Atlanta area. She got her Bachelor's Degree at Furman University in North Carolina and was working on her Master's in Education when she met Dean. She used to love to tell the story of how she and Dean met. Dean walked up to her in the library and said, "Are you married, engaged, or defective?" Wendy responded, "I don't think so," or at least that's how he remembered the story.

Paul was slow in getting up from the bench outside the restaurant because he was cherishing those memories from back in the 1980's. Dean and Wendy didn't see Paul sitting on the bench or if they did they didn't recognize him, since he was slightly grayer. Paul & Dean shook hands and Wendy and Paul hugged, which was something he never would have done 12 years before when they first met. He really missed them both. Paul also missed the two plus years they lived in Northfield, VT. Laura & Paul even investigated the idea of moving back to the New England area, but their investigation didn't go any further than discussing it.

They went into the restaurant and Wendy, in her slight southern drawl, said how she missed us guys and that it was nice to see Laura and the kids two weeks prior. She said Dean was upset because Paul wasn't with Laura and the kids, so this more than made up for it. Dean asked how the hike was going and how he was holding out, so he pretty much filled them in on the hike all except the part about Frank and Sylvia. He mentioned that he really missed certain foods and having the kids around, but that things were going as well as could be expected. Wendy smiled and said, "Well we can't do anything about your kids, but we can give you some banana bread," as she handed him a loaf wrapped in aluminum foil.

Paul had a Chicken Cobb salad for lunch, to make up for his lack of vegetables on the trail. Wendy and Dean both ordered breakfast and the conversation turned to years past and some of their neighbors still on Stage Coach Rd. where they both lived in Northfield, Vermont.

Paul asked Dean how his book turned out because he remembered that it was due soon after Paul and Laura were reassigned in 1985. Dean's book, for his doctoral thesis, was on Alden Partridge, the founder of Norwich University as well as several other private military schools back in the early 1800's. Wendy typed it for him in the days when there were no computers or word processors and it was painstaking work. Paul remembers Wendy having to use a ruler to measure every page; they had to be precise. Dean used to share some of the more interesting facts and anecdotes about Alden Partridge. Dean had a gift for making things interesting, but Paul remembered one anecdote in particular.

Alden Partridge was an avid hiker and walker and he frequently took his students on long marches and quite often up hills. During one of Alden's summers he charted and measured the heights of many of the mountain peaks in New Hampshire and Vermont. Dean based that story on the letters he read in the Norwich University library; they were letters back and forth between Alden Partridge and Thomas Jefferson on the best way to measure the altitude of mountains. Partridge preferred a barometer and thermometer, but Paul couldn't remember how Thomas Jefferson did it.

From memories in Northfield, Vermont the conversation turned to the present day. Dean was a school superintendent and Wendy was a teacher. Laura had already filled them in on what Paul, Laura, and kids were up to, but Paul gave a brief overview of what he was doing.

He told Dean and Wendy that he was taking time out to decide what comes after the military. Wendy said, "Paul, have you ever thought about teaching?" He had of course, but he didn't have an education degree and he really didn't want to return to school. A Master's degree was all Paul ever strived for and he didn't want to have to do any more schooling, certainly not a PhD. Paul often thought about Mrs. Gray, his 6th grade teacher and Professor Edwards, his Spanish Professor in college. He knew how much they did for him and he wanted to give back, but he didn't want to do any more schooling.

The Farmer's girls were doing okay. Elizabeth, there oldest, was Theresa's age and they were like sisters for the two years the Geary's and Farmer's were neighbors. Jennifer, Wendy's youngest, was about three months younger than Dan. Elizabeth and Jennifer, Wendy explained, were with neighbors for the day. After lunch the Farmer's took Paul back to Andover. It was great to see them and difficult to say goodbye, again. He really missed them as neighbors and he felt pretty sure the feeling was mutual. They wished Paul good luck and good health and they drove away after dropping him off at the B & B. He was glad he had the extra day in Andover, so that he could see Dean & Wendy and talk about past experiences.

Paul called Laura right away and told her about his day. He told her about Dan & Sheila and how he saw Frank and Sylvia at Mass, too. Then he told her about Dean and Wendy and some of the things they talked about. Afterwards he talked to the kids and he could hear Heidi barking in the background.

After he hung up he did his laundry and took a nap, something he normally would not have a chance to do. He felt great after the nap and thought about how nice it would be to have a nap every day.

In that it was a Sunday night it was pretty quiet around the B&B, so he decided to go to dinner at the nearby diner. He had a steak and baked potato and a big piece of blueberry pie a la mode. Paul was very full when he left the diner and when he returned to the B&B he asked about getting a lift to the trailhead the next morning after he went to the post office. (256 FK)

Breakfast was simple, but filling. He also bought a sandwich for the trail, so he wouldn't have to stop. Jim said they could stop at the post office on the way to the trailhead, so they left at 8:20. Paul was the first customer and was happy to get the package for a couple reasons. The first reason was that his phone card was just about out of minutes and he needed another one. Secondly, he was out of deodorant; he had just enough when he got up this morning. He thanked Jim and asked him to thank Dan & Sheila again for him. Andover was a nice town.

Back on the trail, Paul passed by a beautiful waterfall after less than a mile. He stopped for lunch at the summit of the East Peak of Baldpate Mountain where he ate his sandwich, some freeze dried bananas and pineapple and washed it all down with several gulps of water. He passed by the Baldpate Lean-to, mile marker 264, and though it was tempting to take a nap, he continued on. He wanted to make it to the Speck Pond Campsite, which was about seven miles away. The trail went right through Grafton Notch State Park and it was beautiful and peaceful. Since it was Monday there weren't many people there, however, Paul was sure it would have been packed the day before.

It was uphill after Grafton Notch and then four-and-a-half miles to the Speck Pond Campsite. There was a side trail to something called Eyebrow Trail which was an 825-foot granite wall of some type, but Paul decided he could do without seeing it. From where the Eyebrow Trail intersected the AT it was about four miles to the stopping point for the day. When he arrived at Speck Pond he was struck by the beauty of it all. According to his guidebook Speck Pond was listed as an Alpine Pond, the highest one in Maine. There was a caretaker collecting $6 for staying the night, so he paid the caretaker and found a tent platform. It was 5:30, so he set up his tent and then prepared dinner.

There were about a half dozen other campers and they looked like boy scouts. When Paul talked to them later that evening he discovered they were Boy Scouts and they were doing this trip in lieu of going to New Mexico, because they didn't register in time. Paul fixed Freeze Dried Turkey Tetrazzini and joined the scouts at their campfire. They were from the Boston area and they had one more night on the trail. If everything went as planned for Paul this would be his last night in Maine because the New Hampshire border was about ten miles away. He wrote in his journal and went to sleep at dusk, which was about 9:45. (271 FK)

The scouts were up and about at 6:00 and they invited Paul for some breakfast and he didn't have to be asked twice, especially since they had fresh brewed coffee for the scout leaders. The scouts were reviewing their weeklong hike while they sat around the campfire. They discussed what to do differently next year, other than register on time, for the Boy Scouts of America (BSA) high mountain camp in New Mexico. That brought back memories of when Paul, Laura, and Theresa were in Garmisch Germany back in the summer of 1982. The BSA had a nice area they leased from the Bavarian Government and it was their equivalent of the high adventure camp in the German Alps. Paul will never forget their visit there and the ensuing adventure.

Paul was attending the NATO School in Oberammergau, Germany, one of the most beautiful places in the world. Anyhow, his next door neighbor from Naples, Italy, who worked with Paul at AIRSOUTH, was a Boy Scout Leader and was in Garmisch with his scout troop. Paul, Laura, and Theresa went to visit Bill and his scouts, one of which was Bill's son, Billy. They had a nice visit and it was nice to see what the Boy Scouts of America did for military dependents serving in Europe. The location was terrific; the site looked out at the Zugspitze, the highest mountain in Germany.

They visited with Bill and Billy for about an hour and then returned to Oberammergau. About a week or so later when they got back to Naples they found out that one of the Boy Scouts had Mononucleosis. Bill remembered that Paul and his family visited them at their camp and wanted to make sure they didn't eat or drink anything during their visit. If they had they would have had to get some kind of shot. Fortunately, they hadn't eaten anything or had anything to drink while they were there and they didn't come in direct contact with the scout in question.

The Boston scouts were also headed to the New Hampshire border and the leader said Paul was welcome to hike with them in that he was hiking alone. The reason for the offer was the Mahoosuc Notch. The scout leader said that it could be very tricky getting through the jungle gym like maze of rocks and trees. He took the scout master up on his offer, since that wouldn't have been a good place to have a fall, not that any place was a good place. They all left Speck Pond at 7:30.

The Mahoosuc Notch was a challenge and Paul was happy he took the scouts up on their offer. After he made it through the notch he went ahead when the scouts took a break. He thanked them for letting him share their campfire, camaraderie, and food. Instead of stopping with the scouts, he ate trail mix and had water while he was hiking. Paul's stride at 6'2" was longer than most 15-yr. olds and he could make better time. After the Notch there was a vertical climb of about 600 feet to the Full Goose Shelter followed by another vertical climb of 600 feet to the East Peak of Goose Eye Mountain.

The view northward was beautiful and worth the small detour from the AT to take it all in. From Goose Eye Mountain he started back down again and from there it was about two-and-a-half miles to the New Hampshire border. He reached the Gentian Pond Campsite at about 6:15 and he was tired and sore. He figured his soreness was from the way he had to contort his body to get through the various crevices back at Mahoosuc Notch.

There were lots of spaces in the shelter, so he put down his sleeping pad and sleeping bag to save a space. And then, as he was now getting used to, he fired up his Svea and boiled water for his freeze dried Beef Stew. For dessert he ate the last of Wendy's banana bread and washed it down with water. He was grateful there weren't many people in the campsite because it was quiet and peaceful. He wrote in his journal and fell off to sleep at about 9:00. (286 FK)

When he awakened at 6:30 it was because of some bird noises. He forgot to write in his journal the night before that he was now one state down with thirteen to go. That was an overwhelming thought, that he had so much ahead of him. It was about 1,880 miles to Springer Mountain, Georgia. It was a depressing thought, but at least the next ten days or so he was looking forward to, especially if things worked out as he hoped and prayed for. His next mail drop was in Gorham, New Hampshire.

If Laura was able to get him lodging at every other hut, then he wouldn't have to worry about carrying the weight of two meals a day times four days. He did plan to stop in Gorham to get the package Laura mailed him. Plus, he liked the town of Gorham which he first visited some 20 years prior.

He went about two miles and then had a 600-foot climb in elevation and then it leveled out for several miles. It was 2:15 when he got to US2 where he hitch hiked the three-and-a-half miles into Gorham. When he got to the road and was taking off his backpack someone happened to stop and offer him a ride. Paul gladly accepted and asked the driver if he would be passing the post office. The guy said no, but he would drop him off there anyhow. There was a package waiting for Paul and when he opened the package there was a phone card, recent pictures of Laura & the kids taken on the 4th of July, and some dehydrated fruit and a couple freeze-dried meals. Next, he called Laura at work and told her he was in Gorham and he just got the mail drop and he appreciated it, especially the pictures.

Then he asked her what she found out from the AMC. Laura was happy to report that she got him what he wanted, but a day later than he had asked for. Paul said that was great; he would be able to take his time getting to Pinkham Notch, since he was unfamiliar with that stretch of the White Mountains.

He phoned the kids next and there was no answer, so he left a cheerful and funny message on the answering machine and mentioned how great the pictures were, especially the one of them giving Heidi a bath. Heidi didn't like baths, so it was always very funny when they tried to give her one because she'd start to howl like a wolf. She did resemble a skinny wolf when she was wet.

When he hung up he changed the itinerary in his head. He would stay in Gorham for the night and then take three days to get to Madison Hut, which would normally take only two. Paul would use a portion of one of those extra days to get his backpack to or near Lonesome Lake Hut the last AMC Hut in the chain of huts and where Laura was able to make him a reservation. He thought of all the possibilities, two of which were hitchhiking or taking the AMC shuttle which went between certain places along the trail twice a day. If it worked out, Paul thought, it would be nice to hike without a heavy pack across the Presidential Range.

Paul found a place a place to eat across from where he was staying. It wasn't great but it catered to backpacker's. When he went to pay for his meal his wallet wasn't in his pants, so he asked the waitress if he could go back to his motel to see if his wallet was there. She agreed, but made him leave something for collateral. He showed her his watch and asked if that was OK, but she said "It's just a Timex, you've got to be kidding. " He tried to think what else he had of value and couldn't think of anything and then the waitress asked "what's that around your neck?"

He was wearing a religious medal, so he showed it to her, and she said, "I'm just concerned you'll run and I'll be stuck with paying your bill. She could tell by the way Paul resisted giving her his medal that that was the best thing she could do for collateral. He would come back for that medal she figured, especially when she saw what kind of medal it was. She had seen many of them before and she knew how important they were to the wearer.

Paul took the medal off from around his neck and handed it to her with the stipulation she had to put it in her apron pocket. Then seeing her put the medal in her apron pocket he was satisfied that it would be safe until his return. What would happen if he couldn't find his wallet?

CHAPTER FOUR

Very Presidential

Paul's wallet was just lying on the bunk in his room when he returned to the motel, so he was overjoyed. He went back to the restaurant to pay his bill and get his medal back from the waitress. Despite her unreasonableness he gave her a tip because after all it wasn't her fault he forgot his wallet.

The unexpected overnight stay in Gorham was nice. Paul had a nice breakfast at the place where he roomed for the night; it was called "Hikers Paradise." Prices were reasonable and they offered rides back to the trailhead. He also bought a couple sandwiches, so he could enjoy the hike and not have to deal with rearranging everything in his backpack. Having missed talking to the kids yesterday, he called first thing Thursday morning. They mentioned that they were swimming at a neighbor's house when he had called the day before. When he finished speaking with the kids he called Laura at work to tell her his plan.

His plan was to take two days to hike to Pinkham Notch and then hitch hike or take the AMC shuttle with his backpack over to where the AT crossed US3. Lonesome Lake Hut, where Laura got a reservation for him to stay, was only three miles from US3. Paul would look for a place to leave his backpack while he hiked across the Presidential Range. Then he would return to Pinkham Notch to spend a night at Joe Dodge Lodge before hiking to Madison Springs Hut which was where Laura made his first reservation. After Paul called Laura he rode back to the trailhead with the owner of Hikers Paradise and started hiking south again.

There were several hikers along the way, but most were headed north. Some looked like they had come all the way from Georgia, while others looked like they were in various degrees in between. There were those who looked like they had been hiking since Pinkham Notch, about 20 miles away, and others who appeared to have been hiking since the Vermont border which was about 145 miles away. They all shared one thing in common; they were all out seeking fellowship and communing with the wilderness. Since he was taking two days to get to Pinkham Notch he decided to stay at Carter Notch Hut, if they had space. Paul had stayed in several of the AMC huts, but never Carter Notch Hut.

The AMC ran eight high mountain huts in the White Mountains. The first, Carter Notch, and the last, Lonesome Lake, were about 62 miles apart. They were all about a day's hike apart and they all offered hikers a bunk bed, blankets, a pillow, and two meals. They had indoor pit toilets and running cold water.

Their season ran from June 1st until about October 14th. The AMC also ran two non-high-mountain places, the first being at Pinkham Notch and it was called Joe Dodge Lodge and a place in Tuckerman's Ravine called Hermit Lake Shelters. Paul's first trip to the White Mountains was between his junior and senior year in college. He and his friend Jeff stayed at Hermit Lake Shelters and he fell in love with the area and went back several times, like the time he went with his father's classmate, Mr. Arthur.

Madison Springs Hut was the first AMC Hut Paul ever stayed in when he hiked with Mr. Arthur. He remembered the treacherous climb up the Parapet Trail in soaking rains and then seeing Madison Spring Hut in the clouds. Madison Springs Hut was in an area called the Presidential Range, which covers a distance of about 25 miles. It goes between Pinkham Notch and Crawford Notch. There was talk some years back of the AMC building another place in Crawford Notch similar to Joe Dodge Lodge, but they had to go thru the permit process that could take years. Joe Dodge Lodge is open to the general public and it doesn't require one to have to hike except from their cars. The Parking area for Joe Dodge Lodge is right on NH16, so you can go from your car to your room in under four minutes.

Most of the Presidential Range is above tree line which refers to the line above which there are no more trees. Tree line is normally at higher elevations in other parts of the world, but due to the strong winds in the Presidential Range it is hard for trees to grow above about 4,700 feet. As the name implies, the peaks in the Presidential Range are mostly named after US Presidents. Paul remembers the first time he and Jeff hiked up Mt. Washington, which at 6,288 feet is the tallest Mountain in the North Eastern United States and home to the world's worst weather. They have the highest recorded wind speed in the world at 231mph. When Paul & Jeff got to tree line there was a big yellow sign that said something to the effect that you were about to enter the most unpredictable weather in the world. If you don't have extra clothing or if the weather appears to be bad, turn back now. And then the sign listed the number of people killed on Mt. Washington due to the weather.

On that particular hike back in 1974 Jeff & Paul continued to the top and it was about 38 degrees at the summit with the wind chill. There was also a snow squall and that was in late July 1974. You can also reach the summit by a cog railway, a tour van, or you can also drive up using the seven- mile-long Auto Road. Anyhow, there were some teenagers at the top and Paul remembered a kid who was in shorts and sandals being told by someone that he wasn't dressed properly. His response was, "well, it was sunny in Boston when we left this morning."

It was about 4:45 p.m. when Paul reached Carter Notch hut. They did have extra bunks for the night, so he picked out a bunk and unrolled his sleeping bag and spread it out on a bunk. The bunks in some of the huts go four high and he didn't want to do that again, so he chose one that was hip-high. After all he wasn't a teenager anymore. Paul was mistaken in that they didn't offer meals at Carter Notch Hut, it was the only one that didn't. They refer to it as a self-service caretaker hut. However, on the brighter side, you could use the kitchen in the hut, so he made some Chili Mac.

The caretaker did offer people some of the bread he made earlier in the day. It didn't look like much, but it was terrific. None of the other hikers were overly social and one couple was upset that they didn't fix your meals for you like they did at the other huts. Paul offered the couple two of his freeze-dried meals, which they appreciated and though they didn't weigh much he figured it would lighten his load. The caretaker gave him extra bread and an appreciative nod for helping the couple out.

After dinner everyone went about doing their own thing. Some played board games and others read. Paul wrote in his journal and figured out his options for the next two days. Since there was no electricity in the hut, everyone went to bed when it got dark at about 9:20 p.m. (313 FK)

Since breakfast wasn't served in the hut Paul fixed coffee, had a granola bar, and started hiking towards Pinkham Notch. He remembered on one of his trips to the White Mountains someone asking a Park Ranger why they are called Notches. The ranger asked the person if they had ever chopped wood and they said yes. "Well," he said, "someone decided at one time that the valleys between the ridges looked like notches when you cut into a log. The notches of course were formed over the course of hundreds of thousands of years as the glaciers cut away the granite by a wonderful thing called gravity." He remembered that Park Ranger's description and used it to explain to others who asked the same question over the years.

He made it to Wildcat Mountain by 10:30 and it was clear enough to see the summit of Mt. Washington, which is in the clouds more often than not. Laura, Paul and three of his high school buddies: Stacy, Tony, and Phillip took the Gondola up Wildcat Mountain before Paul & Laura started their Columbus Day hike back in 1979. It was clear that day also, with no indication of what was to come two days later when Hurricane David worked its way up the Atlantic Coast. However, the day they took the gondola up Wildcat Mountain the weather couldn't have been nicer. It was probably about 40 degrees with a breeze. The five stayed in Jackson, NH that night and then the next day Paul & Laura started their eventful hike.

Paul's high school buddies went along for about the first two miles to make sure Paul didn't leave Laura behind. When they were sure Laura was safe, they went back to the car and then they did their own thing. He was blessed with great high school friends who looked out for one another.

Going down Wildcat Mountain was amazingly steep and obviously why it's a popular ski area. When he still had about a mile to go to Pinkham Notch he saw someone up ahead that he recognized. It was Frank. He stopped and asked Frank how he was and vice versa. Paul said it was comforting to see him and that it was nice to see him and Sylvia at Mass in Rumford Maine. Frank said he would hike with Paul the rest of the way to Pinkham Notch.

Frank started the conversation first. "Paul would you like me to take your backpack to Lonesome Lake Hut?"

"That would be excellent if you can do that for me," he said. "When do you need to leave?"

"I've got all the time in the world," Frank said as he smiled. "It doesn't really matter to me. How about tomorrow morning at 10:00? That is checkout time at Joe Dodge Lodge."

"That would be great and most appreciated. That will give me time to eat, shave and shower, and decide what to take, but I need to buy a small rucksack to carry my stuff."

Frank smiled, and said, "Take mine. I won't need it." Paul hadn't noticed the rucksack on Frank's back. Maybe he had never had it on him before, but he wasn't going to question Frank's offer.

They walked down the mountain and came out at NH16. It was from there that he intended to hitchhike or take the AMC shuttle to Lonesome Lake Hut; he was pleased that he didn't have to do that now. They made it to Joe Dodge Lodge at 3:30. Laura had registered Paul over the phone, but he wasn't sure what Frank wanted to do, so he asked him.

"Frank, they have an extra bunk in my room, do you want to stay?" He wondered whether angels, or whatever Frank was, slept or exactly how that worked. To his surprise Frank said yes. Laura had already paid by credit card for his bunk and meals, so when Paul tried to pay for Frank's, Frank wouldn't hear of it.

"Paul, hold on to that cash, you may need that for something or someone else." Frank took out a $100 bill to pay for his bunk and meals.

It was rare for Paul to be done hiking early, so he thought he'd fit in a nap before dinner. He didn't want to waste his time with Frank, but he figured there would be time to talk at dinner. So, he told Frank he'd like to nap before dinner and Frank said that was fine.

Paul never stayed at Joe Dodge Lodge before, so it was a new experience. The rooms were set up for four people, with two sets of bunks. There was no overhead light, but each bunk had a low watt light for reading. There was no A/C, but you would only need that for the few days when it got hot during the summer. This was one such day; the outside thermometer said it was 87 degrees. Paul opened his window and door for some flow through ventilation and he put his boots in front of the door so it wouldn't slam shut.

Each floor had two communal bathrooms, one for the men and one for the women. He walked down the hall to the men's bathroom to relieve his bladder and then he went back to the room to lie down on his bunk. He took the bottom bunk and left the top one for Frank. It was difficult falling off to sleep because whenever anyone walked down the hall you could hear their hiking boots. A couple of times kids ran down the hall and it sounded like a cattle stampede.

Paul's wrist alarm went off at 5:30 and he must have dozed off because his watch alarm woke him. He put on his clothes and went over to the AMC Visitors Center which was located next door to Joe Dodge Lodge. Besides serving all you can eat meals there, there was a general store, gift shop, and a place for equipment rental. Frank was looking through a book on mountain rescues and when he walked up, Frank said to Paul "hopefully you won't become a statistic."

Paul laughed at Frank's joke and said, "Are you ready to eat?" Frank nodded his head yes.

They both went and got in line because the meal was served cafeteria style. For dinner they had beef & chicken fajitas, Mexican rice, and salad. It was good and plentiful, but Frank didn't eat much. Since there were a number of people at their long table Paul and Frank couldn't talk freely.

The people sitting on either side of them were both from the Boston area and they were up for the weekend. One family was definitely from there because of their accents, but the other family must have been transplants because they had no distinguishable accent. Paul mentioned that his father grew up in Braintree Massachusetts, but that he had not been there since he was five years old. When the two families from Boston left Paul and Frank could talk more freely.

"Frank, I really appreciate your taking my backpack to Lonesome Lake Hut. I was actually thinking about skipping the White Mountains all together because I've been here so many times before, but this is one of my favorite places and didn't want to miss it. Now, without all that weight on my back, I should be able to cover four days ground in two."

"Paul, I'm glad to be able to help you; I see why you like it here so much." And then the two talked about the previous ten days or so, since Frank's first visit. Frank said he was happy that Paul had the chance to go to Mass in Rumford and Frank mentioned that he would have another visitor within the next week, but he couldn't share more than that.

After spending time looking at maps of the White Mountains, Paul decided to buy one. When he went to the checkout, Frank took the map out of his hands so that he could pay for it. The one stipulation was that Paul had to give it to someone else when he didn't need it any more. Frank also bought some snacks for Paul for the next day and when Frank picked up two "Blondie's," that Chocolate Chip type brownie, Paul said he loved those things, to which Frank replied, "I know."

They went back to Joe Dodge Lodge and Paul had an idea. He wondered if Frank was allowed to talk to Laura. He asked Frank if that was alright and he said it was. So, Paul placed the call and Theresa answered the phone. She was excited because she got her list of classes for the coming school year. He asked her to put Mommy on the phone, which she did. He asked Laura if Theresa was still in the room, because she might not understand the conversation. Laura said Theresa went back into the family room and was out of earshot and since the coast was clear, Paul told Laura why he was being so mysterious.

"Honey, do you remember me telling you about Frank?"

"Yes, I do. He's there isn't he?" She always was able to figure stuff like that out. He didn't know how, but it must have been a sixth sense or something or at least a woman's intuition.

"Yes, he is and he said he can talk with you if you'd like," so he handed Frank the phone and he spoke to Paul's wife. Frank mentioned that he would be taking care of Paul's backpack the next day and that they would probably meet up again. Frank told Laura that Paul was in good hands, but to keep praying anyhow. Paul got back on the phone after Frank was finished and he said goodnight to Laura. Then they went back to their room and there was one other person in the room and the guy had a cast on his right arm.

His name was Joe and Frank asked Joe what happened. Joe shared his story of why he had a cast on his right arm. Apparently he was hiking with his son and daughter and he had a fall. Joe said he heard a sound like a stick breaking and he hoped it was just the sound of his walking stick hitting against the rock. However, when he got to the bottom of the rock he knew something wasn't right. Joe said his forearm swelled up immediately to three times its normal size and hurt a lot. They waited a few minutes to see if he was going to be OK, but it wasn't.

His son took Joe's backpack and lashed it to his own while Joe's daughter tried to make a sling out of Joe's Gore-Tex rain jacket. That didn't work, so he found another way to keep his arm immobilized.

Joe said he put his right thumb through one of his belt loops and that helped as long as he didn't take his thumb out. Since it hurt him more to go downhill then to go uphill, they decided to go on up to Lake of the Clouds Hut, which was about five miles from where he fell. Joe was OK as long as he didn't move his arm; unfortunately, the dozen or so times that Joe thought he was going to fall he instinctively put out his right arm to steady himself. When he did that, he had shooting pains which were excruciating. The story got better.

On the way to Lake of the Clouds Hut they got trapped on a ridge during a thunder and lightning storm, which was accompanied by pea sized hail. They crouched behind boulders for protection, but the hail still hit them and it stung. When the hail finished pelting them they got caught in a soaking rain that lasted a good 15 – 20 minutes. When they made it to Lake of The Clouds, the hut master looked at his arm and said she didn't think she could do anything for him. She recommended that Joe continue hiking up to the summit of Mt. Washington, where there would be an EMT. So, Joe and his two kids went outside the warmth of the hut and started hiking up to the summit of Mt. Washington, which was in the clouds.

The summit was about a mile-and-a-half away and 1,200 feet higher. His son and daughter stopped to readjust the son's two packs because the straps were cutting into his shoulders. Joe, however, continued on without them and he took his glasses off because he couldn't see with all the rain on them.

Joe somehow strayed off the trail and he was lost, alone, and couldn't see more than 10 feet. Joe said he panicked briefly and when he regained his composure he realized he was off the trail and that panicking was the last thing he should do. He knew he couldn't backtrack because there were a lot of loose rocks. So, he stood and listened for any noise besides the wind, which was gusting at 30-40 mph. He thought he could hear voices up above, so he walked straight up hoping he would find the trail again. He put his glasses back on and he thought he saw something in the clouds.

Two figures were walking towards him; they appeared gray until they got close enough and then he could see it was two people, one with a red jacket and one with a yellow jacket. They were headed down the mountain to Lake of the Clouds, so Joe asked them if they had seen a girl and boy pass them going up to the summit. They said no, so Joe waited and his two children came along after about three minutes. They continued up Mt. Washington and the closer they got to the top, the windier it got. The rocks near the top were slippery, almost like there was ice on them from the cold temperature combined with the wind. When they did reach the summit they couldn't see the summit house because visibility was only about 50 feet. Fortunately, there were some people who could direct them to the safety of the summit house.

When they got into the summit house Joe went to the Park Rangers Desk and asked if there was an EMT on duty. The women said "yes," she was one, and asked what the problem was. Joe told her he thought he broke his arm in a fall.

She took Joe and his two kids into her office and helped him take off his Gore-Tex jacket which was stuck to his arms because he was soaked from the rain. Joe said, "She literally peeled it off me." When she got the jacket off his left arm she saw blood and asked if that was where he thought he broke his arm and Joe said no, he had done that when he fell a second time. Joe told her it was his right arm which he thought he broke. She got the jacket off his right arm and she agreed that his right arm was broken, but only an X-Ray could verify that.

She called her husband into her office because he was a Park Ranger and she said, "This gentleman needs to be driven down the mountain, he's broken his arm." They would have an ambulance waiting at the bottom to take Joe to the hospital in Berlin. So he and his two kids were taken to the bottom of the mountain and an ambulance was waiting to take him to the hospital. The kids went to get their car at

Joe Dodge Lodge, which was only about two miles from the bottom of the auto road. They showed up at the hospital about 30 minutes after Joe arrived.

The hospital X-Ray confirmed that he fractured his right forearm. They put a temporary cast on him because of the swelling and gave him some pain pills and discharged him. They said he should see an orthopedic doctor when he returned home.

Joe felt bad that his kid's hike had been cut short, so he talked them into finishing the hike to Madison Springs Hut. Joe said his kids should be back tomorrow by 3:00 or 4:00, so they can all drive at least part of the way back to Pennsylvania, where they were from.

Wow, Paul thought to himself. What a story. Joe didn't seem concerned except for the fact that he couldn't sleep on his back and the bunk beds were short and narrow. Joe was about two inches taller than Paul, so he could understand his concern. Joe warned them that if somehow he did manage to fall asleep on his back he was certainly going to snore, but they said not to worry because they had ear plugs. Frank offered Joe help getting ready for bed and Joe was happy to have him take his boots and socks off. A fourth roommate came in at about 8:15 and he didn't have a lot of stuff; they went right to bed.

Joe Dodge Lodge was quieter at night then when Paul tried to take a nap. They left the door open a crack for the flow through ventilation and it actually got a bit cool towards morning, cool enough that he pulled the sheet and blanket over himself. The room was very cramped and almost claustrophobic, which was another good reason to leave the door open. He couldn't imagine if there were four people in the room with all their gear.

Paul wondered if Angels slept. Then again, as Sylvia told him, they weren't really angels. They were created beings with hearts, fingers and toes. They were just never allowed to fully develop because their lives were snuffed out before they were born. He would ask Frank about that sometime when there was a good opportunity. The fourth guy in the room guy was almost as quiet as Frank and his name was Kevin. (319 FK)

Paul was awakened by the sound of a child running down the hall. It was 6:45 a.m. He must have fallen off to sleep because the last time he looked at his watch it was 1:53 a.m. Joe was also awakened and while Paul was checking to see what time it was, Joe swung his feet out over the side of the bed and sat up trying not to hit his head or move his right arm in an unnatural way. The bunks were tight and it was almost impossible not to hit your head, especially for someone as tall as Joe. Frank wasn't in his bunk, so Paul figured he must have gone over to the visitor's center, so Paul, Joe, and Kevin all walked over to breakfast together. Joe needed help tying his shoes, but he didn't wear socks.

Frank was sitting on the front porch of the Visitor Center when the three walked up the steps. He was looking at a copy of the AMC shuttle schedule. Frank looked up at them as they were walking up the steps and he joined the trio when they got to the top of the stairs to enter the Visitor's Center. All four of them went in for the all-you-can-eat breakfast bar and it was pretty much the standard breakfast; they had scrambled eggs, bacon, sausage, pancakes, and two or three choices of cereal. Their coffee was excellent and Paul had three cups. They also had apples and bananas, so Paul took one of each for his hike. Paul also ordered a trail lunch, which consisted of a Turkey & Cheese sandwich.

After breakfast Joe and Kevin returned to their room in Joe Dodge Lodge while Paul and Frank decided on a plan for Paul's backpack. They decided that they would meet outside the Visitor Center at 10:00 a.m. At that point Frank would take Paul's backpack and make his way to Lonesome Lake Hut. He would then hike to Madison Hut by way of the Parapet Trail, which was not technically part of the AT, but it was more difficult.

Paul went back to his room to get his razor and then he went to the men's bathroom to shave and shower. Then he put the things he would need for the next four days into Frank's rucksack. When he was showered and changed he went outside to meet Frank.

Frank was standing outside the Visitor Center talking to Joe when he walked up. Joe was telling Frank that his kids would be there between 3 and 4 in the afternoon. Paul let them finish their conversation and then he walked up to Joe to wish him the best. When it was just Frank and Paul, Paul said to Frank, "I'm not sure about something."

"What's that?" Frank said.

"I don't know whether to take one water bottle or two. Since they don't ever seem to run out, I think I can do with just one."

At that, Frank took the rucksack over to a scale where hikers could weigh their backpacks before starting their journey. He put the rucksack on the scale without the two one-liter water bottles. Then he put the water bottles back in the rucksack and put the rucksack back on the scale. Then he looked and said, "If you're worried about weight you don't have to be."

Paul couldn't believe what he saw. His pack should have weighed at least four pounds more with the two bottles, but it didn't. It weighed the exact same. He never noticed it on the trail because he just assumed it was because he was getting stronger and more used to carrying weight. However, now that he saw the scale with and without the water bottles he knew what a miraculous thing it truly was. After seeing Frank's demonstration, he said, "well I guess I don't have a problem after all."

They both walked over to the white blaze marks that marked where the Appalachian Trail was and Paul stuck out his hand and said, "Frank, I sure appreciate your doing this for me." Frank, shook hands and said,

"Paul I'm happy to be able do it for you. Have a great hike and maybe I'll see you at Lonesome Lake." At that Frank turned and headed to NH16, the main road both into and out of Pinkham Notch. Gorham lies to the north of Pinkham Notch on Route 16 and Conway to the south.

Paul followed the white blaze marks towards Mt. Madison. He planned to recreate part of the hike he went on with Mr. Arthur in 1976, he was closer now in age to Mr. Arthur when they made the hike, so he wanted to see if he noticed a change in his physical condition. The weather looked like it could be a repeat of that particular hike back in 1976 when it rained cats and dogs. Just as he thought that, it got cloudier and started misting.

When he entered what's known as the Great Gulf Wilderness it began to rain and it was at that point where he was supposed to pick up the Parapet Trail. He stopped to put on his rain gear and he also decided to eat his sandwich in case it got soaked from the rain. By the time he finished lunch it had turned into a steady rain. He continued on, now following the blue blazes instead of the white. It was a bit warmer then when he and Mr. Arthur climbed the trail, but similar in terms of rainfall.

As he followed the Parapet Trail up above tree line the footing became more treacherous. He didn't even have on heavy pack and he was finding it difficult. He had a new found respect for Mr. Arthur and the great shape he must have been in.

Paul hadn't seen any other hikers since he got off the main trail, but then he heard someone behind him say, "Excuse us." So he turned sideways and let two hikers could pass. Apparently, they were in such a hurry to get to the top they didn't stop to talk because they passed him and then they were out of sight. It was at about that point when he lost his footing. He fell and slid maybe 20 – 30 feet and he would have fallen further had it not been for someone who was standing there to stop him. When he regained his composure and was sure he hadn't broken anything, he got back up on his feet very carefully. He looked to see the face of the guy who stopped him from having a disaster and it was a familiar face. It was Kevin, one of his roommates from the night before. Kevin spoke first and said, "Are you OK Paul?"

"Yes, thanks to you. I would have been a goner if it weren't for you," he said.

Kevin replied, "No Paul, Thank God. He let me help you and if you don't mind I'll walk with you the rest of the way to Madison Springs Hut and maybe further."

He was happy to have a hiking companion to finish the Parapet Trail and he realized it was stupid of him to try it alone. Kevin must have been the other visitor Frank mentioned, but Paul didn't think it would be so soon. Anyhow, he was happy Kevin was there sooner than later. When Paul's heartbeat returned to a more normal rhythm and he could hold a conversation, he asked Kevin, "So, Kevin, what was God's plan for you?"

Kevin stopped and turned around and waited for Paul to catch up to him, and then he answered, "I was going to be a Chef."

Paul waited before he interrupted, because he knew there was more to the story. As Frank told him, "Don't overlook the simple things of life."

Kevin continued, "I would have been working in a restaurant when someone was choking and I would have given her the Heimlich maneuver; that woman would have lived. Her friends, who were dining with her, panicked and didn't know what to do. They panicked and she choked to death. If my mother hadn't aborted me I would have saved that woman's life and to show her gratefulness the woman would have asked me what I wanted to do with my life and I told her I wanted to be a Chef. She said, "No problem, here is what I'm going to do for you, I will pay for you to go to the New England Culinary Institute and then I want you to come work for me."

Kevin continued by saying, "that woman would have had her own television show that helped a lot of people. I even would have been on her show a couple of times to prepare some heart healthy meals, so her viewers could see how to cook healthy."

Paul said, "It's truly amazing what God can do for us and with us if we give Him a chance. However, we always want to do it our way, we think we know best. It's like one of our priests used to say, "God didn't need us to create us, but He needs us to save us."

Kevin and Paul continued hiking up the Parapet Trail. It was raining hard and in places it looked like small waterfalls coming down off the rocks. When they made it to the top Paul was happy, but soaking wet. That was the hardest rain he experienced thus far in his 25 or so days of hiking. When he saw Madison Springs Hut he felt pretty good despite his fall. However, he was happy to get inside and out of the rain.

Paul decided it was definitely easier hiking without his backpack. He figured it could have been disastrous if he had had his backpack instead of the rucksack because the extra weight and forward inertia would have been his undoing. He would have been lying motionless at the bottom of the ravine were it not for God's intervention.

Kevin, who didn't have a reservation, got a space because there was a last minute cancellation. Paul got a waist-high bunk, which is the second bunk, and Kevin got the top bunk, which was four up from the floor. Dinner was at 6:00 and it consisted of bread, salad, and meatless lasagna. For dessert they had some kind of sheet cake.

It was still raining at 7:30, so they cancelled the nature talk. Paul wrote in his journal while Kevin talked with a couple from New York City. Everybody went to bed at 9:30 when you could no longer see without the use of a flashlight.

As Paul laid there on his bunk he reflected on the day. He was very fortunate to have had Kevin there when he fell. He asked Kevin sometime afterwards why Joe wasn't so fortunate and he said something to the effect that God constantly comes to us in different experiences. He said that Joe's kids helping their father the way they did was as miraculous as his helping me from falling. Paul said his usual evening prayers silently, but he included Mr. Arthur who was now undoubtedly looking down on him from heaven. (327 FK)

The AMC high mountain huts are typically staffed by college age kids who are referred to as the Croo. Some kids work at a hut for just one summer, but many do multiple summers because they have their summers off. The pay from the AMC is marginal, but they can also get tips. For some reason the kids love doing it and that's why the AMC never has a problem staffing the huts.

Besides cooking meals and greeting guests, some of the other duties include hiking down the mountain to get supplies, making sure the pit toilets don't overflow, and giving nature talks to the guests. When the kids go to get supplies they carry out a load of trash, normally consisting of cardboard boxes and aluminum cans and then they bring back fresh food items. Loads can range easily between 30 – 100 lbs., and some kids even boast of carrying a full grown person up the mountain. That's a snapshot of what the Croo does.

The next morning, at about 6:00 the Madison Springs Croo woke everybody by singing a Broadway show tune and making a lot of noise. For breakfast they had scrambled eggs, sausage, bread, butter, and coffee. Then they instructed the hikers how to fold their blankets and leave their bunk beds for the next guests. Paul and Kevin started hiking towards Mt. Washington after they got their bunks in order.

They would have to cover 12 miles to get to Mizpah Hut, intentionally by-passing Lake of the Clouds Hut, which was the next closer hut to Mt. Washington. Lake of the Clouds Hut is the largest of the eight huts and the most popular. Because of its popularity someone once dubbed it Lake of the Crowds and the term stuck. Fortunately, the weather was better than the day before, but the summit of Mt. Washington was still in the clouds, as it frequently was. Paul and Kevin were making good time and made it to the summit by 11:00 a.m.

Paul decided he would get lunch at the snack bar, but Kevin didn't want anything to eat. Instead, he looked at the small museum; as Paul sat in the snack bar watching the various groups of people he tried to count the number of times he had been to the summit of Mt. Washington. He figured this was his fifth time. He hiked up it three times before and drove up on the auto road with Laura and the kids the summer before when he was trying to figure out what they would do after the Air Force. That was a good trip.

They flew from Tampa to Burlington, Vermont and got a rental car. Then they drove to Northfield to show the kids their old house. Paul loved living in Vermont and he liked teaching at Norwich University, but he didn't think he could find a job there. He asked a friend who was still there what the possibility was of getting a job at Norwich and the friend told him he would need a PhD to get a position with the History Department.

He had also thought about teaching Air Force Junior ROTC in Vermont, but there was only one unit in Vermont and it was a highly sought after position in Essex Junction, which is a suburb of Burlington. AFJROTC is the high school equivalent of the college AFROTC program, but the kids don't have any military service obligation and it's more of a citizenship course.

Paul had interviewed for two AFJROTC teaching positions back in the spring. The first opening was in rural southern Virginia. He did well on the interview and they offered him the job, but he turned it down. The high school was in very rural Virginia and none of the Geary family liked the location. The second opening was in Ocala, Florida, where Paul interviewed, but he didn't get offered the job. With future prospects looking bleak, that's when Paul got the idea to hike the Appalachian Trail.

When Kevin came back from the museum Paul was just finishing up lunch, so they started hiking again. The six mile hike down to Mizpah Hut was nice. It was all downhill, a difference of about 2,500 feet. He really enjoyed the section of trail between Lake of the Clouds and Mizpah Hut which was the area where Joe and his two kids weathered the hail storm after he broke his arm. After seeing the ridge in question, Paul had a more profound respect for Joe's dangerous plight.

Along the way Paul asked Kevin if the New England Culinary Institute is in Montpelier, because he seemed to remember seeing it once. Kevin said it was there, just down from the Vermont State Capitol Building. Kevin shared with him that his mother was a college student at Vermont College and she thought Kevin's birth would interfere with her plans. Paul asked Kevin if his mother's plans turned out the way she had hoped.

"They did at first," he said, "she graduated from college and got a job in Albany NY. Then after about three years it finally dawned on her that she had killed a human being. Whenever she saw a child of about three or four years old she would get very anxious and then depression set in. She couldn't sleep and she started taking drugs to help her sleep." Kevin paused as another hiker passed, and then he started speaking again.

"A friend told her she needed to get help, so she visited a psychiatrist. The psychiatrist didn't help much because he was handling it all wrong. He said that she shouldn't worry about what the world thought or what the world had to say because it was her life. In fact, he blamed her difficulty on the world instead of on the problem, which was her decision to have an abortion. Finally, she stopped seeing the psychiatrist when she saw something on television.

As she was flipping through the TV channels she came across the Eternal Word Television Network (EWTN) and it featured a woman who had experienced the same thing she had, but that woman was able to work through her depression and guilt. She tuned in the next day when EWTN had the same woman on explaining how she received healing, so she tried what the woman recommended.

She asked God for forgiveness; she said she was sorry for what she had done and asked for God's guidance..

"Did that help her?" Paul asked.

"Yes, it did. She had a conversion experience of both heart and soul. She started going to church again and got involved in a ministry within her church. She started eating better, sleeping better, and taking better care of herself. She felt like her heart was whole again and that God forgave her. Then she met a man, fell in love, and they will be having a baby on the 15th of next month."

Talking to Kevin made the hike go much quicker; they had only three-quarters of a mile to go before they reached Mizpah Hut. Even though it was downhill, it was tricky because it was like one long staircase that never ended. When you thought it was all over, you rounded a bend and there were more piles of rocks. The tree roots were tricky as well and Paul was glad it wasn't raining because that would have been disastrous. Finally they came into a clearing and the hut was right there, less than 75 feet from the trees. Paul checked in and by chance there was a vacancy for Kevin, too; however, Paul and Kevin's bunks were in two different rooms.

It was 4:45 and he had time for a nap before dinner. He found his bunk, which was in the first room off the common area and he hung Frank's rucksack on a peg, took off his boots, and settled in to a waist high bunk. Fortunately he was able to drift off to sleep and he could feel someone shaking his arm and calling his name. It was Kevin and it was 5:50, dinner was in ten minutes.

It was a full house at Mizpah Hut that night and the Croo fixed their version of Shepard's Pie, in which they managed to fit in all the levels of the food Pyramid, with the exception of fruit. Of course there were tomatoes in it and since tomatoes are technically a fruit, Paul realized they did have the entire pyramid covered. The black beans were an interesting twist to the standard Shepherd Pie recipe. "There would be music tonight in the hut," Paul thought to himself. Of course they also had bread and some kind of sheet cake for dessert. There was a nice couple from Washington DC sitting at their table, so Paul shared some of his childhood memories of growing up in Washington DC back in the 1960's. The couple wasn't originally from there, but had lived there about 15 years. They told Paul that they come up to the White Mountains every year this same week because that's when their kids are at summer camp. The couple, as it turned out, lived about two miles from where his mother still lived.

After dinner Paul and Kevin went outside for some fresh air and that's when Kevin told him he would be leaving the next day after they got to Crawford Notch. He didn't ask why, he just assumed Kevin had something more important to do, but he felt very fortunate to have had Kevin's help the day before, so he didn't ask any questions.

In that Mizpah Hut was below tree line it seemed to get darker earlier than at Madison Springs Hut which was above tree line. He added the day's happenings to his journal and went to sleep. (339 FK)

Day 28 would be a twenty mile day. Paul had to get from Mizpah Hut to Galehead Hut, a distance of about 20 miles. They ate breakfast and then shoved off, taking the Webster Cliff Trail, which he and Mr. Arthur had hiked back in 1976. He remembered it as being very steep and his guidebook backed that fact up. Fortunately, however, it had some beautiful views. Paul was happy not to have the weight of his backpack going down the cliffs. He recalled that back in '76 his pack made him top heavy and once he nearly fell forward off the cliffs. He was thankful to have a lower center of gravity this time as they went down the Webster Cliff Trail.

Kevin and Paul made it to US302 in about two hours and it was there Kevin and Paul said goodbye. Paul didn't ask Kevin if he would see him again, he just assumed he would at some other place and time. He did thank him, however, for all he had done for him.

Paul was pretty sure Kevin stayed for the purpose of getting him safely down Webster Cliffs. He slid in several places and Kevin stopped him from sliding where he shouldn't. He had 14 miles ahead of him after Kevin departed and the first three miles of the 14 brought back memories of his and Stacy's snowshoe adventure many years earlier.

Prior to Christmas in 1977 Paul and Stacy tried their hand at snowshoeing. Neither had ever snow shoed before so the outfitter wouldn't rent them their good snowshoes. Instead, he rented them their heavy plastic snowshoes that secured to the hiking boots with twine. They got a much later start then they wanted, partly due to the runaround at the outfitters and also because of a problem with Stacy's car near White River Junction, VT. The distance from US302 to Ethan Allen Pond was three miles. Paul remembered when he hiked it with Mr. Arthur it took about two hours. However, it took them more than a day-and-half. It was slow going because there was about 14" of snow, with about an inch and-a-half" of ice on top.

Since it was too steep for snowshoes, they took turns breaking trail. Whoever was in front had to break the ice and the person trailing would then step in his footprints. Even though they were wearing gaiters, the ice rubbed away the skin on their shins. When it got dark that first day they had to stop. They patted out a flat area with their snowshoes, put up Stacy's tent, and warmed some water for their freeze-dried meals. In that they sunk down in the snow if they left the tent without snowshoes, they basically had to kneel in the doorway of the tent to pee.

The next day wasn't much better, but they did get to where it was flat enough to try their snow shoes. It got dark again, so they put up their tent and called it a night at about 4:00 p.m. After about one hour of hiking on the third day they reached their destination, Ethan Allen Pond. They were so exhausted they just decided to spend the next two days there. They had the lean-to all to themselves, so it was very peaceful.

It was a beautiful scene back in 1977 with the snow covered trees and snow still falling when Paul and Stacy got to the lean-to. They figured there was about 3" of new snow on top of what they already had. The one real drawback was that the outhouse door had so much snow in front of it they had to dig it out. Once they dug it out they discovered the toilet seat was covered with about ½" of frost. When they left on the third day, they made it back to Stacy's car in about five hours.

With his thoughts back to the present Paul made it to the Ethan Allen Pond cut off in about two hours. He ate one of the "Blondie's" Frank bought him at the visitor's center and some of the trail mix which he bought from the Croo at Mizpah Hut. He washed it down with some water.

Paul looked forward to the next four-and-a-half miles to the Zealand Falls Hut because it was relatively flat and he made it in about an hour-and-a-half because he was walking fast all the way. It was at Zealand Falls Hut where Paul and Laura had their great adventure nearly 16 years earlier on the second day of their Columbus Day backpacking trip.

Paul and Laura, who were both stationed in Ft. Walton Beach, Florida, took a ten-day vacation to go backpacking in New Hampshire. When they woke up that second morning at Zealand Falls Hut the snow was about seven inches deep. Paul asked the hut master if he thought they would have problems getting to Galehead Hut, and he didn't think so, but he said he'd radio ahead to tell the caretaker they were coming. None of the other hikers were going to Galehead because they were all returning to Crawford Notch by way of the Zealand Trail. Paul and Laura were the only hikers on that section of trail between Zealand Falls and Galehead.

When Paul had did that seven-mile hike with Mr. Arthur back in June of 1976, it took about five hours. Laura and Paul had been hiking about seven hours when they got to South Twin Mountain which is just above tree line. The snow was up to Laura's waist, so Paul walked in front of her holding onto the bar on top of Laura's backpack. The snow was so deep they couldn't see the cairns, which are the piles of rocks which show the way above tree line. Paul just prayed they were on the trail and heading in the right direction.

As they started down the mountain and got to tree line, he was ready to take out their tent and sleeping bags. They wouldn't have been able to secure the tent, but they could crawl into it, get in their sleeping bags and try to stay warm. Fortunately, they trudged on and just as it was getting dark Paul thought he saw a man made structure. It was Galehead Hut, so after nine hours of arduous hiking they reached their destination.

When the caretaker opened the door and saw them standing there, she said, "What are you doing here?" It turned out that the Galehead Hut radio was broken and she didn't know they were coming.

Laura and Paul stayed there two days recuperating from an exhausting and scary hike. The next day some hikers came from Zealand Hut and thanked Paul & Laura for breaking trail for them. When Paul and Laura were ready to go they hiked down to US 3 and hitchhiked back to North Conway. It was while they were in North Conway they found out the reason for the heavy winds and snow. Hurricane David made its way up the Atlantic Coast and up the Connecticut River Valley. Mount Washington recorded a wind speed of 179mph on that stormy Columbus Day.

As Paul continued his hike towards Galehaed Hut he thought of how it looked back in October 1979, all snow and ice covered; and how it looked now, all green and lush. He walked up the steps to Galehead hut at 5:30 and he had 30 minutes to spare, but he didn't dare lay down for a nap. If he did lie down he knew he would fall asleep and miss dinner and he knew he would surely need the sustenance after his 20 mile day. Dinner was good, but anything would have tasted good, but the dessert was particularly good.

It was a combination banana bread and zucchini bread and since there were several kids that didn't want any of it that meant more for Paul and the other adults. The kids probably would have eaten it had the hut master not mentioned the word zucchini. There were some interesting people at the hut, but Paul was so tired he didn't feel like being sociable. He climbed into his bunk at 8:30 and drifted off to sleep. (359 FK)

He didn't get a chance to write in his journal before he went to sleep, so he worked on it before breakfast. Breakfast was served at 7:00.

Paul always thought Cracker Barrel made the best pancakes in the world, but the Croo at Galehead made some great ones, too. However, their coffee was better than

Cracker Barrel's; at least that's what he thought. Paul thought everything tasted very good on that Monday, July 17th, 1995. Maybe it had to do with his good night's sleep. He got up once during the night to relieve his bladder and then he was able to fall right back to sleep. Galehead Hut was the farthest southwest Paul had ever hiked in the White Mountains. He had never hiked from Galehead to Franconia Notch, but he understood there were some difficult areas. Apparently there were a lot of granite rocks from listening to people talk at breakfast.

Back during Hurricane David, he and Laura heard that someone died from hypothermia on top of Mt. Lafayette. Paul wanted to make sure he didn't rush this hike, since he was alone. As he reflected back to the day before, he felt he was careless at times and he didn't want to break any bones like Joe, his roommate at Joe Dodge Lodge.

The next hut along the AT was Greenleaf Hut and it wasn't directly on the Appalachian Trail. According to his guidebook it was a mile off the AT and 1,000 feet lower, so that meant an extra two miles of hiking plus the two changes in elevation. He decided on Lonesome Lake Hut, so that he wouldn't have to do the two miles extra. Besides, Lonesome Lake Hut was directly on the AT.

Paul started out at 8:00 a.m. after buying some banana/zucchini bread, trail mix, and some Hershey Bars. The hike from Galehead to Mt. Lafayette was strenuous, but there were some outstanding views from Garfield Ridge. He wasn't prepared for the long rocky staircases which his breakfast mates were obviously referring to. His knees began to hurt from the constant shock against the granite boulders.

The first staircase was up to Mt. Garfield and then there was another one up to Mt. Lafayette. Paul stopped for a 30-minute break on top of Mt. Lafayette. As he ate his banana/zucchini bread and trail mix, he wondered where they found the body of the guy who died there during the hurricane in 1979. It would have been white out conditions, so the poor guy didn't have the great view he did. Visibility was unlimited to the east, but something was moving in from the west.

Paul still had over six miles to Franconia Notch and then another three miles to Lonesome Lake. He was beginning to think he should have planned a night in Franconia Notch before he went on to Lonesome Lake Hut. He was feeling the pain in his knees more and more from all the stepping on the granite rocks. His backpack, however, would be at Lonesome Lake Hut if he did decide to stay in Franconia, but he rationalized that he could rinse out his clothes in the sink or shower.

His knees didn't feel any better by the time he got to the Liberty Spring Tent site which was a little over two-and-a-half miles from US3. By the time he got to US3 it was 5:00 and he knew he couldn't make it another three miles up hill to Lonesome Lake Hut, so he decided to hitchhike to North Woodstock, which was about six miles south. He was too tired to even try to walk alongside the roadway with his thumb out like he normally did.

He hoped he didn't look too scruffy and dirty because he'd been wearing the same clothes since he left Pinkham Notch. He wore them through the soaking rain on the Parapet Trail and his subsequent fall. All he carried in his rucksack was rain gear, a guidebook and map, one extra pair of underwear and snacks for the day hikes.

Someone did pick him up after about ten minutes, so he must not have look that bad. The driver, whose name was Phil, was from North Woodstock and since Paul was tired he asked Phil if he could recommend a place for someone to stay without a reservation. Phil said he knew exactly such a place; it was a B&B and Phil said the owners would even drive him back to the trail the next morning if he wanted them to. Phil said it was close to a nice restaurant called the Landmark, the place where he was a waiter.

Phil dropped Paul off at the B&B and mentioned that his restaurant had some great food. He thanked Phil and said he might see him there around dinner time. They did have rooms available at the B&B since it was a weekday and they had a pay phone in the lobby, so after checking out his room which consisted of a bunk bed and nightstand, with a shared bathroom, he phoned Brandon, Florida. Daniel answered the phone and handed it to mommy after he said "hi, dad. Bye, dad. I'm headed over to Matt's house now."

When Laura got on the phone Paul told her his plan had been too ambitious and he couldn't make it to Lonesome Lake. He didn't think his knees could take it. After making sure she had shipped a package to Glencliff, New Hampshire, he talked briefly with Theresa and Steven. After he hung up the receiver he decided to go check out Phil's restaurant.

He passed the grocery store listed in his guidebook, so he checked out their hours of operation when he passed by. They were open until 8:00 and it was 6:30, so Paul had about an hour to eat dinner. Paul went to Phil's restaurant and they did have good food. He had the special, which was some kind of stir-fry beef and vegetables served on a bed of rice. Paul craved banana cream pie and they had it on their dessert menu, so he had two pieces

After dinner he went to the grocery store, but he wasn't sure how much he could fit into Frank's rucksack, so he got a can of beef stew and trail mix, plus some candy bars. Then he went back to the B&B and the owners offered Paul the use of their washer and dryer, so he took them up on their kind offer. Some of the debris from his fall three days earlier was really imbedded, so their washer did a better job than he could have done in the bathroom sink.

He looked at his map and guidebook to see if there was any way he could make up the lost time. He already forfeited the night at Lonesome Lake Hut. The AMC will let you change the date of your stay at a hut, but only with more of a notice. However, they won't give you a refund. After going through his options, he decided to get his backpack at Lonesome Lake Hut and continue on to Eliza Brook Shelter. When Paul's clothes were done he changed back into them so that he wasn't walking around in just gym shorts. Then he wrote in his journal and went to bed. (373 FK)

His wrist alarm went off at 6:30, which gave him 30 minutes to get ready for breakfast. As he swung his legs out of bed he thought how much better his knees felt than the day before, probably because of the two Tylenol he took before going to bed. Paul had breakfast, used the rest room, and then the owner drove him back to the trail head. He was back on the trail and hiking southwest again by 8:30.

His knees felt OK as he hiked up to Lonesome Lake and he made it to Lonesome Lake Hut by 10:15. He explained to the hut master who he was and why he didn't make it the night before. The hut master understood, but explained that the AMC could not give him a refund, so he got his backpack, used the bathroom, and started hiking again. He stopped for a break at the Kinsman Pond Campsite which was about two miles past Lonesome Lake.

Continuing on to South Kinsman Mountain there was about a 600 foot increase in elevation and he was more worried about his knees on the descent to the Eliza Brook Shelter, which had a drop of nearly 1,900 feet. Fortunately, his knees were

OK. Paul was thankful he took the overnight break at North Woodstock, but he was sorry he paid for two nights lodging instead of one. He got to the Eliza Brook Shelter at 5:15 and there was still space in the shelter, so he staked out his place by rolling out his sleeping pads and putting his sleeping bag on top of it. He had only hiked about nine miles, but he didn't want to stress his knees, which seemed alright now. He was disappointed that he didn't make up any mileage, but there was always tomorrow.

He decided to have the can of beef Stew for dinner and some of the cookies he bought in North Woodstock. The owner of the B&B also gave him some cookies, so he ate hers first and would save the store bought ones for later because he figured the store bought cookies would have had more preservatives and keep longer. It started to rain at about 8:15, so Paul was happy he got a spot in the shelter. He and everybody else in the shelter went to sleep when the sun went down. With the exception of one person, everyone else in the shelter was headed north. The name of the guy going south was Tom and he was from near Baltimore, Maryland. The next day Tom hiked with Paul and mentioned to Paul that he was a sectional hiker.

Tom had hiked the 281 miles of the AT in Maine the year before and this year he was doing New Hampshire & Vermont, which was about another 310 miles. If everything worked out as planned, he would do the next section of about 300 miles from Massachusetts to the Pennsylvania border the following year. He was self-employed, so he could arrange his schedule that way.

About 30 minutes into their hike Tom said to Paul, "Paul I couldn't help but notice this morning when you were changing into your hiking clothes that you have some kind of medal around your neck. I've seen others like it before, but I've never been in the position to ask anyone about it. If you don't mind could you tell me what it is?"

"Yes. It is called the Miraculous Medal," he said.

CHAPTER FIVE

Miraculous

Paul was caught off guard by Tom's question, but he was eager to tell him everything he knew about the Miraculous Medal. "Maybe I can best tell you about the Miraculous Medal by telling you a story I heard once. Then I will tell you what I know about its origin in early 19th century France. Is that okay?"

"Yeah, that's fine," Tom replied.

"I heard this remarkable story about the Miraculous Medal after I started wearing one a couple years ago. I'm sure I won't have all the names and places right, but I'll do my best to tell you what I remember."

Paul glanced over to see how receptive Tom was and Tom's head was turned towards Paul, so Paul began.

"There was a young black man named Claude who was in a prison in Vicksburg, Mississippi back in the mid-1940's. Claude was scheduled to be put to death for murdering his step-grandfather and a couple of months before he was to be electrocuted he urgently wanted to see a Catholic Priest even though he wasn't Catholic.

A priest was sent for and when the priest arrived Claude told him why he wanted to see him. Apparently the night before the priest came to see Claude, Claude was in an argument with another prisoner who was wearing a Miraculous Medal. Claude asked the other prisoner what the medal was and instead of explaining what it was he tore the medal off his neck and threw it on the floor. Claude picked it up off the floor and asked a guard if he could get some string, so that he could wear the medal around his neck and the guard did get Claude some string so he could wear the medal. Claude went to bed that night and during the night he was awakened by someone touching his wrist."

Paul made sure Tom was still listening and then he continued. "Claude said there was a woman standing there in his cell; the 'most beautiful woman God ever created' in Claude's own words. She spoke to him and said, 'If you would like me to be your Mother and you would like to be my child, send for a priest of the Catholic Church.' Then she disappeared. Claude started screaming because he was scared, but he did as the woman asked. The guards called for a Catholic Priest because Claude was causing such a commotion.

The prison guard arranged for a Catholic Priest to come in, so that Claude would calm down because he was screaming and yelling and disturbing the other prisoners.

When the priest arrived Claude told the priest he wanted to become a Catholic and he told the priest why. The priest agreed to give Claude instruction to become Catholic.

Two amazing things happened in regard to Claude's Catholic instruction. He couldn't read, so the priest had to read him everything. When the priest got ready to explain the Sacrament of Confession, Claude said he knew what that was already because the Lady told him all about repentance and Claude explained it to the priest just like the Lady explained it to him. The priest was amazed at the description of Confession that Claude recited back and a few days later it was the same thing when the priest was going to teach Claude about the Sacrament of Communion. Claude told the priest in detail what the Lady told him and the priest was once again amazed at Claude's understanding of the sacraments.

The priest thought Claude was ready for initiation into the Catholic Church, so he gave Claude Holy Communion. A few days later Claude was supposed to be executed, but what Claude didn't know was that a group of people, including a Sheriff and a District Attorney, who were both white, were trying to save Claude from going to the electric chair. They did manage to get him a two-week reprieve and Claude was very upset about that when he got that news. They asked him why he was so upset at the two week extension on his life and Claude told them he wanted to be with the Lady and her son in heaven. When Claude asked why he had to wait for two weeks the priest said that maybe it was because the Lady wanted Claude to win other souls.

There was another prisoner at the prison who despised Claude, so Claude tried to save his soul. When Claude's two weeks were up he died very peacefully. When it was time for the other prisoner to die he too called for a priest. Evidently the prisoner was a Catholic and he wanted to confess his sins before they electrocuted him.

The priest asked him why he had a change of heart and the prisoner pointed to the corner of the room and explained that he saw Claude standing there with a Lady. The Lady let the prisoner see what was in store for him in Hell if he didn't repent and then he saw images of himself in Hell. That was when he screamed for a priest. So, Claude did win the other man's soul; the extra two weeks wasn't for Claude, it was for the other prisoner."

Paul finished the story and turned to Tom and said, "There is more to the story than that. There were other miraculous revelations and one was about something that happened to that Catholic priest during World War II. I have a copy of what actually happened if you want me to send it to you after I get back to Florida; or if you can't wait until December, I'm sure you can find the story in a religious bookstore."

Tom said he would like a copy of it and said he'd leave his address with him once they parted ways. Then Tom said he'd like to hear about how the Miraculous Medal came to be.

Paul told Tom the story of the Miraculous Medal and how it was designed by the Blessed Virgin Mary herself and how she appeared to a French nun by the name of Catherine Labouré. The Blessed Mother appeared to Catherine several times and in the first meeting she told Catherine that she had a mission for her. Catherine's mission was to cast the Miraculous Medal and to both distribute it and explain what it meant to the French people.

On the second visit to Catherine by the Blessed Mother, Mary showed Catherine what should be on the medal, both front and back. On the front side of the medal

Catherine saw Mary standing on what seemed to be half a globe and she was holding a golden globe in her hands, offering it up to heaven. On the back there were twelve stars around the edges and a large cross on top of a big **M** and there were two hearts underneath the **M**. Paul told Tom he didn't want to mess up what everything stood for, so he didn't try to explain further. He did go on to say that the Miraculous Medal is a great testimony to faith and the power of trusting in prayer. "God," Paul said, "uses a Medal as an instrument in bringing certain marvelous things to pass as in the story of Claude."

When Paul finished telling Tom about the Miraculous Medal he looked over at Tom and Tom seemed deep in thought. They walked about one hundred yards before Tom spoke, and then he said, "You know, I was raised Catholic, or at least that's what I always write on paperwork whenever they ask for religious preference. However, I haven't been inside a Catholic Church in a good 15 years or so. Paul, I must admit, I feel this void inside me as if something is missing."

"Well Tom, you know you can always come home to the Catholic Church. I don't exactly know the process, but I don't think it's that difficult. A priest should be able to tell you the process you will need to follow."

They walked along for a while and Paul asked Tom which sacraments he had already received. Tom said he was baptized, made his first confession, and then made his first communion. Tom said that was about the time his mother and father got divorced and Tom explained that his mother stopped going to Mass because it brought back too many painful memories. Tom said he could never understand her logic, but realized his mother wasn't thinking clearly. He did remember that going to Mass always made him feel good. Tom said he didn't necessarily understand everything that was happening, but he knew he felt good inside afterwards.

Paul did some calculating in his mind to see when they would be near a sizable town with a Catholic Church. He was thinking that if he and Tom were still hiking together when they were near a town with a Catholic Church, then they could go to Mass together. Someone told Paul one time that everyone needs companions in their faith journey for encouragement and strength. However, he wasn't sure he could keep up with Tom's pace. Tom was a good 12 to 14 years younger and he was doing his best to keep up. It would have been better if he just had Frank's rucksack, but now he had both. He wondered where Frank was and what he was doing.

He asked Tom what his plans were for that night and Tom said he was enjoying their conversations so much he might stay with him for a day or two if that was alright. Paul was delighted to hear that and he told Tom "that would be great." Paul, however, mentioned that Tom's pace was too fast, so Tom slowed down a bit.

"Tom, I am thinking of hiking to Jeffers Brook Shelter for the night and then tomorrow stopping in Glencliff for my mail drop. After that I don't know. How does that sound to you?"

"That sounds like a smart plan and actually goes along with what I had planned. I also have a mail drop to pick up in Glencliff."

Paul and Tom had their last mountain summit above tree line. It was Mt. Moosilauke and at 4,800 it had a great view. Their guidebooks said you can see five states on a clear day, but this was not one of those clear days; however, they could look back from where they just came from and see the Franconia Ridge. The next 4,000 footer wouldn't be until Killington, Vermont. The hike down Mt. Moosilauke was harder on Paul than the hike up; his knees hurt, but not as much as coming down from Mt. Lafayette two days prior. He mentioned to Tom that he was slower on downhills because of his knees, so Tom was patient and he would just stand there taking in the views until he caught up.

They got to Jeffers Brook Shelter at about 6:45, covering a little over 16 miles since morning. Other than his knees aching, Paul felt pretty good. It was nice talking to Tom along the way because it made the miles go by quicker. Other than talking about spiritual things, when Tom heard Paul mention he had just retired from the Air Force, he said that his grandfather's younger brother was in the Army Air Corps during World War II. Tom said he was a ball turret gunner in a B-17 and never made it home. He said it was hard for his grandfather to talk about it, but from what he could find out he was on his 19th mission when his plane was hit.

Paul could talk at length about the Army Air Corps in WW II because he had been the Military Historian when he worked at AFROTC Headquarters in Montgomery, Alabama back in the mid-1980's. He loved history of any kind, but particularly aviation history.

Paul asked Tom if he had ever seen the movie Memphis Belle and when he said he had not seen it, he told him about it. He thought in some ways it was a better film than 12 O'clock High, though 12:00 O'clock high was a classic and a good case study in Leadership styles. However, in Memphis Belle you got a real appreciation for what the men faced during a bombing run and how the ball turret gunner felt very vulnerable, all alone and underneath the B-17.

He asked Tom if he knew whether his grandfather's brother was short because that was the person who normally got that job. Tom said he thought so because once when his grandfather was talking about his brother he said his parents thought he was switched at birth since they were all over 5'10", but his brother was only 5'2". After talking about the Army Air Corps for so long, Tom made a comment to Paul about how he should be a teacher.

"Paul" he said, "you should be a teacher because you bring things to life with your descriptions and stories."

Paul had thought about that. He loved history and had applied for a teaching job at a community college in the Tampa area. It was a part time job teaching Western Civilization and American History, both of which he had taught for the University of Maryland when he was stationed in Oslo, Norway. There were a lot of applicants for that job in Tampa and it finally went to someone with their PhD. When he didn't get that job, he considered teaching AFJROTC when he retired from the Air Force. He wouldn't need a PhD for that, only a Master's degree.

Paul was thankful he got his Master's degree in History when they lived in Naples, Italy. He shared that story with Tom, the story of how he got a Master's Degree in History. The Air Force expected its officers to pursue a higher degree and he didn't feel like it. However, when they lived in Italy there were three Master's degree programs offered for the military forces and their dependents assigned to the NATO headquarters there. The Master's in Italian/Roman History sounded like fun. So, he took one course to see if he liked it. Paul not only liked it, he loved it. The first course was on Ancient Rome, which included field trips to Rome, the island of Capri, Pompeii and Herculaneum. He stuck with it and passed his comprehensive exams, which were pretty demanding. He needed a Master's Degree in order to teach College ROTC. He applied for ROTC duty and that's how he got to Norwich University in Vermont. All the memories of years past rushed through Paul's mind.

Paul and Tom pooled their resources for dinner with Paul offering up a Chili Mac dinner, while Tom offered up a Lasagna dinner. He also had some bread left that he bought in North Woodstock, plus the store bought cookies. Mixing the two entrees made for an interesting, but not great, dinner. They lucked out because there were two spaces left in the shelter and the weather looked threatening. All the other hikers were headed north, with two hiking all the way to Mt. Katahdin and one only as far as Mt. Washington. Paul added the day's events to his journal and drifted off to sleep. (397 FK)

At 5:45 a.m. someone's wrist alarm went off, but Paul was awakened by a clap of thunder 10 minutes earlier. The trail was messy and slippery going down to the Oliverian Brook, which they couldn't ford. The bridge had been washed away according to the northbound hikers, who mentioned that it would be a problem with the heavy rain. The detour was not too bad and it was relatively flat. Once they made it to Glencliff, they went to the Post Office on NH25 and asked for their packages.

Paul opened his package and took out the phone card, new pictures of the kids, and a granola bar, which he promptly tore into. He and Tom emptied their boxes and put the contents into their backpacks. The postal employee said they could leave their boxes and he would dispose of them. Apparently he had a hobby of collecting the From: addresses and posting them on a map in his den at home. He said that Paul's From: of Brandon, Florida was his first. He said he already had one from Towson, Maryland.

Paul told Tom he would need 15 minutes before they started hiking again because he needed to phone home and Paul's call home was a miss. There was no answer, so he left what he thought was a pretty funny message on the answering machine and sang a short song. Paul returned to the post office and found Tom, who was munching on trail mix. They crossed over NH 25 which would be the first of three times they would cross a road marked NH25. Tom made the comment that they must have run out of road numbers when they were naming roads because they would also cross NH25C and NH25A.

The rain slowed to a drizzle, which made the hike pleasant between Glencliff and NH25C; there was just a slight uphill grade. However, the hike between NH 25C and NH25A was a different story. Although the distance in the guidebook was listed at five miles, it seemed longer and you could tell you were going uphill. Paul sensed he was holding Tom up, but he was doing his best.

When they stopped to take a break about a mile after NH25A Paul told Tom he felt overwhelmed with these 15 – 16 mile days and he said he only had about another two hours of hiking left in him for the day. Looking at the guidebook, he decided he would stay at the Hexacuba Shelter which was at about mile marker 413. He told Tom that he would understand if Tom wanted to hike further, but Paul thought that was as far as he could go for the day, which was his 32nd since leaving Mt. Katahdin. Paul figured it would take him at least another two days, if he was lucky, to get to Hanover, NH and his next mail pick up. Hanover was still 29 miles away.

When they got to the Hexacuba Shelter Tom said he would also stay there. The next possible camping area was another mile-and-a-half away, but the guidebook indicated the water source was considered unreliable. The story behind the name of the shelter was that it was shaped like a hexagon and it was on top of Cube Mountain. The shelter was already full, so Paul and Tom had to use their tents. Apparently the shelter was a popular hangout for Dartmouth architectural students on weekends during the school year. However, most everyone staying there that night was a thru hiker headed north. The people at the shelter invited them to share their fire, which they gladly accepted. Someone from the shelter also hung a clothesline between the shelter and some trees and said anyone was welcome to use it, so Paul hung up his shorts, shirt, and socks he wore during the day's rain. (413 FK)

Paul was awakened at 6:15 a.m. by the sound of boots walking on wooden planks. It was the north bounders in the shelter some 20 yards away, but he could still hear them from his tent. The north bounders were hiking in one day what took Paul & Tom a day-and-a-half. He looked forward to his coffee and some oatmeal with raisins and chocolate chips. Tom wasn't stirring yet, so either he slept with earplugs or he was a heavy sleeper. At 7:05 Tom came out from his tent and was surprised to find that the north bounders were already gone. Their goal for the day was to make it to Moose Mountain Shelter which was 18 miles away, so both Paul and Tom started hiking at 7:45.

Though they had been drinking water as they hiked, they stopped for a big water break after about 2 ½ hours, when they reached Smarts Mountain. Tom asked Paul if he wanted him to fill his water bottles along with his, but he said that wouldn't be necessary because he was still fine. As he watched Tom walk off to the spring to fill his water bottles, he felt a tap on his shoulder. Startled, he swung around to see Sylvia looking up at him. She looked out of place in the wilderness dressed in an orange paisley blouse with khaki pants. Sylvia said, "I'm sorry if I frightened you Paul, but there is something I should tell you."

"Hi Sylvia. What a great surprise."

"You have probably been wondering what to do when Tom or anyone asks you why you never refill your water bottles. You can tell him the truth, but you don't need to tell him everything, at least not yet."

He wondered about that and was a little bit nervous about how he would handle it if the situation arose. It must have seemed odd to Tom that he never filled his water bottles. His thoughts turned to Sylvia and how she was doing.

"Did you get to Dover?" Paul asked.

"No. Not yet. I still have some things to do before I can go there. How are you holding up?"

"Well Sylvia, physically I have some good days and some not so good days, but my spirits are good. It has been fun hiking and talking with Tom. I thought he was one of you guys for a while."

While Paul was talking to Sylvia, Tom came back from the stream, but Paul didn't see him.

"Paul, who do you think you're talking to?" Tom asked.

"Oh, just myself," he said. "I do that sometimes when I'm bored. Are you ready to start hiking again?"

"Yes, I'm ready Paul. Do you remember what we were talking about last?" Tom asked.

Actually Paul drew a blank because he was still thinking about Sylvia and why no one could see her except him. He wasn't sure if he had ever asked her that. Paul made a mental note to ask her, or Frank, or Kevin the next time he saw any of them.

Paul thought he could steer the conversation in any direction he wanted since Tom couldn't remember either what they were talking about before they stopped for water.

"Tom, you know I can't remember what we were talking about. I do remember though that you asked about returning to your Catholic roots." When he looked over at Tom, Tom nodded his head, so he continued.

"I remember when I was driving to work a couple months ago I heard an interview on the Catholic radio station in Tampa. The host was interviewing someone, I think a Presbyterian, and he mentioned a friend of his who was a minister who also was a convert to the Roman Catholic Church. His friend was a man by the name of Scott Hahn and he had just published a book on his conversion experience. The name of the book was *Rome, Sweet Home*. I bought it and I remembered thinking to myself that the information was very valuable to me. I learned a lot about the Catholic Church, things I always took for granted.

My wife and I were asked if we would help sponsor someone in the RCIA program, so I thought what if someone asks me a question about the Catholic Church and I can't answer it. Well, that book helped a lot."

Tom wasn't familiar with RCIA so Paul explained that The Right of Christian Initiation for Adults is an adult faith formation process leading to full reception into the Catholic Church. It used to be referred to as Convert Instruction. The RCIA process helps people grow in faith and understanding on the teachings of Jesus and His Church.

"So how did it go? Tom asked.

"What do you mean? Paul asked in reply.

"How did the person do that you sponsored?"

"It turns out that we were alternates and they didn't need us. However, if they ever do need us, I feel confident we would be up to the task."

Paul and Tom made it to the Lyme-Dorchester Road by 12:15 and they took a break alongside the road. They were falling off their pace and weren't sure if they could make it to Moose Mountain Shelter. They cut their break short and started hiking again after sipping on some water and snacking on trail mix. They would quicken their pace some, trying to get to Trapper John Shelter cut off by 1:30. It was a distance of about three miles, so they felt confident they could do it. The workers in the White Mountain Huts, he thought, can do that carrying twice the weight he was carrying.

The Trapper John Shelter was apparently so named for the fictitious character in the movie and hit TV series M.A.S.H. who was a Dartmouth graduate. Paul remembered back to when he, Laura, and Theresa were living in Naples, Italy. It was probably in late 1982 or early 1983 that everyone gathered to see the last M.A.S.H. TV episode, which was recorded back in the States and mailed to the person hosting the party. A neighbor's son babysat Theresa and Paul remembers that Laura got nervous about one hour into the tape because it was time for Theresa to nurse. The worrying was unnecessary because Theresa was still napping when they got back after the two hour M.A.S.H. party.

The conversation returned to RCIA and Tom wanted to know if he should go. He was worried that he had been gone for so long, that he couldn't remember what to do. He told him to ask a priest; however, Paul shared a joke with Tom about a guy who hadn't gone to confession in 40 years. When the priest told him to say a decade of the Rosary for his penance, the guy told the priest he had been gone for so long he forgot how to say a decade of the Rosary. At that, the priest told him to say three Our

Father's and three Hail Mary's. Again the guy said he had been away for so long that he forgot, at which point the priest asked, "What do you remember?"

The guy said he remembered how to do The Angelus. The priest told the guy then to go and do 15 Angelus'. As the priest was sitting in the confessional he thought about what the guy said. The Angelus was something that was prayed throughout the day and it got its start when the clock in the church bell tower rang and that way people would know when it was time to pray. The priest was curious and since there was no one in the confessional he decided to sneak out to see what the guy was doing. He walked up the side aisle and he saw the penitent kneeling in front of the statue of Mary. The priest listened carefully and he could hear the guy going "bong, bong, and bong."

Paul didn't get the reaction from Tom that he normally got from people, but after about two minutes Tom started laughing, he finally figured it out. Paul knew it was a good joke and he was glad Tom finally appreciated it. There were a lot of jokes about going to confession, but confession was no joke. Paul knew that as hard as it was to go sometimes, he felt relieved and felt better afterwards. Paul had heard or read somewhere that Catholics who went to confession were more peaceful and content with their lives. He would try to make it a practice for the family after he got back. He remembered when he was a kid how he went with his mother, father, and two brothers.

Paul and Tom made it to the Trapper John Shelter cut off by 1:28, two minutes to spare. Since their pace was quicker, they went through more water than normal. When they got to the cut off for Trapper John shelter, Tom decided to get more water. Paul told Tom that in his guidebook it said that water was iffy in dry years. Paul wasn't sure if this was a dry year, but he told Tom he could have some of his water; at which point Tom said, "Paul I have been with you for the better part of three days and I've never seen you fill your water bottle. How can you possibly have more?"

Paul told him about his two one-liter water bottles and how they always seemed to be full. He even demonstrated by drinking a quarter of the bottle and putting it back in his backpack. He waited a few minutes and took it out again and it was full.

"That is a miracle," Tom said. Paul didn't share more than what was required and he figured that was sufficient for Tom to know. When Tom's curiosity was peeked, he said, "OK, can you please fill up one of my bottles?"

Paul poured water from his water bottle into one of Tom's and then Paul returned it to his backpack and took out the other one liter bottle and took a big gulp. Tom was speechless. He couldn't even think of anything to say, but when he did, he said "You know it's terrific not having to treat the water. I can't stand the taste of the iodine in my water. Thank you, Paul."

Paul said not to thank him, but to thank God, which Tom promptly did. Refreshed again, they started hiking. They had one vertical climb up to what was called Holts Ledge and then it leveled off. They didn't stop when they got there, they continued on. However, Paul's guidebook said Holt's Ledge had a nesting site for Peregrine Falcons, which was apparently a rare phenomenon and since neither of them were bird enthusiasts they continued on. They still had about five-and-a-half miles to the Moose Mountain Shelter. That would leave nearly 11 miles for the next day and put them in Hanover, NH. That of course meant they would have to wait until Monday to pick up their packages at the Post-Office.

It was about 6:15 p.m. when they got to the Moose Mountain Shelter and since it was a Saturday there were several people there and no room in the shelter, so they had to set up their tents and prepared dinner. Paul made Beef Stew and Tom had Chicken Stew. After dinner they talked with the people in the shelter and it turned out they were doing a summer program at Dartmouth. The students found it interesting that Paul was planning to hike the entire trail and that Tom was doing it in sections. One of the students said he wanted to do that after he graduated and asked both of them for any tips.

After Paul finished his beer he excused himself and went back to his tent to write in his journal; then he said his prayers, and went to sleep at about 9:15. (431 FK)

The smell of bacon woke Paul up. He threw open the fly of his tent while he was lying on his stomach and he could see that a Dartmouth student was cooking bacon and he wondered if they had any extra. It looked as if he also had a pot of coffee brewing on one of the two stoves set up on a picnic table, so he put on his boots and walked over near the shelter. The student cooking was the one who had mentioned that he wanted to hike the trail after he graduated. Just as Paul finished lacing his boots he could hear the zipper on Tom's tent. When Tom poked his head out, Paul said to him, "isn't that a wonderful smell?"

"I agree. What a great way to wake up. Do you think they have any extra?"

"There's only one way to find out," he said in reply. He walked over near the picnic table where the student had two stoves set up. One was for the bacon and the other was for the coffee. When Paul walked up he said "good morning" and mentioned to the student that nothing smelled better than the combination of bacon cooking and coffee brewing. The student said both he and Tom were welcome to share their breakfast if they wanted. None of the other students were up yet, so they joined the student, whose name was Tim.

While Paul and Tom were eating with Tim they asked Tim some questions about Hanover, like where would be a good place to stay, good place to re-supply, and where the Aquinas House was? Tim said there were places they could stay on campus for free or for a small fee. Tim also recommended the Grand Union Supermarket for food shopping, but that the Dartmouth Co-op was the best place for camping type equipment. Tim had heard of the Aquinas House, but didn't know where it was. As the other students started showing up for breakfast Paul and Tom decided to hit the trail. They left at 7:35.

Tom asked Paul what the Aquinas House was and he told him that on most College Campuses there were various places for religious nurturing. For Catholics it was generally called the Newman Club. However, at Dartmouth it was the Aquinas House. He discovered that tidbit of information while he was researching his hike. Paul also remembered that they had Mass on Sunday evenings at the Aquinas House, but he wasn't sure if that was the case during the summer. Tom said he went to UMBC, which stands for the University of Maryland Baltimore, but that he didn't live on the campus, so he didn't know what they had at his campus.

Paul learned that Tom worked his way through college while he worked at two or three different jobs. He turned one of those jobs into a full-time position when he graduated. His degree was in computer information systems, so it was a natural fit to move into a job he was good at and one that he could name his own hours. His company pretty much left him on his own and he would go in to the company's office only once a week. Tom admitted that he was getting pretty bored with technology, plus he thought it was too impersonal and he was contemplating a career change.

Tom just wasn't sure what he wanted to do, but he said the best thing about his job was that he had a lot of free time; however, the down side was that he didn't have anyone to spend the free time with. Tom mentioned that he was engaged once, but it didn't work out.

For the next hour, or so, Tom shared his life story with Paul. He talked fondly about his high school days and getting his first job. He decided on UMBC because his girlfriend went there. It took them both five years to graduate because they were both working their way through college and then he proposed to her their senior year and she said "yes." When they graduated she went to Europe as a graduation present from her parents, but unfortunately, she met someone there and called off their engagement. He said it took him three years to get over it. However, on a positive note, he said it was because of his break-up he started hiking and camping.

He explained how he went to northern Italy where his former fiancé lived, to see if he could win her back. Tom didn't stand a chance, however, because her new fiancé was a wealthy Italian and he had a beautiful villa on Lake Garda. Tom mentioned that when it finally sunk in, that he couldn't get her back, he went for a hike in the Dolomites and loved it so much he was captivated with hiking and camping. He hiked in Switzerland the next year and he was hooked.

He turned his hiking efforts closer to home because Europe was getting very expensive. He hiked in the Rockies and loved it and that's when he decided to hike the AT a section at a time.

They reached Ledyard Spring and took a short break; Paul had a granola bar and trail mix, while Tom had a Snickers bar he discovered in a side pocket of his backpack. It was all mangled, but he said it still tasted like a Snickers. They still had two miles to go to get to Hanover and that was when Paul brought up what they would do for the night. He said that staying in the Dartmouth College facilities might be OK for college-age-students, but Paul said he didn't feel up for it, so he asked Tom if he would be willing to split the cost of a motel room if they could find a reasonably priced one. Tom said that sounded like a good idea.

They got to Hanover at about 2:45 and they stopped at a motel right in Hanover and the price of a room didn't seem too excessive, so they took it. The motel was centrally located and there were washing machines they could use. They both freshened up and then went to get a bite to eat, but only after Paul called home.

They both had Chef Salads for a late lunch and a slice of apple pie a la mode. Paul wanted to see if the Aquinas House had an evening Mass during the summer, so they walked to the campus and it turned out they did have an evening Mass at 7:30. Paul told Tom he was welcome to go with him to Mass if he wanted and Tom said he'd like that.

Paul and Tom had about two hours before Mass, so they went to the Grand Union first and then to the Dartmouth Co-Op. While they were walking back to the motel Tom asked Paul how he met his wife, so Paul told him they were both stationed at the same Air Force Base in Illinois when he met Laura. Paul already had orders for his next assignment, so Laura didn't think it was a good idea for them to get involved in a relationship. They had several dates though and they both liked each other, a lot. Two nights before he was supposed to leave for his new base, he asked Laura to marry him. Paul told Tom how they got married in December of that year and went skiing for their honeymoon. It then took them five months to get an assignment to the same Air Force Base in northwest Florida.

A young priest by the name of Father Dave celebrated Mass. At the sign of peace when Paul noticed that Frank, Sylvia, and Kevin were two rows behind them. Since Paul couldn't reach to shake their hands he flashed them the peace sign.

After Mass Frank, Sylvia, and Kevin were standing around outside when they were leaving, so they went over to say hi. Paul introduced Tom to Frank and Kevin, but not to Sylvia since he knew Tom couldn't see her. All of a sudden Sylvia stuck out her hand and said, "Hi I'm Sylvia and I don't know what has happened to Paul's manners." He couldn't believe it when Tom stuck out his hand to shake hers. Tom could see her and Paul wondered what it was that changed, so that Tom could see her now.

Frank suggested they all go to dinner together at the Tavern across the street from the campus and at dinner Tom asked how Paul knew everybody. Frank answered by saying they met Paul in various places along the trail and Paul would share that with him later. Paul was sitting next to Sylvia and his curiosity got the better of him. He asked her quietly so that Tom couldn't hear, "Sylvia how is it that Tom can see you now?"

"Paul, my mother's father repented. He asked forgiveness for pressuring my mom to get an abortion. He felt responsible for my mother taking her life. He realized that he didn't have a daughter anymore; he also realized that he didn't have a grandchild either. That's why I couldn't go right to Dover, Delaware. I had to wait until he asked God for forgiveness."

Dinner was nice and the conversation centered on Tom. When asked about his life he shared many of the same things he had already shared with Paul. He said that that was the first time he had been to Mass since middle school and he said he felt drawn to the Eucharist, but he knew he shouldn't receive because he hadn't been to confession in years. He also mentioned that Paul had shared many inspirational stories that "fired him up." Tom said he planned to come home to the Catholic Church once he got back to Baltimore.

Frank picked up the tab for dinner and they all went outside the Tavern afterwards and said their goodbyes. However, Paul walked up to Frank before they left and he asked him, "Frank when you said I could tell Tom later where we all met, can I tell him everything?"

"Yes you can. I just thought it would be easier and cause less of a commotion if anyone overheard you in the Tavern. You see, Tom will be going home sooner than he thought, but don't tell him that until he tells you."

Paul and Tom thanked Frank again for dinner and Tom said how nice it was to meet everyone. It took them less than 10 minutes to get to the motel and once there, he explained everything to Tom. He explained how he met Frank and how it was that after that meeting the water bottles stayed full. Then he told him about how the Svea stove showed up at the pie ladies. Next he told Tom how he met Sylvia one day, but that no one else could see her up until now. In fact, Paul told Tom he was talking to her that time when Tom caught him talking to himself. Then he told him what Sylvia told him at dinner about her grandfather asking for forgiveness.

He saved the story of Kevin for last. He described how he would have fallen off the mountain if Kevin wasn't there to stop his fall. In that Tom had seen how the water bottles always remained full; he didn't doubt any of the other things Paul shared with him.

The conversation then turned to the Mass. Tom mentioned how much he got out of it and he said he felt drawn to the Eucharist and he wished he could receive. Since that wasn't possible until after Tom went to confession, he let Tom copy down the Spiritual Communion prayer to say in its place. Then the conversation turned to the real presence in the host and he shared a story with Tom that he had read somewhere. It had to do with Pope John Paul II's visit to the United States. Paul couldn't remember the year of the Pope's visit, but that wasn't as important as what actually happened. In fact, it was while the Pope was in Baltimore he decided he wanted to visit the seminarians at St. Mary's Seminary. It wasn't on the Pope's schedule and that created a real problem for the security folks.

The police rushed into action when the Pope made his desires known; they had to do a quick security sweep of the school to make sure no one was there who could harm the Pope. The police went into the seminary and did a room by room search and then they brought in those dogs that can find people in the rubble of fallen buildings. They searched the chapel first, because that's where the Pope wanted to go first. The dogs alerted on the tabernacle much like they would have alerted when they found someone in the rubble of a building. The dogs alerted on the tabernacle, where they kept the consecrated hosts, and the dogs were sure that a living person was in the tabernacle. As most Catholics know and believe, Jesus is present in the consecrated host even though they can't explain it. The dogs sensed that presence, too.

"Tom," Paul said, "I believe that is why you are drawn to the tabernacle. Although you can't comprehend it in your head, you know it in your heart and your soul. Like a piece of bread that is shot with a high dose of radiation would affect whoever ate it, the consecrated host is loaded with graces and whoever eats it worthily, will get those graces. I would recommend that you say that spiritual communion prayer until you can receive the real body of Christ."

"Paul," Tom said, "do you think that the priest at the Aquinas House would listen to my confession before we hit the trail tomorrow. I know that will get us on the trail later than expected, but I'd like to try at least."

"I'm sure he would hear your confession, if he is available." Paul replied.

Neither of them had done their laundry, so they took care of that and Paul also called Laura; the kids were sleeping. He told her all about his remarkable day, but since it was late he said he'd write everything down in his journal and she could read it when he got home. It was about 11:30 when he and Tom went to sleep. (442 FK)

The alarm on the clock radio went off at 7:30 a.m. Both Tom and Paul slept straight through the night and both felt well rested when they got up. It was then that someone knocked on their door. It was a motel employee and he asked if either one of them had left clothes in the dryer the night before. Paul confessed that it was him; he forgot about them because he was on the phone with Laura. So, he went and got them and then they went for breakfast at a place nearby.

They both had two eggs, Sunnyside-up, with bacon and sausage, and an order of English muffins. The coffee was great, but Paul really enjoyed his English muffin because it was toasted the way he liked it. They talked about that, how they had never seen a backpacker eat English Muffins on the AT. They had seen French Baguettes, bagels, and Pita Bread, but never English Muffins. They chalked it up to not having toasters along the AT. Who could they recommend that to? They kidded.

Tom and Paul asked the manager if they could leave their backpacks somewhere while they went to Dartmouth. He said yes, and showed them a room off the lobby where they could store them. They passed by the Post-Office, but decided to stop for their packages on the way back to the motel. They got to the Aquinas House and asked if Father Dave was around because they needed to have a confession heard before they could start hiking again. He wasn't there, but they said they would page his beeper. While they waited, Tom asked Paul how to make an act of contrition, because he had forgotten how to. Paul said he remembered the words, but it would be easier for Tom if they were written down, so he got up and looked around. He found a prayer book with various prayers, including the act of contrition, so he gave it to Tom to use when he went in to see Father Dave.

Father Dave showed up about a half-an-hour later and Tom talked to him first, explaining it had been years since he had been to confession, but he really wanted to receive the Eucharist. So, Tom and Father Dave went into Father Dave's office and shut the door. Ten minutes later the door opened and Tom came out first. He had a big smile on his face. He continued past Paul to the chapel and kneeled down in front of the altar. Then, Father Dave came out robed in his vestments and entered the chapel. He was going to administer Tom the Most Holy Eucharist, so Tom came out to get Paul and said, "Father is asking for you." So, Paul went into the chapel and Father Dave asked him if he wanted to receive communion since he would be hiking for a while. "Yes Father; most definitely," he said.

On the way back to the motel to get their backpacks, Tom was overjoyed. He made a confession and received Holy Communion all in the same day. He thanked Paul, to which he didn't know how to respond other than "you are welcome, you deserve it." When they got to the motel to pick up their backpacks the girl at the desk said Tom had a message from his younger sister in Towson, Maryland. Tom read the note and the look on Tom's face turned from happiness to sorrow. He looked up at Paul and said, "My mother died. I have to go home."

Paul felt a sorrow for Tom and would miss his company on the AT. It was then that he mentioned what Frank told him at dinner the night before that Tom would be "called home soon."

Tom made a couple calls to Baltimore and one to Virginia Beach; that was where his father lived, his father who he hadn't seen since he was 14. Paul could tell it was hard for Tom talking to someone he could hardly remember. All the missed memories and special occasions which they couldn't share except through pictures. Tom told his Father he would call again once he got back to Baltimore.

CHAPTER SIX

St. Francis of Assisi & The Wolf

It seemed odd hiking alone after having hiked with Tom for so long. After leaving Tom at the Hanover motel Paul went to the Post-Office to pick up his package from Laura. He opened it and transferred everything into his backpack except for the AT&T phone card which he put in his T-shirt pocket. Then he crossed over the Connecticut River and into Vermont. He paused on the bridge to look at his guidebook and do some figuring. He had gone 442 miles since Mt. Katahdin and still had over 1,700 miles to Springer Mountain, Georgia.

Norwich was the first town Paul would go through in Vermont and it was the original home of Norwich University, but Paul couldn't remember why it was that Alden Partridge started the university there back in 1819. It was a pretty town nestled between two small mountains and sitting on the western bank of the Connecticut River. Since it was already 1:30 he stopped at a nearby deli to get a sandwich and then ate a picnic area which had a great view of Hanover, New Hampshire. He called Laura at work to tell her about Tom's mother and that he was hiking by himself again.

Paul wasn't sure where he would be staying for the 35th day of his Appalachian journey and he wasn't sure how much ground he could cover, but he would try to go 13 miles. That would put him at the Thistle Hill Shelter if he figured right and if he couldn't make it that far he would just camp somewhere along the trail. He was making good progress when he crossed US89 and he remembered when they use to drive past that point on US89, while on their way north towards Montpelier, he always thought how beautiful the view was. Looking down at Sharon, Vermont always reminded him of one of the scenes you'd see on a pharmaceutical calendar, especially when everything was covered with snow. The terrain started to get more difficult on the west side of US89 and the White River.

At 7:50 Paul had had enough for the day, but was willing to try hiking for another 30 minutes. After US89 there weren't many markers and he couldn't tell where he was without a good map, and the map he was using wasn't a good one. As he rounded a bend in the trail he could see the Thistle Hill Shelter, so he was happy, but exhausted. There were two other hikers at the shelter, so he didn't have to set up his tent and he didn't even cook dinner because he was so tired. He had had more difficult mileage days, so he didn't know why it was he was so exhausted. One of the things was that he no longer had a hiking buddy he could swap stories and experiences with and maybe that made the difference. He ate a granola bar and some trail mix that Tom gave him and then he went to sleep. (456 FK)

With the exception of having to go pee at about 1:30 a.m., he slept until 6:15, when the two other hikers were getting ready to leave. They were pretty considerate because he didn't even hear them until they left the shelter; one of them had difficulty putting his backpack on and it hit the wooden floor when he dropped it. Then Paul had the shelter to himself when they left and it was very peaceful.

Paul made breakfast because he was starved from not eating dinner the night before. He made instant coffee and oatmeal with brown sugar and raisins and then he stirred his coffee with the same spoon he mixed the oatmeal with; it gave his coffee a terrific taste.

Once he fastened everything to his backpack he started hiking at 7:35. He planned to make it to the Wintturi Shelter, which was about twelve miles away. To help his miles go by effortlessly he planned to make this a Rosary day. He would say a Rosary for Tom's mother and another one for Tom and his father that they might reconcile all their years apart.

Paul felt pretty good after four miles. He was making good time, but it was mostly downhill. After about another mile-and-a-half he took a break when he crossed Bartlett Brook Road. According to his guidebook there was an Inn only 800 feet from the trail. He couldn't see it from where he was, so he started walking in the direction the guidebook said to go and sure enough, when he rounded the bend it was there. He had a bacon cheeseburger and French fries along with a side salad. The people at the table next to him were very loud and he could hear everything they said. They were an older couple and obviously had hearing problems; they were talking about their next door neighbors and it was sort of comical.

After lunch Paul started hiking south again. When he reached VT12 he took out his map to see if it was the same VT12 he lived near in Northfield, and it was. VT12 went straight thru Northfield and up to Montpelier, the capitol of Vermont. He had fond memories of driving on route 12. There was the Christmas he, Laura, and Theresa cut down their own Christmas tree at a Christmas tree farm along route 12. He also remembered the time his mother-in-law came to visit and they took route 12 to the Ethan Allen outlet in Randolph, Vermont. She found an end table she liked and bought it. In that she couldn't bring it on the plane with her, they brought it down to her that next summer when they visited Bridgeport, PA., which was Laura's childhood home.

Praying made the hiking go quicker, or at least that's how it seemed. Paul made it to Wintturi Shelter close to 5:00 p.m. He still felt like he had some miles left in him for the day, but decided he would stay there since there was only one other person at the shelter. The lone hiker was from Massachusetts and he was taking a week off from work.

He started hiking from US89 two days before and he was planning to go VT103, which was about 36 miles away. Don Bowser told Paul his name and that he was 56 years old. Then he told Paul he wasn't out to set any records, he was just out to enjoy nature and some solitude. Don had a wife and five kids, the youngest of which was about to begin her freshmen year in college. Don was a high school teacher and he taught history, so Don was glad to hear that he was a history major in college and went on to get his Master's degree in history.

Don confided to Paul that he loved teaching, but the BS that went along with teaching was getting him down. He would be returning to the classroom in a couple weeks, so he was using this week-long trip to clear his head and put him in the right frame of mind. When Paul asked for an example of the BS that got him down, Don gave an example. He said that every time they got a new administrator, there were new initiatives because the new person had to make their mark somehow. He gave as an example their school district getting a new administrator who read a book over the summer and that book became the focus of every in-service training day during the course of their school year. The next year the book was out of vogue and they didn't even mention it. He learned to live with it though because as he said "things will come full circle." He loved teaching kids, though; he felt he made a difference, not necessarily with every kid, but with one here and one there.

Paul mentioned to Don that he had considered teaching High School Junior ROTC, but wasn't sure if it was for him. Don said there was a JROTC unit in his high school and the guys who were in charge had a good program as far as he could tell. "They do some pretty cool stuff for the kids," he said, "and they really have helped a lot of kids." Then Don went on to explain that in addition to the regular curriculum courses, they have field trips, their own honor society, and various clubs within JROTC. He was impressed with their rocket club and drill team. Don said, "Let me tell you a story that happened a couple years ago."

"One day I was eating lunch with one of the JROTC instructors in his classroom and one of their JROTC students came into the classroom while we were eating. The student excused himself for interrupting, but he had a question. When the student left I asked the JROTC instructor what kind of a kid he was and he told me he was OK, that he actually liked him, but that he seemed to bother the other students. The JROTC instructor asked why and I told him I had his older brother a couple years prior and didn't really care for him. Then I explained how I made a home visit and when I saw how the kid lived I had a whole new respect for the kid. His parents made him live in the basement, which had a dirt floor, and his bed was right next to the furnace. I was impressed with that kid from then on out. You see Paul, it was the parents who were the problem. Like the old expression 'you are the product of your youth.' The JROTC instructor thanked me for telling him that story because he said it explained why it was the younger sibling had difficulties with the other students."

"How do you mean?" Paul asked.

"The kids didn't always understand his jokes and they thought he was weird. They also thought he looked like an unmade bed which reflected poorly on the whole unit."

There was a pause and then Don continued, "When they started JROTC at our high school I wasn't sure how it would work out. However, they will take an average kid and give him or her better self-confidence then I would have ever thought possible. I remember I was at a function with a middle school teacher and he couldn't believe it when a particular student got up and addressed the city of Pittsfield. He told me she had been one of his students and she was as quiet and shy as they come. Well, that student was in charge of the JROTC unit, I believe they called her the Corps Commander. Yep, the JROTC program is one of the highlights of our high school and community. The amount of volunteer work they do in the community is unbelievable. I guess the kids can get ribbons and awards for doing a certain number of volunteer hours. But you know, I was at one of those community service events and I heard one of the JROTC students come up to the colonel and tell him he had a fun time helping others. The point being, it's not necessarily the ribbons they do it for, but for the pride of it. "

Paul was glad to hear Don's glowing remarks about JROTC and teaching high school in general. When he asked which history courses Don taught, he said he'd taught many different ones over the years, but his favorite was European History. It was 6:40 when the two finally got around to dinner.

Another hiker came into camp and he was a thru-hiker headed south. In the midst of the dinner conversation Paul remarked at how beautiful Vermont was and how he missed living there. Don asked Paul where lived in Vermont, based on his comment and he told Don that he taught Air Force ROTC at Norwich University back in the early to mid-80's. Don mentioned he had a neighbor whose son just graduated from there in May and he said he went with his neighbor to visit the son a couple times.

"Northfield is a very beautiful town," Don said.

Paul, Don, and the other south bounder all went to sleep around 9:00, but not before Paul made his journal entry for the 25th of July, 1995. (468 FK)

The other south bounder was up early and making a lot of noise. It could have been due to his youthfulness, but he was not as considerate as the people in the shelter the night before. He was walking around with his boots on, but they were untied, so it sounded like someone was using a hammer on the wooden planks every time he took a step. He wondered if he had been that inconsiderate back in his younger days. The guy was obviously in a hurry to get on the trail and when he left the shelter Don made a comment.

"Paul, now don't take this the wrong way because it's not directed at you, but some of these hikers are rude and think they're special. No one is forcing them to hike the Appalachian Trail. They do it for some unknown reason to make people think they are more superior than they are. If they want to try something challenging they should get a job, raise a family, and become productive members of society." When Don seemed finished with his rant, he said, "I'm sorry, I just wanted to get that off my chest. I guess that's the civics teacher in me saying what I want to say in the classroom, but can't or else they'd probably fire me."

"That's OK Don. I know what you are trying to say and since your remarks weren't directed at me I'll tell you why I am hiking the AT."

So, Paul gave Don the short version of why he was hiking the AT and told him what he learned so far. Of course he didn't mention Frank, Sylvia, or Kevin, but he did mention Tom and how Tom was different than the ordinary hiker. In fact, Paul said he thought it made more sense to hike the trail in sections than to do it all at once. However, if you have the time and wanted to see what you're capable of doing physically, than that's fine.

Don had a single cup coffee brewer and asked Paul if he also wanted a cup. He didn't have to ask twice. Don also took something out of his backpack wrapped in tin foil and asked if Paul wanted some. It was banana bread and Don said it wouldn't be worth eating tomorrow.

Something clicked between the two men and Don asked if he could hike with him; Don said he'd try not to hold him up. That was fine with Paul, because he enjoyed having someone to talk to. They set off at 7:35.

For a 56 year-old Don did very well. He reminded him a lot of Mr. Arthur on their hike some 20 years earlier. He seemed to enjoy hiking for the scenery and the camaraderie and not to prove anything to anybody and thus Don's earlier rant about hikers made sense.

The conversation turned to history and the American Revolution. Don wasn't sure if Paul knew the Long Trail traced its beginning to that period. He did know that, but he let the teacher be a teacher and after a good two hours they stopped for a break. Paul thought the temperature was pleasant, but Don was sweating a lot, so he kept wiping his brow with a neckerchief. He hoped Don was OK and that he would be able to make it all the way to VT103. He decided that no matter how slow Don was, he would stick with him until his wife met him on VT103.

After a 15-minute break the two were off again. Fortunately, the next couple of miles were mostly downhill and the down hills didn't bother Don as much as the up hills. Don asked Paul if he had any clearer sense of what it was he wanted to do with the rest of his life. Paul mentioned that in addition to his interest in teaching JROTC he liked writing, but he didn't think he could make a living at it. Don asked him if he had ever had anything published, to which Paul replied "no." Paul said he had a couple short stories he wanted to submit, but he didn't think they were ready.

Don asked what the stories were about and Paul said one was about his 6th grade teacher and the other was about a dance he went to in college. Don said he'd like to hear the story about his 6th grade teacher, so he tried to tell the story as best as he remembered it.

Paul started by saying he liked his 6th grade class and he was very fond of Mrs. Gray, their teacher. In late November, of his 6th grade year, his class was playing kickball for recess and the ball got stuck in the low branches of an oak tree, which was next to the ball field. Paul had a terrific throwing arm, so his good friend Billy pleaded with Paul to throw his hat to knock the ball out of the tree because recess was almost over and they were only behind by one run. He tried, but his hat got stuck by the strap that held the earmuffs up. He was very upset because that was the hat his father gave him for Christmas his third grade year, about five weeks before his father died in a car accident. Leading up to Christmas of that year it snowed one morning and he and his brothers sat around the radio to see if their schools were closed. No such luck. They all had school.

Paul said that when he got to school, he was summoned to the principal's office. It was just a plan to get him out of the classroom, so that Mrs. Gray and the rest of his class could surprise him. When Paul walked back into the classroom his hat was sitting on his desk and the class all yelled "surprise." He was so thrilled. It was like an early Christmas Present. It turns out that on that morning when Joe the janitor was checking the school grounds he noticed a branch was down from the weight of the snow. He knew Paul's hat was on that particular branch because he asked Joe if there was a way to get it down and he asked him that question almost every day. Joe gave the hat to Mrs. Gray and she came up with the idea of surprising Paul.

"That is a good story Paul," Don said. "Have you ever thought about getting together with an illustrator and turning it into a children's story?"

"You know, someone else I know said I should do that. So, now that two people have recommended that, so I'll look into it."

They were making better time now because it was a nice trail and there were no switchbacks. Don told him about all his children. Two were still in college and a third one was about to enter. One decided college wasn't what they wanted and they were still searching for what it was they wanted to do. The other son enlisted in the US Navy and was getting ready for a cruise to the Mediterranean.

He told Don that he and his wife were stationed in Naples, Italy, which was the homeport to the US Navy in the Mediterranean. He then explained how he was assigned with the Air Force contingent at the NATO headquarters that was also in Naples.

"How did you like it, Paul?" Don asked.

"We liked it a lot, but that was back in the early 1980's and I'm sure things have changed. You could say that of all our time in the Air Force that was our favorite place to be stationed."

"You know Paul, my wife and I are going to visit my son sometime while he's in the Mediterranean. He said that would be OK, that family members frequently do that sort of thing. In fact, he might be there this Christmas, or at least that's what he thinks. I think we may go regardless of his plans. If he's there great and if he's not there that's OK too, because we're not getting any younger."

"That's a good point. Do it while you're young and healthy." Paul said.

"Paul, where do you think we should fly into? I really haven't looked into it yet, so I don't know. I'm just thinking out loud."

"Don, I would recommend flying into Rome and from Rome going to visit your son in Naples, or he could come up to Rome for that matter to see you. To a historian, Rome is amazing and you'll love it. You have Ancient Rome, Medieval Rome and Renaissance Rome and Rome is central enough that you can go up to Florence and some other cities."

"See Paul, we need someone like you to tell us where to go and what to see in Italy."

Paul went on to tell Don about the first Christmas he and Laura were in Naples. He mentioned how his brother was living in Rome at the time and how their mother came over to visit them for Christmas and New Year's. Additionally, Paul's cousin Jim was also there for Christmas because he was assigned to the U.S. John F. Kennedy and they were anchored in the Bay of Naples.

He explained that his cousin was given two days' vacation and he spent the whole time with them and even went to the Island of Capri with them. Though Jim said the food on the ship was good, he said there was nothing like home cooking, especially Laura's pies.

The time seemed to fly by and they made it to the Stony Brook Shelter cut-off at about 3:30 and they both felt pretty good. Since the shelter was over a half mile from the trail they decided to skip it and continue on. They would try to make it to Kent Pond, which was another four-and-a-half miles. There was a slight vertical climb, but not as bad as what they would experience the next two days. Don started to get noticeably slower, so Paul recommended that they find a place to camp off the trail. Don didn't have a tent, but he did have an interesting rain fly he could use if it rained, so he set up his tent first and then helped Don set up his rain fly. Then they fixed dinner.

They both had the same freeze dried dinners in their backpacks, Chicken A La King, so that's what they had. Don also had some home-made granola bars which he shared, they were great. Paul never had a granola bar that tasted so good because most of the store bought granola bars tasted slightly better than cardboard. Don said they were easy to make and he explained the process to Paul.

During dinner Don asked which three or four places in Italy he would recommend their seeing if they did go over at Christmas time. He said Rome for sure and broke that down into three must see places: The Vatican, The Roman Forum, and the Church of San Clemente. He gave Don a brief overview of each one. The first two in themselves would require a whole day and as Paul explained to do the Vatican "right," might take two. Don said he wasn't Catholic and asked if that would make a difference, to which Paul said, "No." "You see Don," depending on your faith background, Rome is the seat of Christianity. Both St's Peter and Paul were martyred in Rome and that is where the early church continued the traditions of Jesus."

Don asked what is so special about San Clemente, so Paul told him about when he went there on a field trip with his Master's Degree class. "The church at street level was built after the Normans sacked Rome in the 13th century. I remember looking at the outside of the church and thinking, what is so special about this place? Then you go inside and after you see the inside of the 13th century church, which is nice, you go down to the 5th century church built to honor Pope Clement. There are murals about the life of Pope Clement and you think to yourself, or at least I did, well that was nice, but still not great.

Then you go to the back of the 5th century church and go down more stairs and you come out in 1st century AD Rome. The first thing you see is a Mithric Temple. Paul explained that Mithra was a god the Roman legion worshipped in the 1st century. After we saw the Mithric Temple we could walk around 1st century Roman streets. Our teacher pointed out that you could tell it was built after the great fire in 64 AD because there were fire breaks between the houses. She said the fire breaks didn't exist before the great fire."

He then shared similar stories about the Vatican and the Roman Forum. Paul also told Don about some of his favorite Italian meals when he was in Rome and looked over at Don and said, "I never had a bad meal in Rome." After that sank in, Don asked Paul about Florence, so he shared his thoughts on Florence, but recommended that he and his wife try something less congested, like Gubbio or Assisi. He explained that after spending a couple days in Roman traffic that Don and his wife might want to experience the Tuscan or Umbrian countryside.

He told Don all about Assisi and Gubbio and that while Assisi is most associated with St. Francis, Gubbio also has a St. Francis connection. Don asked what that connection was, so Paul told him about it. While St. Francis was visiting Gubbio sometime back in the early 13th century a wolf had been terrorizing the town. St. Francis tamed the wolf while he was there.

Paul said that since Don and Chris would be in Italy at Christmas time it also made since to go to Assisi because St. Francis is credited with creating the Nativity scene or Presepio as they call them in Italian.

Paul went on to describe how Don and his wife would be able to see more of Giotto's and Cimabue's murals in Assisi than they could see in Florence, thus another good reason to get away from the crowds.

Don was getting more and more excited about the prospect of going to Italy and he kept asking Paul questions. Finally, at about 9:20 they both agreed they should call it a night. The weather was nice and cool, so they didn't have to worry about getting wet. In fact, it was a very starry night.

The next day they would cross VT100 and meet up with the Long Trail and then they would cross US4, where Paul would try to phone home. He had planned to phone home today, because it was his 42nd birthday. Oh well, Laura and the kids would understand. It was more important to help out a fellow hiker than to celebrate his birthday. After all, he celebrated 41 birthday's already.

As Paul was trying to fall asleep, he thought back to some of his more interesting birthdays. At least three or four of them involved moving in some way. There was the one back in 1958 when the family moved to San Diego and he remembered his mother had a birthday cake which they ate on top of unpacked boxes; they were joined by the movers. Then the next year it was the same thing on their move back to Washington DC, that too was on his birthday and they were also joined by the movers. Then two years later when they moved to Minnesota it was on his 8th birthday and the movers also joined them for cake and ice-cream. Unfortunately, it was during that year Paul's father died, so they moved back to Washington DC, and it was again on his birthday. Paul's mother always tried to make his birthday special regardless of the circumstances. He only hoped his kids felt that he and Laura tried to do the same thing for all of them. (481 FK)

The birds were all singing at 6:20 a.m. and that's what woke Paul up. When Paul opened his tent he saw that Don was already up and was about to fire up his stove. He offered Don some of his water, which Don cheerfully accepted. Don was traveling with only one water bottle. It was slightly more than one liter, or at least it appeared that way. When the water was ready Don made Paul's coffee first and then his. They both had oatmeal for breakfast and he offered Don some raisins to add to his oatmeal and Don accepted.

They packed up after they finished breakfast and were on the trail by 7:30. They made it to Kent Pond in one hour and to VT100 by 9:00. They were actually making decent time, but Paul chalked that up to the cooler temperature.

Where the AT cut through Gifford Woods State Park they could see a lot of people were there. Don said he would love to get a shower since they had pay showers, so they dug into their packs and took out some quarters. It was a nice treat to get a shower, one which Paul hadn't expected. Don filled up his water bottle and they continued on. At about 11:30 they met up with the Long Trail, which shares over 100 miles with the AT.

He would be on both the AT and the Long Trail until he reached the Massachusetts border, which was 107 miles away. They decided to take a break and have lunch which consisted of trail mix and another one of Don's homemade granola bars. They started hiking down to Sherburne Pass which was where they would cross US4. It wasn't that steep, but steep enough that Don tripped and slid about 30 yards down the hill.

Don was just lying there which concerned Paul, because Paul didn't know what to do, he never took a first aid class. When Paul got to where Don was, he leaned over to see if Don was moving and he could hear Don say, "Boy that really hurt." He continued to lay there and didn't move. Paul took off his backpack and said, "Don that was a nasty fall, where do you hurt?"

"All over, but I'm playing it safe by just laying still."

"OK, Don. Take your time. Move when you're ready."

After seeing if he could move his fingers and toes and arms and legs, Don tried to get up with Paul's help. Some other hikers passed by headed north and they stopped to ask if they could help, but Don said no. He just wanted to know how far away US4 was. The hikers said it was about half a mile further, that if you were quiet you could probably hear the trucks trying to get up Sherburne Pass. Don thanked the hikers for stopping, but said he would be OK after a couple minutes. The hikers continued on leaving Don and Paul with about a half mile hike down the mountain to US4.

Don didn't think anything was broken, but said his left knee hurt. You could tell because his left knee was swollen, or at least it was bigger than his right knee. Don said he was sorry for holding him up, but Paul said not to worry about that. Instead, they had to come up with a plan. Don told Paul he should continue on because he was sure he could make it down to US4 on his own, but Paul said he wouldn't hear of it. He would stay with Don down to Route 4 and then they would decide what to do. He transferred stuff from Don's pack to his own, so that Don didn't have to carry more weight than he had to.

When he was satisfied that Don's pack was light enough they started hiking down the trail. As they got closer to Sherburne Pass they could hear the trucks climbing up and over the pass. It took two hours to go the half mile or so. They stopped about every 40 yards and Don would tell a short story to take his mind off the journey. After the first such stop, Paul found some hiking poles which were just leaning on a tree. Since, they didn't see anyone around Paul took them and gave them to Don. They seemed to help a lot, especially getting up. Don would put them both in his right hand and lean on them as he would get up. Paul wondered how the poles got there and Frank came to mind. Frank must have left them.

When they got to US4 Paul came up with a plan. They would get a ride to the nearest hospital in Rutland, so that Don could be seen. Then they would call Don's wife for an early pick up. Don didn't argue like Paul thought he would, so he must have been in terrible pain. It was close to 4:15 before someone offered them a ride. They explained to the driver that Don was hurt and they needed to get him to a hospital. The driver was kind enough to take them into Rutland and directly to the hospital.

As with most emergency waiting rooms, they waited. As they sat there Don said it was probably a good thing it wasn't winter or the emergency room would be full with skiers. He was right. It could have been worse. Paul went and got some sandwiches from the cafeteria while they were waiting and Don was finally seen at about 6:30 p.m. They X-Rayed him and they determined there was no break, but that Don had a torn Meniscus. Since neither Don nor he knew what the Meniscus was, the doctor got a picture to show how the Meniscus works and why it was that Don was in so much pain. They put a knee immobilizer on his left knee, gave him some crutches, and prescribed him something for pain. One thing was for sure, Don's summer hike for 1995 was finished.

Since it was almost 9:15 by the time they left the emergency room Paul recommended they get a motel for the night and call Don's wife and arrange for him to be picked up in the morning. Paul had called Don's wife, Chris, once they got to the hospital to let her know about her husband's fall. She was standing by for a call back with Don's prognosis and further directions.

Paul also called Laura and the kids to let them know about his adventures and why he couldn't call earlier. They sang him Happy Birthday, which always got Heidi to howling in the background. It never failed, whenever they sang Happy Birthday, Heidi would also join in, by howling. Laura said it was a good thing he was there for Don; she realized it wasn't in his plans, but it was a good thing. Paul also told Laura about how the hiking poles miraculously appeared.

Don and Paul got a motel room in Rutland and Don called Chris and asked her if she could pick them up tomorrow at the motel and then give Paul a ride back to the trailhead. She said she would be there at 8:30 a.m. The pain pills must have started working because Don started sounding a bit loopy. Chris wanted to talk to Paul afterwards and in fact she commented that the painkillers must have taken affect. She thanked him for helping her husband and said she would see them both the next morning. Then Paul helped Don get as comfortable as possible in the full size bed by making a wall with the pillows, so Don wouldn't roll out of bed. There were two full-size beds in their motel room, which Don insisted on paying for.

The motel offered a pretty basic continental breakfast, so they went across the street to a Friendly's, a northeastern restaurant chain, and they both had a hearty breakfast, which was also Don's treat. Then they went back to the motel at 8:10 and Chris was there, she had just pulled up in a Metallic Blue Mercury Grand Marquis. She hopped out of the car and ran up to Don and gave him a big kiss and a bear hug, while trying to be careful with his left knee. Then she ran to Paul and gave him a big hug.

They checked out of the motel and loaded up the car and Paul asked if they could stop at the Grand Union to get some fruit and other perishables for the next day and then to the Post Office in Killington to get his package from home. Chris and Don then drove Paul to the trailhead, which was about two miles away. When they got to the trailhead Don insisted on getting out of the car to see him off.

Paul and Don had exchanged addresses and phone numbers at breakfast and Paul scribbled down some recommended sights to see while Don and Chris were in Rome at Christmas time. So, with all the administrative stuff already taken care of Paul started hiking south again about 10:25.

He figured out in his head that he had fallen a couple days behind, but he realized helping people was more important than accomplishing some feat. He still wanted to hike over Killington Peak before dark. His backpack was heavier then he wanted because Don gave him some of his supplies and some white gas in Paul's gas bottle. Plus, he had the stuff he got from Laura and the kids, which was more than normal. He would have to mail a package back to them eventually because all the pictures were creating a weight and space problem. He made a mental note to mail a package from Manchester Center Vermont, which was about two to three days away.

The hike was all uphill for the next seven or so miles. Once he reached the Killington Peak Trail, at 4,235 feet, it would be downhill or flat for nearly 40 miles. As he was hiking up Killington Peak he remembered back to his honeymoon, some 17 years before. He was going to take Laura hiking for their honeymoon, but her mother recommended that Paul hold off on that awhile and take her skiing instead. Laura liked to ski, but Paul was a terrible skier; however, he was up for an adventure. The whole honeymoon as it turned out was an adventure.

They got married in Bridgeport PA, which is near Valley Forge PA, in December 1978. It was unseasonably warm the day they got married, which was the 16th of December. That night, while they were in the honeymoon suite of the Sheraton, the weather took a turn for the worse. During the night, it sounded as if the wind was going to rip the roof off the hotel. The wind was still strong in the morning and Paul figured their flight to Boston would be cancelled. The flight wasn't cancelled, but it was so windy the stewardesses even had to stay in their seats the entire flight.

When they got to Boston he checked to see if their flight was still going to Rutland, Vermont. It was. It was a small plane with only eight passenger seats and his head hit the ceiling of the plane every time they hit turbulence and when they landed at Rutland, the plane hit the runway so hard it damaged the nose strut. To make matters worse it was 30 below zero with the wind chill.

When they checked into their chalet they were given a room with four bunk beds, so Paul went back down to the front desk to see if there was something more appropriate for a honeymoon. They did; the Chalet gave them a room with one queen size bed. For the next four days Paul and Laura skied, but Paul skied very poorly. He was all over the slope, but mostly on the ground. They left a day early because another front was moving in and they were worried they wouldn't get home for Christmas. It was quite a story and he told it a lot and people always laughed when he mentioned the part about the room with four bunk beds.

When he reached Killington Summit he took in the view, said a decade of the Rosary, the Joyful mysteries, and started downhill. It wasn't the same pounding on his knees, like in New Hampshire. It was a gentler trail, for which he was very thankful.

He was making good time, maybe because of the gentler terrain; he made it to the Clarendon Shelter by 6:50. He could have made it to VT103, but he didn't want to spend money on a motel. Plus, he had loads of food in his backpack.

There were lots of people at the shelter; locals from Rutland. It was after all a wonderful place to have a party on a Friday night, but he wished he had gone the extra mile or so to VT103, or to some other place along the trail. Fortunately, he had a feast for dinner.

He ate the orange he bought at the Grand Union, plus one of Don's freeze-dried dinners, and for dessert some homemade Granola bars which Chris brought for him. Paul heard Don tell Chris that he loved her granola bars if she wanted to make him some. He considered eating both, but decided to save one for breakfast. After dinner he wrote in his journal and went to bed, though the partiers made a lot of noise. It was difficult falling off to sleep, but eventually he did. (503 FK)

When Paul awakened at 6:45 a.m. he had an urge for coffee and donuts. However, a granola bar would have to take the place of the donut. No one else was up, so it was very peaceful. He decided to take it easy on this Saturday, the 29th of July; it was the 40th day of his hike. He planned to go to VT140 and see if he could find some place where they had Mass either tonight or the next morning. He generally didn't like going to Mass on Saturday night, but would go occasionally if the family had some kind of Sunday plans.

Sunday never seemed the same if he didn't go to Mass. As a kid, it was always Mass on Sunday, followed by spending a day with his mother, father, and two brothers. Old habits were hard to break.

He started hiking at 7:45 and none of the partiers were awake. He made it to VT103 by 8:15 and he remembered that was where Don was originally supposed to meet his wife. Paul stopped momentarily at the road and debated if he should walk the half mile to the Whistle Stop Restaurant that Don talked about. He looked at his watch and figured he would have time to go get a good breakfast and still have plenty of time to get to VT140 which was only about six miles away.

He ordered Corned Beef Hash with two eggs Sunnyside up and an apple juice and coffee. It was good and he was happy he took the time. Another patron offered him a ride back to the trailhead and it was a pretty easy hike to VT140; the scenery was beautiful.

Paul stuck out his thumb at about 3:40 and someone picked him up almost immediately. It was the second car to be exact and Paul made it to Wallingford, Vermont by 3:50 and he found a room at a B&B in town. While he was checking in he asked the owner if there were any Catholic Churches nearby. The owner said there were several in Rutland and that he and his wife were Catholic. So, Paul asked the owner whether there was a Saturday evening Mass.

The owners name was Patrick and he said there was a Saturday evening Mass at 5:15. He said that was the Mass his wife went to because she handled breakfast for their borders on Sunday mornings. He said his wife Sue could give him a ride to Mass if he wanted to go, but that she would be leaving for Mass at about 4:30, which gave him about 25 minutes to get ready. Paul went to his room, showered, and was back in the lobby by 4:25. Patrick introduced Paul to Sue and they both left for Rutland at about 4:30. Rutland was closer than he thought and they made it to Christ the King by 5:05 p.m. As Sue and Paul walked into the church, Paul looked around to see if any of his companions were there.

Frank, Sylvia, and Kevin were sitting in the fourth pew on the right side of the church. Sue mentioned on the way to church that she liked to sit in the front because the sound system wasn't very good and she was a bit hard of hearing. Sue picked the third row on the right. Paul nodded to Frank, Sylvia, and Kevin as they walked into the pew.

Mass felt good and Paul was glad he took the afternoon off. At the Sign of Peace, Paul shook hands with everyone around him, including his companions in the row behind. Frank, as he shook Paul's hand said, "Paul you did well yesterday." Paul wondered what he meant by that, it obviously had to do with Don's accident.

The drive back to the B&B was nice. Sue told Paul about herself and her husband. They were originally both from northern Virginia and decided to semi-retire. They saw that there was a B&B for sale in Wallingford a couple years ago, so they decided to buy it and try to make a go of it. They like it.

Patrick worked for a community college in Northern Virginia and Sue worked as a CPA for a building contractor and they both decided they wanted a simpler and less hectic life. She said they loved Vermont, even the long winters. She turned to Paul and said with a giggle, "it's sort of nice to have a reason to snuggle, and there are lots of chances for that." They hit it off so well that Sue invited him to join Patrick and her for dinner.

Dinner was nice and Paul told them all about himself and what he was doing. He shared some of his adventures thus far, especially the one with Don. When he said "Don" he remembered that he should go call Don to see how he was doing. So, he excused himself from the table and went to use Sue and Patrick's phone. Once he punched in the code for AT&T and Don's phone number in Massachusetts, the phone rang and a female voice answered "hello."

"Hi Chris. This is Paul Geary, Don's Appalachian Hiking buddy. I'm calling to see how Don is."

"Oh, he'd love to talk to you. Let me put him on the other extension."

Paul could hear talking in the background and then he heard Don say "Paul how are you? Thanks for calling. Where are you calling from?"

Paul explained to Don that he decided to take it easy, so he stopped in Wallingford, Vermont. He told Don that he had this desire to go to Mass when he woke up in the morning and thanks to the owners of the B&B they made that possible. They talked for a good 10 or 15 minutes and Don said he visited his doctor this morning and said his torn meniscus could be healed by therapy if he was good. The other option was surgery, which no one particularly wanted. Don also said that he told Chris all about Italy and she was really anxious to go. When Don finished talking, Chris wanted to talk again, so when she got on the line she told Paul once again how thankful she was that he was with Don when he fell. She also mentioned how excited she was about going to Italy for Christmas to see their son. Then she said they'd come to visit Paul when he hiked thru Massachusetts, all he had to do was call once he got close to Pittstfield.

He called Laura and the kids next. They were excited to hear from him, but weren't expecting him to call for another two days from Manchester Center. Paul told Laura about his unexplainable desire to go to Mass when he woke up. Then he also told her that he called Don and that his prognosis was good. They said they would come to see him when he got to Massachusetts.

Paul explained to Laura that Don and Chris lived in Pittsfield Massachusetts which was probably less than 5 - 10 miles from the Appalachian Trail. As Paul was telling her that, he wondered why Don would travel so far to go hiking when he lived that close. He could only guess that it was because he didn't want to chance running into anyone he knew. He would have to ask him that when he saw him again. When Paul hung up with Laura he went to find the owners to ask them a question.

Paul found Patrick in the kitchen and he asked him if he could go with him to Mass in the morning and Patrick said yes. Then he did some laundry, wrote in his journal, set the alarm clock which was on the night stand, and went to bed. He slept great and he didn't even wake up to use the bathroom. (510 FK)

Paul ate before he left for Mass because there was still enough time in between eating and receiving the Holy Eucharist. A different priest celebrated Mass, but Frank, Sylvia, and Kevin were in the pew behind him and Patrick. After Mass, while Patrick was talking with some of his friends, Paul decided to talk with his companions. He was still very curious about the hiking poles, so he asked Frank if he left the poles up against a boulder for Don's use. Frank said he did and he added, "Paul we didn't want you to fall trying to help him down the mountain. Besides, you will need those again."

Paul had the hiking poles now because Don said he didn't need them anymore and that they might help Paul on his trip to Georgia. He thought they did make a difference when he used them the day before and he wished he had them when he was in the White Mountains, because they provided him good balance going up Killington Peak. Going downhill was even better; he noticed that his knees didn't take the same pounding. He thanked God for that.

He went back to Patrick's mini-van, because Patrick was still talking to some of his acquaintances and he used the time to take the pant legs off his convertible pants. First he put his left leg up on the rear bumper, and then he pulled the horizontal zipper, which separated the bottom of the pant leg from the top. Then he did the right leg. The whole process took about 30 seconds to convert the long pants into shorts. Paul then rolled up the pant legs to put them in his backpack when Patrick showed up. They were ready to go, but when Paul looked back towards the church he noticed someone waved to him and when he didn't return a wave the person gave a hand signal that they should stop.

"Do you know that person Patrick?" Paul asked. "No, I can't say I do," he said in reply.

"It looks like he wants to talk to one of us." The person waving was in about their 40's and he started walking faster in their direction. As the stranger got closer, Paul thought he looked familiar, but he still couldn't see his face. Paul wondered if it was someone from his Norwich University days and when the guy got to where Paul could clearly see his face he remembered who it was. When the person got to within speaking distance Paul said what a pleasant surprise it was to see him.

"Do you live back in this area again?" Paul asked.

"No, Kate and I are just visiting. Why are you here?"

CHAPTER SEVEN

Green Mountain Boys

It had been nearly eight years since Paul saw his old boss last and when Colonel Woodburn got close enough he shook his hand. The colonel shook Paul's hand with a firm shake and said, "You don't have to call me colonel anymore, please call me Ed. You make me feel old when you say it."

So, Paul and Ed spoke for about 15 minutes while Patrick got out of his mini-van to talk to some of his friends. It gave Paul and Ed a chance to catch up on the previous eight years. Colonel Woodburn was Paul's boss when he was at Norwich University and he was always one of Paul's favorites. When Colonel Woodburn found out what Paul was up to, that is hiking the Appalachian Trail, he mentioned that someone from his town did that and wrote a book about it. When Paul asked who the guy was from his town, he recognized the book and told his former boss that he read it along with several others. "He took his dog, as I recall."

"Yeah, it was a yellow Labrador Retriever."

When Patrick walked back over to his car he asked Paul how much longer he needed and Colonel Woodburn said about five minutes. During those five minutes he wrote down his address and phone number and asked him to keep in touch. They shook hands goodbye and this time they were ready to go.

What a small world Paul thought to himself. Of all the places Colonel Woodburn could vacation and go to Mass, he picked here. It was great to see him and reminisce, but he was sorry he missed Kate. She left right after Mass because she had to go pick up one of their daughters.

Patrick asked Paul if he needed to stop anywhere before they returned to the trailhead, but he didn't need anything because he was in good shape as far as supplies were concerned. They went back to the B&B and Paul got his pack together. The hiking poles were great in that they were telescopic, so they really didn't take up much room when you had to pack them. When he went to the lobby Sue was there to see him off. She had prepared a bagged lunch for him and put some fresh fruit in the bag, too. He thanked her and said he might be back for a visit some day with the family. Patrick was already outside in the mini-van, so Paul joined him for the two-mile drive to the trailhead. The stay in Wallingford, Vermont had been a nice treat.

It was almost 11:00 when Paul said goodbye to Patrick and started hiking. There was another car at the trailhead dropping off some other hikers, so Paul asked them where they were going and they said they were headed to VT11 and then to Manchester Center. They appeared to be in their late teens and they figured the trek would take two days. VT11 was about 26 miles away, so Paul thought they could do that, after all that was his plan. They were traveling light, with just daypacks.

It turned out the three were up and coming sophomores at Middlebury College and they belonged to the Middlebury College outdoor club; they were looking for possible adventures for the new students. They seemed like very bright kids and they were much quicker than Paul, so after about the first mile Paul said they should go on without him because he felt like he was holding them up.

The hiking poles helped Paul a lot because they took some of the weight off his back, or at least that's how it seemed. He stopped at the Little Rock Pond Shelter to eat the lunch Sue made him and it was a ham and Swiss cheese sandwich on some homemade whole grain bread. The bread was terrific and actually the best part of the sandwich. He ate both plums which were also in the lunch bag. They were very juicy and thus very messy, but Sue included a couple napkins in the lunch bag. He was tempted to stay at the shelter for the night since no one was there, but he still had a lot of daylight and didn't want to fall any farther behind in his imaginary schedule. He continued hiking and enjoying the Vermont scenery. He passed the Homer Stone Brook Trail which also led to South Wallingford; he thought of Sue and Patrick and their B&B in Wallingford and how nice it was. He had always thought about doing something like that, but only when their kids were grown and on their own.

Paul crossed over the Danby-Landgrove Road at about 6:05 and continued hiking south. Looking in his guidebook, Danby, was about 3 ½ miles away and it was the town where Pearl Buck died. He didn't think that was a big enough deal to warrant a side trip to Danby, so he continued on. Paul never had to read any of Pearl Buck's novels, but if he had then it might have warranted a special trip. Paul made it to the Big Branch Shelter at 7:15 p.m. The kids from Middlebury College were at Big Branch Shelter and they were very polite when he walked up.

Paul said "hi" and asked how their hike went. They said "great" and said there was still a space in the shelter, but Paul declined the offer and set up his tent in a small clearing about 100 feet from the shelter. After he set up his tent he took out his stove and fired it up. He would have one of the Freeze-Dried meals Don gave him; it was Chicken Almondine. After dinner Paul decided to talk with the students from Middlebury College.

The kids were finishing up their dinner when he approached the shelter and they asked him if he wanted some dessert. Dessert for them consisted of Little Debbie oatmeal and marshmallow cakes. He said, "No thanks, I'm full from dinner." Paul was interested in where they were all from, because he knew that the student body was mostly from out of state, like it was at Norwich University.

One of the kids said he was from Delaware and two said they were from Massachusetts. Paul told them that he taught at Norwich University back in the mid-1980's and he took some of his students to Middlebury to go camping once. They asked where he took them camping and all he could remember was that it was a state park south of town. One of the kids mentioned a State Park name, but he couldn't remember. Paul told them that he also took his students over to Ft. Ticonderoga the second day of the trip.

He asked the kids what they were majoring in and one said French, and the other two said they hadn't declared a major yet. They asked him what he taught at Norwich and he told them. One of the kids, the French major said, "I don't think we offer

ROTC at Middlebury, I think you have to go up to the University of Vermont if you want to take that."

Paul mentioned that when he was at Norwich he got a visit one day from a Dartmouth College student enquiring about Air Force ROTC and why it was no longer offered at Dartmouth. He said he gave the student a short answer, that the Dartmouth faculty didn't want ROTC on campus. Army ROTC got around that by offering classes in the local armory in town. The Dartmouth student, however, told him that he didn't want to go into the Army because he wanted to go into the Air Force because his father had been in the Air Force. The student was so determined that he transferred to the University of New Hampshire and is now flying for the Air Force. Paul said that was a good example of a kid knowing what he wanted to do in life and not letting anything stop him until he got it.

Paul asked the kid majoring in French if he would be spending a year abroad and the student said, "Yes, I'll spend my junior year in France and I'm really looking forward to it. Have you ever been to France?" he asked.

"Yes, once when I was seven years old and it was just for two or three days and again when I was 17 for five days. I also went a third time for less than 24 hours when I was switching airports. You know, it was a funny thing."

"What's that?" one of the students asked.

"When I went there as seven year-old it was very boring stuff. That is, going to the Louvre and seeing the Venus De Milo, and probably thinking to myself, what's the big deal? It's a statue of a woman with no arms. Then in high school art appreciation when the teacher showed us a slide of the Venus de Milo, what a change in perception. It was all of a sudden a beautiful piece of art."

"Where were you going when you switched airports?" one of the kids asked.

"I was going to Djibouti," he said. "Do any of you guys know where Djibouti is?" he asked.

The student who majored in French said, "Yes, it's on the Horn of Africa."

The other students were impressed that there friend knew where Djibouti was, but before he could say anything the student asked him, "Why did you go there?"

"It's a long story, so I'll shorten it as best as possible. When I was in the Air Force I went there to visit our military guys at the US Embassy. No one from our headquarters had visited there in recent history, so my boss volunteered me to go with him. When we arrived on the Air France flight it must have been 98 degrees, and the US Army Major who met us said we were lucky because it was cooler than normal."

"Paul, if I can interrupt, asked one of the other students. Why are there US military at the embassy?"

"Every embassy, or at least I think every US embassy, in the world has some military presence there. There are a couple reasons for that. There are, of course, the US Marine Corps guards who provide internal security for the State Department employees working there.

The guys we were visiting, however, were there to help the Djiboutian military by providing training and equipment. The Djiboutian military had some engineering equipment and so the military guys at the embassy showed them how to use the equipment and how to fix the equipment. Of course, for the more advanced countries that have jets and ships and tanks, there are US military at the embassies in those countries providing that same type support."

Paul continued, "I left out the third type of military people at the embassies and that would be the military attaches. Those are the guys and gals who provide advice to the ambassador on military matters."

The French major chimed in, "so the military also needs linguists."

"Yes they do. So, someday when you are at the American Embassy in Djibouti, if you're having difficulty trying to figure out what the Djiboutian's are trying to say, you can always go to the Army attaché."

"You mean they speak French in Djibouti?" the student asked.

"Yes and some African dialect, either Somali or Ethiopian. I'm not sure which," he admitted.

"What was Djibouti like?" asked one of the other students.

"It was pretty grim. Did any of you ever see the movie The Planet of The Apes?"

All three of them shook their head yes.

"Well, supposedly the opening scene in Planet of the Apes, which showed the Earth after nuclear devastation, was filmed in Djibouti. Let's just say I was very happy when the plane lifted off for the next leg of our trip."

"Which other countries did you get to?" One of the students asked.

"On that trip or just in general?" he asked.

"Let's start with that trip."

"Well from Djibouti we went to Muscat, Oman, which was fascinating. Then we went to Amman, Jordan and while we were there with the embassy personnel we were able to take a day off to visit Petra. That was very interesting and the only place from that trip that I'd ever want to go back to. Did any of you see the movie Indiana Jones and the Last Crusade?"

The three nodded their heads yes.

"Well," Paul went on, "near the end of that movie when they rode down the canyon on horses, where they came out of the canyon that was Petra. What they showed of Petra in that movie was only about 1/50th of what there is to see there. From Jordan we went down to Nairobi, Kenya. The best part of that trip was seeing a former classmate of mine from an Air Force school I went to in Montgomery, Alabama. He took me around the country side showing me the places where he spent his youth."

"You mean he was Kenyan?" asked the French major.

"Yes. That's a long story and it's getting late, so I will make this very short. Suffice it to say, that the US military invites Allied Countries to send students to various military courses we have here in the United States. And in many cases they reciprocate. You might find this interesting," turning to the French major, "but one of my Army bosses went to the French Cavalry School for a year in France and then was invited to stay on as faculty for two or three years. His family loved that experience."

"Well fella's, I'm going to turn in before the sunlight disappears."

He went back to his tent and felt pretty good about the dialogue with the students. It made him realize how happy he was to have had the opportunity to take ROTC in college; of course they didn't have ROTC at Mount St. Mary's, his alma mater, so he drove up to Gettysburg College three days a week. It was a terrific experience for a 19 year-old. He wrote in his journal, said his prayers, and went to sleep. (520 FK)

At 6:45 a.m. Paul could hear the students talking and then it was quiet. He unzipped the rain fly and looked out. No one was there, the students already left. He decided to boil some water for coffee and oatmeal and sit and enjoy the solitude. About an hour later he rolled up his tent, secured it to his pack, and started hiking. The first few miles were uphill and the view from Baker Peak was great, so he decided to sit a while and take in the view. As he sat looking at the beauty of creation he wondered if he should camp on the AT for the night or go to Manchester Center, which was still 13 miles away. He decided on the latter.

As Paul sat there he couldn't help but think of how much he loved the mountains and particularly those in Vermont. He remembered back to when he found out he would be assigned to Norwich University. Initially he was disappointed because it wasn't his first choice of assignments. However, when he got there he loved it and thought about how God always didn't give you everything you asked for. God knows best. It was also a blessing for the family because his son Dan was born in Vermont and on the feast of the Annunciation.

Paul's reminiscing was interrupted by a noise. It was the sound of people and someone was in distress. He continued on to see what was happening and whether he could help or not. About 150 yards down the trail one of the Middlebury students had twisted his ankle. He had never taken the time to learn their names, or least not committing them to memory. The other kids used the injured boys name though and it was Mark. According to his buddies, Mark had actually slipped going up Baker Peak. He thought his ankle was OK, so they continued on. However, after about 100 yards, it was apparent that he wasn't OK. Mark was just wearing sneakers and he twisted his ankle very badly. He tried to go on, but he didn't have enough support.

Paul didn't have much of a first aid kit, but he did have an Ace bandage he inherited from Don. So, they wrapped his ankle tightly with the Ace bandage and decided they would stop every half hour or so to take off the bandage. Since no one really knew first aid they thought that might help so as not to cut off the blood flow to his foot. One of the students said, "The outdoor club was going to teach first aid to the sophomores this week, but we thought we would be alright. I guess we were wrong."

After some discussion, it was decided that Paul and James, the French major, would hike as quickly and safely as possible to the US Forest Service Road 21 at Mad Tom Notch. They would get help while Mark and Ray hiked slowly towards the road. Paul left Mark the hiking poles, thinking they would give him stability as he walked.Paul and James took off at a very quick pace and Paul felt awkward hiking without his hiking poles. As odd as it seemed to get used to them, it was equally as odd to hike without them; he didn't feel as sure footed.

James kept mentioning how much trouble they were all in because they were supposed to have been using the two days for getting in shape. Paul told James not to worry. He said, "You know you guys can give them a lesson plan they can use for years and that lesson plan is to do as you are told, don't take any chances, and bring a first aid kit. Heck, that's actually two or three lessons."

James smiled at that and said something very mature for his age. He said, "Well I guess if someone can learn from our mistake that's a good thing."

They made it to Peru Lake Shelter at 9:45 and they were hiking at a brutal pace and even though James was carrying Paul's tent and sleeping bag, Paul needed a break and he told James that. They took about a five-minute break and drank water and ate some trail mix; then they continued on. It was downhill from Peru Peak and they made it to US Forest Service Road 21. There was no one there, so they waited a bit. Looking at the road it was apparent that nothing drove down it recently because there were no fresh tire tracks. Paul suggested that they continue on to Bromley Mountain because his guidebook said there was a chair lift there, so maybe there was a phone.

As Paul and James continued on Paul couldn't help thinking about mobile phones. If they only had a mobile phone, how much simpler it would be. He didn't know the range of a mobile phone, but figured they had to be better than Walkie Talkie's.

James saw it first when they came into a clearing, saying "There's the top of the chair lift."

James picked up the phone and it was dead, so Paul moved the lever up and down a couple of times and finally someone picked up and said, "Hello, can I help you. Whoever this is shouldn't be on this phone unless it's an emergency."

James said it was an emergency and gave the person on the other end of the line a good summary of what happened to Mark. They said they would send a team to Mad Tom Notch and hike northward and they asked if they were going to come down the mountain to meet up with the rescue team. James turned to Paul relaying the information to see what Paul thought and he nodded his head yes. The hike down the mountain was nice because there were hardly any rocks or boulders to contend with. They made it to the base of the mountain in less than 15 minutes.

Paul and James met the person who James had spoken to and she introduced them to the rescue team. Bob and Jim, the rescue team, took them to their vehicle and they drove to Mad Tom Notch. As they got closer it was apparent why the road wasn't used. It was actually a trail assessable by four-wheel-drive-vehicles, which they were driving in. They reached the AT and Bob told James and Paul to hike south in case Mark and Ray already passed by the Mad Tom Notch intersection.

Bob and Jim on the other hand would head north and would fire their pistol, which was loaded with blanks, if they found them. After about 20 minutes they heard a shot, so thinking that Bob and Jim found their friends they turned and headed back to Mad Tom Notch.

Once they reached the road they started heading north on the AT. They came upon the four after about 15 minutes. Bob and Jim were looking at Mark's foot and were putting an inflatable cast on his foot as they walked up. After they put the inflatable cast on Marks foot, Bob, Jim, and James carried Mark towards their four-wheel-drive at Mad Tom Notch and Ray and Paul followed behind. As they were walking Ray filled Paul in on the ordeal and it was looking like Mark may have broken a bone in his foot. When they reached the four wheel drive, they loaded Mark into the vehicle first, which only left room for five. Someone would have to walk, so Paul said he didn't need to ride along and he wished Mark and the others well. Paul asked for a contact number, so that he could check up on Mark once he made it to Manchester Center.

The ankle ordeal took a big chunk of time out of Paul's day, but it was unavoidable and he was glad that Mark was safe and in good hands. Paul didn't think the students would get into the trouble like they thought they would. In fact, his belief was that one of them would probably get an award of some type at one of their club meetings. The hike up Bromley Mountain was beautiful the second time around.

The first time up it he and James walked so fast they couldn't appreciate the surroundings.

When he made it to the top, for the second time, it was almost 5:30, so he decided to go another two miles to the Bromley Tenting Area to camp for the night, but unfortunately, his legs gave out on him after a mile or so. He found a flat area where he could pitch his tent, which he did. Then he prepared dinner, which was beef stew. At 7:45 he couldn't keep his eyes open, so he laid his head down on his makeshift pillow and drifted off to sleep. (534 FK)

At a little after midnight he was awakened with Charley Horses in both legs, plus he had to pee. He unzipped the tent and went outside to relieve himself. Once he got rid of the Charley Horses he thought he would go back in the tent and massage his legs, but he looked up and the sky was amazing. He could see the northern lights which he had seen a handful of times before. So, he sat there on the side of Bromley Mountain and watched the northern lights for about ten more minutes as he massaged his calves. Then he was ready to go get some more sleep before it was time to get up. He zipped up his tent at 1:05 a.m. and laid there. He couldn't sleep so he said a decade of the Rosary, the *Joyful Mysteries* and when that didn't work he said another, the *Sorrowful Mysteries*. He only made it to the third sorrowful mystery, when Jesus was crowned with thorns and then he fell off to sleep.

He awoke at 7:15 a.m. from all the sounds of nature. He was happy he didn't have any other Charley Horses during the night, but his legs were still a bit fatigued and felt heavy. Paul figured he only had two-and-a-half miles to VT11 and then it was about a five mile hitch to Manchester Center. His next mail drop pickup would be in Bennington, Vermont, which was still another 40 miles further, so he didn't need to stop. However, after yesterday's events Paul felt he would love to sleep in a real bed and call Laura and the kids. He figured out that with all the commotion and adrenaline involved with Marks possible broken foot, he had hiked 20 miles or more the day before and his legs could attest to that. He had a cold breakfast, rolled up his tent, and started hiking at about 8:00 a.m.

He made it to VT11 by 9:00 o'clock and he stuck out his thumb; the second car picked him up. Otis, the driver, was from Londonderry, Vermont, but worked in Manchester Center, at the Grand Union Supermarket. Otis said he was originally from Connecticut, but moved to Londonderry because it was too congested in Connecticut. He was attracted to the area because of Bromley ski area, where he worked as a ski lift operator during the winter.

Otis dropped Paul off at a lodge in town and told him he knew the owners, so he should mention his name for a deal. When he walked into the lodge he went to the desk and asked whether they had any rooms and they did. Paul mentioned Otis' name and the owner smiled and said, "So, Otis is picking up hitchhikers again and sending them here. What a great guy that Otis is!" The lodge had several vacant rooms, probably because it was a Tuesday during the summer.

Driving through town on the way to the lodge Paul saw a McDonald's and while he never had an urge for a Big Mac since leaving Florida, he had a Big Mac attack, so he retraced his route back to VT11 to find the McDonald's. Since it was before 11:00 a.m. he had to settle for two egg McMuffin's with extra Canadian bacon. They tasted good, but their coffee really was quite exceptional. After Paul ate at McDonald's he went back to the lodge and used the phone in the lobby to phone home.

Theresa answered and was happy it was her father. They had expected a call the night before, but of course he didn't make it to Manchester Center as planned. He talked to Theresa for a while giving her a much abbreviated synopsis of what happened the day before and then he spoke to the boys. They all seemed pretty happy about going back to school. Theresa wanted to talk again after the boys were finished, so she got on the phone and had a question. "Dad," she said, "Where is the University of Notre Dame?"

He told her it was in South Bend, Indiana, and then he asked why she was asking. She just said, "Oh, I was just wondering, but be sure to call Mommy next." Paul said goodbye and that he might call again in the morning if he had a chance, but he would call for sure when got to Bennington.

Paul placed a call to Laura, but she was busy with a patient and couldn't talk. The person who answered said to call back in about 15 minutes and she would let her know he called. Paul thought back to Theresa's question about South Bend and why she was asking. Maybe it was soccer related. Perhaps she was thinking ahead for a possible place to go for soccer camp next summer. After all, she had gone to a soccer camp at Clemson University the summer before and she loved it.

While Paul was waiting to call Laura back he asked the owner if he could do some laundry, so he showed him where the washing machine was and exchanged some of Paul's bills for quarters. He put a load of clothes in the washer and just threw everything in together. He went back to the phone in the lobby and called Laura again and she answered the phone.

First he told her about the adventure the day before and why he couldn't call. Next he told her how nice a town Manchester Center was and that maybe they should add that to their list of places to come back to someday. When he was finished, Laura told him something which made Theresa's question make sense. She said that something came in the mail the day before and she wasn't going to mention it because she knew Paul was intent on finishing the hike.

So Laura told him they received a postcard from AFJROTC Headquarters notifying him of an instructor opening in South Bend, Indiana. She said the opening was for the November timeframe. He asked how Laura and the kids felt about it and she said she was ready to leave Tampa, Theresa was excited about Notre Dame, and Daniel didn't care. Steven was the lone holdout. Paul asked Laura when he would have to let AFJROTC know and she said she thought he had about 10 days to respond. Paul realized he was being selfish with his AT trip, but he was thinking more clearly now, at least more clearly than 43 days prior. He said he would think about it and pray about it and call Laura in the morning.

Paul looked in the phone book for a list of churches in town. He saw that there was a Catholic Church called Christ our Savior on Bonnet Street, which from the town map looked like it was two or three streets away, so that is where Paul headed.

Christ Our Savior Parish was only about an eight-minute walk from the lodge. He walked up the stairs to the church and pulled on the front door which was open. He walked in, dipped his hand in the Holy Water, and walked towards the altar. With the exception of one other person, Paul was the only one in the church, and of course Jesus was in the tabernacle. The glow from the red candle indicated where the tabernacle was and inside the tabernacle is where they kept the consecrated hosts, which is the body of Christ. Paul picked the third pew, genuflected, blessed himself, and then moved into the pew where he kneeled down. He was quiet at first, trying to get in the right frame of mind and then he spoke to Jesus in the tabernacle. He asked for guidance as to what he should do.

Paul stayed about an hour and was interrupted by people coming into the church. Someone in a suit came forward and asked Paul if he was there for the funeral. He shook his head no and the man in the suit walked to the back of the church; he followed him.

"What time is the funeral?" Paul asked.

"It will start at 2:00 o'clock," said the man in the suit.

"Is it a funeral Mass?" Paul asked.

The man nodded his head yes.

He decided to go back to the lodge to shave and shower and put on the best clothes he had. Unfortunately his best clothes weren't appropriate for a funeral, but he would sit in the back and try not to stick out. It took about seven minutes to get back to the lodge, so that meant Paul would have to leave the lodge no later than 1:53. He shaved, showered and put on his clean long pants and shirt. He tried to get the dirt and mud off his hiking boots as best as he could and then he left for the church. Paul arrived back at the church and he could hear the music. He stood outside until he was sure the priest was up to the altar and when he could see the priest at the altar Paul moved into the most inconspicuous seat in the church.

The funeral Mass was beautiful. It was for a young mother who died during child birth. The priest, in his homily, said that as a child his heroes were always the ones who tried to save lives, like police, firemen, and soldiers. He went on to say that Judy, the baby's mother, died to save a life, the life of her son.

Father went on to say that in this day and age most people would have told Judy to save herself, but she believed in what Jesus told His Apostles. And the priest quoted John's gospel and read the verse, "There is no greater love than to give your life for a friend." He said that Judy gave her life so that her baby would have a life and in his eyes and Jesus' eyes that was heroic.

At the sign of peace, Paul noticed that Frank, Sylvia, and Kevin were there, but too far away to shake their hands, so he flashed a peace sign. Paul left after the final blessing because he felt underdressed and out of place. He started walking back towards the lodge, but it took a little longer because he was thinking about the beautiful ceremony. He never liked funerals and tried to avoid them. He was sure his disdain for funerals was because his father died when he was eight and he still remembered his father laying there in the casket in the funeral home and he would have frequent dreams about that. Additionally, certain smells reminded him of the funeral home. When he got to the lodge, he got his laundry from the dryer and went to his room. He wrote in his journal about the funeral and then he took a nap.

Paul decided to splurge for dinner, so he went to a steak house. He ordered a house salad and a sirloin with a baked potato and squash casserole. It was delicious and he had the blueberry pie a la mode for dessert. It was a great dinner and as he sat there eating his pie he reflected back to the conversation with Laura. It sounded like she was ready to leave Florida. Theresa was eager and Daniel was up for anything. Steven was the one who wanted to stay in Florida. If Paul told Laura to send the post card back to Air Force JROTC headquarters he wondered when he would have to go for the interview. He was assuming he would be one of the three people recommended by JROTC. He knew the process well, from the interview in southern Virginia and the one he had gone for in Ocala, Florida.

The logistics of it all was confusing. Would he go back to Tampa and then go to South Bend for the interview? Or, would he have Laura mail his Class "A" uniform to South Bend and then he would go right there? Who would she mail his uniform to? Perhaps she could mail it to the NCOIC and Paul would pick it up from him or her. The one good thing was that his uniform would fit him well. Paul figured he lost 15 pounds since he began his hike. Whereas his uniform had been a bit tight at his retirement ceremony, that wouldn't be the case now. It might actually be a bit loose and baggy.

Paul returned to the lodge and called Laura. He told her to mail the post card to JROTC Headquarters and she asked if he was sure and he said "well you know, I can always decline the interview." They talked for a while about all the possibilities and the one that made most sense was for him to return to Tampa before going for the interview. Paul did some rough calculations in his head and figured the earliest he would be asked to interview was at the end of October. What he wasn't sure of was whether the position was vacant already or if it was a planned vacancy. If it was vacant already the school might want him there sooner than later. He would make a mental note to ask JROTC Headquarters that question if he was selected for the interview process.

After he finished talking to Laura he took out the map and figured out his next couple of days. Bennington, his next mail pickup, was about 40 miles away and that would take him three days. Some people could probably do it in two, but there was no sense in overexerting himself because there would be a price to pay. The price of overexertion in Paul's case seemed to be Charley Horses. Stratton Mountain was his goal for the next day and it was about 14 miles once he got back on the trail. Paul wrote in his journal, set the alarm clock, and went to sleep. (536 FK)

The alarm woke him out of a sound sleep. It was 6:00 a.m. when his feet swung over the side of the bed searching for the floor with his feet. There was no one else staying in the lodge, so the owner said Paul could help himself to his own breakfast. He went down to the kitchen and had a look around.

The coffee was already brewed, so Paul helped himself to a cup while he decided what to eat. He helped himself to three eggs which he scrambled and added some cheddar cheese which he found on the shelf above the produce drawers. He also made some wheat toast and smeared peanut butter and jelly on them. There were some bananas and apples, so Paul took two of each, saving them for his lunch. At 7:45 the owner drove Paul back to the trailhead.

The lodge sort of reminded Paul of the lodge that Laura, Theresa, and he stayed in while they were waiting for the house to be built in Northfield. That lodge was in Moretown, Vermont, which was about a nine-mile drive over the mountains to Northfield. The road was rough and was called a washboard road by Paul's contractor because he traveled the same road. Paul had never heard that term before, but it was sort of like an old fashioned washboard.

The owners of the lodge in Moretown were great and they made Paul, Laura, and Theresa feel at home. They lived there on and off, for about two months, while their house was being built. There was a full breakfast every morning and they could use the kitchen for their other meals. It was really a ski lodge, but since Paul & Laura needed a place to stay in July and August the owners were happy to have someone there.

Paul remembered how on one Sunday they went to Mass at the church nearby and someone walked in wearing Bavarian clothes. Laura leaned over to Annie, the owner, and asked who that was. It turned out to be one of the Von Trappe children. The Von Trappe's, of *Sound of Music* fame, moved to Vermont back after World War II and settled down in Stowe, Vermont. Paul also remembered back to one of the Sunday readings, the one where Jesus was invited to Mary and Martha's house and Martha was disturbed that Mary wasn't helping her. Both Laura and Annie laughed at something the priest said in his homily, but Paul didn't get it. Whenever Paul heard that reading, it took him back to Vermont in 1983 and Laura and Annie finding humor in something the priest said. Paul chalked it up to being one of those girl things.

It was a productive stop in Manchester Center in a number of ways. First, he got to go to Mass and receive communion, second, Paul decided to try for the AFJROTC position in Indiana, and lastly, Paul checked on Mark's status before he left the lodge. James answered the phone and said the prognosis was a badly sprained ankle. Paul marveled at God's plan. If Mark hadn't sprained his ankle then Paul wouldn't have stopped in Manchester Center, he wouldn't have gone to Mass, and he wouldn't have made the decision about AFJROTC. From VT11 the trail southward had a vertical climb of about 400 feet.

At Prospect Rock there was an excellent view of Manchester Center, which was about two miles away as the crow flies. The trail was fairly level until he got to the Douglas Shelter cut-off and then the trail started to climb up to Stratton Pond which was listed as 2,565 feet. Fortunately, the trail didn't go over Stratton Mountain which was listed at 3,936 feet. Paul stopped to eat one of his bananas and some trail mix along with a couple healthy swigs of water.

It was beautiful hiking through the Green Mountain National Forest. He used to talk with Dean Farmer about hiking all or part of the Long Trail, but neither had a job which would allow them to take off. It definitely would have been easier as a 31 yr.-old, Paul's age when he was at Norwich. Paul's attention returned to the trail because it was getting steeper. He couldn't figure out which mountain it was, but he figured that it was the highest mountain he would have to cross before getting to Virginia. The view was great and he could see that there would be a major weather change headed his way. He didn't think he could make it to Story Spring Shelter, so it would be a wet night by the looks of the sky. He looked for a sheltered area where he could pitch his tent.

To the best of Paul's calculations he made it a little past the spring mentioned in his guidebook. He was probably at about 551 miles, the distance from Mt. Katahdin, Maine. He didn't know exactly, but he didn't care because he found a nice spot going down the mountain.

He pitched his tent and pulled over a downed stump, so that he could sit while he was cooking his dinner. Then he selected an entrée which he inherited from Don; it was lasagna. He hoped it was better than when he and Tom combined meals, since that was the only time he ate Lasagna. He ate the other banana for dessert and after dinner he wrote in his journal, including his memories of when they stayed in the lodge in Moretown, Vermont, about 12 years prior.

Paul could see lightening in the distance and he hoped he was sheltered enough from the approaching storm. When it started to rain at 7:55 p.m. he sought refuge in his tent. The storm approached fast and he was barely in his tent before he could hear a branch hit the tent. The branch hit pointy end first and it punctured the rain fly and the mesh screen roof of the tent. Water started as a drip, but then as the intensity of the storm got worse the flow of water got worse. He wrapped his journal in two plastic bags and then inside his sleeping bag for added safety. He could hear the thunder and it was terribly loud as some of the lightning strikes seemed very close. The storm kept up for 45 minutes. Paul gave up trying to sop up the water from the tent floor and started to pray; he reflected on the gospel passage of when the Apostles were in a fishing boat and there was a terrible storm, but Jesus was sleeping. After about another 20 minutes the rain slowed down and then stopped after about another 10 minutes.

Even though it was dark, he thought he'd check things out, so he unzipped the tent and crawled outside. He was very careful when he pulled the tree branch out of his tent. There were other tree branches nearby and he realized he was very fortunate because many of them had longer pointy ends than the one that came through the roof of his tent. Even though it was dark he could see all the destruction around him. One huge tree fell over within 15 feet of his tent. There was nothing he could do except pray that the rest of the night was safe. So, he went back into his tent and tried to dry it out as best as possible. He used every piece of dry clothing he had to sop up the water. Finally at about 11:20 p.m. he was able to get into his sleeping bag, which was somewhat damp, and go to sleep. (551 FK)

Paul thought he could hear people talking and that's what woke him up. He could also hear the unmistakable sound of his Svea 123; how could that be he thought? He looked at his watch and it was 7:57 a.m. He felt well rested and though he was upset he had slept so late, he was happy he had a good night sleep after the storm. He unzipped his tent and peered outside. Someone was sitting on the log he pulled over so that he could sit while he ate dinner the night before. There was a guy was using his stove, well technically it wasn't his, he thought.

"Hello," the guy said. "That was quite a storm last night; it really made a mess of things. Didn't it"

Paul said, "Yes, I was very fortunate."

"No," the guy said. "You were much blessed. The Lord was looking out for you."

Paul surveyed the surrounding area. In addition to the two trees he could see that were downed the night before, it looked like about one quarter of the trees on the mountain were blown down or twisted. Paul said, "Yes I am much blessed. Now I know you know who I am, but who are you?" In addition to the words the visitor spoke, Paul sensed that this was another companion sent from God.

"My name is Will, and I'm from Montgomery, Alabama."

"Hi Will it's nice to meet you."

Will looked like he was about 25 years old. He had a scrubby beard and was a big guy. He must have been 6' 5" tall, taller than Paul by a couple of inches.

"Was there a tornado last night caused by the thunderstorms?" Paul asked.

"No, they were just very strong winds." And then standing up he said, "Take these they'll help your tent."

Will handed Paul some weather proof tape to put on his rain fly and some screen repair tape for his tent roof. He took both from Will and thanked him. Then he took the rain fly off the tent and checked the puncture and said, "This should work. You know Will, I lived in Montgomery for about four years."

"Yes, I know that" Will responded. "How did you like it?"

Paul thought about it a while and said, "Except for the heat during the summer, it was nice. From May until October I couldn't stand it. However, I must say the people were all very nice and polite."

Paul could tell Will was thinking about what he said. It was sort of like he could see the wheels turning in his head. Paul was curious about Will's story, but he didn't rush him.

Then Will said, "Yes, I heard the people are very nice and I hope to get there someday soon. My life was snuffed out at 12 weeks in my mother's womb; my mother was almost a quarter through her pregnancy. She and her boyfriend, my father, got nervous and he talked her into having an abortion. They were both students at Auburn University in Montgomery and thought it was more important to graduate than to have a baby."

Will had difficulty speaking, Paul could hear it in his voice, and his eyes began to tear, but he continued. "A couple years later my mother was killed in an automobile accident and my father was devastated. He started thinking about me and what if he hadn't pushed my mother into having the abortion. He realized that she would probably have been at home taking care of me. The 'what ifs' started gnawing at him and he second guessed everything as a result. It got so bad, he lost his job.

He's in another job now that he is overqualified for. When he comes to realize that we have an all merciful and forgiving Father, then he will ask for forgiveness. Until that time he will continue to doubt. I was told that I could ask for your help."

"How can I help?" Paul asked.

"Here is my Dad's name and phone number. The next time you are near a pay phone please call him and tell him about me. He won't believe you at first. In fact, he will undoubtedly hang up on you. However, you need to be persistent and he will eventually come around when you mention some personal things I'll share with you about my mother."

Will handed Paul his father's name and phone number, plus a phone card. Paul reached out and before he took it he said, "Are you sure this is OK? Is this part of God's plan?"

"Yes, Paul. This is OK. You won't get into trouble if that's what you're thinking."

"Will, you know that's exactly what I was thinking. Why didn't any of the others ask for any help?" Paul asked.

"Paul, sometimes men don't see the cause of their problems. They are too proud to admit it and sometimes they need a little push. God thinks my father has suffered enough; however, he has to ask for God's help and he has to want it."

Paul considered everything Will told him and when he reached for the slip of paper he asked, "And what was God's plan for you if I may ask?"

Will said, "I was going to be a High School teacher and I would have helped many youth through some tough times and situations."

Paul thought about what Will said and remembered back to what Don Bowser said. The youth of today were in trouble because of all the choices they had to face.

Will said to Paul, "now let me give you a hand with your tent. Let's shake it out. Then I'll walk with you a while to tell you about my mother."

It was about 8:50 by the time Paul and Will started hiking and Will shared some things about his mother and father; things which he could use to help convince Will's father. Will offered to carry Paul's pack and he readily accepted the kind offer. They made it to Story Spring Shelter by 11:30 and on the way they met several hikers headed northbound. The topic of conversation was the storm the night before. They said they were glad they were in the shelter and when they found out that Paul spent the night in his tent they were impressed. He told them about the tree branch puncturing his tent and how it came to within inches of his head.

When the hiker's continued hiking north Paul said to Will, "How come they could see you? Sylvia said they couldn't see her because her grandfather hadn't asked for forgiveness."

"Paul wouldn't it seem unusual for a backpack to be floating through the air? That is what it would have looked like to them if they couldn't see me. Remember Paul, your ways are not God's ways."

Will hiked with Paul until 1:15, reaching the Kid Gore Shelter and then Will said goodbye and walked off. Paul thanked him for the repair tape and for carrying his backpack and Will turned and said, "Don't thank me, thank God."

Paul took out what was left of his trail mix and finished it off. He also ate the last of Don's food, which was a snicker's bar and then he washed it down with water. He felt re-energized.

He figured he would hike to the Goddard Shelter and see how he felt. It was too far to the Melville Nauheim Shelter, which according to his guidebook was nearly nine-miles further than Goddard. Still, that would leave him a 20-mile hike on Friday to get to Bennington, Vermont. Though the weather was beautiful, Paul didn't want to spend another night in his tent because it needed a good drying out.

Paul thought it would be easier going south and he thought the most difficult was behind him, but the last mile to the Goddard Shelter seemed as hard as ever. His legs were sore, so that solved that issue. He would stay at the Goddard Shelter. There were four other hikers there. Two were headed north and the other two were just hiking to Bennington. He picked a spot in the shelter to sleep and then found a place to dry out his tent. It was a good sized shelter and one of the people from Bennington was sharing some cheese, it was a huge piece of a Gouda Cheese wheel. He said it was the last day it would be edible, so Paul took some. It was delicious and he saved some for his Chili Mac, which he would try to melt over the top. The memories food can bring are amazing.

He remembered back to his hike with Mr. Arthur when they were at Ethan Allen Pond in the Presidential Range. A guy in the lean-to had a huge Gouda wheel and he was sharing it with everyone who was seeking shelter from the storm. Paul was thankful that friendly hiker, who was the bearer of Gouda Cheese, didn't slice off part of his finger like Joe did that Memorial Day Weekend back in 1976.

After dinner the two guys from Bennington were going for a hike to see the sunset. They invited Paul, but he didn't feel like doing any more hiking that day, which was Thursday, the 3rd of August. It seemed so long since he was in Manchester Center, but it had only been two days. He really wished he could make it to Bennington in one day, but that would be more than his body could handle.

It was starting to get tedious and it was the same thing every day. One day runs into another and one scenic view is just like the next scenic view. He would ask the two from Bennington, when they returned from the summit, if it is possible to hike to Bennington safely in one day.

Paul tried to stay awake, but it was difficult. He fell asleep and didn't wake up when the two came back from the summit. He slept well and didn't even get up during the night, which was unusual. He must have been somewhat dehydrated, but fortunately he didn't have Charley Horses; he would be sure to drink enough water this Friday, the 4th of August. Everyone was up in the shelter and the two north bounders were already gone. He asked the Bennington guys if it was possible to hike to Bennington in one day and they said, "It better be, because that's what we plan to do. Do you want to join us?" Paul said he would like to try and they said "it's all downhill."

They set off at 7:05 a.m. and they set a killer pace. One of the guy's names was Jeff and the other was Ryan and they were nice enough to carry some of Paul's equipment. Like Otis, the guy who picked him up in Manchester Center, both Jeff and Ryan fell in love with Vermont. They both graduated from college and decided to take a couple years off before thinking about settling down. They worked at various odd jobs to help with expenses and both worked at nearby Mt. Snow during the winter.

Both Jeff and Ryan were nearly out of control going down the mountain, one misstep could have been disastrous. Paul was glad he had the hiking poles for stability, though a couple times the tips slipped off the rocks and he stumbled, but fortunately never fell. They made it to the Melville Nauheim Shelter by 12:45 and took a 15-minute break and then continued their high-spirited pace. The last mile and-a-half was just as quick as the first eight-and-a-half and they made it to VT9 by 2:05. What would have taken Paul over a day, took only seven hours.

Jeff had a car at the trail head and they offered Paul a ride to town. On the way to town they asked Paul where he was staying and he asked if they could recommend a motel. Jeff said they wouldn't hear of his staying in a motel and said he was welcome to stay with them. While Jeff and Ryan were both nice guys, he didn't want to impose. But when Jeff said Paul would have his own room with a private bath, then it seemed too good a deal to pass up.

Jeff and Ryan lived in a three bedroom house in town that they were house-sitting for a professor from Bennington College who was on sabbatical for a year. It was a nice house and Paul had his own bedroom like Jeff told him. They told Paul to make himself at home.

The first thing he did was shower. He didn't feel right after the storm, it was hard to explain, but he wanted to change out of his clothes. Jeff showed him where the washing machine was and Paul dumped all his clothes in except for the gym shorts he was wearing. After his shower, he asked if he could use their telephone. He called home and Laura answered; she had just gotten home. He told her he was OK and in Bennington, Vermont, and that he would call back after dinner. Jeff and Ryan said he was welcome to join them for dinner and he said OK. He offered to help cook, but they said they had it under control, so he folded his laundry while they were putting the finishing touches on dinner.

Jeff and Ryan explained at dinner how they met the professor whose house they were staying in. He frequented the ski slopes at Mt. Snow and Jeff gave him private ski lessons. They both marveled at the fact that the guy never learned how to ski and then all of a sudden at age 55 he thought it was time to learn to ski since his wife and kids skied a lot. One thing led to another and Jeff, Ryan, and the professor became the best of friends.

The professor, John, was an English literature Professor at Bennington College and he asked them if they would take care of his house for ten months while he was in

England. They said "yes." It was a good deal because they didn't have to pay for rent or utilities and they figured that if John liked the way they took care of his house they could fall into other house sitting opportunities for other Bennington professors who were on sabbatical.

In that Jeff was going into town after dinner, Paul hitched a ride. He mentioned during dinner that he had been to Bennington once before and that was for only overnight. Paul thought the name of the motel where he and Laura stayed was the Paradise Motel, so Kevin drove past the Paradise Motel and Paul said it looked vaguely familiar, but it had been 12-13 years. On the way into town Jeff mentioned that he and Ryan were both from Connecticut.

Both Jeff and Ryan went to the University of Connecticut and went on a ski trip their senior year to Mt. Snow and that is when they both fell in love with Vermont. They had both skied in Colorado and admitted that the skiing was tremendous; however, they didn't want to live in Colorado.

Jeff said they could be home in three hours or less, so if there was a family event, they could go. Jeff said he was from the Danbury area and Ryan was from Bridgeport. On hearing that Jeff was from the Danbury area, Paul told him that as a teenager he used to spend part of his summer in New Milford, Connecticut, and specifically on Candlewood Lake. He told Jeff how he loved going to his Aunt Ellen and Uncle Bill's lake front house. Paul also explained that he was born in New London, Connecticut, but left when he was one.

Jeff was going to the Price Chopper Supermarket, so Paul picked up some things he would need for the next week to complement his mail drop stuff. He would pick that up as soon as the Post Office opened in the morning. Then Jeff gave him a tour of Bennington and Bennington College; it was a beautiful campus. Afterwards they returned to the house.

It was a little before 7:45, so Paul called Laura and the kids first and then Don Bowser. When he called earlier, Laura said she had something to pass on from his brother Dave, who was serving with the Air Force in the Middle East.

CHAPTER EIGHT

Foxes and Cats

The first thing Paul did was to tell Laura about the terrible storm two nights prior and his heavenly companion after the storm. Then he told her about the two guys he was staying with in Bennington and his plan to call Don Bowser after he hung up with her. He planned to stop to see them when he got to Dalton, Massachusetts, in four or five days, so he told her that was where she should send his next package. After he said it, he thought of how that must have sounded, so he said, "So let me make sure I'm clear, you're going to mail my next package to Dalton, Massachusetts and not Pittsfield. I don't even know if they will be around next week until I call them. Dalton, Massachusetts is right on the Appalachian Trail."

Laura said she would send the package the next morning and then she let him talk to the kids. Laura got back on the phone after the kids each talked and she passed on the information from his brother Dave. The information was that he was being assigned to the base in Tampa, Florida, in the October time-frame. That was great news because Paul would get to see his brother more often and the kids would get to see their uncle. Besides being the kids uncle he is Theresa's and Steven's Godfather. After he hung up the phone he looked for Don & Chris' phone number. When he found the paper with Don's phone number he placed the call.

Don answered and when he found out it was Paul he said, "Paul where are you?"

"I'm in Bennington, Vermont, and I think I'll also stay here until tomorrow. So, if my calculations are right, I will be in Dalton by Tuesday late or Wednesday around noon." He figured it was 44 miles from Bennington to Dalton, so he would do about 15 miles a day.

Don said, "That's great Paul, either way Chris and I would love to have you stay the night with us. I will wait to tell you about our proposed Italian trip, instead of using your minutes on the phone. I'm looking forward to your visit because I'm going stir crazy around the house."

"Don how about if I call you from Williamstown when I get there? That way I can give you a better indication of my progress. I'm looking forward to the visit as well and I have some experiences to share with you."

After Paul hung up he went downstairs to the kitchen and Ryan was sitting at the kitchen table looking at maps. He looked up as he walked into the room and said to Paul, "I'm starting to plan our next trip."

"Where are you planning it to?" He asked.

"Well, you've given me something to think about. I've never hiked the Presidential Range, but I don't want to go now, I'm leaning more towards the end of September when all the kids are back in school."

"Ryan, I was wondering if I could stay here until Sunday because I'd like to go to church tomorrow afternoon. When Kevin was giving me a tour of town I saw a Catholic Church, it was close to the college."

"Yeah, I know that church. It's called St. John the Baptist. Yeah, that's alright if you stay until Sunday."

"Then let me at least give you all some money for food. After all, if I wasn't staying with you guys, I'd be in a motel somewhere in town."

Ryan said, "How about this? You take care of dinner tomorrow night and we'll call it even."

"Thanks Ryan. Well, I think I'll go to bed now. Thanks for everything."

Paul went back upstairs to his bedroom, wrote in his journal, and went to sleep. (576 FK)

At 8:15 a.m. there was a knock on his door. He couldn't believe he slept that late; he had to get up once to use the bathroom, but he was able to fall back to sleep. The knock on the door was Jeff and he was headed back into town and he wanted to know if Paul wanted a ride to the post office and grocery store. He said he did want a ride, so he got dressed and met Jeff at his car.

They got to the post office at about 9:00, so he went in and got his package. When he went back to the car he said to Jeff, "How about I treat you to breakfast somewhere?"

Jeff thought that sounded good so they drove to the Blue Benn Diner. Paul ordered Eggs Benedict with home fried potatoes and Jeff thought that sounded good, so he had the same thing. As they sat there drinking their coffee Jeff said, "I understand you are going to stay until tomorrow. Ryan said something about you want to go to church this afternoon."

"Yes, that's right. I was thinking of going to Mass tonight; Mass is at 4:30 p.m. according to the church recording and that means I can't fix dinner before 6:30. Is that alright with you guys?" He asked.

"Yes, that's fine. Maybe I'll go to Mass with you." Jeff replied.

"I'm Catholic," Jeff said, "but I don't get to Mass very often. I go for Christmas, Easter, and other special occasions." Jeff looked around to make sure no one could hear him and when he was sure it was safe to talk he said, "Now I haven't told Ryan this yet, so please keep it confidential, but I'm planning to get married next summer. My girlfriend is Catholic and we want to get married in the church. So, I think I should get back into the habit of going to Mass more regularly. I'd feel like a hypocrite on my wedding day if I didn't."

"So why haven't you told Ryan yet? Paul asked.

"I don't know. He's one of my best friends, but I don't think he would agree to be in the wedding party. He has this thing about organized religion and I think he would feel uncomfortable in church. My brother will be my best man, so that's not the problem. Maybe going to Mass with you this evening will be a good reason to tell him. I can spring it on him during dinner."

Paul thought about that a while and then said, "it sounds like a good plan to me."

The waitress brought out their Eggs Benedict and refills on their coffee. They dug right in and it was good, particularly the home fried potatoes. Paul asked Jeff where his girlfriend was from and how he kept this a secret from Ryan for so long.

Jeff's girlfriend was a high school sweetheart and when he went away to college they stayed in touch. During his senior year in college he realized he really loved her, but didn't think he was ready to settle down. He wanted to get the skiing thing out of his blood, but when he went home over the 4th of July, he proposed to her and she said yes. They set the date for June 1996.

Jeff said he would drive Paul to the supermarket after breakfast, so he could pick up stuff for dinner. He said he would make chicken parmesan with a salad and garlic bread and that sounded good to Jeff and he was sure that Ryan would be happy, too. He said he never knew Ryan to turn down a meal, especially if he didn't have to make it. Jeff mentioned that Ryan didn't like to cook, so Jeff did most of the cooking. Ryan kept the Professor's house looking nice, both inside and out. According to Jeff, that was Ryan's contribution to their living arrangement.

They drove by St. John the Baptist Catholic Church to pick up a church bulletin, but there was a wedding in progress and they didn't want to disturb anyone, so they returned to the house to put the cold things in the fridge.

Paul was thinking how Jeff reminded him of someone he knew, but he couldn't think who it was. If it had been someone he didn't care for, it would have come right to mind and since it didn't come right to mind, Paul thought that was a good thing. Paul wondered why that was, why he always remembered annoying people, but couldn't think of nice people's names right off the bat. It took him two trips to carry his stuff in. First he carried in the groceries and then he got the box from Laura and the kids. He put the food in the fridge that needed to be refrigerated and left everything else on the counter. Ryan was outside mowing the lawn and Jeff decided to go for a jog.

Paul went to open his package from Laura and took out the phone card and travelers checks. He needed both because he was low on minutes and on cash. Then, since he was by himself he thought he would make a private call. He got the slip of paper out of his wallet that Will gave him with his father's phone number in Montgomery, Alabama. He dialed the number and no one was there. The answering machine picked up after five rings. He debated as to whether to leave a message, so he left a very brief message saying he would call back later. He hung up and prayed for Les, Will's father. Since he couldn't reach Will's father he went into the kitchen to start dinner.

His plan was to do the chicken breasts, but not to fully cooking them. Then he would finish them when he got back from church. Then he made the salad and garlic bread ahead of time. He made two boneless chicken breasts for each person, plus two extra, so there were a total of eight. One of the chicken breasts would make a good lunch for the trail the next day. Paul thought how great it was to be working in a full size kitchen. Actually, he thought, it was the perfect kitchen. It had a food island, pots and pans galore, and two dishwashers. He figured the Professor or his wife were gourmet cooks because it was the perfect kitchen.

Ryan came in and asked what was up, so Paul told him the plan, not mentioning however, that Jeff would be going to Mass with him. Jeff came in a short while later and said he was going to shower. He told Ryan he thought he would go to Mass with

Paul. At 3:45 p.m. Paul tried to call Les again, however, there was no answer. This time he didn't leave a message.

Jeff and Paul left for St. John the Baptist church at about 4:00. It didn't take long to get there, less than ten minutes. Paul thought back to when they lived in Northfield, Vermont. Their parish was also called St. John the Baptist, but whereas their church in Northfield was made out of wood and painted white, the one in Bennington was a beautiful red brick building. It looked sturdier than theirs in Northfield. Mass started exactly at 4:30 p.m.

Paul glanced around the congregation to see if he knew anyone. He did; in the pew behind his were Frank, Sylvia, Kevin, and Will. When they saw him looking they each nodded their head and smiled in recognition. The homily was on the sacrament of marriage, which had to have been a good thing for Jeff. The priest talked about the wedding that afternoon and how everyone was so full of life and optimism. He talked about marriage and how the successful ones, at least from his standpoint of 20 years, were those who put their spouse before themselves. He said the marriages that didn't seem to work out were those that went from being selfless to selfish. During the priests homily he asked if there was anyone in the congregation who was contemplating marriage within the next year. Jeff looked at Paul and Paul nodded his head to Jeff, so that Jeff would raise his hand, which he did.

The priest looked at Jeff and the one other couple who had their hands raised and smiled. He didn't put anyone on the spot by asking them a question, but continued on with his homily on the sacrament of Holy Matrimony. At the Sign of Peace, Paul shook hands with everyone around him, but it was too difficult to reach any of the companions. The priest was standing outside the church after Mass and when Jeff passed by he shook Jeff's hand and said, "Are you getting married in this church?"

"No father," Jeff replied. "I'm getting married down in Connecticut, where I'm originally from." The priest said in response, "I've seen you around town, so if you need anything, I'm here."

As they walked to the car Jeff said, "That was nice of the priest, but his comment about seeing me around town was a bit awkward. He knows I don't attend Mass regularly, but he still offered his help."

They walked through the back door at 5:55 p.m. and Paul went right to the sink to wash his hands. He took the mostly cooked chicken out of the fridge and put it back in the oven. Then he put water on for the noodles. The salad was already made, so all that needed to be done was to grate some parmesan. He always liked to put fresh parmesan over the top of the chicken. He took the chicken back out of the oven, sprinkled some parmesan cheese over the top and put the pan back in the oven. He also put the garlic bread, which was wrapped in foil, into the oven as well. Dinner was on the table by 6:40, a little later than he planned. Jeff opened a bottle of wine to have with dinner and Ryan asked what the special occasion was. Jeff looked at Paul and Paul just smiled.

"Ryan, I have some news for you and I thought considering the news, you might want to offer a toast."

Ryan said, "what's your news Jeff?'

"Ryan, I've asked Susan to marry me and she said yes." There was a pause and then Ryan said, "Well, when's the big date."

For all the worrying Jeff did about Ryan's reaction, everything seemed OK.

"We'll be getting married next June, back in Connecticut. Susan is still checking with the church and with some banquet halls, so I can't give you a firm date yet."

Ryan raised his wine glass and said, "I'd like to toast my good friend Jeff and I wish both he and Susan all the happiness in the world."

Paul and Jeff raised their glasses and touched them together and then they both touched their glasses together with Ryan who was at the far end of the table. Jeff said, "Thank you Ryan."

Ryan and Jeff said the chicken and pasta were great at which point he told them his intentions of taking one of the leftover chicken breasts for lunch. The conversation then turned to Jeff and his going to church.

"You know Jeff I had a suspicion that something was up when you said you were going to church. I thought to myself, why out of the blue would he do that? The first thing I thought of was you and Susan. I was right."

Jeff said in reply, "You mean you're not mad at me for not telling you sooner?"

"Maybe just a little bit," said Ryan.

Ryan washed the dishes after dinner and Paul said he was going to use the phone if that was alright. Jeff said he wanted to call Susan first to let her know he went to Mass and what the priest said in his homily. Jeff was on the phone for about ten minutes and when he was finished he told Paul the phone was available.

Paul called Laura first and told her about his day and then he talked with his kids. He hung up the receiver and tried to think about what he would say to Les. After looking at the phone for what seemed like an eternity, he had an idea. He wasn't sure if it was a good idea, but it was worth the try. He dialed the 334 area code and then the seven digit number. It rang three times and someone picked up the phone and it was a male voice. "Hello," said the voice on the other end. Paul took in a deep breath and said, "Hello is the Les?" "Yes it is. Who is this?"

"This is Paul Geary and I'm calling because an acquaintance of ours gave me your name. I believe I'm coming to Montgomery sometime in September or October and I wonder if you can recommend a church to attend while I'm there."

Les didn't answer right away and then he said, "Who did you say you are?"

"This is Paul Geary and I'm a friend of Will's. He said back in college you and Bethany used to go to a church in Montgomery and you were always bragging about it." He kept talking because he didn't want to give Les time to think about what he was actually saying. "I used to live in Montgomery, but I can't remember any of the street names."

"Well," Les stammered, "I used to go to Frazier Methodist. It's on the Atlanta Highway."

Paul interrupted, "Hey Les, someone here needs to use the phone. Can I possibly call you back tomorrow when we can talk more? I really need more information on the Montgomery area if you can help me."

"Yes, that would be fine."

"Is 7:30 a.m. too early? I know there's a one hour time difference, but I have to leave for Massachusetts in the morning."

Les responded, "I'm actually playing golf tomorrow morning, could you call at 6:45."

"Consider it done," he answered in reply.

Paul hung up and thought about everything he told Les. He figured if he was very vague about what he said then at least he could plant a seed in Les's mind. He also figured he didn't lie; he would actually be in Montgomery in October or November if he did get the JROTC teaching job. He thought too that by mentioning Bethany, along with Will's name, then Les would find the conversation plausible. Of course he wouldn't have a clue that Will was his son, but it was also the name of Bethany's father. Paul had to think about what he is going to say in the morning.

Paul went back down stairs to see if Jeff and Ryan were still up. Ryan had already tidied up the kitchen and had moved into the den to watch TV. Jeff was nowhere to be seen, so he said goodnight to Ryan and mentioned that he would be getting up early to hit the trail again. Ryan said, "OK, see you in the morning. By the way, Jeff said he would drive you back to the trailhead whenever you want."

Paul went up to his bedroom, set the alarm clock on the nightstand, and wrote in his journal. When he said his evening prayers he asked for God's guidance on what to say to Les in the morning. Paul tuned off the lamp and looked at the clock; it was 10:10. As he lay there he thought about the significance of the time 10:10 and he remembered the radio show he listened to every weekday morning in Tampa on his drive to work at MacDill Air Force Base; the program always started out or ended with that verse from John's Gospel. "…I came that you might have life and have it more abundantly…" In fact, he remembered that the name of Johnette's program was the *Abundant Life*. He also remembered sharing that with Richard who was in the choir with him at St. Stephen's in Brandon and Richard wanted to share a similar story with Paul regarding the significance of 10:10 to his family.

Richard's wife had had several bouts of cancer. During one of the periods of chemo therapy she stopped at a church to pray. As she had her head bowed in prayer something came over her. She felt like Jesus was telling her she would be OK. She looked up at the cross suspended over the altar and on that particular cross Jesus' arms, as He hung on the cross, were at the position of 10:10 as you would look at a clock. She was familiar with the verse from John's Gospel and she knew she would be alright. The cancer was in remission and she was later told that she was cancer free.

What can he tell Les in the morning that would convince him he would be alright? He rolled over in the bed and dozed off to sleep.

The alarm rang at 7:00 and Paul used the bathroom to shave and shower. He also packed up his stuff and brought it all downstairs. He looked at his watch and it was 7:40 a.m., so it was 6:40 in Montgomery, Alabama. He could smell that someone had brewed coffee, so he went and poured himself a cup. Actually, no one was up, the coffee maker was set to make coffee at 6:30, so Paul took his coffee and went into the den, where he could make his call in private. He dialed the number in Montgomery and Les picked up on the third ring and said, "Hello."

"Hi Les," Paul said. "How is the weather down there this morning?"

"It is hot as Haiti," was Les' reply. "Paul I was thinking about what you said yesterday and I'm somewhat confused. You mentioned a Will and Bethany. I can't remember a Will, but I remember Bethany. She was my wife."

Paul tried to find the words and said, "I don't know that you ever met Will, but he certainly knew Bethany. Will is the one that mentioned you and that church you went to in Montgomery. I was just calling to see what the name of that church was, but I think you said it yesterday before I had to go. You said it is Frazier Methodist and that sounded right. As I remember it's on the east side of town and on Atlanta Highway."

"That's the one Paul, but I still don't understand about this Will guy. How do you know him?"

Paul was at a loss, but he tried. "I met Will a couple of days ago and may have mentioned that I will be going to Montgomery sometime in the fall. He said I should call you, so that's what I'm doing." It didn't seem to be working, so Paul thought he's try the direct approach.

"Look Les. Let me ask you a question. Do you believe in God?"

There was a hesitation on Les' end. Then he finally said, "I do, but I'm mad at God."

Paul said he could understand why Les was mad at God, but then Paul asked Les if he believed that anything was possible for God and Les said, "Yes."

"Les" Paul said, "I'm going to tell you something which is unbelievable, but it is believable because God can do anything." Do you believe that Les?"

"Yes."

Paul went on to tell Les how he was helped by Will during a storm and Will asked for his help in return. Paul asked how he could possibly help, but all Will said was, "you will find a way."

"Paul I don't know if this is some kind of a scam, but I'm going to hang up." And he did hang up. He slammed the phone down.

Paul figured he wouldn't call right back, he would wait about a half an hour to make sure that Les was gone. He would then leave a message on the answering machine.

Paul went back into the kitchen and Jeff was stirring up some pancake batter and asked if Paul wanted any pancakes and sausages. He said he'd love some pancakes and maybe a couple sausages and then he ate the three pancakes and two sausages and had another cup of coffee. The pancakes were above average and the coffee was great. It was Green Mountain Coffee, something Paul remembered fondly from his days at Norwich University. He didn't drink brewed coffee before they lived in Vermont, but that was what they served in the Lodge in Moretown while they were waiting for their house to be built. Jeff asked him when he wanted to leave for the trailhead and Paul said in another half hour if that was OK.

Paul finished his coffee, used the bathroom, and placed another call to Les. The answering machine picked up on the fifth ring. Paul left a message and he said "Les this is Paul again, please don't hang up. Please hear me out. Will is yours and Bethany's son; he told me some things that only you and Bethany knew in case you didn't believe me. You made love after an Auburn football game and that's when she got pregnant. When she started to show, you both got nervous about it being your senior year. You decided she should have an abortion and she reluctantly agreed. You got married two weeks after graduation, but hid it from your families and then Bethany died in an automobile accident about a month later. Now I have to go and I won't be near another phone for several days because I'm hiking on the Appalachian Trail. I'll call when I can, in case you feel like talking. I'll tell you what your son's real message is. Goodbye."

He would save some of the other details Will shared with him for the next time he called Les. However, if Les didn't want to talk, he didn't know what else he could do.

Paul picked up his backpack and put it in Jeff's car. Then he went to say thanks to Ryan for letting him stay there. He took the chicken breast from the fridge and the two bananas he bought the day before at Price Chopper and he was ready to go.

Jeff drove him back to the trailhead and wished him luck and Paul wished him well in the coming year and hoped everything worked out. Then he said that even though he had not met Susan, from what Jeff said, she sounded great. They got to the trail head at 8:50 and Paul thanked Jeff for their hospitality and the great conversations.

It was a steady uphill climb to Harmon Hill which afforded a great view of the Bennington Monument and Bennington College. After another four miles he reached Congdon Shelter. He ate the leftover chicken breast and had a banana, while he sat at the shelter. He thought he saw a beaver, but couldn't be sure. His guidebook mentioned a beaver pond above the shelter, so it could have been. As he sat there he was thinking that he felt pretty good and the terrain wasn't too difficult, so he was making good time. He made it to Seth Warner Shelter by 2:30 p.m. and decided he would go on to the Massachusetts border or a little beyond. He hiked the three miles or so in a little over an hour-and-a-half and it was just 4:05 when he stopped to check his map.

Pulling out his map he looked for the next shelter or campsite. The Sherman Brook Campsite was another 2 ½ miles and he still felt relatively good. It would be a 16 ½ mile day, which he had done before, but he felt well accomplished for the day. He had done what Will asked of him by contacting Les. He just hoped that Les would come around, sooner rather than later.

He toyed with the idea of going all the way to MA2, but decided against it. Even though it was only an additional two miles and the terrain was more or less downhill, he thought he'd play it safe. He didn't want to get any more Charley Horses. He got to the Sherman Brook Campsite at 5:35 and was the only camper. Being a Sunday, he figured everyone was headed home. The seclusion was welcomed, so he set up his tent on one of the four tent platforms and then got out his stove to cook dinner.

Paul saw a fox walk through the campsite, about 50 feet from where he was. He would need to secure his food when he went to bed. He felt very fortunate in that he had only one animal problem so far and that was all the way back in Maine, which was 300 miles ago.

The fox was probably a regular to the campsite and was counting on some easy prey, perhaps some leftover spaghetti that was left out or some Smore's which someone left near the fire pit. He thought to himself that the fox would be disappointed tonight. With the exception of a banana, which he would eat after dinner he had only freeze-dried food. Then Paul remembered he had some trail mix which had peanuts, M&M's, and raisins, and he also had some dehydrated fruit. So, he would have to be careful after all.

The solitude came to an abrupt halt when a group of Boy Scouts came into camp at about 7:15. Paul thought it odd the scouts would get there so late, but they did their best to be quiet, but with a dozen scouts and three adults, there was bound to be noise. Since there were only three other tent platforms, the adults used two of the three and the scouts used a large open area for their tents. One of the adults, as he was setting up his tent, introduced himself and said they were from Pittsfield. The scout master said he was welcome to join them for their snack, which they referred to as a "cracker barrel," and he said he might take them up on that.

While the scouts were putting up their tents one of the other leaders got a fire started in the fire pit. When he got the fire blazing, he threw in the Smores, which was surely a disappointment to the fox. The smell of the fire was nice so he went and got a seat next to the guy who started the fire. Paul mentioned to him that he saw a fox walk through the camp shortly after he got there at 5:30 and the leader said he would be sure to make an announcement, but to please remind him if he forgot.

The kids were on a three-night campout. Their destination was Bennington, Vermont. Apparently they got there late because they had to drop three boys off who were completing something for an award, which they called the Order of the Arrow. The leader said the Order of the Arrow basically involved a night in the woods, but they were sort of sketchy on that because they didn't want to ruin it for any of the others who would be making it the next summer. They would pick the three kids up in the morning and continue on to VT9. It was nice sitting around the campfire with the scouts and the subject of school came up. Paul asked if any of them went to Pittsfield High School and five boys raised their hands.

Paul mentioned how he had run into Mr. Bowser up in Vermont; however, he didn't mention Don's accident, thinking he would leave that to Don when school started in a couple weeks. The kids said Mr. Bowser was the greatest and one of the scouts said he had some of the funniest sayings, for instance he once heard him say, "I can't wait till tomorrow, because I get better looking every day." Another scout said Mr. Bowser was someone you could trust and yet another said he had great stories. All five students agreed that Mr. Bowser made an impact on their lives in some way, shape, or form. One of the adult leaders, who taught at Pittsfield High School, said that the high school wouldn't be the same when Mr. Bowser retired. Paul asked if that was soon and the scout leader didn't know.

Some of the other scouts went to the Catholic High School in Pittsfield and two were from a town close to Pittsfield, but outside the school's boundaries. All in all they were a good group of kids. They shared their snacks which consisted of cheddar cheese, summer sausage, and crackers. They also made up a big batch of lemonade, but Paul stuck with water. He didn't want to be kept awake from the sugar.

They doused the campfire at around 10:00 and the scouts went to their tents. One of the senior scouts stayed a while to make sure the fire went out. The leaders went to their tents and Paul went to his as well. He wrote in his journal by flashlight and when he turned off the flashlight he fell right to sleep. (596 FK)

"Hey get out of here!" Paul could hear someone shout, waking him from the early stages of sleep. His heart was beating fast from the sudden noise. Then he could hear other voices saying the same thing, "Hey get out of here!" Paul unzipped his tent to see what all the commotion was about, thinking it was the fox. Then in the distance he could see a person running away from the camp. Everyone, including Paul gathered to discuss the incident. "Who was it?" someone asked. While another said "I couldn't tell." Paul's adrenaline was pumping for a good twenty minutes and no one could go to sleep. After about 30 minutes the scout master said, "Gentlemen that is enough excitement for the night. Let's return to our tents."

Paul couldn't figure out what it was. He thought he could make something out, but he couldn't be sure. When he went back into the tent he had difficulty falling back to sleep, so he said a decade of the Holy Rosary, it was the *Glorious Mysteries*.

He made it all the way through without falling asleep, so he said the Joyful Mysteries, too. He thinks he fell asleep during the fourth decade, or *The Presentation at the Temple*.

Paul woke up when he could hear a crackling sound, which he figured was a fire and then he could hear some scouts talking. He looked at his watch and it was 6:15. The scout leaders offered Paul some coffee when he stuck his head out of the tent and he accepted. He walked over with his orange Tupperware mug and held it out. When it was about three quarters full the scout leader said "do you want me to leave room for milk." To which he replied, "Yes please." He was trying to get used to drinking coffee black on the trail, but since they had milk and sugar he took both.

They also invited him to join them for breakfast which consisted of diced Spam and scrambled eggs. They also had some cheddar cheese left over from the cracker barrel, so they threw that in with the eggs. It was nice not to have to fix breakfast three mornings in a row now.

Paul sensed a presence while they were eating, but he looked around and couldn't see anyone. He rolled up his tent, secured it and his sleeping bag to his backpack, and lifted it up onto his shoulders. Then at 7:25 he thanked the scout master and the scouts for their hospitality and shoved off. He made it about a mile out of camp when he saw someone sitting on a log up ahead; as he got closer he could tell it was Will.

"Good morning Will, how are you?' Paul said.

Will stood up and at the same time while turning towards Paul said, "that was quite some excitement last night wasn't it?"

"Was that you?" Paul asked in disbelief.

"No, but I saw it all. It was the kids who are getting their Order of the Arrow. They were hungry and figured they could get something to eat after everyone went into their tents. The ring leader had a feeling that the rest of the troop was staying there, so they listened and walked towards the light from the fire and the noise of fifteen or so people talking."

Paul and Will hiked side by side down the hill towards MA2 and Will said, "Paul thank you for calling my father. I don't know if it did any good, but if you could please keep it up I would appreciate it."

"Will, that's OK. I was happy to do it for you. I'll call again when I get to Don and Chris' if that is OK?"

"Yes, that's fine."

Will stopped where he was and Paul continued on. Williamstown, Massachusetts was at the bottom of the hill, but Paul looked north, back up the AT, and Will was gone. He felt sorry for Will, but didn't know why. Will seemed outwardly happy, but he sensed sadness within.

MA 2 went directly through town, so he stopped for a bite to eat at the Friendly's which he could see as he was crossing the road. He ordered a bacon and cheese omelet with hash brown potatoes and wheat toast. You would have thought that Paul didn't eat breakfast with the scouts, but he had a healthy appetite. Dalton, Massachusetts was 23 miles away and would take Paul two days to hike it. He would do the difficult part today, which meant going over Mt. Greylock, and save the rest for tomorrow. He used the pay phone in Friendly's to call Don Bowser to let him know his intentions and Don answered the phone on the fourth ring. Paul said "Hi Don, this is Paul."

He told Don he would be in Dalton, Massachusetts tomorrow at about 4:00 p.m., hopefully in time to pick up a package at the post office which closes at 4:30 according to Paul's guidebook. Don said he would be waiting at the trailhead at about that time.

Next he walked next door to the Price Chopper and bought some fresh fruit, two bananas and an apple. They had Blondie's in the bakery, but he resisted thinking that Chris would have some for him tomorrow. At least he hoped so. So instead of the Blondie's he bought some huge oatmeal raisin cookies. After he paid for his groceries and put them in his backpack, he headed to the trailhead. Williamstown was a nice town from what he saw of it and the people were friendly and he liked the way the AT went directly through town. It was about six-and-a-half miles to the top of Mt. Greylock and once Paul left the town the vertical climb was noticeable. He left Williamstown at about 11:15 a.m. and figured he wouldn't get to Greylock before about 3:00 p.m.

Paul ran into some north bounders headed to Bennington and he wondered if they would catch up to the Boy Scouts. His mind wondered back to the evening before and whether any of the scouts would fess up to their transgression. He wasn't familiar with the Order of the Arrow because his sons were still cub scouts. He would find out soon enough when Daniel became a boy scout in a year or two. Paul enjoyed the four or so campouts he went on with his boys. There was the Dad & Lad which was always in the fall and over near Cypress Gardens.

The first year he went he remembered two things about that campout. First, it rained very hard and two of the Dad's weren't prepared. One of them had gone out the night before to buy a tent and didn't realize that it was a kid's tent for use only in the house; it didn't have a floor in it, so they had to sleep on the ground. They got terribly soaked once the rain started, but fortunately Paul had extra tarps to loan both unprepared dad's. Secondly, the guy who bought the kids tent, was the loudest snorer Paul had ever heard, so he didn't get much of any sleep that night. Fortunately, it was only a one night campout.

Paul had never been to the Berkshire Mountains before and he thought they were beautiful, as beautiful as the Green Mountains, but in a subtler way. He stopped to drink some water and eat a banana at the Wilbur Clearing Lean-to. He gained almost 1,700 feet of elevation since leaving Williamstown and still had nearly 1,200 feet to the top of Greylock Mountain which was still three and-a-half miles further. He thought he had crossed his last 3,000 footer up in Vermont, so he was somewhat disappointed to see that Greylock was listed as 3,491 feet. He took the opportunity, while he was taking in the view, to say a decade of the Rosary; since it was Monday he said the *Joyful Mysteries*. After the fifth Joyful Mystery, *Finding Jesus in the Temple*, Paul continued hiking.

The trail up Mt. Greylock was not as harsh as those he had hiked in Vermont, New Hampshire, or Maine. It was easier on his joints. There wasn't the constant jarring on his knees like in the White Mountains. There was definitely less granite, which meant less chance of tripping or falling. Like Mt. Washington in New Hampshire, you could ride your car to the top of Mt. Greylock, so he expected there would be a lot of people on the summit. As the trees got shorter, the views got better. He was looking forward to the views from the summit. At about 3:10 Paul reached the top of Mt. Greylock and the views weren't as good as he was hoping because it was hazy, so he stayed about 15-20 minutes at the summit. He read the history of the

Veteran's Memorial that was dedicated back in the 1930's. It reminded him of a chess piece, or chess pieces, a cross between a rook and a pawn. Paul wondered if his father, a native of the Boston area, had ever hiked up the mountain. There was probably no road back in the early 1930's, so if he had gone up Mt. Greylock it would have been on foot. And, if he had gone up Mt. Greylock to read the Veteran's Memorial Paul wondered if he had any idea of the time he would serve the nation during WW II and beyond. He would ask his Mom if she ever heard Dad talk about Mt. Greylock. Maybe Paul would call her tomorrow from Pittsfied because he owed her a call since it had been two weeks since his last call.

It was a pleasant hike to the Mark Noepel Lean-to. The three-plus-mile hike took less than one-and-a-half hours. It was 5:10 p.m. when he got there and he still felt pretty good, so he decided to hike on towards Cheshire, Massachusetts. He wasn't sure if he would make it all the way, but he would attempt it. He ran into some hikers at about 5:30 p.m. and they had just come from Cheshire. They talked awhile and mentioned they were headed up to Rutland, Vermont. They said there was a nice place down the trail about a mile-and-a-half if he was looking for a place to spend the night. They mentioned that there were going to be bad thunderstorms before midnight. Paul thanked them and continued on. He wondered where they planned to spend the night, he assumed the Mark Noepel Lean-to.

After what seemed like a mile-and-a-half Paul looked for the good camping site the two guys talked about. After walking another 50 yards or so, Paul thought he could see a place that other campers had used to camp. Five or six huge granite boulders formed a nice shelter. Paul would be able to set his tent up underneath them and not get wet. First he set up his tent and rolled out his sleeping bag, then he got out his stove and dug into his pack to look for a freeze-dried meal, he had three. There was a Chicken a la King, a Sweet and Sour Pork, and a Spaghetti and Meat Sauce. He hadn't had a Spaghetti and Meat Sauce yet, so that's what he picked. He wished he'd bought some rolls at Price Chopper, but he still had the Pita bread he bought in Bennington.

It was sort of lonely sitting there under the boulders, so he got out and walked around a bit. At about 10 minutes past nine he felt the first raindrop, so he emptied his bladder and went back under the protection of the boulders. By the time he got there it started to rain heavier. He was fortunate to have talked to those hikers because the boulders protected him from the rain, the lightening, and falling branches. The wind was pretty considerable and fortunately the boulders protected him somewhat from that as well. He could see far into the forest with every bolt of lightning.

Paul wondered about the two hikers he met. Were they sent to help him? Was that their mission? Well, like Paul told Les on the phone, anything is possible with God. The storm continued and since he was well protected he tried to go to bed. He wrote in his journal, put in his ear plugs, turned off the flashlight and tried to drift off to sleep. (605 FK)

The quietness of it all was strange. It was so quiet that Paul woke up. He took out his earplugs and listened; he could hear the birds sing and the other animals making noises, too. He looked at his watch and it was 6:05 a.m. and also according to his watch it was Tuesday. He slept so well he had lost track of where he was and what he was doing. Looking in his journal it was the 50th day of his Appalachian Adventure. He unzipped the tent and looked out and there were a lot of downed trees and branches. He thanked God for the two hikers whoever they were because if he hadn't run into them he doesn't know what would have happened. He got out of his tent and decided to have breakfast in Cheshire, Massachusetts, which he figured was about two miles away.

He made good time to Cheshire and it was 7:55 when he walked thru the door of the diner. He left his backpack outside as he always did, but one of the employees said, "We don't serve hikers here."

You could have heard a pin drop. Paul looked around and said "What? Oh, I'm not a hiker. I'm a paying customer."

Everyone started laughing. It turned out to be a joke they played on all backpackers when they saw them take their packs off outside. After the practical joke, Paul found that the people couldn't have been friendlier and the food was great, too. The topic of conversation in the diner was the storm the night before. It had made a mess in and around the town. They said the wind was so strong it created gigantic waves on the lake many of the boats became dislodged and were crashing into one another; a couple of the boats sunk because they took on so much water. After breakfast Paul returned to the trailhead and continued his journey south towards Dalton, Massachusetts, which was a little over nine miles away. After hiking up the trail about two miles, to a place called The Cobbles, there was a nice view back down on the town of Cheshire and the reservoir, which must have been the lake the locals were talking about.

Continuing on he stopped at the Crystal Mountain campsite for a break. He was doing fine on time. It was 12:15 p.m. and he had about five miles to go before Dalton. He stayed about 10 minutes and started hiking again. It was downhill to MA9 and his ride.

Paul wondered if both Chris and Don were going to meet him or just Don. He began to think back to some of his conversations with Don and he wondered if he had been conscientious with his physical therapy. Paul got so overconfident with his stride that he clipped a rock sticking up, which sent him flying forward because he was so top heavy; he landed badly. Remembering Don, he just lied there until he could move his fingers and toes. Convinced he didn't have any strains or breaks he got up. Unfortunately, his right leg was bleeding where he landed on it. He must have cut it on some of the rocks, so he took off his pack and put it on a boulder. He looked at the scrape and got out his first aid kit he bought in Manchester Center. He first cleaned off the scrape with water and then took out some antiseptic. He put the antiseptic on and then a couple band aids. They were the last of his Band-Aids so he would have to buy some or borrow some from Don and Chris.

Paul put his backpack on and started hiking again, angry that he had been so careless. He met some hikers going north and they just had rucksacks, so they were obviously out for a day hike. They were probably in their 60's and walking with hiking sticks, so he asked them how far MA9 and they said it was less than a mile. He looked at his watch and it was 3:45 p.m., so he quickened his pace. He got to the trailhead at about 4:05 and he saw that familiar blue Mercury Grand Marquis which he had ridden in back in Rutland, Vermont. Don was standing next to the car and when he saw Paul he waved. When he got closer to the car they shook hands and Don said, "We better get to the Post Office because they close in 20 minutes."

Don was still wearing the knee brace, but one with a hinge, so that he could drive. On the way to the Post Office Don pointed out some local points of interest in

Dalton, the most interesting of which was the Currency Museum. It turns out that the paper company in Dalton was the sole supplier of currency paper for the US Treasury.

As Paul walked into the post office one of the postal workers had the closed sign in his hand, so he was just in time. He walked up to the window and said he was there to pick up a package. He showed some identification and the postal worker gave him the package. He would open the package when he got to Don's, so that he didn't hold up the postal employee. From the post office they drove directly to Don and Chris' house, which was a Cape Cod. As they drove into the driveway Don said, "This isn't where we've always lived, now that the kids are gone we downsized. The taxes on our other house were killing us and we wouldn't be able to sustain it on retired pay."

Chris walked out of the kitchen when Don and Paul came in and she walked up to Paul and gave him a big hug and said, "We're so glad you stopped by to see us. Can I get you something to drink?"

"Do you have Sprite or 7Up?" Paul asked.

Chris nodded yes and went back to the kitchen. When she came back out she handed Paul the Sprite and asked, "Paul how do you like cats?"

Paul answered, "Well done and with Sweet & Sour Sauce." The look on Chris's face was a Kodak moment and she had difficulty even finding words, so Don chimed in.

"Paul I guess I should have mentioned that we like cats. We have seven, but we know that not everyone likes them, so we keep one guest bedroom totally cat free."

Paul didn't know what to say. He had obviously embarrassed Chris, so he said, "It's not that I'm allergic to cats, but I had a bad experience when I was about 19 or 20. I won't go into specifics, but I'll be alright."

Paul wasn't sure if that softened the blow or not, but it was too late. He had said it and couldn't take it back. That response normally got a laugh or two, so Paul changed the topic quickly, "So Don, what's the prognosis on your knee?"

"Well like the doctor I saw in Pittsfield said, if I do the therapy, I shouldn't need surgery. I've been very good about the therapy and I should be able to take the knee stabilizer off when school starts."

"I'm glad to hear that," Paul said.

"Let me tell you about some of the interesting happenings since I last saw you guys."

CHAPTER NINE

Pittstop

Paul started the overview of what happened since Rutland by telling Don and Chris about the Middlebury College students and how one of them got hurt. Then he told them about how he and one of the other students went to get help, while one stayed behind with the injured student, who by the way used Don's hiking poles. He described how they got help at the Bromley ski area and explained how that all worked. Then Paul continued by saying he was worn out from that experience and decided to stay in Manchester Center and he told them about going to a funeral Mass and the circumstances behind the young mother's death.

Chris got him a Sprite refill and then he continued recounting what else happened on his journey. After telling the Bowser's about the beautiful funeral Mass in Manchester Center Paul told them how he got trapped on a mountain top during a terrible storm and Paul described the storm and how he almost got speared by a tree branch, not to mention the soaking he got. He didn't tell them about Will, but instead mentioned that he ran into another hiker who had some repair tape.

He continued on and talked about hiking with Jeff and Ryan and how he stayed with them in Bennington for two nights. He told Don and Chris how Jeff and Ryan were house-sitting for a Bennington College Professor who was on Sabbatical. Then he also told them how he wanted to go to Mass Saturday night and how Jeff went with him.

"Why did he want to tag along?" Chris asked.

Paul told them about Jeff's future wedding and how he thought it would be hypocrital of him to get married in the church if he never went.

Then Paul told them about his hike up Mt. Greylock and of how he ran into two hikers who told him about the looming storm and how they recommended a safe place for him to stay. He described how he set up his tent under boulders and they kept him safe from rain, wind, and falling debris. Paul said he believes that God sent the two, because it was just sort of weird how they showed up out of the blue. Don and Chris looked at each other, but didn't say anything.

Don said they got that storm the night before also, but that it must have been worse higher up. Paul forgot about the scouts, so he backtracked and told them about that, too. Don said he knew the scout master of that troop and said he was a good guy. However, he really didn't know the teacher from Pittsfield High School that well, because he was relatively new. "Did they ever figure out what the disturbance was?" Chris asked.

"No they didn't." Paul didn't share what Will told him because it could get some of the boys in trouble if it ever got back to their scout master.

"Well Paul, you've had an exciting and eventful time," Don said as he stood up from his recliner. Then he said, "Chris made Taco's and Burrito's for dinner, figuring that was something you haven't had for a while."

During dinner Paul found out that Don and Chris weren't originally from Massachusetts. Don was originally from Plymouth, New Hampshire and Chris was from Lancaster, Pennsylvania. They met at a teacher's conference early on as teachers and both were looking for teaching jobs in the same school. Pittsfield High School just happened to be looking for teachers in their two disciplines. Don, of course, taught history and Chris taught English Literature. Then they had five kids pretty soon after moving to Pittsfield, so Chris took time off to be with the kids. When the Bowser's youngest started high school, Chris returned to teaching. She mentioned that it was more difficult the second time around for a lot of the same reasons Don already mentioned. Chris said the layers of bureaucracy had tripled since she first started teaching.

Paul asked about their Italian plans and they both smiled. Chris said they booked their flights to Italy for mid-December, with a return date on the 5th of January 1996. You could hear the excitement in Chris' voice especially when she said their son put in for vacation, so he can join them in Rome like Paul recommended. Don excused himself to get dessert while Chris continued on about their travel arrangements. Don brought out a Boston Cream pie which was one of Paul's favorite desserts.

Chris said, "Paul, I made you some Blondie's to take with you." Since Don was up already he got some maps of Italy that they could look at while they ate dessert. They opened up the Rome map first and Paul made some recommendations. Then they looked at the map of Italy and Paul circled Assisi and Gubbio.

After they looked at the maps awhile, Don said, "Paul can I ask you a question?"

"Sure Don, what is it?"

"I have an older sister who is a nurse. She is a Catholic and I wanted to do something nice for her because she always does so much for other people. We were thinking of making a Christmas Gift of this trip to her."

"I think that's wonderful, so what's the question?" Paul asked.

"She is very frugal and might see this as something too extravagant for her. We don't want to buy her the tickets and then have her turn it down. What if she does turn it down? Do we lose everything?"

"I believe so. I don't think trip insurance covers that kind of cancellation. Did you ask the travel agent?"

"Yes. She basically said we would have to get a note from her doctor or something saying she couldn't go due to a medical situation and you don't know my sister, she can't lie."

Paul thought about it for a couple of minutes and said, "Does she have a husband and family?"

"Her husband is deceased and she has two grown children. Why do you ask?"

"I was thinking you could enlist their help."

"What do you mean Paul?"

"You need to find a reason so that she will want to go and maybe they can help you."

"We're not that close to her kids and that's why we were thinking you might have some religious reason for her to want to go."

Paul thought a while and asked, "Is she very close to your son who is in the Navy?"

"Yes. She's his favorite Aunt."

"Well then here is a possible solution. Tell her you are going to see your son for Christmas. Tell her you would like her to go too, to make it seem very special to him. Also, I'm assuming she has never been to Rome; tell her you would like to go to church at St. Peter's for Christmas."

"That might work," Don said. "It's worth a try. Thanks Paul."

Paul thought of something as they were sitting there and said, "Let me see that map of Rome again." He showed them where the key hole was, the one you can look through and see St. Peter's in the distance, but it appears as if it is at the end of a long row of cypress trees. "It's worth a ride up there just to see that," he said.

After talking to Don and Chris about Don's sister and what they could do, he felt like he hadn't really helped them, so he went back to that topic. "You know Don," Paul said, "I don't know that I was of any help regarding your sister and how you could get her to go with you. Might I suggest you pray on it? We could even pray now for guidance."

Don had a puzzled look on his face and said, "Would you lead us in prayer?"

Paul nodded and started the prayer, "Oh heavenly Father we seek your help and guidance. Don's sister, who has done so much for others by feeding the hungry, caring for the sick and providing consolation to the broken-hearted. Lord, let her know how much her brother and sister-in-law care for her by their generous act of kindness. Let her see a good reason to go to Italy where so many saints have trod and where the Seat of the Holy Catholic Church is and also where so many saints have received inspiration for the good works they accomplished here on Earth and continue to do in Heaven by their prayers of intercession. We ask this of you in the name of Jesus, Amen."

Don and Chris sat there for a while in silence, obviously offering up their prayers and then Don said, "thank you Paul that was very beautiful. I will call my sister tomorrow, which is her birthday and ask her to go with us."

After the three retired to the living room, Paul told them of his decision to apply for AFJROTC. He mentioned that Don had had a little part to play in that decision, but that his family, with the exception of the youngest, was ready to leave Florida.

"Won't you be able to finish your hike?" Chris asked.

"It depends on several things, like whether I get nominated for the job, how I do in the interview, and lastly if I get chosen and accept it."

"I thought you were counting on finishing the Appalachian Trail." Chris said.

"No. It's not essential for me anymore because I have sort of figured out some things. That was the purpose of the hike, to figure out what I will do next. And besides, it's not entirely fair to Laura and the kids. However, there are still too many what ifs." Changing the subject, Paul said, "Don, now that I have some new phone cards from Laura, can I use your phone please."

"Yes Paul, now if you want to talk privately, there is one in your bedroom."

Paul excused himself and went upstairs to the guest bedroom, which was also the "cat free room." He called his phone number in Brandon and Theresa answered. When she heard his voice she said, "Hi dad are you at the Bowser's?"

"Yes, honey. How have you all been?" She went on to tell him that the boys were over at one of the neighbors and she would get Mom, but first she had to tell him about the Girl Scout picnic. When Laura got on the phone he filled her in on the last couple days of hiking and what he anticipated for the days to come. After he got off the phone with Laura he placed a call to Les.

Les picked up on the third ring, and said, "Hello."

"Hello, Les. This is Paul. Do you want to talk?"

"Yeah. About that," Les stammered as he tried to find the words. "I'm sorry for hanging up on you the last time. I just couldn't handle it."

"That's OK, I understand."

"Paul if what you say is true, that you have actually met my son, then what is it I'm supposed to do?"

"Les, from what I understand, God is worried about you. Worried about some choices you've made or were going to make."

There was a silence on the other end, but Paul waited for Les to talk, which was a bit awkward. He must have taken a full minute to compose what he was going to say.

"You know Paul. I was contemplating taking my life. I was thinking that life wasn't worth living, especially without Bethany. If I hadn't pushed her then she would probably be here with our son."

"Les I don't know what God wants you to do. He probably wants you to ask for forgiveness."

"Forgiveness from who?" Les asked.

"I'd say for starters, forgiveness from God. You know Les, God has a plan for everyone; he knew us in our mother's wombs. He knows you are sorry for what you did, but being sorry is not the same thing as asking for forgiveness. Will didn't tell me what God wants you to do, but that's what I believe, at least. It is obvious God doesn't want you to commit suicide. He must have other plans for you, but you'll never know unless you ask Him for forgiveness."

"Paul, can I ask you something?"

"Yes. Did Will tell you God's plan for him?"

"He mentioned to me that he was going to be a high school teacher and help troubled youth."

"So was everything you told me just an excuse to get to talk with me? Les asked.

"Some was true, like I might be in Montgomery in the October, November time frame."

"Why are you coming to Montgomery?

"Well, I've applied for a job and if I get the job I will come to Maxwell AFB, for training."

"How did you know about Frazier United Methodist?" Les asked.

"I was familiar with Frazier because when we lived in Montgomery back in the mid to late 1980's our daughter went to preschool there."

"So Les," Paul asked, "if I do get that job do you want me to give you a call when I go through Montgomery?"

"Yes, by all means. I'd like that a lot."

"So, if you would like, I will give you a call in a week or two to keep you apprised of the job situation."

"Yes, I would like that too, thank you Paul."

After Paul hung up he felt good. It was also good that Les seemed to understand that God loved him and suicide wasn't in God's plan for him. It was just another instance of the saying that "God didn't need us to make us, but He needs us to save us."

Paul made one more call, he called his mother.

"Hi Mom. This is Paul, how are you?"

"I'm fine honey, how are you?"

The conversation lasted for probably 15 minutes while he caught her up on everything since he called her last. He told her about hiking up Mt. Greylock and wondered if his dad had ever hiked up it. She said she wasn't aware of his ever hiking up it, but she was glad Paul did and really appreciated his phone call.

Paul went back down to the living room after making his calls and Don was sitting in his recliner. He looked up as Paul reached the bottom step and said, Chris wants to know what you want for breakfast."

Paul went into the kitchen to tell Chris he missed Corned Beef Hash with eggs Sunnyside Up served on top. She walked over to the pantry, looked on the shelf, and said, "You're in luck. We have a can." She looked for an expiration date on the top and it is still good. Chris mentioned that they never ate it because of the high sodium and fat content, but they kept a can in the pantry for when their son came to visit. She said he loved Corned Beef Hash.

Paul said he would take them up on their offer to do laundry, so he went to get his dirty clothes and Chris showed him where the washer and dryer were. While the clothes were in the washer they went back into the living room to talk. Don asked him his plan for the next day and he took out his map and guidebook.

Laying the map out on the living room floor, he said, "I think I'll hike to the October Mountain Lean-to. Are you familiar with it?"

"Yes. It's far enough away where you don't have to worry about a lot of people, especially mid-week. It can be a bit crowded if you are there on a weekend, though. Another guy and I actually look after that section of trail all the way down to US20 and we walk it once a quarter for our chapter of the AMC."

Then Don said, "What time do you want to leave for the trailhead in the morning?"

"How is the terrain between Dalton and there?"

"It's not as tough as what you've been through, but it would take me at least eight hours."

"Does 9:00 a.m. sound OK?" Paul asked.

"That's perfect. So breakfast at 7:30 then?" Don asked.

"That would be great, too. Thank you all for the dinner and the good company. It's sort of like being at home."

After his clothes were dry he packed everything in his backpack except for what he would wear in the morning. Then he wrote in his journal, said his prayers, including Don's sister, and went to sleep. (618 FK)

He woke up once during the night, but was able to get back to sleep. When he went out in the hallway there were three or four cats, but it was so dark he couldn't tell and he was sure to shut the bedroom door while he was in the bathroom. The bed in the guest room was a sleep number bed which he never slept on before and he slept great. At 7:15 his alarm went off and Paul went down to breakfast; he could smell the coffee and Corned Beef Hash from upstairs.

Paul walked in and said good morning to both Chris and Don and Don handed Paul a mug of coffee and motioned for him to sit down. Paul sat down and asked, "How did you all sleep last night? I had a great night's sleep. That's a terrific bed."

"Great," both replied. "I do love the morning," said Don, "but Chris is more of a night person."

"Chris I'm sorry I took one of your few mornings where you can sleep-in before you go back to school."

"Oh, that's alright Paul. We're actually using the opportunity to go to Springfield today after we drop you off. We make a trip there every so often to shop at one of those warehouse places."

After breakfast Paul shaved and showered and he was ready to go at 8:45. Don and Chris were both in the kitchen when he came downstairs and Chris handed him two foil wrapped items. One foil wrapper had Blondie's and the other had a ham & cheese sandwich, so he thanked Chris and they all walked out to the car together. Don popped the trunk, so Paul could put his backpack in, but first he wanted to know if Don wanted his hiking poles back. He said, "No they're yours now. I hope they keep you safe."

There was hardly anyone on MA9, so they were back to the trailhead by 9:10. Both Don and Chris got out of the car to wish Paul well and Chris gave Paul a hug and a kiss on his cheek and Don gave him a bear hug. Paul said he would keep them posted from time to time and when he put his backpack on Don said "Thanks for all you have done for us. We'll say a prayer for you in St. Peter's."

It was a bit warm, but it was after all the 9th of August, so it should be warm. Still, Paul was hoping for cooler temperatures. He stopped at the Kay Wood Lean-to in order to readjust his pack. As he was redistributing the weight he thought he would have one of the Blondie's Chris made for him. It was delicious and he couldn't stop at one, so he had another. He took several gulps of water and then returned the water bottle to the side pocket. He continued on, saying a prayer to the Blessed Mother for her intercession to help with Don's sister.

The trail didn't have many vertical climbs, for which he was thankful. He stopped at a nice spot near a stream and ate his ham & cheese sandwich. He sat their taking in the surroundings when he saw something out the corner of his eye. It was a hiker, who was also headed south. The hiker stopped too, and said "This is a beautiful spot. I've stopped here many a time." The guy only had a day pack, so Paul figured he was probably hiking to US20 where someone would pick him up.

The guy took off his shirt and wiped his brow with it because he was sweating so much and then he turned back towards Paul and said, "I've got to go, so have a nice hike." Paul watched as the man walked away. He thought of Tom Michie because when the hiker took his shirt off to wipe his brow he saw that the man was wearing a Miraculous Medal around his neck. He wondered how the funeral turned out for Tom's mother and how things were going between him and his father.

Paul sat there for another 15-20 minutes because it was so beautiful and quiet. Then he put his backpack back on and he continued hiking. After about two miles he crossed a road, which according to his map was the Pittsfield Road, but according to his guidebook it was called the Washington Mountain Road. Regardless of what it was called it was a road and he didn't care because it didn't affect his hike.

As he continued south on the AT, about a quarter miles past the road, he saw something on the trail ahead. It was the hiker who had passed him at the spring. He was trying to get up, but he fell back down again. Paul rushed up to him and said, "Are you OK?" and when the guy didn't answer, Paul asked again "Are you OK?" This time the guy looked up at Paul and said, "I feel lightheaded."

"Can you make it to the boulder over there to rest? Paul asked.

The guy said, "Maybe with a little help."

Paul took him under his right arm and helped him to the rock. The guy sat down and looked back up at him and said, "Thank You." Paul reached into the guys pack to look for his water bottle and it was empty, so he took out one of his bottles and poured some from his bottle into the stranger's bottle. Paul then offered the bottle to the guy who said, "Thanks again. I'm sorry to ruin your hike, but I feel light headed for some reason." After he said that, he slouched over towards the ground.

Paul figured he wouldn't be able to get him up again so he let him lie right on the trail. The guy slipped into unconscious, so Paul gave him CPR. Paul revived him once and when the man looked around he said, "Where did all these angels come from? Is it time?" Then he put his hands up towards the sky and said, "I'm ready Lord." Paul started CPR again when the man's head hit the ground again. Finally after about three or four minutes he could hear someone say, "Paul you can't do anything for him now, let him go."

Paul looked up and Kevin was standing there. Kevin asked if he knew the blessing and sending forth for the dead and Paul said, "No."

Kevin took a book out of his pocket and said, "Here read this." So, he read the blessing while doing the sign of the cross over the man's forehead.

Paul looked up and said, "Wow. That really caught me off guard. What should I do?"

"Well, you can't leave him here on the trail." Kevin said.

Paul said, "There was a road back there a little bit. I'll go signal for help."

Kevin said, "That sounds like a good idea. I'll stay here with him," pointing at the man on the ground.

Paul left his backpack with Kevin and went back out to the road. He figured that if he had his backpack on people might not stop. It took him less than four minutes to get to the road. He looked both ways and he thought he could make out a car in the distance. It was a car and not just any car, it was a police car. As the car got closer he started to wave the car down; the police officer saw him and came to a stop, so Paul walked up to the police car and the police officer put his window down and said "what can I do for you, sir?"

Paul said, "Officer there is a dead hiker down the trail about a quarter of a mile. I'm pretty sure he had a heart attack." The police officer said, "Could you repeat that." And he did repeat it, but adding some details.

The police officer parked his car and followed Paul down the trail. The body was lying there, but Kevin was nowhere in sight. Paul was glad he didn't mention Kevin, because he would never have been able to explain him. The officer said to Paul, "Do you know who he was?" To which he told the officer about their first encounter at the spring and how the guy took his shirt off because he was sweating profusely. Then he mentioned how he could see something or someone on the trail and it was the man who passed him at the spring.

Paul told the officer how he helped the man back to his feet and then to the boulder, which he promptly fell off of, but he repeatedly said he was sorry for inconveniencing me. Paul told the police officer he administered CPR and revived him once and told the officer what the man said and did, throwing his hands towards heaven and saying, "I'm ready Lord."

The officer looked for the man's wallet and when he found it in his rucksack he pulled out his driver's license. The man's name was George Murray and he had a Pittsfield address. The officer said to Paul, "we're in a bit of a dead zone here, so could you stay with Mr. Murray? I'll go phone this in."

"OK." Paul said.

The police officer came back in about 20 minutes, but other help didn't get there for nearly 45 minutes. It was about 2:45 before they loaded Mr. Murray into the ambulance to take him to Pittsfield. It was at about that time that the police officer asked Paul to come with him to file a report and they took Mr. Murray to the hospital in Pittsfield to determine the cause of death.

The police officer didn't suspect any foul play because Mr. Murray had $108.00 in his wallet, a gold religious medal around his neck, and a gold wedding band on his ring finger. The police officer, whose name was Sgt. Kranking, said it was just standard procedure to fill out an incident report. Sgt. Kranking said they could fill out the report at the hospital because the family might like to hear about Mr. Murray's peaceful passing.

Paul saw Mr. Murray's wife and kids when they got there. They wanted to hear from him what happened, so he told the story again. When he got to the part of his reviving Mr. Murray and what Mr. Murray said, their sorrow turned to joy. When Paul mentioned that he said the sending forth prayer, they were overjoyed that George Murray, husband and father was in a better place.

It was already 5:45 by the time everything was complete, so Paul asked if he could leave. Paul stopped at the payphone near the cafeteria to call Don Bowser. It rang five times and then the answering machine picked up, so Paul figured they were still in Springfield. He left a very brief message.

As he continued walking towards the exit, Sergeant Kranking saw him and said, "Mr. Geary would you like a ride back to the trailhead? It's the least we can do for you." Paul accepted the ride from Sergeant Kranking to the trailhead and the ride was sort of quiet; when the sergeant saw Paul looking at his watch he said, "I bet you didn't expect this when you got up this morning."

It was 6:25 p.m. when they got back to the trailhead. Paul thanked Sergeant Kranking for the ride and he reiterated what he had said earlier, that it was the least he could do. When he got to the place on the trail where George Murray died he stopped a minute and said a prayer for George and his family. It was a solemn walk for the next two-and-a-half miles and it was 7:45 when he got to the Lean-to. There was one space left in the lean-to, so Paul put his sleeping pad and sleeping bag down in the space. Then he got out his stove and a freeze-dried meal. It wasn't as good as the Tacos and Burritos he had the night prior, but it was filling.

The other people in the shelter were all headed north and they were section hikers completing the Massachusetts to New Hampshire section. One of them had hiking poles and his friends were kidding him about how dorky he looked. Paul chimed in and said, "They may look dorky, but they do the trick. I find they help my knees, give me more stability, and they take some of the weight of my back." The hiker with the poles said, "See I told you so."

Aside from that verbal exchange it was pretty quiet in camp. They were upcoming sophomores at the University of New Hampshire and were all reading the same book for English Literature. Paul thought back to his college days and although he intended to get ahead by reading certain books before the semester started, he never did. He commended them for doing that. He wrote in his journal about George Murray, Kevin, and all that happened on his 51st day of hiking, August 8th, 1995. He and the other hikers turned off their flashlights at about 9:45 and went to sleep. (630 FK)

It was raining lightly in the morning and everyone, including Paul, was up at 6:15. There was a bit of commotion in the lean-to after they got moving and tried to put their boots on. Apparently something came into the lean-to and gnawed through two of the hikers' boots. It was odd that no one heard anything, especially chewing through a boot. One of the guys said he had read that Porky Pines will do that because they are attracted to the salt in your sweat. So, the two hikers whose boots were gnawed were each given a nickname because of the incident. One was called "sweaty" and the other one was called "salty." They didn't think it affected the strength or integrity of their boots, so they shoved off after packing.

Paul was moving a bit slower than the north bounders, but he figured it was because of the events of the previous day. When he ran to the Pittsfield Rd. he must have strained a muscle because his right quadricep bothered him. Paul had pulled his right quad once before and fortunately this wasn't quite as bad. He still treated his right leg carefully, deciding not to do anything that would make it worse.

He looked at the map and guidebook and decided he would try to go to the Upper Goose Pond Cabin, which was a little over nine miles away. Nine miles seemed like kids play, but Paul wanted to make sure he didn't aggravate his right quad any more than he already had. In getting to Upper Goose Pond Cabin he would cross over US20 which had places to eat. That's where he planned to have lunch or dinner whichever the case may be; it all depended on his right quad. Wearing just shorts and a T-Shirt he started out at 7:30 and he made sure his stuff was safe from the elements.

He was glad he had the hiking poles because some places were slick from the light rain. Paul remembered when he pulled his quad before; it was back in 1986 when he played softball in Montgomery, Alabama. It happened when he took off down the first base line to get to first. For some reason, the action of turning and running towards 1st base pulled his right quad. Once he got to 1st base he was fine; however, he had to start wearing a neoprene support for his right quad whenever he played. The neoprene support was hot, but it worked. Unfortunately he had to leave it on the whole game because his team wore uniforms with long pants. He wished he had that neoprene support with him right then.

Paul could hear people talking behind him and when he turned it was two guys. They were hiking at a pace similar to Jeff and Ryan, so he stood to the side so they could pass. As he stood there to let the two men pass he noticed that it was raining harder. He stayed in his shorts and T-shirt because there was no good place to stop to take out his poncho. A chill went through his body, but he continued on. It was 2:15 when he got to US20 and the place closest to the trail, which was a Tavern, was only open for dinner. Paul didn't feel like hitching the five miles to Lee, Massachusetts to the other eating establishments, so Paul continued on without eating. He could hear the cars whizzing by on Interstate 90 when he crossed underneath and he thought he should put his poncho on before something bad happened.

He was soaked to the bone, so when he crossed under I-90, he used the shelter of the highway for taking off his backpack. Then he took the rain cover off the backpack and pulled his poncho out of the back pocket. He also took out two Blondie's and ate them and washed them down with water.

Even though he was cold and soaked to the bone, his poncho helped him and the calories from the Blondie's heated him up somewhat. He looked at his watch and it was 2:25. He figured he would probably be to the Upper Goose Pond Cabin within an hour and-a-half. There was a bit of an incline after he crossed under I-90 and Paul slipped, but didn't fall. The slip caused enough of a jarring sensation to send a message to his brain; the message was pain in his right quad. He stopped underneath a huge tree which sheltered the trail and he took off his backpack and then the rain cover and he reached into the lower pocket that had his first aid kit. He took out two Tylenol and popped them into his mouth and swallowed with a big gulp of water. Why he didn't take them earlier he wasn't sure.

He could tell he was getting slower and the terrain wasn't that difficult. He got to the Upper Goose Pond Cabin at 5:00 and he was exhausted, but he knew he had to take off his wet clothes. He did that and put on dry underpants, T-Shirt, and his one pair of long pants. After he changed his pants and hung up his wet clothes he climbed into a bunk, wrapped himself in his sleeping bag and went to sleep. He woke up at about 8:15 p.m. and it was light in the shelter because they had propane lanterns and not only did they make the cabin bright, but someone made a fire in the fireplace to take the chill off. He asked the caretaker if he could make some hot water on their gas stove to which the caretaker replied "be my guest."

While the water was heating Paul dug into his backpack to look for a freeze-dried meal. He saw a Turkey Tetrazzini and figured he'd go with a sure thing. After he poured the hot water into the pouch he thanked the caretaker and went to a table to eat. He felt better after he had eaten, so he joined in with some people playing a game of Hearts.

Most of the people in the cabin were just camping for two days. US20 was close enough so that it was an easy hike, providing you didn't have any muscle pulls. Most of the other hikers were high school friends that were in college and they used the cabin get together as a mini class reunion. Various colleges were represented; there was one from Holy Cross, two from University of Massachusetts, one from the University of New Hampshire and two from Mt. Holyoke. Paul thought how great it was hearing young people laugh and share stories and he thought of his high school friends and how he formed life-long friendships with many. It wasn't the same case for some reason with his college friends because Paul could only think of one college buddy he kept in touch with. Of his high school buddies only Stacy, Tony, Phil, and Nate were the only camping types.

They turned off the propane lights at 10:00 and everyone got ready for bed. Paul was worried he wouldn't be able to get to sleep because of his long nap, so he took two more Tylenol, wrote in his journal, said his prayers and went to sleep. (638 FK)

Paul's concern that he wouldn't be able to sleep was unfounded because he slept well. He just got up once to use the outside bathroom at 2:45 a.m. and fortunately, it wasn't raining anymore. The sky was very clear and he felt like he could reach out and touch the stars. He tried not to shine his flashlight in anyone's eyes as he went back to his bunk.

When it was time to get up, the caretaker had the stove going and offered everyone pancakes and coffee. The pancakes were good and the coffee was terrific. Paul ate Chris' last Blondie with his coffee and felt guilty he didn't have enough to share with the other hikers. The clothes he wore the day before weren't quite dry, but he put them back on again and saved the dry ones. He figured he would be wet with sweat soon enough, so it didn't matter. The caretaker said the weather was supposed to be friendlier today. Paul left a donation and started hiking at 8:05 a.m.

Paul's right quad felt better than the day prior, but before he left the cabin he looked at different scenarios for the day. The 1st scenario was to go to Shaker Campsite which was about 10 miles away. The 2nd scenario, if his leg didn't give him any problems, was to go to Mt. Wilcox North Lean-to, which was about 14 miles away. Paul's next mail pickup would be in South Egremont, Massachusetts, which was 33 miles away and he figured it would take him three days to get there. He wondered if there was a Catholic Church in South Egremont because he would be there on Sunday.

For some reason Les came to mind. Paul wondered how he was doing and whether he was still contemplating suicide. He hoped and prayed that he would be alright. After he prayed for Les he thought of something sort of funny. It was a story, not necessarily true, about Caller ID in its infant stages. Paul remembered that names sometimes got abbreviated or shortened on the 1st generation Caller ID's. The story was about a minister of the Almighty God Tabernacle Church who was working late and called his wife to let her know he would be home later than expected. He called her and there was no answer, the phone rang and rang and then the answering machine kicked in and the minister didn't leave a message, but hung up.

As the story went there was a man who was contemplating suicide and he had just said, "Dear God, if you don't want me to do this, give me a sign." That's when the minister called the wrong number, just as the guy was about to hang himself. The guy went over to the phone and looked at the Caller ID, and it read "Almighty God." The guy figured that was his sign from God, so he didn't hang himself and when he got up the nerve a day later, he called the number on the Caller ID and when the minister answered he said, "What do you want me to do?" The minister didn't recognize the voice and said, "Who is this?" The guy said to the minister, "You called me last night and hung up. What do you want?" Paul hoped his call to Les had the same effect.

Paul was feeling good because it was cooler. He knew he did better in cool temperatures than warm temperatures, so he was feeling like he was up for scenario number two. Since there weren't any serious vertical climbs or descents his right quad felt OK. He crossed the road to Tyringham, Massachusetts at 11:45 and decided to go with scenario two for sure. He reached the Jerusalem Road at 12:15 and took a break and since he didn't have any Blondie's left he ate trail mix and dehydrated pineapple. After he drank half of one of his water bottles he resumed hiking at 12:40 and still felt strong.

The Shaker Campsite was next at mile marker 648, according to his guide book. It was beautiful when he got there, especially the waterfall. If it weren't for the fact that he still had a lot of daylight he would have stayed there for the night, but he took another 15 minute break to take in the beauty of it all. He had just four miles to go until he got to the Mt. Wilcox North Lean-to, but there was an elevation change.

He got use to the fairly level terrain and now all of a sudden he was going uphill again. It was 5:15 p.m. when he arrived at the Mt. Wilcox North cut-off. The lean-to was three tenths of a mile further on and when Paul got to the lean-to there were only three people there. As he unrolled his sleeping pad and sleeping bag one of the other hikers came up to talk and during the course of the conversation he mentioned that the water source wasn't that great. The guy said you could boil it and boil it and even though it was safe to drink, it looked terrible. He figured that was the reason there were only three other hikers there on a Friday night in August. He saw it mentioned in his guidebook, but water wasn't a concern of his, so he didn't pay it any attention. Since his water was plentiful he offered the hikers water from his water bottles and they were very thankful.

Paul looked through his freeze-dried food choices and decided on Beef Stroganoff and he would also splurge and have the French Vanilla Mousse for dessert. He talked to the guy who was hiking alone and it turned out he was from the same town in Connecticut where Jeff was from. His name was Charlie and he was headed to White River Junction, Vermont, or wherever he ended up in two weeks. He mentioned that he tried to cover 20 miles a day, but stopped short today because his right calf was hurting for some reason. Paul asked him if he took anything for the pain and Charlie said, "Nope, I'll just tough it out." Charlie was going into his junior year at the University of Vermont and his plan was to meet his best friend in White River Junction, Vermont to get a ride back to school in Burlington, Vermont.

Paul told Charlie he taught at Norwich University about 10 years prior and he loved that part of Vermont. He also told Charlie about his fondness for taking the Grand Isle Ferry just north of Burlington over to Plattsburgh, New York. He told him about the winter crossings and standing on the front of the ferry, watching as the bow of the ferry broke through the ice. Charlie said he had never taken that ferry because he takes the one right from Burlington. Paul talked with the other two hikers for a while and then decided he would write in his journal before the natural light was gone. He noticed the night before that his flashlight seemed very dim and he would need to buy batteries before too long. He made a mental note to get batteries in South Egremont. (653 FK)

Paul could hear Charlie walking around in the morning and it sounded like he was limping from the way his leg was coming down on the wood planks. Paul looked up at Charlie and said, "Do you want some Tylenol?"

Charlie said, "Yes. I think I better take you up on that. I can't believe I didn't bring anything like that with me."

Paul handed him four and said "Two for now and two for later." Charlie popped two Tylenol into his mouth and got out his water bottle and took a long sip.

"Are you going to be OK?" He asked him.

"To tell you the truth, I don't know," Charlie replied.

Paul thought about that for a minute and said "I know you want to make it to White River Junction, but you may want to make other plans."

"Like what, for example?"

Paul told him to take it easy for a couple days and see how he feels and if it's still painful he should see a doctor. The look on Charlie's face was one of sadness, but he said "Yeah, you're probably right." Paul said he would hike with him to

MA23 which was about five miles and he would even let him used his hiking poles. Charlie took him up on his offer, so they both packed up and started hiking at 7:45. After a while Charlie commented on how much better it was hiking with poles, but his right calf still hurt.

They made it to the Mt. Wilcox South Lean-to in about an hour and they took a break and each had a snack. Charlie had sunflower seeds in his trail mix instead of peanuts, which Paul thought he would try sometime. About a mile past the Mt. Wilcox South Lean-to was a place called Benedict Pond. It was beautiful and spotless, so they took another break. Charlie told Paul he was a Civil Engineering major and was considering going into the military because one of his friends from college was on a full Army ROTC scholarship and it was a "sweet deal."

"It's amazing the opportunities he's been given." Charlie said. "I wish I'd known about that my freshmen year."

Paul said that he might want to check that out because in the Air Force there are two year scholarships and as Paul said, "You have nothing to lose by asking the question. They have an Air Force ROTC program at St. Michael's College and UVM students can enroll in their program."

They got to MA23 at 11:30 and Charlie thanked Paul for his help; he gave him back his hiking poles. Charlie started hitch hiking on the side of the road where he and Paul parted company. Charlie's plan was to go to Great Barrington or wherever the nearest motel was and then he would swallow his pride and phone home for a ride. On parting, Charlie said he would definitely ask about two year scholarships or any other possibilities.

Paul continued south on the AT and he wondered whether he could still do 12 miles in that he was hiking slower than expected. He also wondered whether his right quad would give him problems and put him in the same dilemma as Charlie. He thought he would press on it give it a try and that way he would be able to go to Mass tomorrow, which was Sunday, August 13th. He quickened his pace while still being mindful of his right quad. As the trail began to ascend he could see someone up ahead. It looked like Will and as he got closer he could tell that it was.

"Hi Paul. Do you want me to carry your pack?"

"That would be great. Thanks Will."

As Paul handed the pack over to Will he figured he would be able to make it to MA41 since he wouldn't have to carry the pack. "You've had a busy couple of days." Will said.

"Yes, they've been interesting to say the least."

As they hiked along, Will thanked him for his help with his Dad and said that he'd be OK now. He also said that if Paul gets the AFJROTC job he should indeed stop to see his father when he goes through Montgomery.

The miles seemed to fly by and he was amazed at how much easier it was without his backpack and they made it to US7 by 3:50 p.m., but still had over three-and-a-half miles to go. Fortunately there weren't many ups and downs; it was relatively level. They made it to MA41 by 5:15, but there was still a hitch of a little over a mile to South Egremont.

Will gave Paul his backpack and said he would see him later. The first car that drove by picked Paul up, as he was walking along backwards towards South Egremont, with his right arm and thumb stuck out. Jack, the guy who picked him up, was headed to Great Barrington and he mentioned that there were better choices of motels there; he said there was only an Inn in South Egremont and it was a bit pricey, especially since it was a Saturday. When Paul asked Jack about Catholic Churches Jack said there was one in Great Barrington, but not in South Egremont. Jack knew that because his neighbor was Catholic, so Paul decided to trust Jack's recommendation and go to Great Barrington instead of South Egremont.

The only reason he had for going to South Egremont was to pick up his package. South Egremont appeared closer to the AT, at least on his map and maybe that's why Laura sent his mail drop there. The guidebook said there was a post office there, but since it was late on a Saturday he knew he would have to wait until Monday at 8:00, so he decided to stay in Great Barrington. Jack recommended an Inn that a friend of his owned and from the Inn it was an easy walk to the church.

As they were driving north towards Great Barrington he was struck by the beauty of Southwestern Massachusetts. It reminded him a little bit of the second Bob Newhart TV show, the one where Bob and his wife owned an Inn.

St. Peter's was the Catholic Church in Great Barrington and as they drove by it, Paul couldn't help but think how much it resembled his childhood church in Washington DC, but on a smaller scale. It was built of gray stone, probably granite. Jack slowed down as they passed the sign listing Mass times and there was a 10:30 Mass on Sunday's. Then Jack drove through town, giving Paul a windshield tour of the town and it seemed like a nice place to grow up. Jack mentioned that as the population has grown older many people who vacationed there during the summer moved back full time. Jack parked the car in front of his friend's Inn and said he'd come in with Paul to make sure Russ, his friend and owner, gave him a decent rate.

The Inn was nice and Russ was a great host. He took Paul to an available room, they agreed on a rate, and he checked in. Russ asked Paul what brought him to Great Barrington and he said, "Jack." Jack laughed, but Russ didn't, so Paul explained that he was hiking the AT and he was going to stay in South Egremont, but Jack recommended Great Barrington. "So, here I am," Paul said. Paul thanked Jack for his hospitality and recommendation and when Jack left, he went back to his room. Once he unpacked he went back down to the lobby and asked about laundry facilities. Russ said they don't normally provide that service, in fact to Russ's knowledge no one had ever asked, so Russ showed him where the washer and dryer were. Paul decided laundry could wait until Sunday and he mentioned that to Russ. Russ was short for Russell, which Paul guessed, but he confirmed that when he saw Russ' full name on a plaque on the wall in his little office. It was a plaque from Bard College, which was in Great Barrington and a college he had never heard of.

Paul asked Russ about places to eat in town and Russ took out a brochure from the Chamber of Commerce and gave it to Paul. Looking through the brochure Paul decided on one, an Italian restaurant. He wondered if they had Cannelloni because for some reason that's what popped into his head. He went to put something more presentable on and left for the Italian restaurant which was about four blocks away. The restaurant was crowded, but it was a Saturday night. Since he was alone they cleared a table for him that they had been using as a staging area. Just as Paul was ready to sit down someone came up behind him and put their hand on his right shoulder and said, "Hello, Paul."

He turned to see who it was and it was Jack and Jack asked, "Would you like to join my wife and I, there's room at our table."

"I don't want to impose," Paul said.

"You won't be imposing." Jack replied.

Jack introduced Paul to his wife Trisha and then one of the waiters moved Paul's place setting to Jack and Trisha's table which was all the way across the restaurant. When Paul sat down Trisha said, "Jack tells me you are in the process of the hiking the Appalachian Trail. That sounds exhausting."

"I've been very fortunate so far," he said.

"So when you're not hiking the Appalachian Trail what do you do?"

Paul never told Jack what he did in the car, so Paul told them what he did in the Air Force. He explained how he was trying to discern what he should do with the rest of his life, but he also mentioned the trip could be cut short if he got the high school teaching job he applied for. Paul asked what Jack and Trisha did and they both worked at Bard College. That explained how Jack knew Russ.

"What do you all do at Bard College?" Paul asked.

"Trisha works in the admissions office and I work in the overseas programs office."

"So do you get to travel a lot?" Paul asked.

Trisha and Jack looked at each other and they both smiled and then Trisha answered that question. "I think he does. He has to go visit each overseas site every year and there are fourteen places where students can study."

Jack then listed all the locations and said that not every site had students every year, but he had to keep current and make sure students are getting what they paid for.

Paul told them how he wanted to do a year overseas in Spain, but couldn't because he took ROTC when he was a college student. Then he said if he really pushed for it, he was sure there was a way he could have done it. However, he told them his Spanish was not that good and he probably would have struggled.

"That's too bad," Jack said, "Studying overseas is an education in itself."

"I don't know that this qualifies as studying overseas, but I did have a great opportunity my sophomore year in college," he said.

"Where did you go?" asked Trisha.

"I went to Spain for three-and-a-half weeks during Christmas break. You see at that time my college had a six-week break between semesters, so students could take a mini-semester. I don't believe they do that anymore, which is a shame."

"Excuse me Paul, but what college did you go to?" asked Trisha.

CHAPTER TEN

Maximilian & The Legion of Mary

"I went to Mount St. Mary's College, a small Catholic College in north central Maryland. It's just below Gettysburg, Pennsylvania if you can picture that in your mind. Anyhow, during the first week of my sophomore year our Spanish Professor, Mr. Edwards, told us he planned a trip to Madrid, Spain for our mini semester if anyone was interested in going. That sounded like fun, so I decided to go."

"How many students went?" Trisha asked.

"There were a dozen of us and we left on the 3rd of January 1972 and we flew from JFK in New York, to Madrid. We stayed right behind the Plaza de Mayor in downtown Madrid, so we were centrally located. We were given a day to recuperate and to get over jet lag, but my roommate and I hitchhiked to Toledo. What we didn't know was that while hitchhiking wasn't illegal in Spain, there had been a rash of incidents where hitchhikers robbed whoever picked them up."

"So how did you get to Toledo?" Trisha asked.

"We had to walk at least five miles, but eventually someone picked us up. We were a little luckier on the way back because we only walked about a mile from Toledo before someone stopped to pick us up. It was that driver who told us about hitchhiking in Spain. Anyhow, it was a fun adventure and our course started the next day."

"What do you mean course started?"

"Yeah, I guess I didn't explain that very well. Professor Edwards, our Spanish Professor, went to Madrid during the summer of 1972 and found this guy who had a school for secretaries and he asked him if he could put together a course for some American students. The guy, Señor Sampere, was happy to help us out. So, for the first day of school we started out with a placement test. My roommate and I decided to intentionally do poorly on the test, thinking we'd be put in the beginner's class and not have to work that hard. We went to lunch after the test and then back to the school to see how we did on our placement test. To my roommates and my surprise we were put in the advanced class. There were about six students who did even worse on the test than Burke and I."

"Was Burke your roommate?"

"Yes he was. So after we were put into our classes, Señor Sampere talked to both classes. He told our class that we would only have school for half a day, in the morning. Then before we were released he would give us an index card with something written on it, for instance the Prado museum. We then had to go to these places and report back the next day. He wanted us to get out and about in Madrid and use our Spanish. The other kids had to come back after lunch, so it worked out better for Burke and me."

"So then you did speak some Spanish?" Jack asked.

"Yes, but not well. However, Burke was better than average, so between us we did OK on our assignments. Señor Sampere took us on weekend field trips to Segovia and the Valley of the Fallen. One other day when we didn't have class I wanted to go to Avila, but no one else wanted to do anything; so, I went by myself to Avila."

"Are you familiar with Avila?" He asked.

Both Jack and Trisha shook their head no.

"Avila is special for a couple reasons. First, that's where Saint Theresa was from and secondly, they say that Avila is the biggest walled in city in Spain. I almost got snowed in there, but made it back very late."

Trisha said "That's good that you were comfortable enough to travel by yourself."

"To tell you the truth I don't think I knew any better, I just knew I didn't want to waste my money just sitting in my hotel room. The last week we were in Spain we could do anything we wanted, so Burke and I decided to go over near the Portuguese border and work our way back to Madrid."

"Do you remember the cities you visited?" Jack asked.

"Yes. The farthest west we went was Caceres, which back in Roman times was an important Roman colony and from there we went to Trujillo. Trujillo was the home of the Conquistador Francisco Pizarro and after seeing the town I know why he wanted t leave."

"Did you and Burke hitch hike or had you learned your lesson by that time?" Trisha asked.

"Yes, we learned our lesson, so we took the train to Caceres and then from there we took the bus all the way back to Madrid with two other stops besides Trujillo."

"What other cities did you visit?" Jack asked.

"We had a bus transfer in Telavera de la Reigna and then we spent two more days in Toledo because we liked it so much the first time. Actually, on our first visit there we barely had enough time to walk around the town, so we both wanted to go back and that was our chance."

"It sounds like you had a fun time, but did you get any academic credits?" Trisha asked.

"Yes. We got one credit."

When Paul saw Jack looking at his watch he said, "Let me share one more thing about that trip with you that happened the last morning we were in Madrid. I went out to the breakfast room and Professor Edwards was sitting there alone, so I sat down with him. He said to me, 'JP, that's what he called me, how have you enjoyed your three weeks here?"

I said, "It's been great."

"He said, yeah, you've been a good group of kids, but there's just one thing. I haven't had a hot shower the whole time we've been here."

I looked around the room to make sure no one had come in and said "Professor let me fill you in on something. I was upset the first morning when I couldn't get any hot water and the next morning I had to go to the bathroom at about 5:00 and when I washed my hands the water was warm. So, I went back to the room to get my towel and a bar of soap. I showered and then told Burke about my discovery and every morning thereafter I set the alarm for 4:45."

The Professor looked at me and said "why do you think there's only hot water at that time?" I replied that it was probably because the hot water heater was the stove in the kitchen and that's when the cook got there and fired up the stove. Two years later, my senior year, the Professor took another group of students for a mini semester and stayed in the same place. I asked him if he got any hot showers while he was there and he said that he and his wife got up every morning at 4:45. "He never shared that tidbit of information with the students because he thought everyone should have to experience cold showers sometime in their life."

Jack said, "It sounds like you did in three weeks what would take a student today three months or maybe even more."

"Yeah, it was a fun time."

The waiter brought out Paul's main course and since Jack and Trisha had finished their meal already, they each ordered dessert, to keep Paul company. When they all finished dinner Jack wanted to pay for Paul's dinner, too. He said Paul's story was well worth the dinner and he'd like to share it with some of the students who are nervous about going to a foreign country.

After dinner Jack and Trisha invited Paul back to their house for a nightcap, but Paul was tired and wanted to go back to the Inn. He thanked Jack and Trisha for dinner and walked back to the Inn. Jack offered him a ride, but it was too beautiful a night. Besides, it was a pretty town.

When Paul got back to the Inn he called Laura, but the kids were already in bed, so Paul said he would talk to them tomorrow morning. Paul did however, fill Laura in on the past two or three day's events, including the nice time he had at dinner with Jack and Trisha. Paul looked at his watch and it was already 10:00 p.m. and probably too late to call Don and Chris to follow up on the phone call he made from the hospital and thank them again for their hospitality in Pittsfield. He jotted down a couple things in his journal, said his prayers, and went to sleep. (670 FK)

Paul slept very well and just got up once during the night. He thought he could smell toast and coffee, so he looked at the clock and it was 7:45. He reached over to turn off the alarm since he was wide awake and so he used the bathroom, put on shorts and a T-Shirt and went down for breakfast.

There were about 10 other guests in the breakfast room and they were all well-dressed. Paul felt out of place and was sorry he didn't put on more presentable clothing. He nodded to the people at the table next to him, but didn't talk. When Russ came into the breakfast room to replenish everyone's coffee he said he hoped everyone had a good night's sleep.

Russ walked over to Paul's table and said, "Jack called to say his neighbor will pick you up for Mass at 10:15." He shook his head and said, "Thanks Russ. I'll be ready." After eating Paul went back up to his room to shave and shower. Fortunately, he had a clean pair of convertible pants and a clean polo shirt to wear to church.

He placed a call back home to talk with the kids before they went to church and they were all excited because their next door neighbor said they could come over to swim about 1:30 p.m. He asked how Heidi was and one of the kids said "she's great" and they all got her to bark and howl so he knew she was OK. Looking at his watch he figured he still had time to call Don and Chris. Chris answered on the third ring and was excited to talk with him and he could hear her say, "Don Honey, Paul is on the phone; pick up on the other extension."

Paul could hear Don fumble with the phone as he picked it up and he said, "Paul where are you?"

"I'm in Great Barrington, why?" he asked.

"We'd love to see you. We have two pieces of news which may interest you. Can we come down and go to lunch together?"

"Okay, but I'm headed to church right now. When would you come down?"

"Does 12:00 noon sound good to you? Don asked.

Paul said that that was good, and asked if they felt like breakfast or dinner. Chris said she'd like lunch, but told Paul to decide. He told them where he was staying and said he would see them at noon and after he hung up the phone he went downstairs to see if his ride was there.

At exactly 10:15 a brown Ford Taurus pulled up the circular drive and stopped in front of the front steps. The woman in the passenger rolled down her window and asked "are you Paul?" He nodded and got into the back seat. The driver introduced himself as Andy and the woman introduced herself as Joan. Paul thanked them for picking him up and said they didn't have to because the church was within walking distance. They said it was no problem and they were glad to help.

Andy pulled up in front of St. Peter's and found a parking space in the street. Paul walked into church with Andy and Joan and he was delighted when they sat up front in the third pew; Paul sat with them. After he showed reverence to the tabernacle he looked around. It was crowded enough that Frank, Sylvia, Kevin, and Will were towards the back. Paul had difficulty concentrating during Mass. He wondered what Don's and Chris' news was. Then after a while he figured out what one bit of news was, probably that Don's sister agreed to go with them to Italy. He was able to focus again on the homily and just in time because the priest asked if there were any visitors and a few hands went up, including Paul's. He didn't turn around to see if Frank, Sylvia, Kevin, or Will had put their hands up, but he wished he had.

After Mass he told Andy and Joan he wanted to walk back to the Inn, but he appreciated the ride to Mass. He walked back to the Inn and still had 15 minutes until noon. He walked up the steps to the Inn and opened the screen door, but as he did that he could hear a car pull into the driveway and he turned around to see whose it was. He recognized the blue Mercury Grand Marquis as the Bowers.

They parked the Mercury, so he walked back down the stairs to the driveway. The car doors opened and three people got out. Was the third person Don's sister he asked himself? No, the woman was vaguely familiar. He saw her at the hospital in Pittsfield, but couldn't remember who she was. He thought that she might be part of the medical staff, but then Don introduced her as George Murray's wife, Judy.

It was too much for Paul to comprehend. He couldn't figure out why she was there, but Chris said they will explain everything at lunch or brunch whichever Paul wanted. Paul took Chris' place in the front seat while Chris got in the back seat with Judy; then they set out to find a restaurant in town. They didn't have to drive far because it was two streets over and they had an American menu.

Don started out by saying, "when we got back from our shopping trip in Springfield we heard your message on our answering machine. Then when we read about George's death the next morning in the paper we pieced it together. George and I were friends and occasionally hiked together, we volunteered to take care of the trail between Dalton and US 20 and I think I mentioned that to you, but I never said who my friend was. I was originally supposed to go with George that day, but couldn't because of my knee. When I called Judy to pass on my condolences she said that it was easier on her and the family knowing that George was in heaven, or at least with Angels in a better place. When I asked what she meant, she told me what George said to you before he died."

Paul didn't know what to say. Instead of crying Judy seemed outwardly happy and at peace. Paul asked, "Have you had the funeral already?"

Judy looked across the table at Chris and Chris looked at Don. Don nodded, but not to Paul's question, he nodded as if he had been given the assignment of telling him something.

"Paul" Don said, "Judy would be honored if you can attend the funeral the day after tomorrow." Paul looked at Judy and Chris and then back at Don. They sat poker faced, not saying a word.

Paul thought that would put him even more behind schedule then he already was, but then again it was only an artificial schedule in his mind. He remembered something he heard one time, but he couldn't remember from whom. It went something like "God constantly comes to us in different experiences." In an instant he could see all the ways God came to him in different experiences on his trip thus far. He turned to Judy and said, "I would be honored to attend." Judy gave Paul a hug and said "Thank you so much, this will mean so much to the whole family."

Paul waited a minute or so, but then he said, "I will need to get a suit or something for the funeral." Judy gave Paul a once over and said, "you can if you want and I'll pay for it. However, we would love for you to come as you are. You were pretty muddy as I recall when we saw you in the hospital and that was the way George saw you in this life and the next."

"Let me think on that a while before I decide what to wear. Do I need to let you know before the funeral?" He asked.

Judy answered, "No, however you show up will be fine with us."

Paul let it sink in a while and then it dawned on him. Hiking the AT wasn't the most important thing in his life right now. Helping others was more important.

The silence was broken when Don said, "And the other piece of news is you will get to meet my sister at the funeral. She is driving down tonight from New Hampshire. She knew George and Judy through Chris and I and she would go to Mass with them whenever she visited."

"Don," Paul said, "I thought you were going to tell me that she's going to Italy with you."

Don had a sheepish grin on his face and he said "we're going to ask her Monday."

As Paul was sitting there it dawned on him that Tuesday was the Feast of the Assumption. Could you even have a funeral on the Assumption Paul wondered? He was sure Judy's priest would have said if they couldn't, so he didn't ask the question. The more he thought about his attire for the funeral, he didn't want to stick out. The funeral he attended in Manchester Center was different, he had no choice. Here at least he had a day or so to prepare. Before they got up from lunch, Paul made an announcement.

"I've thought about it and I would feel more comfortable in a suit."

Judy said, "Okay I can understand that. Now I have a son about your size, you can borrow one of his if you'd like, or like I said, I will buy you one."

The plan was to check out of the Inn and go back to Don and Chris' for the night, stopping somewhere along the way for a blazer and slacks, or if need be a suit. While Paul went to pack Don took care of Paul's bill with Russ and since a lot of Paul's stuff was dirty he just stuffed it into his backpack thinking he would do laundry at the Bowser's. When he went back to the lobby, Don said "we're all set here," and he looked over at Russ and Russ shook his head in agreement.

Pittsfield was not that far as the crow flies, it took only 45 minutes to get there. The conversation in the car was about George and his love of the outdoors. Judy and Don shared some of their fond memories of George and Paul sat there quietly taking it all in.

Then it dawned on him that he didn't call Laura about his change of plans. He thought about his package sitting in the South Egremont post office and figured it would still be there Tuesday afternoon. However, he was a little low on calling card minutes, so he would need to buy another one. Since they didn't pass any men's clothing stores on the way to Pittsfield they went right to Judy's house, so that he could try on one of her son's jackets and pants.

Judy lived about a half-mile away from the Bowser's and her house was a flurry of activity getting ready for the funeral. He remembered meeting some of the family at the hospital, but it was sort of awkward nonetheless. Paul tried on several of her son Roger's jackets and they found a blazer that fit. He also fit into a pair of Roger's pants, thanks to Paul's weight loss since he started his hiking adventure. A shirt and tie was no problem, but her son's feet were a size and-a-half bigger than Paul's, but nothing an extra pair of socks or two couldn't fix. They left the Murray's at 5:15 p.m. and when they got home there was a car in the driveway, it was Don's sister Donna.

Donna was very nice, like Don said. She was a few years older than him, but you could tell they were brother and sister by the shapes of their faces and the nose was a dead giveaway. Fortunately, Donna liked cats, so Paul got the cat free guest room. Chris said that Paul could do his laundry while she started dinner. Don and his sister caught up on family matters and Paul could hear them laughing from the laundry room and it reminded him of when he got together with his brothers.

Paul went up to the guest room and called Laura and told her about his change of plans. She thought it was a nice gesture on the family's part to want him there and of course it was a sacrifice on his part to be there for the funeral, or as Laura preferred, "a celebration of life." He spoke briefly to the kids and then went down to put his clothes in the dryer.

Chris made Lasagna for dinner and it was great. After dinner Don and Donna wanted to go get ice cream, so Paul went along. They drove to the Dairy Queen on the outskirts of Pittsfield and they all got a small vanilla cone dipped in chocolate and after the ice cream at DQ they returned home. When he wrote in his journal that night he seemed to be regressing, that he was going backwards mileage wise. Every night he would write down the day's events and mileage where he was on the trail. He figured he would resolve that when he was finished his Appalachian journey.

Monday morning there was a knock on Paul's door and he opened it to look out and see Donna. "Hello," Donna said, "I'm going to Mass, would you like to go, too?"

"I'd love to," he said.

He put on some clean clothes and met Donna downstairs. They left for the short drive to St. Mark's and 8:00 o'clock Mass. It was a big church at least compared to St. Peter's in Great Barrington. It was August 14th and the Feast Day of Maximilian Kolbe, one of Paul's favorite saints. Paul would occasionally use Maximilian Kolbe as an example when talking about the Christians faith. Some people have difficulty relating to what Jesus did 2,000 years ago, but they can relate to what Maximilian Kolbe did in 1941. He gave up his life for another person in a Nazi Concentration camp.

The priest walked in at 8:00 and even though homilies aren't required for daily Mass, he talked about Maximilian Kolbe. It was short, but fitting. At the sign of peace, Frank, Sylvia, Kevin, and Will were in the pew behind him, so he shook all of their hands instead of the normal nod. Paul and Donna returned to the Bowser's after Mass and Don had breakfast waiting and it was one of Paul's favorites, Corned Beef Hash. Donna made a comment about how unhealthy it is because of the fat and high sodium content, but said "I don't think you have anything to worry about. How many miles have you hiked?"

"It was about 670 miles to South Egremont," he replied.

While they were finishing up breakfast, Don handed Donna an envelope. She took it from him and said, "What's this?" She read it and her eyes began to tear. She looked up first at Don and then at Chris and said, "I don't know how I can."

Chris said, "Donna honey, we want to do this for you because you of all people deserve it. One of the good things about having Paul here, other than he's a new friend, is that he has lived in Italy and he knows Rome like the back of his hand. He has already shared with us some of the special places to visit in and around Rome. Now we know you still have to check with work and such, but you need to do this for yourself. You're not getting any younger and this would be the perfect occasion. The travel agent needs to know by Friday. She can only hold your reservation for so long."

Donna thanked Don and Chris and said she had already made up her mind. She said "yes" and agreed that she's not getting any younger. Don looked at Paul and smiled and he nodded his head in approval. Chris stood up to clear the table, leaving Don there to tell Donna the itinerary. They would leave the evening of the 15th of December from Boston, arriving in Rome on the 16th and their return flight on the 5th of January 1996.

Paul, Don, Chris and Donna spent the day in preparation for the funeral. As Paul was helping out he thought back to St. Maximilian Kolbe and how he died. Paul thought he read somewhere that St. Maximilian started the Legion of Mary, of which George Murray was a member, or at least that's what his obituary said.

When Don rode to the store later that afternoon Paul asked if he could ride along. He bought an AT&T phone card with 250 minutes and Don went to a nearby bookstore and bought two Michelin Guides for Rome, one for them and one for Donna. He also bought Donna another card which he was going to put inside the Michelin tour guide. After Don was finished shopping they went back to the house and Paul excused himself to make a phone call.

Paul dialed the 800 number for AFJROTC and when he got the person he wanted to talk to he explained his situation. He just wanted to make sure that if he was nominated for the instructor's position in South Bend, that it could be difficult to track him down to let him know he was selected. Janice said she would put a note in his personnel file with everything he told her. Confident that Janice wouldn't let him "fall through the cracks" and miss out on the job, he thanked Janice and hung up.

Paul helped Chris put the finishing touches on the fruit tray for after the funeral and, of course, sampling some as he went along. The four of them sat up until nearly mid-night playing cards with Donna. Donna dominated the card games, but it was fun sitting there at the table and laughing together.

He went to the guest room at about 12:15 a.m. and got ready for bed. He skipped his journal entry since he had written something earlier when he and Don returned from their shopping trip. Paul glanced at the clock as he turned off the light and it read 12:35, which was the last thing he remembered. The alarm sounded at 7:15 and Paul jumped out of bed because he had to relieve his bladder in an urgent way. As he ran down the hall in his skivvies, past all the cats, he hoped Donna wasn't in the bathroom because he didn't think he could make it to the downstairs powder room. He turned the knob and went in, he was fortunate to have made it and the sound of the pee hitting the toilet water must have been very loud. He was embarrassed, but got over it quickly remembering Donna was a nurse.

Paul put on some gym shorts and went downstairs. He could tell that someone was up because he could start to smell that wonderful aroma of coffee as he went down the stairs. When he walked into the kitchen he was surprised to see Donna standing over the coffee machine waiting for it to finish. The "beep, beep" went off as he said hello. Donna reached for the coffee pot and an empty mug and said, "Would you like a cup?"

His eager reply of "yes please," gave away his fondness for coffee. He took the milk and sugar which Donna already had on the counter and put both in. He liked his coffee with about an ounce of milk and a heaping tea spoon of sugar. Donna did the same thing. Donna turned her head both directions to make sure no one was there and said, "Paul I'd like to thank you for all you've done for Don."

Paul said in reply, "Oh, any hiker would have done the same thing."

Donna said, "That's not what I'm talking about, however, if that had never happened you wouldn't be here. I'm talking about the spiritual aspect of your friendship. Let me explain if I can."

Taking a sip from her coffee, she set her mug back down and looked at Paul and began where she left off.

"As children we weren't brought up in a particularly religious family. We went to church two or three times a year and that was it. When I went to nursing school I met a wonderful man and we got married. He had no particular religious affiliation, but he was a good man. We decided to search together and we found the Catholic faith. Don and Chris always seemed a bit uneasy whenever the topic of religion came up, but now he seems very comfortable talking about religion. I don't know what you talked about on your backpacking adventure, but I believe it has been the catalyst for his faith journey. I believe the fact that he wants to go to Rome is great and that's one of the reasons I'm going. I have hope for my brother and sister-in-law that they will find the peace I have in the church."

Paul thought about what Donna said and he let it sink in a while and said in response, "Well, anything is possible with God. I'm just glad he is doing well both physically and spiritually. I'll tell you Donna, he gave me a real scare when he fell in Rutland."

He had just gotten that out of his mouth when he heard Don and Chris' door open. Chris came through the kitchen door first and said, "You guys are up early, but I'm glad because now the coffee is already made."

The funeral was scheduled for 11:00 and since it was August 15th and the Feast of the Assumption, there were earlier Masses. It was unusual to be able to have a funeral Mass on the 15th of August, but in George's case there was a good reason. George was indeed very involved in the local Legion of Mary and when they were deciding on the funeral date the family and the Legion of Mary group decided on Mary's feast day, if the parish priest would agree. He did.

On the way to church they dropped the fruit tray off at the parish social hall; Chris asked where the refrigerator was and someone said they would show her. After they dropped the fruit tray off they went over to the church and the church was packed. There were reserved seats for the Bowser's, Donna, and Paul and the funeral Mass started promptly at 11:00.

The music was uplifting and when the priest walked past the casket he stopped at the first pew, said a few words to Judy and then continued up the aisle and on to the altar. During the homily the priest made mention of how the day before was the Feast Day of St. Maximilian Kolbe and he was one of George's role models not because of how he gave up his life for another, but because he had a great devotion to the Blessed Mother whose Assumption into heaven was celebrated today.

It was after the Mass that various people got up to give their remembrances of George's life. Paul was amazed that Judy had composure enough to get up and speak, though she did stop twice and wipe the tears from her eyes. It was during her son's eulogy that the manner of his death was mentioned. He pretty well summed up what happened in his father's final moments on the AT and how they were sure he was looking down from heaven. After Mass Paul rode with the Bowser's to the cemetery and then back to the church again for the reception. Several people came up to Paul to introduce themselves and share stories of hiking with George.

The God incidences of the last couple days went through his mind as he was sitting there eating some of the fresh fruit; they were too numerous to remember and he hoped he captured them all in his journal. At 2:30 Paul went over to Judy to say goodbye. She gave him a hug and mentioned how much the family appreciated his being there. "I'm just so happy that you were there to say the sending forth prayer," she said. He told her he was honored to be a part of it all. Don came over and said, "Paul we can leave whenever you would like, but Chris and Donna will stay here."

Paul went and said his goodbyes to Chris and Donna and then he and Don rode off in the Mercury Grand Marquis. The plan was to go back to the Bowser's to change and get his gear. He would leave the borrowed clothes with Don and then Don would drive Paul down to South Egremont before the post office closed. Originally thinking he would be in Great Barrington for two days the two days turned into four. It was actually like a mini-vacation of sorts. His legs were well rested and he had his dinner fixings for that night. He was particularly glad to get lots of fruit.

They got to the post office at 4:30 and Paul went in to pick up his package and mail one back to Laura and the kids. Thanks to one-hour photo at the drug store he was able to send several pictures of himself taken by Don. He also sent back a lot of the photos that Laura and the kids sent him. The package he picked up was heavier than usual because of the new boots Laura sent. He figured he would need new boots by this point in time, so Laura sent one of the other pair he had already broken in, but he decided to put them on at the trailhead, so he wouldn't hold up Don.

He went back out to the car and Don drove him the mile to the trailhead. Instead of just a handshake Don gave Paul a big bear hug and thanked him. Paul said he would keep in touch and wrote Don the phone number for their house in Brandon, just in case he needed to get in touch sooner than later. After Don drove off he sat on a big boulder by the side of the trail and tried on the new boots. They felt a bit stiff even though they had already been broken in, so he put some moleskin on the places where there seemed to be rubbing. He walked about a quarter of a mile with them tied loosely and then he readjusted them, making them tighter. His backpack seemed heavy, probably because he was carrying his old boots and the food from the reception.

The area near MA41 was nice, but as he got about a mile away he started a vertical climb and the extra weight he was carrying was very noticeable. There was an elevation gain of about 1,200 feet, but the view was excellent. The location was called the Jug End, but his guidebook didn't say why it was called that. His guidebook, however, did list two lean-to's within a tenth of a mile of each other and he decided on the first one, which was his original plan. He chose it over the other because he was the only one there when he got there at 6:45. He took his backpack off and put it in the lean-to and sat down on the front ledge and he took off his boots because his right foot was bothering him. There weren't any hot spots where his boots normally rubbed, so he couldn't explain why his right foot was giving him problems. He put his legs up for a while and then he put his old boots back on.

Paul took the two sandwiches out of the bag that Chris fixed for him and there was one ham and cheese and one turkey and cheese in addition to the fresh cut up fruit. Chris had also snuck in some Blondie's which he would save for breakfast. He wrote in his journal trying to capture the general summary of the funeral Mass, eulogy, and reception.

He was still in a quandary as to how to mark the mileage, so he figured it wasn't worth the stomach acid. He just enjoyed the spirit of the moment and thought back to some of the events of the past four days. Another south bound hiker came at about 8:45 p.m., so he put his journal away and talked to the guy for a while and then went to bed. (674 FK)

There was a clap of thunder that woke him at about 4:30 a.m. Since it wasn't raining yet, he thought he'd relieve himself because it was never a pleasant thing to do in the rain. The thunder was accompanied by lightning and a bolt of lightning struck a tree about two hundred yards from where he was watering a tree. Paul had never seen a tree get struck by lightning and it was a spectacular sight with all the sparks and smoldering of tree bark.

It started to rain, slowly at first, but then it was a downpour right after he got back to the lean-to. The other south bounder was sitting up, obviously startled by the closeness of the lightning strike. Paul got back into his sleeping bag and fell back to sleep about 15 minutes after the last thunder clap. He awoke again at 7:15 from the noise of people talking and he looked up and saw three hikers headed north on the AT. Paul figured they must have spent the night at the lean-to which was only a tenth of a mile away. The other south bounder, whose name was Phil, was also awakened by the hikers that passed by and as he sat up he said, "Well I guess it's time to get moving. Where are you headed today Paul?"

"I haven't decided. My foot was giving me a problem yesterday, so I think I'll take it slow and see how it cooperates."

Paul fired up his stove and asked Phil if he wanted a Blondie, holding them out as he asked.

"That would be great. I love those things," he said.

Phil ate his Blondie and drank his coffee and then shoved off. He decided he was going to try to make it to the Limestone Springs Lean-to, which was about 19 miles away. Phil, as Paul learned the night before, was a section hiker who was hiking the Massachusetts and Connecticut portion of the AT.

Paul packed his backpack after Phil left, but decided to wear his old boots for the day and it was 8:15 when he started hiking again towards the Connecticut border. Paul had gone about 100 yards when he heard someone say, "Can I carry your backpack for you?"

When Paul turned around he saw Kevin walking up. Paul said, "I would really appreciate that." He took off the pack and handed it over to Kevin. They started hiking side by side, but would occasionally walk single file because the trail was narrow in places. Kevin commented on the funeral Mass the day before and how George's family took his passing well. He said, "That's how it should be."

"What do you mean?" Paul asked.

"Most people see death as a sad thing and I suppose for some it is. However, for those who follow the Father's commandments and live their lives accordingly, as if every day was their last. Heaven is beyond human words and descriptions."

"Kevin, can I ask you a question?"

"You can ask." Kevin responded.

"How do you discern what God's plan is for you?"

"Paul, all I can tell you is that if you pray for God's guidance and don't let your own thought's cloud the issue, then you will know. Sometimes people forget what lessons they've learned in life. Let me recommend something to you. You should include in your evening prayers an examination of conscience. You should look at how you have been blessed over the course of the day and how you can improve on them for the next."

Paul and Kevin talked about the funeral and other things that had happened since George Murray died. The hours and miles seemed to go quicker with someone to talk to, but at 3:30 he was ready for a break. Kevin took off the backpack set it on the ground, leaning it up against a rock. He then said, "You should be OK now. I'll see you later."

Paul said thank you to Kevin as he walked off and disappeared in the woods. He went over and sat next to his backpack and was sorry he stopped, because it was a real luxury to have his backpack carried. He did notice, however, that his foot was OK. He decided not to put the new boots on again. They had hiked up Mt. Everett and Bear Mountain, without his even noticing anything in regards to his foot.

Paul realized when he took out the map that he was in Connecticut, the place of his birth some 42 years prior. It looked like he was just shy of the Brassie Brook Lean-to. Paul figured he would spend the night at the Riga Lean-to, which was about four miles further.

He picked up the backpack, rested it on his left knee, and then sort of slung it around and up on his right shoulder. Once he got both straps on, he buckled the waist belt and started hiking again. He already missed Kevin. One of the things Paul saw while he took the break was that he wouldn't cross over another 2,000 footer until Pennsylvania, so that was good. He passed the Ball Brook Campsite just before he crossed a brook on a footbridge. He still had over two miles to the Riga Lean-to and fortunately it was mostly a level trail. When he reached the Riga Lean-to at 6:30 p.m. he noticed only one hiker and it was Phil, his lean-to mate from the night before. He figured something must have gone wrong with Phil because the Limestone Springs Lean-to was still five and-a-half miles away.

Paul said, "Hi Phil," as he walked up to the lean-to.

"Oh, Hi Paul," he said in reply.

"Are you OK Phil?"

"I have boot problems." Phil said.

"What happened?" Paul asked.

"You know those annoying little granite rocks which you stumble over from time to time? Well, I caught one in such a way that it tore the sole off my right boot."

"What size shoe do you wear?" Paul asked.

"A size 11 ½."

"Well, if you think you can fit your feet into a size 11 I can give you a pair of boots."

Phil had a puzzled expression on his face, so Paul told him about his boots and how he had to go back to wearing his old ones. "They're yours for the taking" he said smiling.

Phil's response was "Really, you'd do that for me?"

"Yeah, then I won't have to carry the extra weight."

"Well, OK, but only if I can pay you."

Phil reached around and took his wallet out of his back pocket and said, "Does $60 sound fair? That will leave me $20 for getting home."

"Yeah, that's fine. I would have given them to you for free. So, let's say $40 and then you'll be able to eat, too."

So, Phil tried on the boots and they fit him well. He walked around a bit, making sure there weren't any hot spots, and then he shoved off again. He would hike until it got dark and if he made it all the way to Limestone Springs Lean-to all the better.

He was the only one at the lean-to now, so he took out his stove, poured water in his pot, and turned on the stove. While he was waiting for the water to boil he looked through his pack for a freeze-dried dinner. He decided on Beef Teriyaki for his entrée and thought that he should also have some vegetables, so he picked peas and carrots, which he would mix in with the Beef Teriyaki.

Paul enjoyed the solitude because it had been a busy couple of days, so he wrote in his journal, looked at his map and guidebook to decide what he would do the next day. Then he said his prayers and went to sleep. (686 FK)

At about 7:15 a.m. Paul was awakened by some loud birds. With the exception of getting up once to relieve himself, he slept through the night. He decided not to heat up his stove because he actually wasn't that hungry. He just ate some trail mix and dehydrated apples; he also drank a half liter of water to make sure he was well hydrated.

At 7:45 he was ready to hike, so he started out and made it to the Plateau Campsite, which was a little over a mile, by 8:25. There were some tents set up there, but he really didn't pay attention. He made it to CT41 a little after 8:30 a.m. and generally felt good; his right foot and right quad hadn't given him any problems. When he reached CT41 he took out his map to see how far the town was. Salisbury, Connecticut was about a half mile and he considered walking there for some coffee and breakfast.

He noticed in his guidebook that there was a place that sold Coleman fuel by the ounce and since he was running low, he thought he would get coffee and some white gas for the stove. The first restaurant Paul came to he stopped to eat and get a cup of coffee. He had the special which was a three egg omelet with any three fillers and hash browns. He chose cheese, bacon, and tomatoes for his fillers. The coffee was OK, but he had had better.

What he liked best about the restaurant were the signs hanging on the walls. His favorite was "Unattended children will be given an espresso and a free puppy." After he paid for his breakfast he walked to the hiking store for some white gas. In addition to buying Coleman fuel for his stove, he bought some moleskin for his feet, just in case his old boots gave him any problems.

He walked back to the trailhead and as he was walking he wondered how far Phil made it the evening before. Paul's destination for the day, at least he hoped he was up to it, was the Sharon Mountain Campsite. Well-fed and well rested Paul felt good, but he wished it were a little cooler. He didn't have a thermometer with him, but he thought it was close to 85 degrees and that wasn't a good sign. He could already tell that the atmosphere was unsettled; at least that's how it felt, as if there would be a storm later in the day. He remembered back to his days in Montgomery, Alabama, and you could practically set your watch by the weather. It seemed to rain at 4:00 p.m. every afternoon during the summer.

The topography was pretty pleasant; there were no strenuous up hills and Paul made it to the Limestone Springs Lean-to cut-off by 1:05 p.m. As he passed the sign saying the lean-to was .5 miles to the right, he wondered about Phil and if he made it there before dark the previous evening. He thought he would do something he hadn't done for a while, and that was to soak his feet. According to his guidebook there was a spring with very cold water three miles past the Limestone Springs cut-off. When he got there he took off his backpack and leaned it against a tree and then he took his boots and socks off. The water was very cold as his guidebook said, but the air temperature felt like it was at least 90 degrees if not hotter.

He sat there about 20 minutes soaking his feet and then he took his feet out and let them air dry before putting his socks back on. He looked at the map and guidebook while his feet were drying. Paul was having second thoughts about staying at the Sharon Mountain Campsite because it looked like there would be a late afternoon storm and he didn't want use his tent in another storm. There was a lean-to two miles past the Sharon Mountain Campsite, but Paul didn't feel confident he could make it without re-injuring his foot or leg. He decided he would leave it up to God. After putting his socks and boots back on he started hiking again.

The terrain was generally level, so he was making good time. He hiked the three miles to US7 by 2:45 p.m. and still felt strong, but he was sweating a lot. Paul made sure he drank a lot of water because he knew you had to in that extreme heat. After he crossed over US7 it got more difficult because there was a change in elevation of about 600 feet, so he kept one of his Lexan water bottles handy, so that he could drink as he hiked. He decided to strap the hiking pole, which he used in his right hand, to his backpack because he almost fell once while he was drinking water while he was hiking. He was making good time and when he got to the Sharon Mountain Campsite he decided not to check it out. It was 4:45 p.m. and The Pine Swamp Brook Lean-to was only two-and-a-half miles away.

Between the time Paul left the Sharon Mountain Campsite cutoff and hiked to the Pine Swamp Brook Lean-to the sky grew eerily dark. He reached the lean-to at 6:20 and there were three hikers there and they were waving their arms around. It wasn't until he got closer that he could tell what they were doing, they were swatting at something. When he got even closer he could tell they were swatting mosquitoes. Paul walked up to the lean-to and when they saw him, someone said, "That makes four, but it looks like he has a tent, too. So, if it's OK with him we can still set up in the shelter."

The flies and mosquitoes were so bad around the hut that the three other hikers wanted to set up tents in the lean-to. There was easily room for two tents, but no more. If a fifth person came they would have to figure something out. Paul's tent was really a one-man tent, with gear; however, if you left your gear outside you could squeeze two people in. They asked him if he was agreeable to sharing a tent and when he saw how bad the mosquitoes were he agreed.

Paul and the other person with a tent set up their tents while one of the other's boiled water. They asked him if he had a water filter by any chance because the quality of the water was so bad. Paul said he didn't, but said he had just filled both of his bottles up, so they could use his.

It started to rain at about 7:45 p.m., plus it was thundering and lightening. The lightening didn't seem as bad as the last storm Paul experienced, but the one good thing about the storm was that the bugs didn't seem as bad.

The three people were from Waterbury, Connecticut, and their names were Matt, Mike, and Jon. Since Jon was the shortest, at about 5'3", he became Paul's tent mate for the night. The other nice thing about the rain was that it cooled it down, so that it wasn't oppressively hot anymore. Of course, when it stopped raining the bugs would be worse and it did stop raining at about 10:30 p.m. and about 30 minutes after they crawled into their tents when the mosquitoes swarmed around the lean-to.

Paul didn't even bother using his sleeping bag other than to lie on top of it. Paul and Jon talked for a while and Paul found out that Jon was an Elementary School teacher in Waterbury. He had been teaching for about eight years and he liked it. He enjoyed teaching the younger kids because to them he wasn't short. He realized when he was student teaching in college that he got teased about his height and how the kids were taller than him. The kidding got to be so bad he decided to switch to Elementary Education, so all the kidding probably worked out for the better.

Paul told Jon that he was considering teaching high school and Jon told him that Matt and Mike were high school teachers. The trio was doing one last campout before school started. Someone had warned them about Pine Swamp Brook lean-to with the bugs, but they didn't believe it. Paul and Jon finally fell off to sleep, but they were awakened about two hours later by a loud crashing sound outside. The guys in the other tent started shouting, "Hey get out of here, get out of here."

Besides shouting, Matt and Mike were shining their flashlights around so that it gave an almost strobe like effect. Paul and Jon looked out and saw Mike and Matt standing in front of the shelter shining their lights into the trees. When Jon asked what happened they said they thought it was a bear that tried getting into one of their backpacks. It was sort of hard getting back to sleep after all the commotion, but they tried. (703 FK)

When they got out of their tents in the morning they could see where the bear shredded Matt's backpack looking for food. Everyone else's was OK. They all agreed that it was a terrible night and not worth staying around to cook breakfast. The mosquitoes seemed particularly vicious at that early morning hour. They were all eager to start hiking, so Matt, Mike, and Jon headed north on the AT while Paul headed south.

Paul hiked about two miles and stopped to eat a snack. He ate some peanut butter crackers which were smashed from being in his backpack. He also ate his last candy bar and washed it down with water. He made it to CT4 by 11:15 a.m. and he pulled out his map to see how far the nearest town was. It was about one mile to the town of Cornwall Bridge. He was ready for a prepared meal, so he thought he would hitch in that general direction. The fifth car, which was a pickup truck, stopped to pick him up and he settled for the first place they came to which was a general store. Paul had bacon, eggs, hash browns, toast, and coffee. After he ate he used the public telephone outside to make a couple calls.

He started out towards the trailhead and had to walk the entire way because no one picked him up. Fortunately it was a quick mile and it was a beautiful walk. When he got to the trailhead he looked at his watch and it was 1:35, he had taken longer than he thought on his phone calls. It was a little less than four miles to the Stewart Hollow Brook Lean-to and he figured he could be there by 3:30 at the latest. He hoped the fact the shelter had the word Brook in it wasn't a bad sign as far as bugs were concerned. The lean-to the night before had the word Brook in it as well, but it was more likely the word swamp that should have been the clue.

When Paul got to the Silver Hill Campsite he started going downhill and he was happy about that. After the trail flattened out a bit he was walking along a trail next to the Housatonic River. It was very beautiful and teaming with wildlife; he could see a couple wild turkeys and what he thought was a bobcat. The thing Paul liked best about the trail along the river was how less stressful it was on his legs. The dirt trail was easier on his joints and muscles and he wished it was like that all the way to Georgia. However, there wouldn't be anything special about the AT if it were like that. Although it was tedious and boring at times, there was something to be said for challenging oneself. He got to the Stewart Hollow Brook Lean-to at 3:45 and was feeling good and he thought about going further, so he took out his map and looked at what was ahead.

There were no major changes in elevation between Stewart Hollow and Kent, so he thought he would give it a try. He took a fifteen-minute break and continued hiking southward towards Kent. Paul remembered Kent from when he was 13 or 14 when his Uncle Bill took him there to see the falls. All he could remember though was the falls, so maybe his Uncle Bill never took him into the town of Kent.

Paul remembered those summers fondly and in great detail. His Aunt Ellen and Uncle Bill lived on Candlewood Lake about 15-17 miles south of Kent. His Aunt Ellen was a great cook and Uncle Bill was a nice man, who told good stories of times back in the 1930's and 1940's. Uncle Bill's family had all been involved in yachting and so when World War II came along Uncle Bill was given a direct commission in the US Coast Guard.

Uncle Bill's wartime experience consisted of cruising up and down the Long Island Sound, in a commandeered yacht, looking for German U-Boats. He actually saw and reported two to the Navy. The stories Aunt Ellen used to tell about Paul's father always brought tears to her eyes. She missed Paul's dad and would get teary eyed whenever she heard the Dion song about Abraham, John, Martin, and Bobby played on the radio, especially during the part that said "only the good die young."

As he got closer to CT341 Paul thought he could make out a church steeple. Kent was just a half mile away, so he walked instead of hitch hiking. As he walked along CT341 he thought back to his call with Laura at about 12:15 and she had some good news. Janice called from AFJROTC the day before and said the closeout date for applying for the job in South Bend had come and gone. There were two others who were interested, so they would send all three packages to the high school. Laura asked Janice when she thought the school may want to interview, but she couldn't say. She said it was entirely up to the school.

Paul looked at his watch when he got to the outskirts of Kent and it was 7:15, so he went right to the outdoor store listed in his guidebook, hoping they were still open. It looked closed when he got there, so he pushed on the door handle and the door opened. A little bell at the top of the door signaled his arrival and someone from the back of the store said "we're closed." A young girl in her early twenties came forward and said again, "we're closed, but we forgot to lock the door. I was just coming to do that when you walked in."

He explained that he didn't want to buy anything he just wanted some information. He told her he was looking for a place to stay because his guidebook mentioned that the few Inn's in town were pricey for thru hikers, so to go to the outfitters to see if they had any recommendations. The girl, whose name was Rachel, said there were a couple of places she could recommend. She said, "Come on in, let me just lock the door."

After she locked the door Rachel got a Chamber of Commerce map of Kent and circled the places that put up thru hikers. She rank ordered them. Paul chose the one closest to the store for a couple of reasons; it was close to almost everything and in particular the Catholic Church. He thanked Rachel and said he would be back the next day to buy something. It was a short walk to the first place on Rachel's list. He knocked on the door since there was no doorbell and when the door opened there was an older gentleman standing there. Paul told him why he was there and the guy, whose name was Tobias, asked him in. Tobias did have a room which he could have for $30, so he took it without even seeing the room.

Tobias, as Paul found out, had been an avid outdoor enthusiast in his younger days. He loved camping and fishing. He was a retired high school teacher who rented a room to supplement his retirement income. The one drawback was that he didn't have a phone which Paul could use because it was broken. Tobias said they had had a bad storm a couple nights before and a tree took out the phone lines and the phone company hadn't gotten around to fixing them. During the course of their conversation Paul learned that Tobias was an usher at Sacred Heart Catholic Church. Paul figured that was just another case of a God incidence. Paul went up to his room, unpacked as best he could, and went to eat at a restaurant one street over.

After dinner Paul walked two blocks to where Tobias said there was a pay phone. He called Laura to tell her where he was and she was a bit surprised. "We didn't think you would make it to Kent until tomorrow," she said. He said the trail was easier than he was expecting and he felt like sleeping in a bed after the terrible night sleep the night prior. He told her about Tobias and his being an usher at the Catholic Church, which you could see from his house. After Paul talked with Laura, he spoke with the kids. They were the ones who mentioned getting the package that he sent from South Egremont. They liked the pictures Chris took, especially the one of all her cats sitting at Paul's feet in their living room.

He went back to Tobias' and they sat around and talked for a bit. Paul shared with Tobias that he had spent several summers as a teenager at Candelwood Lake and how his Uncle drove him up to Kent Falls once or twice. Tobias wanted to hear more about Paul's hike in the White Mountains, so he obliged. The "Whites" as Tobias referred to them were one of his favorite places, too. After they both sort of ran out of things to say, Tobias said, "I have a thought Paul. If you can stay through Monday, we can go to Mass here tomorrow evening and then I'll take you down to New Milford for Mass on Sunday. I belong to their Knights of Columbus Council and there is a picnic after Mass. Then, if you'd like, we can see if we can find your Aunt and Uncles place on Candelwood, so you can see how it looks."

"That sounds like a great idea, but I don't want to impose." he said.

Tobias replied back, "That's no imposition at all. I would love to do it. It's generally a very nice picnic and you'll meet a lot of nice people."

Paul said goodnight and went to his room. The bathroom which was two doors away from his room was pretty old fashioned, but it was clean. There was no shower, but there was one of those hoses that you held over your head as you knelt in the tub. He tried to shower without getting water all over the bathroom and he was mostly successful and then he went back to his room and wrote in his journal. One of the books Tobias had in the guest room was one which listed all the Saints. Paul flipped it open to August 18th to see who the Saint of the Day was and it was St. Helen, the mother of Emperor Constantine. He read about St. Helen and made a mental note to tell Don, the next time he talked to him, to see the Sacred Steps while they were in Rome. (721 FK)

Paul set the alarm for 8:30 a.m., but he didn't need it. He woke up at 7:45 and felt refreshed. He figured he would eat breakfast first and would plan out his day while he was eating. He went back to the same restaurant where he had dinner, and though it was bit pricey, Paul felt like a nice breakfast. First, he'd stop at the post office to pick up his mail drop and then he would go back to the outfitter to buy a different sleeping pad.

Rachel saw Paul walk into the store and she came right up to him and said, "Did you get a room at Tobias'?"

"Yes, I did and he's great like you said."

"What can I help you with?" Rachel asked.

"I think it's time to buy a different sleeping pad. I need a thicker one now that I don't have to worry as much about weight. What would you recommend?"

Rachel replied, "It's really a case of how much you want to spend. They all do the same thing, but there's a price for comfort and convenience on the trail."

Then she showed Paul the different options and he settled for another closed foam pad, but keeping one of the ones he had. He would keep the thicker of the two and combine them, which would give him a sleeping pad one-and-a-half inches thick. The wooden floors had definitely taken their toll on Paul's hips and they were a bit tender to the touch and his backpack waste strap didn't help any and it was always a struggle to find the best place to wear it. After buying the pad he went to the nearby barber. He hadn't had a haircut since Manchester Center and it was easier having short hair when you couldn't wash it every day.

After he got the haircut he went back to Tobias' and Tobias was sitting outside reading the newspaper. He sat with him for a while and opened the package from Laura and the kids while they sat there. Paul looked through the contents and commented on each one.

Tobias said, "I've never gone for that freeze-dried stuff, but I guess it serves its purpose. I always brought frozen food and it thaws out and I cook it in tinfoil on the fire. I've had some tasty dinners camping, but my wife always thought the food tasted burned."

That was the first time Tobias mentioned his wife, so Paul asked him about her and whether there were any other family members. He said his wife, Martha, had died two years before and they had three grown children, none of whom lived nearby. He said the closest one lived near Woodstock, New York. When Tobias mentioned Woodstock, Paul said he had a cousin who lived in Woodstock, but couldn't remember the exact name of the street. Paul and Tobias sat outside for about two hours talking and laughing at jokes and stories. At about 3:45 Tobias said, "Well, we better get ready for Mass."

Paul went up to shave and shower. After drying the bathroom floor, where the spray had strayed from the bathtub, he went to put on his long pants and a Polo shirt. He met Tobias in the kitchen and they walked over to Sacred Heart Church.

Paul walked in with Tobias and Tobias introduced Paul to the priest who was in the sacristy. Tobias explained that he was a thru hiker staying with him for a couple days, so Father Greg welcomed Paul. Then Tobias said he had to go meet with the other ushers.

Paul sat in about the third pew and by Mass time the church had filled up. He looked around after Mass started and he saw that Frank, Sylvia, Kevin, and Will were in the next to last pew. Right before Mass started there was a commotion in the back of the church and someone ran up to the altar and said, "Is there a doctor in the church?"

CHAPTER ELEVEN

Candlewood & Corn on the Cob

Paul found out what all the commotion was in the back of the church. Tobias had a heart attack about 30 seconds before Father Greg was going to process up the aisle. There was a paramedic in the congregation and he went to administer CPR, but was unable to resuscitate him. Mass was cancelled and Father Greg gave a general absolution to anyone who couldn't make it to Mass the next day.

Paul stayed because he didn't know what to do and he certainly didn't feel right about going back to Tobias' house. Finally, when the crowd thinned out, he went to see Father Greg to see if there was anything he could do. He didn't know what a visitor could do, but he should at least make the offer to help.

Father Greg knew that he was just passing through town, but asked if he would contact Tobias' son in Woodstock, New York. Paul said he would, but would need to use someone else's phone because Tobias' still wasn't working. Father Greg said he could use the one in the rectory, so he returned to Tobias' house and looked around for phone numbers. He found Tobias' address book on the desk in the kitchen right next to the telephone, so he grabbed the address book and returned to the church rectory.

Paul thought it odd that Father Greg asked him to place the call, but he didn't question Father's request. Father Greg walked into the church office as he was about to place the call and he said "You know, that wasn't fair of me to ask you to do this. I should do it." And Father stuck out his hand for the receiver and placed the call as Paul read the number out loud. Someone picked up right away, it was Tobias' son.

"Jim, this is Father Greg from Sacred Heart. I have some difficult news to pass on to you. Your father collapsed during Mass this evening and he died, they tried to resuscitate him but they couldn't bring him back."

Father stopped talking to let it sink in and then he started speaking again. "Now I don't know any of the funeral information so I need you to contact the funeral home right now. Let me find that number." Father opened a book with contact numbers in it, found the funeral home number and read it to Jim. Paul put his hand up to get Father's attention because he wanted to talk with Jim after Father Greg was finished. Father told Jim that he was sorry for his loss, but his father died in the place he and Martha loved so much over the years. When Father finished speaking he handed the receiver back to Paul and Paul got on.

Paul explained the situation to Jim, that he was a thru hiker staying with his father and that he went with him to Mass. Paul said if there was anything he could do he would be happy to help out. Jim told Paul he was welcome to stay in the house for the night and he would be over first thing in the morning, so he went back again to Tobias' house and it felt sort of strange. It was strange in the sense that Tobias was dead and would no longer return to the house. Looking in the refrigerator he saw what appeared to be leftovers from Tobias' lunch, so he took it out, pulled the cover off and saw what looked like Chicken & Rice. He also took out a bottle of beer.

He put the container with the Chicken & Rice into the microwave and heated it up and then Paul twisted the top off the Michelob and sat down at the desk. He flipped through the address book and wondered who some of the people were and how they knew Tobias. A little paper fell out of the address book and onto the desk and it was the Mass card for Martha's funeral. It said she died on August 14th, 1993. Was that another God Incident or what? It was the same date that Maximilian Kolbe died, just over 50 years apart.

Paul kept looking through the address book to see if he could figure out who Tobias' other children were besides Jim. He couldn't tell, so he decided to do some exploring after he ate. The microwave beeped signaling that his dinner was reheated, so he took it out of the microwave and put it on a plate to let it cool down, so that he wouldn't burn the lid of his mouth. He had some time for exploring before he ate, so he went into the dining room first. It was sparsely decorated, but there was a buffet table with pictures on top. He picked up the one with people in it and there was nothing on the back to indicate who was who, so he put it back down. Then he moved into the living room and there were various pictures on the mantel. One of the pictures had Tobias in it at someone's graduation. Paul turned it over and it said "Jen" on the back. Then he found similar pictures with his other children, at least Paul thought they were his children.

The other two pictures also had names written on the back, one said Jimmy and the other said Annie. Jim was a big guy or at least he looked big in the photo. Jen and Annie were beautiful girls and sort of looked like Martha, whose wedding picture with Tobias was also on the mantel.

Paul returned to the kitchen to eat and see if he could find any Jenny's or Annie's in the address book. There was a Jen listed who lived in Colorado Springs and an Annie living in Clearwater, Florida. Paul wondered why Tobias never said he had a daughter who lived in Clearwater, which was only about 20 miles from where they lived in Brandon. He was sure he mentioned that he was from the Tampa Bay area to Tobias. Well, he figured he wouldn't explore any more, he might find something he wasn't prepared for. Paul took another Michelob from the refrigerator and went into the Living Room to write in his journal. As he was sitting there, in what was probably Tobias' Lazy-Boy, there was a knock on the door.

He got up from the recliner and went to see who it was and as soon as he opened the door he recognized the guy from church. He was from the funeral home and he wanted to look through any photo albums which were around. Paul told him to help himself, but said he didn't know where any of that kind of stuff was. Matt, the funeral home owner, said he knew Tobias and Martha from church and had a pretty good idea where they kept them.

Matt, as it turned out, said he grew up with Tobias' children and they went to CCD together. Tobias was also his biology teacher in high school and one of the reasons he went on to study biology in college. He said that when Martha died two years prior, Tobias took it very hard. "It was his faith that pulled him through," Matt said.

Matt found some pictures and other stuff he would use for the funeral program and the obituary. He said he would wait until Jim got there the next day to look through Tobias' clothes. As Matt was leaving, Paul went to the door to let him out and there was a woman standing on the porch, she had just walked up. She introduced herself as Liz from church and she said Father Greg called her and said that Mr. Geary might need some dinner or something and at that she held out a picnic basket. Paul thanked her, instead of explaining that he had already eaten, and took the basket from her. When he looked at his watch, it was 10:45.

Paul went back inside and looked in the picnic basket. Liz had something in there for both dinner and breakfast. That was very thoughtful of her and Father Greg and since he was still hungry, he took the dinner plate out to eat and then he put the breakfast items in the fridge. Paul sat down at the kitchen table and ate the dinner plate which Liz brought; it was beef stew. It was great, but then any home cooked meal would be better than freeze-dried food. He washed his dishes and looked for the washer and dryer to do a load of laundry.

Since he couldn't ask Tobias, and there was no working phone to call Jim, Paul figured it would be OK to do his laundry. The washing machine and dryer were in the basement, so Paul put a load of clothes in the washer and would put them in the dryer when he woke up. The first Mass was at 8:30 a.m., so he set the alarm for 7:00 a.m. and went to sleep. (721 FK)

Paul heard a car drive up the driveway and then doors opening and closing. He looked at the clock and it was 6:15 a.m. He jumped out of bed and looked out the window. There was a man, a woman, and two children. He recognized Jim from his graduation picture and figured the woman was his wife. The kids looked like the ones in the picture on the mantel, with the picture frame that said "We love you Grandpa."

Paul put on his shorts and went downstairs barefoot and Jim was just coming through the door when Paul reached the bottom of the stairs. Jim looked up at Paul and said, "Hi, you must be Paul. I'm Jim."

It was a bit awkward since Paul didn't have a shirt on, but he said in reply, "Hi Jim. I'm sorry for your loss."

After he met Jim's wife, whose name was also Laura, and their children he went back upstairs to put on a shirt, but he realized they were all in the washer. Feeling embarrassed Paul went back downstairs through the kitchen and down the basement stairs. He put his clothes in the dryer and went back upstairs and apologized for not having a shirt on and explained how he was doing laundry and hoped they didn't mind. Jim said he understood and said he was sorry for getting there so early.

Laura, brewed some coffee and Paul filled them in on the happenings of the day prior, including Tobias' and his great conversations; he didn't leave anything out including the part where they were going to drive to Candlewood Lake and go to Mass at St. Francis Xavier, in New Milford, followed by a Knights of Columbus picnic. Laura asked if there were any indications that he wasn't feeling well, and Paul said no. In fact, to the contrary he was happy and full of life. Paul took advantage of the awkwardness and mentioned that his wife's name was Laura and she too was a brunette.

Paul told Jim and Laura that he planned to go to 8:30 Mass, then come back and pack, and then he would leave right away if that was alright with them. They said that was fine. Jim looked through his father's important papers while Laura went upstairs to look through Tobias' suits; she had to pick out what they bury him in.

Father Greg was standing at the front entrance of the church when Paul walked up and he asked how Paul's night was. He told father that Jim arrived very early and that he would come by the church later in the day. Then Paul started to walk into the church, but he remembered to thank Father Greg for sending Liz over with the meals. Father Greg said that was the least the parish could do for him. He went into the church and sat in the third pew where he sat the evening before. After he prayed he looked around as he sat back into the pew and he saw the four companions in the pew directly behind him. He smiled at them and they smiled back. During the homily Father Greg mentioned what had happened at the Saturday evening Vigil Mass and said that the funeral would probably be on Wednesday.

After Mass Paul went back to Tobias' house and Jim was sitting on the front porch looking through scrapbooks. Matt, from the funeral home, returned them while Paul was at Mass. Jim looked up as Paul walked up the steps and there were tears in Jim's eyes. Jim closed the scrapbook and said, "We had some good times in this house growing up. I'll miss dad a lot."

"Jim, for what it's worth, I could tell your dad was a great guy and well-loved in the community. In fact, I found out about this place from one of the employees at the outfitters. She actually gave me a list of where hikers could stay and she rank ordered them and she listed your dad first because she thought he was the best. And, Matt from the funeral home said it was your father who was the reason he studied biology in college and was probably responsible for his getting into the mortuary business."

Jim smiled at that and nodded his head, so he continued.

"I also spent a good two hours yesterday talking and laughing with your father; he sat where you're sitting and I sat in that chair," pointing to the chair to Jim's left. "In that two hour period of time I could tell he was happy with his life and had no regrets, with the exception of your Mom dying before he did. I know it's hard to understand, but I think he was ready to leave this life and start his next life with God."

"Thanks Paul. That means a lot coming from someone who only knew my father less than a day. I'm happy that Dad met you and laughed with you."

When Jim started looking through another scrapbook Paul turned to go into the house. He walked up the stairs to his room, changed into his hiking attire for the day, grabbed his backpack and hiking poles and went back down stairs. He opened the front screen door and stepped out onto the porch; Jim was still flipping through a scrapbook and when he saw Paul come out he looked up. Paul reached around to get his wallet to take out $60 for the room and when he started to hand the $60 to Jim, Jim said, "I won't accept that. I should be paying you. You've given me a lot. You showed me a side of my father I didn't see and more importantly, you shared with us Dad's last hours in life."

Paul put the money back into his front pocket and stuck out his hand to shake Jim's hand. Jim said, "Can I at least offer you a ride to the trailhead? It's the least I can do."

"That would be great, but could we stop at a store first? I'd like to pick up some fresh fruit."

"Sure, but let me just tell Laura where I'm going."

While Jim went into the house Paul put his backpack in the backseat of Jim's car and he could hear the front screen door open and both Jim and Laura came out. Paul walked over to say goodbye to Laura and when he put his hand out she was tried to give him something. It was a rosary.

"Paul I think you are supposed to have this," Laura said.

"Why?"

"I had a dream three nights ago that someone, a stranger, would come into Tobias' life. I could see the stranger knock on his front door and then I could see the two talking and laughing on the front porch. I also had the same dream two nights ago, but it was slightly different. In that dream I could see Tobias take a rosary out of his pocket and hand it to the stranger and then Tobias disappeared, but the stranger was still on the porch. Last night I had the exact dream again with the addition of Jim and the stranger talking on the front porch."

"You didn't tell me that honey," Jim said.

"That's because it didn't dawn on me who the stranger was until I looked out and saw you and Paul talking on the front porch. Anyhow, while I was looking through Dad's things I came across this. It was Dad's Knights of Columbus Rosary and that's why I'm sure you are meant to have it."

Paul didn't know what to say. The best he could come up with in response was, "well, thank you. This means a lot to me because your dad was a devout man from what I witnessed."

When Paul put out his hand to shake Laura's again, she said, "let me give you a hug," which she did. Then she said to Paul and Jim, "I've never had dreams like that. I think God was trying to tell me something, too."

Paul climbed into the front seat of Jim's car and Jim backed out of the driveway and they went to the store. So at 12:45 p.m. on August 19th, 1995, Paul continued his trek; it was the 61st day of his Appalachian Adventure. On the way to the trailhead he picked up some fruit, two bananas and two apples. He also bought a deli sandwich and some oatmeal raisin cookies from the bakery. Since it was late he couldn't take time to stop for lunch, so he would eat on the go. His plan was to make it to the Ten Mile River Lean-to, which was just a little less than 10 miles. He ate a banana before he started and washed it down with water. Having had two beers the night before, he didn't want to risk getting dehydrated because he would surely get Charley Horses.

The trail started to climb once he got away from the Housatonic River and he almost immediately passed by the cut-off for the Mt. Algo Lean-to, so he stopped there to readjust his boots. There was still someone sleeping in the shelter and from the beer cans all around the shelter it was obvious he would have a serious hangover whenever he got up. He continued hiking and it was a pretty strenuous vertical climb for the next three miles, but the reward was a great view from the top. His guidebook called it Indian Rocks. There was a beautiful view of the Housatonic Valley and the Schaghticoke Indian Reservation, which his guide book said was the only Indian Reservation the Appalachian Trail went through.

From Indian Rocks it was a vertical descent of nearly one thousand feet. Paul's knees hurt from time to time as he descended, but the hiking poles helped. He got to the Ten Mile River at 5:25 and crossed over on the Ned Anderson Memorial Bridge. Paul stopped to read the plaque about Ned Anderson, who actually mapped out the Connecticut portion of the AT. It was 5:45 when he got to the Ten Mile River Lean-to and there was no one there. He was the only one, or at least he was the only one there at 5:45 and no doubt someone would still show up. Anyhow he took off his pack while sitting on the front ledge of the lean-to as he normally did. He took his sleeping bag and pads out and spread them out. He put the new pad on top of the old one. It wouldn't be as comfortable as a mattress, but certainly better than it was before. He tested it out, but he couldn't find a comfortable position.

He took out his stove and fired it up and he used up the last of his freeze-dried meals which he had from his South Egremont mail drop; he took out a BBQ Beef with mashed potatoes, which was a first for him. When the water came to a boil he poured it into the pouch with the freeze-dried meal and he let it sit awhile and then he stirred it. He took a spoonful and it wasn't bad; it was probably one of the better tasting freeze-dried meals he ever had. He also ate one of the giant oatmeal raisin cookies after dinner and felt that it was a bit dried out. Fortunately the raisins were still moist, but the cookie lacked the chewiness he enjoyed in a oatmeal raisin cookie.

Paul finished dinner and at about that time another hiker showed up. So much for having the lean-to all to him; the guy was a thru hiker who started out from Georgia in May. He looked and smelled like he'd been on the trail for the better part of four months. The guy wasn't very talkative and Paul respected that, so he wrote in his journal, since he never finished the night before. He treated Laura's dreams as a providential experience because he couldn't explain it; he just wrote it down as she described it. He wondered how she would change her life as a result of it. He had a lot to write about including his not being able to call Laura before he left Kent. He just plain forgot, so Paul ended his journal entry by saying this was his last night in Connecticut, the state where he started out life on the planet Earth. (729 FK)

Paul had difficulty sleeping. It could have been for several reasons; he wasn't used to the thickness of the pad, the odor in the lean-to from the thru hiker, or more likely the acid indigestion from his dinner. As good as the BBQ Beef and mashed potatoes tasted the first time, it kept repeating on him all night. He wished he had some antacid, but since he didn't he got up because lying down and that didn't help the reflux. It was 5:45, so he tried to be quiet because the north bounder was still sleeping.

Paul thought he could eat something bland to help with the acid indigestion, but he didn't have any bread or anything. He considered eating his other banana, but remembered that those occasionally repeated on him as well. The acid indigestion was so bad he just wished he could vomit and get it over with. He rolled up his sleeping bag and pads, drank some water, and started hiking. The north bounder woke up while Paul was packing and just nodded and rolled over.

Paul figured he hiked about a half mile when he sensed that someone was behind him. He turned around and there was a young Latino looking girl, probably in her early twenties. She was traveling light with just a rucksack. She caught up to Paul and said, "Hello Paul. I have something for you."

When he turned around he could see the girl was holding something out in her right hand. It was Gaviscon, which was the antacid he normally took for reflux. He reached for it and said, "Thank you. I really need this. What's your name?"

When he stopped to take the Gaviscon the girl said "My name is Gloria."

Paul took out one of the water bottles and then two Gaviscon to start with. He chewed the tablets and drank about four ounces of water. It felt refreshing on his throat as it made its way down his esophagus into his digestive tract. He took one more sip of water and put the lid back on the Lexan water bottle. Then he asked Gloria where she was from and she said Ybor City, Florida, which was a suburb of

Tampa. He knew the place well because one of his and Laura's favorite restaurants was there in the Wyndham Harbor Hotel.

Paul was ready to start hiking again and Gloria walked by his side and she was the first one to talk.

"It was a shame you never had a chance to go see your Aunt and Uncle's place on Candlewood Lake, but I can remedy that if you are up to it."

Paul was curious as to what she meant, so he asked her what she was implying.

"I know that Tobias was going to take you to New Milford today, but his time to meet the Father was yesterday. We're not that far from New Milford if you want to go."

Paul figured that all the details were probably already worked out so he said he would love to. He didn't question her any further because he knew she would tell him how they would get there, and she did.

"When we get to Route 55 Kevin will be there with a car and he will take us to Candlewood Lake, which is less than 20 miles to your Aunt and Uncle's old place."

"Sounds good to me, let's do it." Paul said.

In the roughly mile-and-a-half to Route 55 Gloria told Paul all about herself. She had been aborted at 11 weeks because her mother already had two children and she didn't think she could handle a third. Gloria was aborted in May 1994, a little over a year ago.

"How exactly did our paths cross?" Paul asked.

"If you remember back to the day you broke your ribs you were at the Wyndham Hotel on Harbor Island attending a conference. You were in pain and you felt a cough coming on and because your broken rib would jab your lung, you had excruciating pain. You left the conference early to go to the hospital and on your way to the hospital you saw my mother having a fight with her boyfriend. You wanted to give her a word of encouragement after her boyfriend left, but you couldn't because you were in so much pain. However, you did include her in your prayers."

"And what was God's plan for you Gloria?" Paul asked.

"It was very simple. I was going to get a job in a coffee shop in Tampa and just help people."

"What do you mean just help people?"

"Something as a simple as giving someone encouragement when they're feeling depressed and all alone. That can make all the difference. For one person that would have made a difference between life and death. You see, he will end up taking his life in another 18 years because I won't be there."

"And God is going to let that happen? He can't still change that?" He asked in disbelief.

"You have to understand that sometimes a greater good can come out of bad. I don't question the Father's reasons for doing or not doing something. Nor do I question why He allows certain things and disallows others. Free will is very dear to Him."

Paul shook his head, but said," Hopefully I'm not in the Tampa area 18 years from now, but is there anything I can do to help him, like I did for Will's father?"

"No. There's nothing you can do."

Kevin was waiting when Paul and Gloria got to route 55. He was driving an extended cab pickup truck, which made it nice for Paul because he could just toss his backpack and poles into the truck bed without having to struggle getting it through the door. He shook Kevin's hand as he got in the front seat while Gloria climbed into the back. Kevin did a U-turn to get them headed in the right direction towards New Milford and after a few miles there was a sign which said they were in Connecticut. Kevin talked about Tobias and what a beautiful thing Paul did yesterday.

"You know you didn't have to do all that," he said.

Paul tried to think of a response but all he could think of was, "I couldn't think of what else to do. You would have done the same."

Kevin spoke again and it was to say that they should stop by a phone so that Paul could call Laura, since he didn't get a chance to call before leaving Kent. Paul wasn't quite sure how to say all he had to say in a phone call, like Tobias' death, so he would just keep it simple.

When they got to New Milford Kevin knew exactly where to turn, so Paul didn't have to tell him. They followed signs for Linn Denning Park because Aunt Ellen and Uncle Bill's place was almost right next door to the park. It was about a mile and-a-half off of Route 202 and when they got to the park entrance Paul didn't recognize anything because things had changed so much in the 21 years since he was there last.

The entrance to Ellen and Bill's was only about 15 feet past the park entrance, so Kevin found the driveway and drove down it. Their entrance changed too since Paul's last visit in 1974; it looked very nice. Whoever bought the property from his Aunt and Uncle had done a total reconstruction. Instead of a three bedroom, one bath Cape Cod, it was now a two story colonial. It was huge in comparison to what it used to be. It must have had four or five bedrooms plus a lot of other rooms. Instead of being a weekend getaway for his aunt and uncle it was now probably someone's permanent house.

Kevin parked the truck and got out and Paul got out and said "what if someone's home, what do we say?"

Kevin said "no one is home and won't be for twenty minutes." They walked around to the front of the house and Kevin said, "Why don't you come and sit on a chaise lounge and relax. Gloria sat across from him on another chaise lounge and Kevin walked behind Paul and put his hands on his shoulders and said, "Shut your eyes and let's go back to some of your fond memories of the time you spent here with your Aunt and Uncle."

When he closed his eyes he started seeing images in his mind. He saw Aunt Ellen cooking in the kitchen and Uncle Bill coming in to see what was for dinner. Then he could see Uncle Bill and himself walking down to the lake and it was a snapshot image of the day Paul tried to go waterskiing, but was never able to get up on the skis. Fortunately, he didn't have to relive the falls or the pain of falling again. Next, he saw his older brother skiing on one ski and he was good. After that they were all sitting around the table on the patio eating something, it looked like Aunt Ellen's Chicken Cacciatore, which was Paul's favorite. They were all laughing and having a good time. Then Paul's Aunt Martha was there and two of Paul's cousins playing Crazy Jack's and they were all laughing uncontrollably.

The next image had Paul's brother Bill and Bill's brother-in-law Mike and Bill's friend Reggie getting ready to go on Uncle Bill's boat. Reggie didn't know how to swim, so they were putting two life vests on him to make him feel more secure. Next Paul was out on Uncle Bill's Chris Craft when the engine housing caught on fire and he could see his Uncle, who was a hulk of a man, pick up the engine housing and dip it into the lake to put the fire out. From there the next image was of Uncle Bill and

Paul going to the airport at the north end of the lake, he could read the sign as they drove in, it said Candlelight Farms. Then he could see a snapshot of himself and Aunt Ellen going to Mass in town, he could read that sign also as they drove up and it read St. Francis Xavier Catholic Church. Then they were back at the house on Candlewood eating hamburgers and hot dogs and corn on the cob. When Kevin took his hands off of Paul's shoulders the images stopped. Paul opened his eyes and could see Gloria sitting across from him smiling.

Kevin said, "How was that Paul?"

"It was great, can we do it again?" he asked.

"No, I'm afraid we don't have enough time. The owners are just turning off of Route 67 in New Milford and they'll be here in less than five minutes."

Paul stood up and scanned the shoreline and it was still very beautiful. The last time Paul visited his Aunt and Uncle there were only a few boats on the lake, now there were lots of boats. It didn't have the same charm, but it was beautiful nonetheless. Gloria started walking back to the truck and Kevin and Paul followed and he thanked Kevin for the chance to see that all again. He wondered how Kevin did that, but then he remembered anything is possible with God.

Just as they turned left out of the driveway onto the main road they could see a car put its right turn signal on. It was a Black Mercedes Benz and they turned into the driveway they just came from. It was the new owners and they just missed them.

Gloria tapped Paul's shoulder once they were out on the road and when Paul turned around Gloria asked, "Did the Gaviscon work?"

"Yes, it did." Paul answered. "Thank you."

"Well than how about we get you some breakfast and then you can call Laura?"

"I like that idea," he responded.

Kevin turned the truck right at the bottom of the hill and drove into New Milford and they stopped at a diner about a half mile down CT7. Paul ordered Eggs Benedict and Hash Browns, plus coffee and Apple Juice. Gloria and Kevin both had pancakes with peaches, pecans, and whipped cream. The three talked about various topics and Kevin said what a great comfort Paul had been to Jim and what a great gift for Laura to be able to see you and Tobias laughing. That will start them both on a journey back to God.

Kevin and Gloria remained seated at the table while Paul went to call Laura and when he got her on the phone he started out by saying he was sorry he didn't call the day before and explained why he couldn't. He talked about Tobias' heart attack and then how odd it felt staying in Tobias' house afterwards. Paul shared the talk he had with Jim on the front porch after he came back from Mass and also Laura's dreams. Then he told her about the terrible night with acid reflux and how he thought it was caused from the freeze dried dinner. He then shared with Laura how his day went after he woke up, meeting Gloria on the trail and how she had Gaviscon for his acid reflux.

Then Paul told Laura about Gloria and Kevin and their offer to bring him to Aunt Ellen and Uncle Bill's place on the lake. Paul turned around to make sure no one was behind him and then he told her about the miraculous thing Kevin did for him.

"It sounds like an exciting day," Laura said.

"Yes, so far."

Before he hung up Laura told him about their neighbors with the two boys. They were moving south to Bradenton, Florida because that's where the dad's job took them. She said Daniel and Steven would miss playing with them.

So, Paul went back to the table where Kevin and Gloria were and Kevin had already paid for the meal, so they were ready to go. Kevin asked if there were any other places he wanted to go, so they went to a grocery store to buy some fruit and Blondie's, if they had any. After he bought two more bananas and some dehydrated pineapple, Kevin and Gloria took him back to the trailhead. It took less than a half hour to get back to where he and Gloria met Kevin on Route 55 earlier in the day. Paul thanked Gloria and Kevin for all they did for him and then he started hiking again at 1:30 in the afternoon.

Paul enjoyed his day with Kevin and Gloria, particularly the relived memories of summers on Candlewood Lake. On the ride back to the trailhead he asked Kevin how he was able to do that and Kevin said, "God knows all things and He sees the past and the future as present. He let you experience that for helping Tobias and his family." Paul thought about many of the images he was allowed to see, but the image of the ride to the airport brought back to mind a story Aunt Ellen used to tell.

She said Uncle Bill got his pilot's license, but she was scared of flying. One day Uncle Bill showed up in a float plane and tied it right to their boat dock. As the story continued Uncle Bill went up to the house to get Ellen and she said "no" she won't fly. So, Uncle Bill told her they would only taxi around the lake, to which Ellen agreed. She got in the plane and Uncle Bill started taxiing and the next thing Ellen knew they were up in the air. Aunt Ellen was furious and she screamed "you promised me we'd just taxi," and Uncle Bill responded by saying "We ran out of lake."

It was good to see the image of them at the table on their patio eating corn on the cob. Paul remembered the corn on the cob eating contests that he and his Uncle used to have. Uncle Bill always won. Yes, Paul thought, those were good times.

Paul stopped for a break after about three miles to look at his map and guidebook. There weren't many camping shelters or lean-to's in New York and in fact, New York seemed to have a lot of camping restrictions, so he arbitrarily picked the number 10. He would see how he felt at mile marker 742, which was 10 miles from route 55. His guide book indicated a shelter near there called Telephone Pioneers Shelter. So, with that thought planted in his mind, he started hiking again. What amazed him about the area was how green everything was.

He remembered when he used to drive up to Candlewood with his Aunt Martha they would take the Taconic Parkway out of New York City and cut over somewhere into Connecticut; it always amazed him how green it was. He was more amazed because it wasn't that far from New York City, which he always considered dark and depressing.

He crossed over County route 20 at 6:30 p.m. and from there it was less than a mile to the shelter. As Paul stood on the side of route 20 he took a big swig of water before he continued. Someone drove by as he was standing there and wanted to know if he wanted a ride. He said, "No thank you, but thanks for stopping." He continued on and got to the Telephone Pioneers Shelter by 7:00 and there were two other hikers there, so Paul took off his backpack and claimed his space in the lean-to. The two hikers, a guy and a gal in their late teens or early 20's, were cooking dinner as he arrived. They said hi and asked if he wanted some dinner. It was kind of them to ask, but he declined because he thought he'd play it safe and have as bland a dinner as possible. Paul did take them up on their offer of hot water and he ate some hot oatmeal for dinner. He explained to the two hikers what had happened as a result of the dinner he had the night before. He just told them another hiker gave him some antacid and that seemed to take care of it.

The couple was from East Stroudsburg, Pennsylvania, and they were completing the New York-New Jersey section of the AT. They were both school teachers from that area, which was near the Delaware Water Gap. While Paul was writing in his journal a third thru hiker arrived right at dusk and he was going all the way to Katahdin. Paul tried switching the order of his sleeping pads to see if that would help, because he couldn't tell any difference from before. He said his prayers and fell right to sleep. (742 FK)

The thru hiker was up early and so was the couple from Pennsylvania. This would be the last day of the couples hike, but the thru hiker still had at least 45 days to Mt. Katahdin, although it had taken Paul 63 days to get to the Telephone Pioneers Shelter. Paul heated up some water after they left and had some more oatmeal, but added raisins and brown sugar. Even though it promised to be a hot day, the warmth of the oatmeal was soothing on his throat as it made its way down. Paul looked at the map as he sat on the front ledge of the shelter and the next shelter was about seven and-a-half miles away; it was called the Morgan Stewart Shelter and that didn't seem like a long enough hike, so Paul would try for the next shelter after that, which was 10 miles further and called the RPH Shelter. It dawned on Paul, as he was loading up his backpack that he never asked the Pennsylvania couple how long it took them to get to that point. He was upset with himself that he didn't ask them, but he would find out soon enough.

It was eight o'clock when Paul started what would be the 64th day of his journey. He wondered when Tobias' funeral was; it would have to be today or tomorrow, he thought. He also wondered if the daughters made it in to Kent because they both had to come a long way. It was good Jim lived relatively close. Paul looked to see how close he would come to Woodstock, New York because he considered taking a day to go see his cousin Jim, but it looked too far away. He didn't even know if his cousin Jim would be home.

It was a very pretty hike, even as he passed Nuclear Lake. Paul was curious when he saw that on the map, so he looked it up in his guidebook. The lake was named Nuclear Lake because there was a facility there back in the 60's and 70's that processed low-level radioactive materials, which seeped into the surroundings. Paul wondered if the AT was rerouted during that time period while they cleaned up the area, because the trail went right up to the lake. His guidebook said the National Park Service still monitored the lake.

Crossing over NY55 Paul took a short break before continuing and he ate one of the bananas he bought the day before. He could tell the temperature was climbing because of how much he sweated, so he took off his T-Shirt and that helped. Paul couldn't remember the last time he said a Rosary, so he said all three mysteries: *The Joyous, The Sorrowful* and the *Glorious*. When he finished the *Glorious Mysteries* Paul thought about Gloria and how she got her name.

Somewhere in the Psalms it says that God knew us in our mother's womb. Did that mean God named us in our mother's womb? He wondered if that was something he could ask one of the companions. It was 11:45 when he reached the Morgan

Stewart Shelter, so he stopped for lunch. He had trail mix, the other banana, and about a pint of water and then Paul started hiking again at noon.

About four miles after leaving the Morgan Stewart Shelter Paul happened on a hiker; he was just standing in the middle of the trail. He was looking up in the sky, so Paul looked up, too. Paul didn't see anything, so he wondered what the guy was looking at. When he got up to him he said, "What are you looking at?"

The guy turned towards Paul and said, "I don't know, but something definitely flew overhead." Paul stayed and talked to the guy for a while. His name was Andy and he was from West Chester, Pennsylvania. Andy was probably about 50 years old, but maybe older. As Paul came to find out, Andy was a section hiker trying to finish up the New York and New Jersey section. He had to do it before the Labor Day Weekend or at least that's what he told Paul. When Paul asked him why he had to finish by Labor Day weekend, Andy said, "Oh, it's just a goal I set for myself. It won't be the end of the world if I don't finish, but it will be easier for the family. What I don't finish this year I'll have to finish over one of the long weekends."

Andy started walking again, to the south; in the same direction Paul was headed, so Paul answered, "Would you like some company?"

Andy said he'd like some company because hiking was really pretty boring and if there was something noteworthy, it was nice to share it with someone else. Paul walked to the left of Andy because that's what Andy asked him to do. It turned out that Andy was hard of hearing in his right ear and he said it would be a tiresome experience if he always had to say, "Huh?"

"Where are you headed?" Andy asked.

"I'm headed to Georgia or maybe not," Paul said in reply.

"What do you mean maybe not?"

Paul told Andy his intent for the last 24 years was to hike the entire AT, but then he told Andy that he might have a job offer before he got to the Maryland border. Andy nodded his head like he understood, but then there was a pause and he asked another question.

"So let me understand this, you've wanted to hike the Appalachian Trail for 24 years or so and you would give it up if you got a job?"

Paul thought about how to respond and said, "Yeah, that's pretty much the case. I decided to hike the trail to discern what I'm supposed to do with the rest of my life. It all boils down to this; I took this hike because it was all about me because I was selfish and not thinking about others. However, now I think I know what I want to do for the rest of my life, so why should I finish the trail if I know now what I want to do? I think that would be unfair to my family, my friends, and, well, to God. Who am I helping by finishing the trail? I would be just another number in a statistic."

Andy didn't say anything in response; he just walked along, occasionally looking up towards the sky. Then he said, "Well what is it you want to do for the rest of your life?"

"I want to share my love for God and all He does for us, but in a way people can understand. Now mind you, it wouldn't be in a burning bush kind of way like Moses experienced, but more like a compassionate understanderer, if there even is such a word." After Paul said that out loud he didn't know where it came from; but it definitely came from his mouth.

Before he could figure out what prompted him to say that Andy asked him in response, "How will you do that?

"I will strive to live my life so that it is pleasing to God. I will help others in whichever profession God sends my way. And thus far, on my journey, I'm sensing that I should teach high school."

"That's a noble cause, but what if you don't get the job?"

Paul thought about it for a while and then said, "Then I'll continue my journey as far as the money lasts."

They talked more as they went along and every once in a while Andy would stop to look up. Paul didn't know what that was all about, so he didn't say anything, but he too would also stop and look up. Andy, as Paul came to find out, had his own business in the West Chester, PA area, which is a suburb of Philadelphia. He loved hiking and he was doing the AT in three or four week segments. He had done from Maine to the New York border already in previous summers and he planned to start at the other end, Springer Mountain Georgia, the next spring before it gets too hot. When he found out Paul loved history, he said, "You would love the Philadelphia area." He told Paul about Valley Forge, the Brandywine Battlefield, and Philadelphia, where the American experience traces its roots. "And of course," he said, "Gettysburg is only 75 or so miles away."

They went along talking about the Revolutionary period and then the Civil War. The time flew by and they were at the Taconic Parkway by 6:25 p.m. There was a lot of traffic on the Taconic Parkway, so they had to be very careful crossing it because there was no under or overpass like there were on the other major highways that crossed the AT. The RPH Shelter was only three tenths of a mile from the Taconic Parkway, so they were both concerned they would be able to hear the parkway noise. When they got to the shelter, they both decided it was the nicest shelter either of them had ever seen on the AT.

It was constructed of cinder blocks and was painted off-white. It had a small front porch and the inside was clean and spacious for up to at least six people. More could sleep, and probably have, on the floor. Andy tried the water to see if it was as bad as the guidebook described; after tasting it, Andy said it tasted like iron. There was no one else at the shelter, but both had grown accustomed to thinking they would have the place to themselves just to have someone else show up.

Paul took out his stove to boil some water for dinner and he told Andy he could have some of his boiled water if he wanted to use it for his freeze-dried dinner. Andy said he'd love some. While they waited for the water to boil they spread out their sleeping bags on a bunk bed of choice and they both chose a top. In case someone came in late, they figured, it would be less troublesome and less likely to get a foot in the face. They had dinner on the porch and their entrees were very similar. Paul had Chicken a la King and Andy had Chicken Gumbo.

Andy asked Paul what some of the more memorable parts of his hike were, so Paul shared the story of Tom, Don, George, and Tobias. Paul didn't, however, mention anything about his heavenly companions.

When Paul told Andy about Tom, Andy's reaction was that Paul was a gift from heaven at least in the life of Tom. It was then that Andy told Paul he was Catholic. When Paul told Andy the story of Don, he said that Paul did a noble thing. Of course the story of Don ran into George's story, and Paul found it difficult to draw the line between talking about George and talking about Don. After Paul shared the story of Tobias, Andy said, "I think you have found out what you need to do with the rest of your life. You are called to be an instrument in God's redemptive Mercy."

"What does that mean?" Paul asked.

Andy thought about it for a minute and then said, "I think in short it's sort of what you said, being a witness to others of God's great love for His children."

He was still unclear as to what Andy meant, but he didn't want to say he didn't understand, maybe it would come to him in time. Paul gazed over at Andy and when Andy looked back at him he said, "Was Tobias' first name Tobias or was that his last name?"

"You know I asked the funeral director that because that was all I ever heard anyone call him."

"What did the funeral director say?" Andy asked.

"Matt said that Tobias' last name was so hard to pronounce people always had problems with it. It was the longest Italian name I ever heard and I'm pretty good with Italian names. Suffice it to say it began with a B and it had 12 letters following it. Matt said Tobias didn't want to be called B12 like the vitamin, so he always introduced himself as Tobias. Matt said the students called him Mr. T, but he preferred Mr. Tobias and it caught on."

As Paul and Andy got more comfortable talking with each other, Andy asked Paul if he belonged to the Knights of Columbus. Paul said he wasn't, but shared the story of Dan McNeil in Maine and how after meeting Dan he wanted to become a Knight.

Andy said "some people are like that, they are the kind of people who draw you to the Lord. We should all inspire others to follow God, but sadly we get caught up in the world and what the world expects us to do."

Paul also shared with Andy how he was supposed to go with Tobias to a Knight's of Columbus picnic near where his Aunt and Uncle used to live. Then Paul told Andy about Laura's dreams and how she gave him Tobias' Knights of Columbus Rosary.

"You see Paul, that's an example of how God is using you as an instrument of God's redemptive Mercy.

"How do mean."

"God was using you to reach Laura."

For the next hour or so Andy talked about his Knights of Columbus council in Downingtown and when he said Downingtown, Paul said, "I thought you said you were from West Chester."

"I did," Andy said. "I said that because most people have heard of West Chester, but might not be familiar with Downingtown."

"I'm pretty sure that is where one of my wife's brothers lives in Downingtown and they go to a Catholic Church there."

"Well, if he does go to a Catholic Church in Downingtown, we belong to the same parish. Do you know if he's a Knight?"

Paul said, "I don't know, I've never heard him talk about it."

"It is a small world. You'll have to write down his name for me before we part ways."

Andy described what he did in his business, but Paul didn't fully understand what he was talking about. Andy's firm did some kind of financial consulting, which is something that confused Paul and he freely admitted so. Andy told Paul that if he ever came to visit his brother-in-law he would take him to Valley Forge and to the Brandywine Battlefield.

No other hiker did come that night to the RPH shelter, so at 9:45 they both turned out their flashlights and went to sleep. The bunk was actually pretty comfortable; it was definitely better than sleeping on foam pads on a wooden floor. (761 FK)

While Paul and Andy were sleeping they didn't know it started to rain during the night. The temperature dropped about 10 degrees and because of that fact it was foggy. The fog wasn't a problem for Paul and Andy, but it was for the cars on the Taconic Parkway. Visibility was reduced to about 75 yards and a Chevy Blazer couldn't see the deer crossing the road. The Blazer hit the deer and the driver lost control of the car; he crossed over the median and into incoming traffic. Fortunately at that time of the morning it wasn't busy. However, the noise from the accident and the sound of the emergency vehicles was enough to wake up Paul and Andy.

The accident occurred at 5:30 and the sirens went continuously for 15-20 minutes. It wasn't until Paul and Andy got to NY301 they found out what had happened three hours earlier from a tow truck that was on the side of the road. The tow truck driver said it was a real mess, the Chevy Blazer took out five cars and the Taconic Parkway was still closed down. The tow truck driver also mentioned how bad it would have been if it were rush hour.

Paul offered up a prayer for everyone involved in the accident and when he took out Tobias' rosary to say the Rosary, Andy took out his and joined in. After they said the *Sorrowful Mysteries* Paul put his Rosary beads back in his pocket and Andy said to Paul, "You would make a good Knight. Make sure you join when you have a chance. Both Tobias' and my Rosary beads were given to us when we become Knight's;" showing Paul that his Rosary beads were the same one's Laura gave Paul. "They told us to always carry them with us. Now I have a better appreciation of why."

Andy told Paul about his council in Downingtown and some of the things they did for their community. What seemed most impressive about Andy's description of his brother Knight's, as he called them, was their support for life. Paul didn't know whether he could ever stand out on a street in a prayer chain, at least not before he began his hike. He remembered one Sunday in Tampa when he drove by a prayer chain. It was the October before, because Paul remembered going to a Tampa Bay Buccaneers game and seeing people with their Rosaries and some of them were holding up signs about Abortion. He mentioned that to Andy and asked whether they did that in Downingtown and Andy said they did.

They stopped to take a break at half past noon and during their break Paul pulled out his map and guidebook to see what their opportunities were for overnight camping. The next AT shelter was over 20 miles away, which Paul didn't think either one of them were up to. However, Paul saw there was an opportunity when they got to the Old West Point Road, which was still about 8 miles away.

According to Paul's guidebook there was a place there they could stay; it was an old Monastery turned into a retreat center and it was called the Graymoor Spiritual Life Center run by the Franciscans. Paul asked Andy if he thought they could quicken their pace some and Andy asked why.

"Well, according to my guidebook we can stay on the grounds of the Franciscan retreat center, and if we are there before 5:00 p.m. we can eat dinner there."

Andy had a quick mind and said, "Than why are we dilly dallying around here, let's get going."

162

They set a nice, quick pace; Paul just prayed his right quad and right foot cooperated. Once they left the Dennytown Road the trail was nice because it was fairly level and not many elevation changes. They continued their conversation from where they left off, but neither could remember what they were talking about last. Paul thought Andy was talking about his Knights of Columbus Council in Downingtown, but Andy didn't think so. So, he said "let me tell you what happened to one of my Brother Knights in the spring.

"We got word that one of our Brother Knight's was in the hospital, so we prayed for him. The next thing we know he is home and OK, in fact I saw him at Mass right after he got out of the hospital. Then less than a week later we get word he is back in the hospital for brain surgery because a CT scan showed four spots on his brain. The prognosis wasn't good, but he had the surgery and then he had to go to rehab. One of our Brother's, who was a Eucharistic Minister, went to see him in order to give him communion and according to that brother Knight he had difficulty talking and reasoning, so we prayed all the harder. He had to go thru speech therapy for about a month, but by the grace of God he's OK now. The only thing that's noticeably different is that he's just very deliberate in his speech."

"Is that a bad thing?" Paul asked.

"No, but I guess it shows that he had something happen to him and he's grateful to God for his second chance at life; in other words he doesn't want to mess up."

Paul and Andy made excellent time, covering the close to eight miles in less than three hours. He figured that Jeff and Ryan wouldn't have considered that quick, but Paul and Andy were pleased. When they got to the Graymoor Spiritual Center there were already 10 people there, so Paul and Andy found a place near the shelter by the ball field and they both pitched their tents. The Franciscans served dinner at 5:30 and they were invited since they were among the first 14 people to show up. Paul decided to stretch out for a nap on one of the picnic tables, but set his wrist alarm in case he drifted off to sleep.

Paul's alarm went off at 5:15 and he had fallen asleep and Andy likewise fell asleep on the next picnic table over. They both used the bathroom facilities and then went to the retreat house. The meal was simple, but hearty. The fresh bread was particularly good with real butter on it. The pound cake for dessert with real brewed decaf was the highlight of the meal. The group, of ten students, was from the Franciscan University at Steubenville, in Ohio. They finished their hike at the Graymoor Spiritual Center, having started out at the Massachusetts border and they chose to end their hike at Graymoor because two of the students were trying to discern if they wanted to become Franciscan Friars. The two would stay on for three days after the others returned to Steubenville, Ohio.

The student sitting next to Paul was from Washington DC, so he and Paul had a lot to talk about. He went to St. John's College High, the same high school Paul attended. The student sitting across from him had gone to their rival, Gonzaga High School.

They were an impressive group of kids and Paul thought they were more mature than when he was their age. He shared with them that when he was looking for colleges Steubenville had a real reputation as a party school and he was glad to see that they got a president who came in and restored the college to one of great Catholic Morals. They asked Paul if he was accepted and he said he never applied because he thought it was too far away from home. He did share with them that he ended up at

Mount St. Mary's College and it seemed to be the best place for him. When one of the students asked why and he told him it was primarily because of one of his Professor's, who was a great mentor and role model.

After they finished eating dinner, the Friars invited them to evening prayer. Anyone who wanted to attend could, so Paul and Andy and about half dozen students took them up their offer. They were impressed with the evening prayer service and they both agreed it put them in a very peaceful frame of mind. On the way back to their tents Andy said something that was very interesting and yet another God incident.

"Paul, I didn't know you went to the Mount. I don't know why I never thought to ask. That's where I went to college. When did you graduate?"

"1975," was Paul's reply.

"I graduated in 1968. I'm sure we had some of the same professors, but that can wait until tomorrow. It might be fun to compare notes while we're hiking, but I just want to go to bed now."

Before Andy went into his tent Paul asked him a question about the following day. The kids from Steubenville wanted to know if they wanted to be a part of their West Point Tour. They had one scheduled for 10:00 the next day and since two of their members would stay behind with the Friars, they made the offer to Paul and Andy.

Andy left the decision up to Paul, so whatever Paul decided was fine with him. (780 FK)

CHAPTER TWELVE

Mounties

The friars served breakfast at 7:30 and everyone was at the table by 7:25 enjoying coffee and apple juice. The friars had cheesy scrambled eggs and toast with a choice of jams which were made by the friars. Paul decided to go for the West Point tour, but only if they would give Andy and he a ride back to Bear Mountain, New York. Both had to pick up their mail drops at Bear Mountain, New York and Paul didn't want to risk the post office being closed since their hours were different than most others. Paul and Andy packed before breakfast as did the Steubenville students, so they were ready to go after breakfast. They each left a $25 donation for the friar's hospitality.

It was pleasant to spend the time at Graymoor with such group of thoughtful people and it was also good to see that Paul's high school turned out mature students with a good sense of moral values. He felt as if he had been given a foretaste of heaven with the evening prayers, the sacred music, and the holy people whose company he was in.

The bus picked them up outside the spiritual center at 9:15 and the bus driver assured Paul he would take both he and Andy to Bear Mountain after the tour. West Point wasn't that far, but with traffic it took 35 minutes. Someone from the academy tour office hopped on the bus and told the driver where to park and then gave them a walking tour of the academy, followed by a question and answer session.

The kid from Paul's high school had at least three or four questions and after the question and answer session the academy gave everyone a chance to shop in the cadet store. It was a nice tour, but not as thorough as Paul would have liked. However, since he and Andy wanted to get on the road, so to speak, it was probably just the right length. Perhaps, it was an abbreviated tour because the Steubenville students requested it because they still had at least a seven-hour bus ride back to Ohio. The bus dropped Paul and Andy off in Bear Mountain at 1:30.

They thanked the Steubenville group and then went to find a place to eat because the post office didn't re-open until 2:30. They walked to the Bear Mountain Inn and ate in the restaurant; it was more upscale then most other places they had eaten on the AT. They finished lunch and then walked down to the post office and were there when the doors opened. After they got their packages and disposed of the cardboard, they repacked their backpacks and got back on the trail. If everything worked out right they would be to the West Mountain Shelter, which was five miles away, by 5:30.

Since it was a Thursday they felt they would have a good shot at one of the six spaces in the lean-to; whereas, if it were a Friday or Saturday night they probably would be out of luck.

Going from the Hudson River up Bear Mountain had a gain in elevation gain of over 1,000 feet. Andy was struggling a little bit, so Paul gave him his hiking poles, which seemed to help a lot. "So Paul" Andy said, "Who taught Philosophy while you were at the Mount?"

"I can't remember them all, but I had Father Redmund, and Monsignor Kline."

"I had them too," he responded. "Did Father Redmund still smoke his pipe in the classroom?"

"Yeah. In fact we used to guess how many times he'd burn his fingers while he talked and tried to light his pipe. I believe the record for one class was three times. Of course that was for the 75-minute class, I don't know what the record was for a 50-minute class."

"That's funny; we used to do that, too. Wasn't Monsignor Kline great?" Andy asked.

Paul thought about it awhile and said, "Yes he was, but I tried not to get him because I heard he was hard. I tried to get whoever the lay teacher was because they said he was an easy 'B'; however, once I got into Monsignor Kline's class I found out it was all hype. What I liked about him was that you got the grade he thought you were capable of, not how you did on tests. I didn't do well on his tests, but still pulled a 'B'. Class participation helped for sure and I guess he thought I made a positive contribution."

Paul and Andy talked about the Mount and all their teachers on the way to the shelter and it made the time go faster. They got to the shelter at about 5:45 and no one was there, so they had their choice of spots in the shelter. Paul liked being on an end, so he rolled out his sleeping pads and sleeping bag and then got out his stove to boil water for dinner. Paul just automatically boiled extra water for Andy and when it was ready he poured his own water into the freeze-dried meal he selected, which was Chicken Almondine. Andy was having Beef Teriyaki.

It was a very impressive view from the lean-to and you could see the Hudson River very well. When the sun set to the west you could see the sun reflecting off the glass skyscrapers in Manhattan and when it got dark that night they could see the lights in those very same skyscrapers.

No other hikers ever showed up, so Paul and Andy had the shelter to themselves. When Paul took out his journal to write, Andy asked him what kind of things he wrote down. He answered that he wrote down memorable events of the day and particularly the "God moments." Andy thought about that for a while and said that sounded like a good a good thing to do, then he asked him what he would do with his journal afterwards and Paul couldn't really give him an answer because he wasn't sure himself.

They both turned out their flashlights at about 9:45 and the view southward towards New York City was great. Besides seeing the lights in the buildings you could see their reflections on the Hudson River. Paul figured he fell off to sleep around 10:15. (790 FK)

Paul woke up around 3:45 a.m. to relieve himself and Andy was up. He was sitting on the edge of the lean-to and he was looking out towards the city. When he saw Paul's flashlight go on he said, "It's amazing to think there are millions of people out there where we see those lights and yet it is so peaceful here."

Paul agreed, but didn't say anything. After he relieved himself he went back to the lean-to and sat on the front ledge next to Andy.

"I had to relieve myself too a little while ago, but I just wanted to sit here for a while."

"Yeah, it is an amazing site when you think about it," Paul said. Then he climbed back into his unzipped sleeping bag and went right back to sleep.

It was 6:07 when Paul checked his watch. He rolled over and Andy was still asleep, or at least that's how it appeared. Paul quietly got dressed, but didn't put on his boots, but his sneakers which he kept for around camp. He went behind the lean-to to brush his teeth because he didn't want Andy to see him wasting water because the water at the lean-to, according to Andy, was awful. When he walked back around to the front of the shelter Andy was sitting up in his sleeping bag, so Paul didn't have to be quiet anymore.

Paul fired up his stove and boiled some water for oatmeal and Andy had some freeze-dried eggs. They were both quiet at breakfast, just taking in the views of Manhattan. It was hazier than the day before, so they were both happy they had the chance to see the skyline when it was clear.

They shoved off at 7:35 and crossed the Palisades Parkway, which was about a mile away, at 8:00. They were sort of all talked out from the day before, but Paul shared a story that Monsignor Kline used to tell and wondered if Andy had heard it before. He had. However, Andy still asked him to tell the story as Paul remembered it because it was a great story about when Monsignor Kline was a student in the seminary back during World War II and how one of his classmates saw Winston Churchill at a truck stop in nearby Thurmont, Maryland. When Paul finished the story Andy said that was exactly as he remembered the story.

Andy asked Paul about something the kid from Paul's high school had said at breakfast the day before.

"Paul, let me ask you; did you go to a Catholic High School?"

"Yes it was Christian Brothers and back then it was an all guy's school. It's co-ed now."

"How was that?"

"I liked it, though I didn't to begin with, but it got easier and I realized my Mom made the right decision. I think when you're in high school you really don't have a good grasp on things; at least I know I didn't. I'm sure it was the strict regimen of it all that got me through."

"What do you mean the regimen of it all?"

"The military regimen along with the way the Christian Brothers taught."

"You mean it was a military school, too?"

"Yes. In fact, I remember one of the military instructors talking with one of the Christina Brother's one day about how the two lives were similar. They are both well-ordered life styles and since I was never a good student that helped me out. The military stuff came easy, but the academics were a challenge. I thought very highly of the Christian Brothers I had as teachers and even the one I didn't care for taught me an important lesson on life."

Paul and Andy walked along continuing their conversations about the Mount and life in general. One of the things Andy shared with Paul was that he got married at the end of his junior year in college. He figured he was safe from the draft as long as he was doing well in college, but he was worried about after college. He and Mary had been dating for two years and were serious about spending the rest of their lives together, so he proposed. They wanted to have a child right away, so that he wouldn't be drafted and Andy said their first son was born on March 25th, 1968 and that they had three other children. Andy said he is always embarrassed to mention that, particularly around veterans.

When Paul heard that one of Andy's children was born on the Feast of the Annunciation, he said "One of my sons was born on the 25th of March, too."

They were hiking well and covering a lot of ground. They stopped for a break after eight and-a-half miles at the William Brien Shelter. Paul took off his shirt because it was hot, but Andy left his on. They started out again at 12:45 and there was a vertical climb of about 300 hundred feet, but everything seemed to be OK. However, when they got to a place which was referred to in Paul's guidebook as the Lemon Squeezer, Andy was having difficulty. They both made it through the tight crevice and Andy said he needed to take a break, so he sat down on a boulder and took off his ball cap and said, "Paul I'm feeling nauseous and dizzy. You can go on without me because I don't want to hold you up. I think I'm dehydrated."

"Andy I'm not going to leave you alone because I think you have heat exhaustion because your skin is sort of pasty. We need to get you in the shade and cool you down. Let's go over there." Paul was pointing to a big boulder in the shade of the crevice.

When they got over to the boulder in the shade Paul helped Andy take off his backpack. Andy was a bit clumsy and having difficulty with his fine motor skills, so Paul suggested that Andy take off his shirt and lay down on the boulder, figuring the coolness of the boulder would help cool Andy down. Then Paul took one of his water bottles out of his back pack and poured it into Andy's empty water bottle. Andy had drunk very little since they left the shelter, probably because of the foul taste. When Andy saw him pour water into his water bottle, he said, "I don't want to take your water."

"Andy, I'm pretty sure you're dehydrated. I should have offered you some water before. Don't worry about me because I'm going to show you something miraculous." Paul put his empty water bottle back in his pack and waited about a minute, while Andy just sat there with a deer in the headlights sort of look. When Paul took it out again his water bottle was full. Paul took Andy's other water bottle which still had the foul water in it and poured it out; then he poured new water from his bottle into Andy's and then returned his empty bottle to his pack. Then he left it in the backpack about a minute and when he took it out again it was full.

The look on Andy's face was one of amazement. "How is that possible?"

"The simple answer is that anything is possible for God. He has blessed me on this trip with a lot of help and at times when I needed it most. Now drink some more water we need to get you re-hydrated; you don't have to worry about the water because it won't run out."

Andy drank about a quarter of a liter and looked up at Paul who was sitting on the boulder next to his. "You know that explains something."

"What's that? Paul asked.

"I wondered why I never saw you fill your water bottles when I filled mine, yet you always seemed to have water for re-hydrating the food and even brushing your teeth."

"You mean you could hear me brushing my teeth this morning? Paul asked.

"Yes. I was awake when you went behind the lean-to and I heard a noise that sounded like you were brushing your teeth. I thought to myself 'why is he wasting water like that' and then I saw you when you put your toothbrush back in your pack along with your water bottle."

Paul and Andy stayed near the Lemon Squeezer for about 45 minutes, until they were sure Andy was fine again. Paul took out his map and guidebook and Andy said "what are thinking Paul?"

"We're about two-and-a-half miles from NY17 and then Southfield NY is less than two miles from there. We might get lucky hitchhiking and it looks like there is a cheap motel there according to my guidebook; we could share a room for the night and get you re-hydrated and cooled down."

"That sounds good to me, but I hate to ruin your hike."

"OK then, it's settled. We'll take it easy to NY17 and see how lucky we are at hitchhiking."

Paul and Andy started hiking again at 2:30 and fortunately it was mostly downhill. They made it to the road at 3:45 and Andy didn't show any signs of heat exhaustion along the way. They stood alongside NY 17 and stuck out their thumbs.

NY17 wasn't nearly as busy as the New York thruway, which was less than a quarter of a mile away and whose traffic they could hear. When they passed underneath I-87 Paul remembered the number of times he, Laura, and the kids drove down that road from Vermont.

Very vivid in his mind was their rear tire blowing out in the Plymouth Mini-van. He was able to get the spare tire down, but then he couldn't get the flat tire back up in its place. It turned out that the cable was rusted, so it wouldn't crank back up. They had to ride with it in the mini-van to Philadelphia where Laura's dad fixed the tire and the rusty cable, so that they could put the spare where it belonged up underneath the car.

Paul and Andy got a ride after about 15 minutes from a guy in a Ford 150, so that made their backpack situation a breeze. They simply tossed both packs in the back and climbed into the front with the driver. The guy was headed to Southfield which was where Paul and Andy would look for the motel mentioned in Paul's guidebook. The guy dropped them off right in front of the Tuxedo Motel and they got a motel room with two full-size beds. The room was clean, but very basic.

They spotted a restaurant within eyesight of the motel, but they figured they would both shower first and then take a nap before they went to eat. While Andy was showering Paul called Laura and told her about the past two days.

Andy said he felt much better after his shower, so Paul took one next, thinking his shave could wait until tomorrow. The water streaming down on Paul felt good.

He started with the water a little bit warm and then he gradually made it cooler. He wore his underwear into the shower and took them off and rubbed soap on them. Then he rinsed them and wrung them out before getting out of the shower. Paul put his wet underwear over the shower rod when he got out and Paul then went for a nap, but Andy was still on the phone with his wife, Mary.

As he walked back into the room he heard Andy say, "OK let me know tomorrow morning; I'll call before we leave."

He hung up and said "Everything's fine on the home front; how is your family doing?"

"They're fine, too."

After sharing news from back home Paul and Andy took a nap, but didn't set an alarm clock. When Andy lay down he said, "This is so much more comfortable than that boulder you had me lie on this afternoon."

It didn't take long for them to drift off to sleep and they both napped about an hour and-a-half and felt good when they woke up. They dressed and decided to walk to the restaurant down the road.

The restaurant was pretty informal. There was no waitress service, so you ordered your meal and then took a seat. They both went with the same thing, soup, salad, and a bacon cheese burger. The best part of the meal, however, was the Jamocha milkshake.

There wasn't much to do in Southfields, NY, so after dinner they returned to the motel and decided to watch some TV. Since it was a Friday night there wasn't anything worth watching, so Paul recommended they play some word games. Both games just required paper and pens, which they found in their room's desk. While they were playing *Instant Boticelli* the conversation turned to the Mount again when Paul asked if Professor Edwards was there when Andy was a student.

"No. That name doesn't ring a bell. What did he teach?" Andy asked.

"He taught Spanish. I had him every semester I was there, not that I was any good at Spanish." Paul went on to explain how they dropped the foreign language requirement his sophomore year, but he decided to stick with it. Paul gave a brief account of the trip to Spain, sharing the same shower story he told Jack and Trisha in Great Barrington, Massachusetts.

"He was also a man great of faith," Paul said. "I remember that he and Mrs. Edward's went to Mass every day when we were in Madrid. You know Andy, he was the reason I went into the Air Force. I had always planned to follow in my father's footsteps and go into the Navy, but Professor Edward's reminded me that they didn't have a Navy ROTC program at the Mount, but they did have an Air Force ROTC program up at Gettysburg College where we were allowed to enroll."

"What was his Air Force connection Paul?"

"He was a retired Air Force officer. I never found out what he did while he was in the Air Force, but I know he taught Spanish and German at the US Air Force Academy before he retired. He was a great mentor and role model."

They both got tired around 11:00 and went to bed, but Paul got up and turned the air conditioner fan on high because the road noise from the interstate was too loud. The white noise helped drown out the noise and he fell asleep. (803 FK)

They had set the alarm for 7:00, but they were both wide awake at 6:30, so they went to breakfast at the place they had dinner. Then they came back to shave and shower. While Paul was showering Andy called his wife and when Paul came out of the shower Andy was looking at the map and looked up when he came into the room.

"Paul, it looks like it may be a tent night tonight because there isn't a logical place to stay."

Andy laid the map down on the desk and showed Paul what the best prospects were. There next mail drop pick up was in Vernon, New Jersey, which was 28 miles away. Since the post office would be closed tomorrow, Sunday, they could take two days to get there. They decided to see how they felt when they got to Wildcat Shelter, which was less 10 miles from the trailhead.

They went to check out and Andy insisted on paying for the room, just like he had done for their meals. While they were in the lobby Andy noticed a pair of hiking poles behind the desk, so he asked the desk clerk whose they were. The desk clerk said someone left them in their room and they were holding them in case anyone claimed them. Andy asked the clerk if he would accept $30 for the poles and the desk clerk said "sure, it's been over two weeks since housekeeping found them."

Traffic was light out on NY17, probably because it was a Saturday morning; so, they started walking towards the trailhead with thumbs outstretched. Someone did stop to pick them up after about 100 yards because the driver had seen them both at breakfast earlier that morning. From NY17 the trail started to climb and Andy had to stop to adjust his poles. Once they got to the top of the ridge they were doing OK. Andy was about four pounds lighter because he emptied out his water bottles because he could get water from Paul whenever they took water breaks. It was hotter at 10:45 than it was at the same time the day before, so they needed to drink lots of water.

When they got to Fitzgerald Falls, Paul asked Andy if they were named after his family. "No I don't think so," he said, "maybe a distant cousin." The water looked so refreshing, the way it cascaded down. They decided to eat lunch there. They had trail mix, peanut butter crackers, and water. Andy was still amazed at the way the water bottle refilled itself once Paul put them back into his backpack and he had offered to carry one of the two bottles, but Paul explained how they didn't weigh anything either. Plus, he didn't want to relinquish control of the water bottles because they were entrusted to him.

Despite the heat, both Paul and Andy felt good and decided they would try to make it at least six more miles and see how they felt. Paul poured water over his bandana and then put the bandana inside his ball cap and Andy did the same thing because he didn't want to run into heat problems like the day before.

Wildcat Shelter was about two miles past Fitzgerald Falls and they didn't think it was necessary to stop, since they cooled off near the falls. It was 12:55 and the heat was unbelievable; it was at least 5 -10 degrees hotter than the day before. They made it to NY17A at 2:00 and they were tempted to stop, but it was Andy who wanted to continue on. They decided to see where they were at 5:30 and if there was a nice area for tenting they would stop.

At about 4:45 p.m. Andy said, "I don't know how much more I can do today. I'm worn-out and my legs are feeling weak." The duo continued on and all conversation between the two stopped.

"Andy, I believe Prospect Rock is at the top of this section of trail. If we can make it to the top I would suggest camping there. This heat is really bothering me too and I think we will get more of a breeze on top."

Paul was correct; they were hiking up to Prospect Rock and it was marked as such when they got there. The view was great, so they started looking for a place they could pitch their tents well out of sight of the AT. They surveyed the area first to make sure they couldn't be seen from the trail and they found such a spot about a quarter of a mile past Prospect Rock.

Paul and Andy couldn't wait to get their backpacks off and when they did they put their tents up and then took it easy enjoying the view from their campsite. After looking at the view for a while, Paul took out his stove to boil water for their freeze-dried meals. Paul decided on Sweet & Sour Pork with Rice and Andy had Chicken Stew.

They were both so tired they didn't do much talking during dinner or afterwards. Paul wrote in his journal and then asked Andy if he wanted to say a decade of the Rosary. They chose the Glorious Mysteries with each one alternating the lead. When they finished Paul told Andy they probably would miss Mass tomorrow, but not to worry because he had a copy of the spiritual communion prayer. They both went to sleep at 8:45 and it was still light. (820 FK)

Paul got up once during the night to relieve himself and he thought he could see a reflection of some sorts down on the lake, possibly from the light of the quarter moon. Something must have caused a ripple on the water, either a fish or a bird, but it was enough to catch his attention. He went back into his tent and fell back to sleep.

Both Paul and Andy were awakened by birds singing. Paul laid there for a while listening, because it sounded beautiful. Finally, at 6:15 a.m. Paul went outside his tent and Andy was sitting in front of his tent looking at the lake down below. Neither one of them felt like a warm meal, so they just had some de-hydrated fruit and Yogurt covered raisins, which were mushy because they didn't do well in the heat.

They packed up their tents and sleeping bags and loaded then onto their backpacks. Paul looked at his watch as they started down the mountain and it was 7:05. They made good time to the Wawayanda Shelter Cut-off and were now in New Jersey. Paul didn't see a marker telling them they were in New Jersey, but Andy and he were engaged in a conversation about Gettysburg and could very easily have missed the marker. They took a break at 10:45 and filled up on water. It wasn't as hot as the day before, but they weren't going to take any chances on becoming de-hydrated.

They started hiking again after a 15-minute break, figuring they would make it to NJ94 by 3:00 p.m. They talked about what they would do when they got to Vernon, New Jersey. In that it was Sunday the post office was closed, so they would have to wait until Monday morning. Their guide books listed a hostel in town, so they decided they would try that for the night.

Paul and Andy made it to NJ94 by 2:50 and immediately picked a place alongside the road to hitchhike. They decided to try hitch hiking for 15 minutes and then if no one picked them up they would start walking towards town, which was almost two-and-a-half miles away. Just when they were about ready to give up on hitch hiking an RV stopped to pick them up; they couldn't believe it. They were riding in style.

The RV owner was headed to the New Jersey Shore for Labor Day weekend, but a week early. He explained that it was their annual family reunion and he was in charge of it this year and thus the reason for getting there a week early. Listening to the guy talk about the shore brought back some fond memories for Paul.

Paul went to the beach twice while he was in high school and he went with his friend John whose family had a house in Bay Head, New Jersey. It was a huge house, but then they had a huge family when all the cousins would converge on Bay Head for the weekends. John, Paul, and Mike, another friend of John's had the run of the house during the week, so it was a lot of fun. One of Paul's fond memories was lying in bed at night and listening to WABC radio out of New York City. They played all the great hits during those summers of '69 & '70. You could even tell when it was going to storm by the static on the AM radio. The more frequent the crackling meant the storm was getting closer and then it would rain and cool things off. Those were some fun times.

Paul was thinking about Bay Head and those summers nearly 25 years ago when all of a sudden Paul could hear his name. "What?" Paul said.

Andy repeated what he asked Paul, "Where do you want him to drop us off?"

Paul looked out the window and when he got his mind focused again he said, "Here's fine."

They thanked the driver and wished him well at the shore. Then they got out of the RV and started walking to the hostel, which according to Paul's guidebook was two blocks away. The hostel was in the basement of an Episcopal Church, which could take up to 15 hikers a night. Paul and Andy were fortunate because there were only two other hikers. Andy asked the volunteer where a pay phone was and she told him, so Andy found a place to put his backpack and Paul followed suit. They got out of their hiking boots and put their sneakers on and then they went and found the pay phone which was a couple blocks away.

While Andy was making his calls Paul went into a store to get a candy bar and when Paul came out of the store Andy was finished his call. Andy had a big smile on his face. Paul got out his AT&T card and called Laura and the kids. She sounded happy, but when Paul asked her why she was so happy, she said, "I just had a call from a former classmate that I haven't talked to in years." Paul didn't press her for any more information because he really didn't know any of Laura's classmates.

Andy and Paul picked up some food and supplies at the A&P and brought it back to the hostel because the volunteer said they could use the kitchen and laundry facilities. They bought frozen lasagna and salad fixings, plus they picked up some things for breakfast the next morning. During dinner Andy told Paul that is if it was OK with him he wanted to try to make it to the Delaware Water Gap by Thursday night. That would be 64 miles in four days, which would make it 16 miles a day.

Paul said they could try, but added that it was an ambitious endeavor. That meant they would have to be at the post office when it opens at 8:30 the next morning. Andy said that was no problem because he arranged for a ride back to the trailhead, so they didn't have to worry about their time. Three other hikers came in that night which made for a grand total of seven. Paul and Andy joined the other twosome in a game of hearts and they were better than either Paul or Andy. Everybody was pretty tired, so no one was up past 9:30. (830 FK)

Someone walked into the basement at about 6:05 not realizing there were seven people sleeping on the floor. When they realized what they had done, they turned and left again. It was probably a good thing that someone did come in by mistake because the other hikers, who were all headed north, wanted to start hiking by 6:30. However, since it was so dark in the basement no one woke up until that interruption. Paul and Andy continued to lay there for a while since the bathroom was occupied by the departing hikers.

When the hikers left at 6:40 Paul and Andy got up, made breakfast, used the bathroom, and packed. They made a donation to the hostel and made their way to the post office. Their ride, which Andy had arranged, was waiting outside and it was the same guy who had come in at 6:05. Paul wondered if that interruption was planned by Andy.

The doors to the post office opened a few minutes early, so Paul and Andy went right in. They got their boxes, unloaded the contents into their backpacks, and disposed of the boxes in the recycling bin; then they went back outside and got into the Dodge pick-up, throwing their packs into the bed behind the cab. It took about five minutes to get to the trailhead and Andy settled his account with the driver.

Paul and Andy started hiking at 8:47 and it was a nice day; it wasn't hot like the two previous days and fortunately it was a relatively easy trail. There were no big elevation changes, so they made it to County Road 565 by 10:20, which they were both happy about. They both took a water break and each ate a banana, which they bought at the A&P the day before.

The next six miles went as quickly as the first four, but Andy had a problem with one of his hiking poles, so they stopped. Somehow one of the tips came off and when he inspected them he noticed the other had almost come off, too. Andy shook his head and said," Well, I guess that's why no one ever claimed them at the motel." Since it was relatively level Andy figured he didn't need them, so he strapped them to his pack and was ready to go.

At that point the AT practically straddled the New York and New Jersey border. The Wallkill River Valley was beautiful and according to Paul's guidebook the soil there was one of the richest in the nation and it was teaming with wildlife when Paul and Andy hiked through it. When they crossed over Lott Road they decided to take a water break. They were standing in New Jersey, but Unionville, New York was less than a quarter of a mile away from where they were standing.

They started hiking again after about 10 minutes and if things continued as they had, Paul and Andy would exceed their goal. Just as he had that thought, the trail began to climb. Paul figured if he was having difficulty, than Andy certainly must have been struggling. When they got to High Point Shelter it was nearly 7:15 and they were exhausted. There were three other hikers there and they were all headed north to the New York border, so they took their backpacks off, put their sleeping pads and sleeping bags down and then had dinner. Paul was so tired he didn't even write in his journal, but he did say his prayers and thanked God for the day; he fell asleep during his examination of conscience. (850 FK)

There was a fuss during the night because one of the north bounders left some food out, instead of using the bear box near the shelter. They awakened to the noise of the bear bending back the aluminum foil trying to get the food out. They couldn't tell if it was a brown bear or a black bear, but it didn't matter because it was so dark, but they could catch a glimpse of it in one of their flashlight beams. Paul and Andy didn't put their freeze-dried foods in the bear box, but they did put the "real" food in it like their trail mix and candy bars. Paul wondered what would happen to a bear if it ate a freeze-dried meal. Would it have stomach problems the next day? Would they even associate their stomach problems with what they ate? That was the topic of conversation at breakfast about three hours later.

The north bounders shoved off at 7:45 and Paul and Andy started southward about 30 minutes later. This was the 71st day since Paul left the summit of Mt. Katahdin and 70 days since he last saw his family. He really missed them. He wondered how the school year was stacking up for the kids. Theresa was in 8th, Daniel in 5th, and Steven in 2nd. They were making good time and decided to use the showers at the High Point State Park.

The showers were free and it was near a concession stand, so both Paul and Andy had a hamburger, fries, and a milkshake. It felt good to get a hot shower because the shower at the hostel didn't have hot water by the time Paul or Andy got to it. From the time they arrived at the park, showered, and ate it took only 45 minutes. They were on their way by 10:30 and Andy didn't let up on trying to get to the Delaware Water Gap by Thursday.

They passed by the Rutherford Shelter cutoff at about 11:45 and took a ten minute break to drink water. Once they were sure they drank enough water they began hiking again. They figured it was about 7 - 10 degrees hotter than the day before at the same time, so when they took their water break Paul poured water on his bandana and put it under his ball cap and Andy did the same; by that time they were both hiking without their shirts. However, when they stopped for their next break at the Mashipacong Shelter Paul tried something he used to do when he jogged in the south during the heat of the summer. He took out one of his undershirts, poured water on it, and put the undershirt on. What always struck Paul about that, when he did that in Tampa, was that his undershirt would be dry by the time he finished his three mile jog. The wet T-shirt acted like a radiator and he recommended it to Andy, which Andy was eager to try, especially if it worked like Paul said it would.

The initial sensation of the wet T-shirt took your breath away, but felt great after about a minute or so. It worked so well their pace quickened. When their T-Shirts were dry, they did it again. They made it to the Gren Anderson Shelter Cutoff at about 4:15 and Andy thought they should take a break; Paul agreed, but waited until Andy made that decision. Andy took out his map and looked at it while Paul just sat there with his pack off. It felt good just sitting there. Andy looked up from the map and said, "I suggest that we stop at US206 for the day. Then when we get there we can decide on whether we want to stay in tents or a motel." Paul said that sounded good to him and that he actually felt like calling home if they were near a phone.

They completed the three miles to US206 by 5:45 and though the terrain didn't look difficult on the map it was tricky, so Andy tried to fix his hiking pole. To accommodate for the missing tip, he lengthened the pole that was missing a tip. That worked for about a mile or two and then all of a sudden Andy fell. Paul heard him fall, but Andy was walking behind Paul when it happened. Andy was lying there still and Paul was concerned until he noticed Andy move his head and then his arms. When Andy felt sure he was OK to walk again he said, "Well, that settles it, we're staying in a motel tonight. It's my treat."

When the two got to US206 they stuck out their thumbs. Their guidebooks listed a motel less than two miles away and there was also a restaurant nearby the motel. They stood there about 20 minutes before someone picked them up and it was a park service employee who said he was headed to Layton, which was about three miles past Tuttles Corner, where the motel was located. The park service employee dropped them off in front of the motel and continued his drive to Layton.

There were several rooms available, so they checked into the room and Andy said, "I'd like to use the telephone first and it's private if you don't mind stepping outside." Paul thought that was odd, but he went to see what kind of food they had at the nearby restaurant while Andy used the phone.

When Paul got back to the room he asked if everything was alright and Andy said it was. Then Paul called Laura and told her about the past two days and why they had stopped for the night. Paul assured her that Andy was OK with just some minor scrapes and bruises. Paul talked with the kids very briefly because they were on their way out the door to CCD. He asked about his next mail drop and verified that it was in Delaware Water Gap, Pennsylvania.

After Paul hung up he and Andy went to the restaurant down the street where they both had salad, Rib Eye steaks and baked potatoes. Andy let Paul pay since he insisted that he had to pay for something, sometime. After dinner they walked back to the motel and found something to watch on the TV; Paul wrote in his journal while they watched TV. Paul caught up for the day before when he was too tired to write. Andy fell asleep before the show was over, so Paul got up to use the bathroom and turned off the TV before going to bed. (866 FK)

The alarm went off at 6:30 a.m. and Andy reached it first. Paul was in the midst of a dream and was sorry he couldn't finish it. They decided to shower and shave after they ate, but Andy asked Paul to go to the restaurant and order for him and he would be along shortly. Paul did as Andy asked; he walked across the street to the restaurant and asked for a table for two. Then he ordered two of the omelet specials, which was a Greek omelet with bacon and a side order of hash browns.

Andy came through the door about two minutes before the waitress brought their order out and it was perfect timing on Andy's part. During breakfast the conversation centered on the Mount and some of the lessons they learned there and whether either of them had any regrets. Andy had no complaints, but regretted that none of his kids went there. Paul said he had a couple regrets, the first of which was his not sticking with the Glee Club.

Paul told Andy that he and the Glee Club director had a falling out midway through Paul's sophomore year and he had to choose between going to Spain or going on a cruise with the Glee Club. Since Andy already knew that Paul chose the trip to Spain, he asked

"And what were your other regrets?"

"I regret not being able to explain our faith better."

"I don't understand what you mean," said Andy.

"You know all those Philosophy and Theology classes we had to take at the Mount?" Andy nodded. "Well I can't articulate that information and put it into words to explain the Catholic Faith. All those books and papers we read on Augustine, Aquinas, Aristotle, Plato and others I can't explain to others the core of the faith."

"Paul I see what you mean. I think what you lack in being able to explain the faith you make up for in action. I believe it was St. Francis of Assisi who said something to the effect, 'preach always and if you have to, use words.' I wouldn't sell yourself short, and as my father used to say "deeds matter more than words.""

After some peach pie a la mode, for both, they returned to the motel to shave, shower and pack. Andy picked up the tab for everything which Paul was thankful for. Someone leaving the motel at the same time as Paul and Andy offered them a ride to the trailhead.

It was 8:45 when they started hiking. Paul asked if Andy wanted to use his hiking poles and Andy said he would try it without them for a while. The trail was on top of a ridge for the most part and they walked single file, so as not to cause the other to fall. Paul was fortunate that he didn't get taken out by Andy when he fell the day before. Paul was surprised at how beautiful New Jersey was, at least that part of New Jersey. Instead of skyscrapers, cars, and pollution it was unspoiled. Andy had commented on that very same thing the day before when they were straddling the New York border.

They were making good time and they both felt strong and they made it to Rock shelter by 1:15. Rock shelter wasn't the name of an AT shelter, but had to do with the Native Americans who lived there some 5,000 years before; at least that's what the sign said. Andy took out his map, so Paul knew that Andy was about to make a suggestion on where they should stay the night. He didn't make a suggestion, though; he just folded the map back up and put it in his front pocket. They began hiking again after about 30 minutes and after another 45 minutes Andy said, "Paul, I think I'd like to stay the night at the Mohican Outdoor Center. I don't know if you've ever heard of it, but it's run by the AMC, and I've always been curious about it. They occasionally run some interesting outdoor programs there."

"OK Andy, that's fine with me," he said.

They hiked along for the next five or six miles talking about camping and backpacking. Andy shared a story about him and his family renting an RV for a family vacation one year and going all the way to the Grand Canyon in Arizona. Andy looked over at Paul and said his wife said she would only go camping if it was in an RV.

So, there they were at Cortes, Colorado and the RV caught on fire. Andy said it happened so fast they lost almost everything they had brought with them except for what they could grab as they exited the RV. He said the people of the town were very friendly and it was the people from the Catholic Church there that put them up and fed them; however they did have difficulty with the RV company. However, the RV company changed their tune when another RV like theirs caught fire up in Wyoming the next day and so then the company was very accommodating. Andy said the bright spot of the fire was that they got to see Mesa Verde.

Andy said they never would have seen it if it weren't for the RV fire in Cortes, Colorado. Paul asked what Mesa Verde was and Andy told him it was an amazing Indian cliff dwelling civilization that up and vanished at about the same time Christopher Columbus discovered America.

Then Andy shared a story about when he and his oldest son went to Alaska. They were camping along the side of a river and looked out their tent one morning to see a mother Grizzly and her two cubs. They quietly put the zipper back up and lay down without making any noise. They could hear some sniffing outside the tent, but didn't dare check to see which one of the bears it was. About an hour after hearing the sniffing sounds they looked outside the tent and the mother bear and her cubs were gone.

Paul shared his story of him and Laura backpacking in the White Mountains of New Hampshire during a blizzard and also the story of the family campout at Disney World. The stories made the time go quickly.

They got to Camp Road, the turn off for the Mohican Outdoor Center, at 4:45, so Andy checked to see if they had anything available for the night. They did. The girl who helped Andy said we would have been out of luck if we had gotten there tomorrow or Friday because of the Labor Day weekend. They were currently offering a first aid course for first responders, so that's who else was there, about a dozen people. The girl said Andy and Paul could eat dinner with the first aid class for $9 each. Andy said that was too good a deal to pass up, so Paul and Andy decided to eat dinner with the first aid class. The girl said dinner was at 6:00.

The sleeping accommodations at the Mohican Outdoor Center featured cabins with bunk beds. Andy and Paul both got top bunks, not by choice, but because that's all that was left. They went to their cabin and unrolled their sleeping bags out on their respective mattresses and then they went to wash up. Andy asked the girl earlier where the pay phone was and he went to make a call, obviously to check up on his ride for the next day. Paul played horse shoes with one of the students from the first aid class and Paul won. When Andy was finished his call he asked to play the winner. It was a close game, but Paul won because he got some great tosses when he needed them.

Dinner was served promptly at 6:00 and it consisted of salad, enchiladas, and pound cake. It was simple, but filling. The first aid students, who all happened to be over the age of 25, were nice folks. Many of them were there for their respective AMC clubs. Everyone turned in at 10:30, but Andy used the phone before he climbed into his bunk. (884 FK)

In that it was the last day of the First aid class the students were up early. Paul looked over at Andy's bunk and he wasn't there, so he hopped out of his bunk to look for him. About the time he finished tying his shoes Andy came back into the cabin. He said he went to check about whether they could eat breakfast with the first aid students and they could.

Paul and Andy went to where they had dinner the night before and they were the last ones to sit at the table. It was family style and the food was already on the table and the selections were scrambled eggs and sausage, hash browns and toast. They also had coffee and orange juice. Since Andy and Paul were last the last ones to eat there wasn't much left, but the server brought out some left over pound cake from the night before and gave them two pieces first before offering it to the first aid class.

The first aid students all got up to leave by 6:55, so Paul and Andy stayed and talked.

Andy said, "You know Paul I've been thinking. The AT will be crowded because of the Labor Day weekend, so why don't you come and spend a couple days in Downingtown with Mary and I and then we'll drive you back to the Delaware Water Gap on Monday."

Paul sat there awhile before he spoke, going over in his mind Andy's proposition. He could visit his brother-in-law in Downingtown and maybe see his in-laws in Valley Forge. He could also do some laundry and maybe break in a new pair of boots.

"OK, but are you sure that won't be too much of an imposition?"

"No. I've already run the idea by Mary and she thinks it sounds like a great idea. I'd like you to meet her. She'll pick us up at 4:30 at the post office in Delaware Water Gap, Pennsylvania. That way you can get your mail drop and not have to worry about that over the weekend. You know, Mount St. Mary's is only about 80 miles from Downingtown, so maybe we can go to the Grotto this weekend."

It was a little over 10 miles to Delaware Water Gap. Paul had always heard it referred to as the Delaware Water Gap thinking it was a recreational area along the Delaware River. However, Paul was mistaken, there was an actual town called Delaware Water Gap, with its own zip code, which Paul discovered when he was looking at logical places for mail drops along the way. Paul and Andy figured it would take eight hours to make the trek, so they left at 8:30 on the 73rd day of his Appalachian adventure.

As they started hiking Paul couldn't help but think of the National Grotto of Lourdes at Mount St. Mary's. As a student he went there frequently to pray and to find solitude. It is modeled after the Grotto in Lourdes, France; at least that's what they say. The grotto was built in that location partly because of St. Elizabeth Anne Seton; she used to go to the mountain to meditate, to pray, and to have picnics, soon after her arrival in Emmitsburg, Maryland. His association with the area around the grotto went back to the summers between 4th and 6th grades. His mom used to rent a neighbor's summer house right next to the grotto. Those were fun filled summers with his best friend. Paul thought it would be nice if they could drive over there sometime over the Labor Day weekend. He wasn't sure if he had ever mentioned his childhood memories of Emmitsburg with Andy, so he did as they hiked along.

They took a break at Sunfish Pond, which was about halfway to Delaware Water Gap. As they started their descent towards the Delaware River Andy asked Paul if he could use his hiking poles because the footing was tricky for about a half mile. However, once they made the descent the trail got wider and they didn't have to go single file anymore. The area was very plush and green and they started seeing some day hikers. Paul and Andy used the rest rooms at the Delaware Water Gap visitor's center before they crossed over the bridge and into Pennsylvania. It was 3:05 when they reached Pennsylvania, so they had plenty of time until Andy's wife picked them up.

The post office was about two blocks from the Delaware River, so that's where they went first. After Paul picked up his package he and Andy got a bite to eat at a café across the street from the post office. Andy cautioned Paul not to ruin his appetite because they would be stopping to eat in Allentown after Mary picked them up. At about 4:15 Andy looked up and said, "There she is. Let's go out so that she doesn't have to park that beast." The "beast" was a large Ford burgundy colored van.

They went outside and Mary saw Andy signal, so she just put the van in park where it was and got out. She ran up to Andy who was taking his backpack off and she threw her arms around him and planted a big kiss on his lips. When Andy finished kissing her he turned and said, "Honey, this is my friend and fellow Mountie, Paul Geary."

Instead of shaking hands Mary gave Paul a hug as best she could because Paul still had on his backpack on. She looked up at Paul and said, 'Hi Paul it's so nice to meet you. Andy has told me all about you and some of your God incidences."

Andy opened the back of the van, so that he and Paul could toss their backpacks in and Andy climbed up into the driver's seat, put on his seatbelt and put the van into gear. Paul was sitting in the front passenger's seat and Mary was sitting behind them on the bench seat, so she could see them when they talked. Paul didn't comment on the van, but it seemed like an awfully big vehicle for just the three of them. They got on PA33 towards Allentown and the conversation turned to the hike. Andy's treatment of his brush with heat exhaustion was embellished a bit, but then again heat does play tricks on the mind. Paul didn't correct him, but he was a bit embarrassed by the way Andy made it look like he would have died if Paul hadn't intervened.

Afterwards the conversation turned to family because Mary wanted to hear all about Laura and the kids. Paul told them the story of how they met at Chanute AFB in Illinois, and then told them about their wedding in Norristown, Pennsylvania. After that he told her about their various assignments in the Air Force and where each of their kids was born. Mary liked the story about Theresa's birth in Naples, Italy, and how it was a miracle that she lived. She also enjoyed the stories of Daniel's and Steven's births and the fact that Paul had been involved in some big way with each child's birth. When he mentioned that Daniel was born on the 25th of March, she said that was her oldest child's birth date as well.

When they got to Bethlehem, Pennsylvania, they picked up US22 to Allentown. Andy said they would stop to eat in Whitehall near the mall. As they passed the exit for the airport Andy looked in the rearview mirror at Mary and smiled. At the Whitehall exit they went north about two miles and pulled up in front of a nice looking diner. They all got out and as they were walking up to the door, Andy said, "We come here a lot when we go skiing at Blue Mountain which is about 12 -15 miles north of here. If you like Greek salads this is the place."

The restaurant was such a popular place there was a 10 - 15 minute wait. The salads looked great, but Paul decided on Pot Roast with all the fixings, plus asparagus and it also came with a side salad. The Pot Roast was good and Paul couldn't remember the last time he had eaten asparagus. Andy and Mary both had Chicken Caesar Salads, which were huge. While they were eating Andy told Paul that when he rejoins the AT, he will eventually be hiking over the top of the Blue Mountain Ski area. In fact, Andy said the Blue Mountain runs very far west and you'll be on it until you get to Harrisburg, where you'll make a turn to the south."

They finished dinner at about 7:00 and neither Mary nor Andy seemed to be in a hurry. When they saw Paul keep looking at his watch, Andy said, "Paul we have to make a stop at the Lehigh Valley Airport to pick up some friends, so that's why we're not in a hurry. Their plane gets in at 9:15. We hope you don't mind."

"No not at all," Paul said.

Andy picked up the dessert menu and decided to have peach pie a la mode and Paul had the same. Mary just had decaf coffee. The pie was good and the vanilla ice cream was excellent. It was Hershey brand ice cream, which Paul; wasn't familiar with. He was familiar with Hershey Chocolate, but not Hershey Ice Cream. Andy insisted on paying for dinner and then they were ready to go. Traffic wasn't as bad on US22 and as when they were on it before and it was only an exit or two before they got off for the Lehigh Valley Airport.

Andy pulled into the parking lot and found a parking space. He tried to back it in, but couldn't manage it, so he just pulled in straight. They walked into the terminal at 9:05 and the plane they were meeting from Atlanta was still on time. By the time they got to the gate it was 9:10 and Paul asked Andy who they were picking up and Andy said it was friends of theirs from Florida. As Paul stood there he started sorting through what had happened the last couple of days, but he didn't think anything more about what Andy said. The plane pulled up to the gate and started to unload.

Paul couldn't believe it when he saw Laura and the kids walk through the door with big smiles on their faces. Tears of joy automatically started to flow from all of their eyes, including Mary's and Andy's. It was Steven who spoke or yelled first, "Daddy, Daddy!" Paul ran over and picked Steven up and then when he got to Laura and the kids he put Steven down and they had a group hug. After the group hug Paul kissed Laura and held her tightly in his arms. Laura then stepped back and asked, "Were you surprised?"

CHAPTER THIRTEEN

Gathering

"You bet I'm surprised! I'm amazed and actually and I don't even know what to say other than I've missed you all so much."

Paul had just figured everything out in his mind, all the secretive phone calls Andy made and the ploy to come to their home for the Labor Day Weekend. He turned and looked at Andy and Mary and by the smiles on their faces they were just as happy as Paul, Laura, and the kids. Paul took his family over to meet them and when Paul introduced Laura to Mary, Laura said, "It's nice to meet you face to face instead of talking over the telephone."

As Paul came to find out, Andy thought the whole scheme up back on the day he was experiencing heat stress. While Paul was showering Andy saw Laura's work phone number written down on the nightstand and thought of the idea. He called Mary and told her everything that happened that day, except for the miraculously filling water bottles; then he told her his recommendation, which was to fly Laura and the kids up to Philadelphia. He left the planning in Mary's hands and she was the one who arranged everything, including their flying into the Lehigh Valley Airport. When Paul asked Andy what he would have done if he hadn't accepted their offer to come to their home in Downingtown, he replied, "I would have thought of something or another."

Laura and the kids traveled light; besides a carryon each, they had two small suitcases between them. After they loaded everybody and everything into the van they drove to Downingtown and it was well after mid-night when they all got to bed.

The Fitzgerald's had a five-bedroom house and all their kids were grown and gone, so Paul and Laura got the guest room with the queen sized bed and private bath and the three kids got the room with the bunk bed and a twin. However, the kids were so excited to see Daddy they wanted to sleep on the floor in Mommy and Daddy's guest room. It was probably 1:30 a.m. before everyone was able to drift off to sleep. (894 FK)

The kids were up first in the morning and realized that mommy and daddy needed some alone time. Theresa took Daniel and Steven back down the hall to the guest room and they decided to get dressed and go downstairs. Mrs. Fitzgerald was in the kitchen starting to get breakfast ready and when she saw the three kids come thru the door she was happy to have young kids in the house again. She asked them what they liked for breakfast and when the kids hesitated Mrs. Fitzgerald said, "Don't be shy. How about eggs and bacon and pancakes with chocolate chips? That's what my grandchildren like when they visit."

Laura and Paul laid there for about 45 minutes and then decided it was time to get up. When they walked into the kitchen the kids were just finishing up breakfast and Andy was walking in from outside with the newspaper. The adults sat around the kitchen table while the kids went out in the yard to kick a soccer ball around. It was decided that the first thing they should probably do was to see Laura's parents, but the Fitzgerald's had yet another surprise.

What Laura didn't know was that Mary called Laura's mom when she knew for sure they would be coming and Laura's parents were going to have an open house at noon on Saturday. The open house was a great idea because they wouldn't have to worry about offending any family members. Mary got up from the table and said, "Paul, I'm going to do a load of laundry, I can do yours also if you'd like." Laura wouldn't hear of that, so she got up and joined Mary and they both worked on the laundry together. When Paul and Andy were done with breakfast they went outside and kicked the ball around with the kids.

Watching the kids have fun made Paul see what he had missed the past two plus months. He wondered how they accepted what their dad was doing. A feeling of selfishness came over him and he thought to himself that he would somehow find a way to make it up to Laura and the kids. Laura and Mary came outside, taking a break from the laundry, and sat down to chat. Both Laura and Mary were laughing, so it was good to see that they got along as well as Andy and Paul did. After about 30 minutes Mary stood up and said it was time to get ready for the day's activities. The plan was to take everybody to Valley Forge, then have lunch in King of Prussia, and then just go back to the Fitzgerald's to relax and recuperate.

The kids enjoyed Valley Forge, especially the people who dressed up like Revolutionary War soldiers. Laura had actually grown up less than five miles from Valley Forge and she had a lot of fond childhood memories from there. Some of her fondest memories were of her Girl Scout group and their leader, who was her mother. They ended up at the visitor center because that's what Andy recommended; he said everything would make more sense if they did it that way, so they did.

On the way to lunch in King of Prussia they stopped at the Washington Chapel, which had a very nice gift shop. Paul had shared with Andy at some time during the course of their hike that they liked to hang little dolls on their Christmas tree from various places they visited. Laura bought two Revolutionary War soldiers to add to their Christmas tree collection. She bought one Colonial soldier and one British soldier.

It was only about a five-minute drive to the restaurant from Valley Forge and it was nice and homey. It was an old Tavern that had a lot of Revolutionary War memorabilia like pictures and guns.

After lunch they drove back to the Fitzgerald's house in Downingtown. It was a relaxed afternoon and since Laura was curious about all the people and events Paul encountered on his hike, she wanted to read his journal. Paul took the kids to a playground down the block while Laura read his journal and Mary and Andy worked on dinner.

When Paul and the kids came back after about an hour-and-a-half Laura ran up to Paul and gave him a big hug and a kiss. Then she said, "You're journal entries are amazing and you need to do something with it when you're done."

"What would you recommend?" He asked.

"I don't know, but I'll think about it," Laura replied.

Paul and Laura asked if there was anything they could do to help and Mary said just to relax and enjoy the kids. It was a terrific dinner; it was a casserole with crab, shrimp, mushrooms, artichoke hearts, and cheddar cheese melted over the top, and then served over a bed of wild rice. Since Paul said he loved asparagus the night before at the Greek restaurant, Mary had those as well and peas for anyone who didn't like asparagus. They all stayed up very late, even the kids. They went to bed at 11:15, but Paul and Laura insisted the children sleep in their own beds down the hall. (894 FK)

Everyone slept in a little later Saturday morning and it was actually Paul and Laura who were up first. They went to the kitchen at about 8:45 and helped themselves to the coffee which had already brewed because the coffee maker was on a timer. Paul walked outside and got the newspaper which was on the front side walk and when he came back in he saw Andy walking out of the first floor master bedroom.

"Good morning Paul. Did you sleep well?"

"Yes, I had a great sleep. We just got up about 20 minutes ago and helped ourselves to coffee."

"I'm glad you did. Mi casa es su casa."

Andy was in charge of breakfast so when he heard that everybody loved Corned Beef Hash, that's what he fixed and just like Paul liked it served with the eggs on top. Laura and Theresa didn't want their eggs runny, so Andy cooked theirs longer. Then at about 10:45 it was time to get ready for the open house at Laura's parents' house near King of Prussia. Providing the traffic wasn't bad in King of Prussia, Andy said it should take 30 - 35 minutes to get to Bridgeport. While the kids were getting ready Laura handed Paul a wrapped gift and said, "Happy Birthday honey."

He unwrapped the present and it was a pair of slacks and a polo shirt which Laura had already washed. 'The waist might be a bit loose," she said, "but I can live with that. You had a little bit of a gut before the hike."

Paul said, "Thank you," and then gave her a kiss. Then he shaved, showered and got dressed and he was the last one downstairs. Laura and the kids looked fabulous and Mary said she wanted to get a family picture before they left. Laura invited Mary and Andy to go to the open house the night before, but Mary said to Laura, "you go have some fun family time and so will Andy and I."

The drive to King of Prussia went well and the Mall traffic didn't seem that bad. Everyone was probably at the shore. When they pulled up to Grandma and Pop Pops there were already a lot of cars parked there, but Pop Pop had saved a parking space in the driveway for the Geary family. Grand mom and Pop Pop were the first to come outside and the kids ran up to Pop Pop whose arms were outstretched and after he gave them a hug, they all went and gave Grand Mom a big hug and a kiss. Laura then hugged and kissed her father and mother and when Paul walked up to his father-in-law and put out his hand to shake it, his father-in-law gave him a bear hug.

When they went into the house several of Laura's sisters and brothers were there. An added surprise was that Paul's brother Bill was there with his wife, Maura, and their mother. Bill and Maura had driven their mom up from Washington DC, but Paul's other brother couldn't be there because he was deployed to Iraq.

It was great seeing everyone and so that Paul didn't have to tell his story more than once, they gave him the chance to tell it to everybody all at once. Everyone, even the kids, sat on the floor and listened as Paul described his experiences. He recounted a lot of what happened on his trip, thus far, but he couldn't remember everything without his journal to jog his memory. Of course he didn't mention any of the supernatural events which occurred along the way, but Laura knew everything and when he occasionally looked over at her, she was aglow.

The open house lasted until about 3:30, but Bill, Paul's mother and sister-in-law left at 2:15 because they had to drive all the way back down to Washington DC. Paul, Laura, and the kids decided to stop at the King of Prussia Mall before going back to Downingtown, so they called the Fitzgerald's to say they wouldn't be back until around 5:30 – 6:00. There were a couple of sports stores at the Mall, so he figured he'd try on a couple different pairs of boots. However, the traffic at the mall was such a mess they decided to skip it.

On the drive back to Downingtown the kids said how great it was to see all their cousins, something that was difficult to do because of where they lived while they were in the military. When they got off US30 near Exton, they decided to go to the Exton Mall to see if there were any sports stores. When they found one, Paul tried on a couple different pairs of boots, but none felt quite right, so they just went into a regular shoe store to see what they had.

The first pair of hiking type boots Paul tried on fit just right; however, to make sure, he walked around the store and even asked if he could go outside to walk up and down some stairs. The stairs were in view, so the sales girl said it was OK. When Paul was sure the boots were right he bought them and even wore the boots out of the store and Paul's cordovan oxfords, which Laura brought from Florida, were in the shopping bag.

Paul wore the new boots because he wanted to be sure they fit right, so that he didn't have the problem he had in Massachusetts. He was glad he got the new boots even if they cost more than he wanted to spend.

It was 5:15 when they got back to the Fitzgerald's and Mary and Andy were putting the finishing touches on dinner. Andy was outside at the grille and Mary was in the kitchen making a salad. Paul went outside to join Andy while the kids went and played with the Fitzgerald's huge Lego collection they kept for their grandchildren when they visited.

Laura stayed in the kitchen with Mary and helped with the salad by slicing cucumbers and carrots. Laura asked Mary about their kids and Mary filled her in on what their five children were all up to. When Mary said everything was ready inside that was Andy cue to throw the steaks on the grille. Andy said he enjoyed grilling because it was the closest thing to camping he could do without leaving home. The dinner was great and Laura told the kids they would have to get to bed because the adults needed some time alone.

After the kids got in their own beds, Paul and Laura came back downstairs and joined Andy and Mary. It was nice just to sit there, not having to worry about what to say or do. The four seemed comfortable in each other's presence. Eventually Andy spoke up and recommended they go to 9:00 a.m. Mass at St. Joseph's and then go to the Mount for a picnic. Paul and Laura said that sounded great, but wanted to help in some way, so Mary said if they wanted they could take care of the picnic lunch.

So, Paul and Laura borrowed Mary's car again and went to the Giant food store which was about three miles away. When they got into Mary's Ford Taurus they were all alone and it was the first time in nearly three months since they had been alone together and their passions were strong for each other; they hurried through their shopping, so that they could get back to the Fitzgerald's. (894 FK)

In the morning the kids came into the bedroom and jumped on mom and dad's bed. It was 7:15 and they were hungry, so they all went downstairs to the kitchen. The kids had pancakes and sausage and Paul had something he really had missed the past two months, and that was peanut butter and apricot jelly on an English muffin. He had two whole English muffins and Laura had a poached egg with sausage. They were finished breakfast by 8:10, so that they could still receive communion.

The kids got dressed while Paul and Laura showered and got dressed. The Fitzgerald's lived only five minutes away from St. Joseph's and they made it to Church with two minutes to spare. That was a pet peeve for both Paul and Andy; they didn't feel right if they were late for Mass.

Paul turned around at the sign of peace to see if he saw any of his Appalachian Companions, but he didn't see them. He wondered what that meant. Did it mean that he wouldn't see them anymore? Did it mean he had somehow fallen out of grace? Or, more importantly did it mean he wasn't doing God's plan? All during Mass Paul could feel something different. It was something he had felt a handful of times before, but he couldn't put it into words if anyone had asked him how he felt; it just felt right to be there at that church at that time.

After Mass, Andy introduced Paul to some of his bother Knight's while Mary introduced Laura and the kids to some of her friends. As they walked to the van, Laura said to Paul, "you know I get a good feeling here." Paul didn't say anything, but he knew what she meant.

After Mass they returned to the Fitzgerald's and changed into more comfortable clothes and picked up the coolers which had the picnic lunch. Andy took US30 west, passing through Lancaster, York, and at PA94 Andy turned south to Hanover. Once they got to Hanover he took PA116 west to US15 south. Mount St. Mary's was on US15, so they only had about 15 miles to go from where they got on route 15. Once they got into Maryland they could see the mountain where Mount St. Mary's was located and when they passed the first Emmitsburg exit they could see the statue of Mary about a quarter of the way up the mountain. Andy passed the Mount and took the first right after the sign for the National Grotto of Lourdes.

When Paul was in college at the Mount he used to walk up the 100 or more steps to the Grotto from the college. He always started to feel at peace the closer he got to the top. He got the same feeling as Andy drove closer to the Grotto parking lot.

The kids hopped out of the van as soon as Laura opened the doors. They were excited to be at dad's college, but even more excited to eat. So, before going into the grotto they found a secluded space for a picnic. There was a tour bus there, so it wasn't as quiet as Paul and Andy would have liked. However, the people were very respectful of the surroundings. After the Geary's and Fitzgerald's ate lunch they went into the grotto and Paul pointed out various things to Laura and the kids.

If, per chance, Paul forgot to mention something then Andy spoke up. As they walked back to the van, Andy mentioned that he goes to a Men's retreat at the Mount the last weekend in July every year. He told Paul it was nice to spend a weekend with men of faith who love the Lord. Andy gave them a quick windshield tour of the campus after leaving the grotto and said, "It wasn't this splendid when your father and I went here. They've built a lot a new buildings and facilities since then."

After the Mount tour Andy suggested they go to Gettysburg and visit a couple of the less congested sites. The two sites he recommended were Devil's Den and Longstreet tower, generally the two places he always took visitors who had never been to Gettysburg. It didn't take long to get there and Andy took the same route that Paul used to drive when he attended AFROTC classes at Gettysburg College from 1973 -1975. Since Andy was driving and he was the host, Paul didn't voice his concerns regarding Devil's Den.

Paul's concern was about something that happened when he was a Cub Scout, about thirty years prior. One of the scouts from his den fell off one of the huge boulders and cracked his skull. His friend never seemed quite right after that incident, so instead of saying anything Paul would have to be more vigilant while his kids were climbing on the boulders. After an incident free trip to Devil's Den, they drove to Longstreet Tower and walked up the stairs.

The walk to the top was tough for anyone not in shape because it was about 121 steps to the top and for anyone who was scared of heights the look down could be intimidating. However, the views from the top were amazing and gave a bird's eye view of the battlefields below.

The kids were worn out after the day's events and the two boys fell asleep before they reached US15 which was about two miles away. Theresa fought falling asleep, but eventually drifted off as well. They got back to Downingtown by 6:00 p.m. and were surprised to see Laura's brother Edward, or Eddy as they called him, and his wife JoAnne waiting at the Fitzgerald's front door. Eddy and Joanne missed the open house the day before, so they decided to drop by the Fitzgerald's with the hope of catching them. Their timing was good because Andy was just pulling the van into the driveway as Eddy and JoAnne were walking up the front walkway to the front door. Mary told everyone she was going to fix dinner and there was plenty if Eddy and Joanne wanted to stay.

It was nice to see Eddy and JoAnne and talk over dinner, but Paul let the kids do most of the talking, because they didn't get to see their Aunt and Uncle very often. It was about 8:45 when Eddy and JoAnne left and Paul had this feeling of sadness come over him because the weekend was nearly over. Laura and the kids flight was scheduled to leave the Lehigh Valley Airport at 3:00 the next day, so they would plan their Monday around that. After Laura and the kids left on Monday, Andy would drive him to Delaware Water Gap. Paul planned to use the first shelter he came across, which was called the Kirkridge Shelter and it was about six-and-a-half miles from where Andy would drop him off.

Paul decided to call Don and Chris to see how they were doing, but there was no answer and the answering machine kicked on after about the 5th ring. Paul left a pretty long message. He told them all about the surprise visit by Laura and the kids and he said he would call next weekend if he was near a phone. After Paul said goodnight to the kids he went to bed. (894 FK)

Paul tossed and turned that night as did Laura. They were both anxious and couldn't sleep, so they laid there and talked about if Paul got the AFJROTC instructor's job. He felt pretty sure he would hear in the next couple weeks if he got the interview or not. He would request the interview around the beginning of October and then Paul would fly back to Tampa about a week before the interview to make sure his uniform and grooming standards were all in order. Paul and Laura lay there for quite a while doing "what ifs" and finally after about two hours of that they drifted off to sleep.

Steven was the first up in the morning and he took a running jump onto mom and dad's bed. Then within about a minute Daniel and Theresa joined in, now everybody was wide awake. Steven said the Fitzgerald's were up and in the kitchen fixing breakfast, so everybody went downstairs. In honor of their last morning there, Mary made Eggs Benedict and pancakes. Paul and Laura said they wished they could stay longer because they felt so at home.

Laura promised to stay in touch with Mary and would come visit whenever she came to visit her parents. After breakfast everybody went to pack and Paul gave Laura his journal for safe keeping. He would start a new composition book/journal at the Kirkridge Shelter. When they were ready to leave Andy just happened to check on traffic and the news wasn't good.

The Northeast extension of the Pennsylvania Turnpike was closed because of a terrible accident. A fuel truck caught on fire when it was rear ended by a Jeep Wrangler, at least they think it was a Jeep Wrangler. The fire was so bad they decided to let the fire burn itself out. The turnpike would be closed for at least three hours, but maybe longer. When Andy heard that he said they should leave right away; he knew another route to Allentown, but it would take significantly longer.

They left the Fitzgerald's at 11:45 and went up Route 100 towards Pottstown. It was a nice drive through Chester County and when they crossed over the Schuylkill River they were in Montgomery County. The drive north of Pottstown was pretty and the traffic coming south was heavy, obviously re-routed from the Pennsylvania Turnpike. Once they crossed under the northeast extension the traffic lessened somewhat. Andy said they should stop to eat in Emmaus, so they did.

At 1:15 Andy said they should finish lunch because they still had about 12 miles to the airport and he didn't want to take any chances of Laura and the kids missing their flight to Atlanta.

They got to the airport at 1:55, which was later than Andy was counting on. They all went into the airport and walked to the gate with Laura and the kids. Laura thanked the Fitzgerald's for their generosity and hospitality and said she would never forget them. Andy and Mary watched the kids while Paul and Laura said their goodbyes.

When they started boarding at the gate, Paul talked to each of the kids and told them to help mommy. Then he gave them each a hug and a kiss and said it shouldn't be much longer. When Paul and the Fitzgerald's saw them shut the door to the plane they turned to leave; Paul was teary-eyed and all choked up. He turned towards the airport exit and walked out with the Fitzgerald's. Paul was quiet for most of the ride to Delaware Water Gap and when he had his composure back he said, "Andy and Mary this was so nice of you to do all this for us. I feel a bit uncomfortable though with what it must have cost you."

Andy said in response, "Paul I'm glad that I could do it. We've been blessed over the years by God. And now we're blessed with your friendship. So, don't even think like that. Think of it as all the people who you've touched on this trip giving back to you. You've been a blessing to so many people and, you probably saved my life, too. I think you take what happened to me too lightly, but I know I wouldn't have made it without your help. After all, you gave me 'Life Giving Water."

When they got to Delaware Water Gap Andy stopped the van. Paul thanked both of them for about the 50th time and opened his door. He got out of the van and walked to the back to get his backpack. Andy and Mary got out of the van as well and walked around to where Paul was to say their goodbyes. Andy gave Paul a bear hug and a handshake and then Mary gave Paul a hug and a kiss on his cheek.

Wearing his new boots now, Paul started hiking at 4:15 p.m. on the 4th of September 1995. It was the 78th day of Paul's Appalachian Adventure, providing he didn't miscalculate the days. The long weekend really threw his miles per day out the window, but it didn't matter anymore. He would try to make it to the Maryland border and see whether he heard from the High School in South Bend.

Paul reflected back on the Labor Day Weekend and how great it was. He couldn't believe the Fitzgerald's did that for them, regardless of what Andy said. The cost alone of four roundtrip airfares from Tampa, plus all the food, renting a van, not to mention all the planning required was certainly over and beyond what Paul and Laura could have paid. What good and generous people they are, he thought to himself. Most importantly he got to see his wife and kids, plus his mother and brother, plus most of Laura's family. He was glad that Laura's folks had the open house. It had been years since he had seen many of his nieces and nephews and he was amazed at much they grew.

Paul had to stop after about an hour-and-a-half to adjust his boots. He considered putting mole skin on, but upon closer inspection the skin wasn't red or pink where he felt the hot spot. Since leaving Delaware Water Gap he had been climbing ever so subtlety, but enough that he had a good view of the Delaware River. He came to a nice flat space that would have been good for camping, but he decided against it. The day started out cloudy and by late afternoon there was a heavy cloud cover. He wanted the security of a lean-to just in case it rained. He didn't see any other hikers since leaving the water gap, so he figured he might have the lean-to to himself and he made it to the lean-to by 6:45, but he was wrong about being the only hiker there.

There were two north bounders and one of them had a dog. They were cooking dinner, so Paul sat and talked for a while, before getting out the sandwiches Mary packed for him. The north bounders had the same feelings as many of the other hikers he had met and that was that, "I have to finish, I have to finish." Paul shared some of his experiences with the two and they seemed oblivious to helping others in need and though they never said it in words he could tell by their tone, like why would you bother to help someone you didn't even know?

He figured that these guys were clueless on what it was to be a Good Samaritan, so he gave up trying to explain. It did rain that night, but not hard and he was glad he didn't have to use his tent. He wrote in his brand new journal before going to sleep. He thanked God for his family and friends and even his two lean-to mates that they would experience the gift of giving. (901 FK)

The dog was up and sniffing pretty early. Paul looked at his watch and it was 5:30 a.m. He felt well rested, but still lay in his sleeping bag with the zipper half-way open. The two north bounders got up about 15 minutes later and they dressed, packed, and were on their way not even bothering to eat. He figured they would wait until Delaware Water Gap before they ate.

Unfortunately, for the two hikers, they may have been ready to leave but their dog wasn't. They called her "Tasha" and "Come Tasha" and she did not want to leave the lean-to. They tried everything to get her to go and couldn't believe that she just wanted to sit next to Paul. He wondered why she was staying; maybe he was wearing something the kids brought that had Heidi's smell on it. He searched in his mind what that could be and he couldn't think of anything.

Deciding to help the north bounders Paul put out his arm and pointed to the two guys while saying, "Go Tasha; go on girl." It didn't work, so one of the guys took off his backpack and got something out of the side pocket. It was a leash.

The guy walked up to Tasha and said, "Come on girl, come on." The dog turned away from the guy and ran in the opposite direction. Paul asked, "Do you want me to try?" He said, "No that's OK. She doesn't know you."

So he went about his business while the guy tried to get the dog on the leash. Paul ate a banana and had a handful of trail mix as he was watching the drama of the dog and her master. He got one of the water bottles out of his backpack and took several swigs and he was happy to see that the water bottles still worked as they had since the 100 Mile Wilderness. Paul had seen enough of the Tasha show, so he put his sleeping pad and sleeping bag back on the backpack. Then he picked it up and set it near the lean-to ledge. Then he sat down in front of the backpack and reached back to put his arms through the straps. He attached the waist belt and stood up.

He looked at his watch and it read 6:43 a.m. He looked at the second backpacker and said, "Good luck" and started hiking southward. He noticed the dog's master just about catching the dog and then the dog would take off. It looked like the dog was playing with him, but by the tone of the master's voice and the profanity that came forth from the guy's mouth. Paul could tell the owner was furious.

Paul got about a half a mile from the hut and he could hear the dog panting from behind. He stopped and turned around and he could see the dog running towards him. Paul waited to see what the dog would do and when she caught up to him she stopped, sat down, and put out her right paw like she wanted to shake. Paul shook her paw and said, "Good girl." The owner finally caught up and said to Paul, "Do you mind not moving?" Paul stood motionless, but talked to Tasha in a calm voice. As Paul was talking to her, the dog's owner put the leash on her. Then he looked up and said, "You are the first stranger she has ever taken a liking to. I don't know what's gotten into her."

He turned around with the dogs leash in his left hand and started to walk away; however, he stopped after about 15 feet and turned around and said, "I apologize for some of the things I said last night. I could tell that you didn't take them the right way." Then he and Tasha started hiking north together side by side.

Paul turned southward and continued his hike. He sensed a presence after about 200 feet so he stopped. Gloria came walking along and when she got to Paul she said, "Maybe he'll have more respect for people now."

Paul was happy to see Gloria and he said, "Was that you that made the dog do that?"

Gloria smiled and said, "Yes."

Gloria walked along with Paul for the better part of five minutes and when Paul finally got up the nerve to ask her why he didn't see Frank, Sylvia, Kevin, Will or her at Mass in Downingtown. She thought about it for a while and said "we thought you could use some time alone with your family. You were in good hands. That's all Paul, don't read anything into it."

Paul nodded his head in understanding and said, "Thank you and thank God."

Then as they hiked towards the next lean-to Paul talked about how wonderful the weekend was; Gloria just listened and from time to time smiled. When Paul took a break at 10:45 Gloria said she had to go, so he thanked her once again.

Paul ate some trail mix and drank some water and then he readjusted the way he had his boots tied. He started hiking again once he was sure his boots were fine and his boots did feel good now, there were no hot spots. He figured he would toss out his boots in the next day or so to lighten his load. He had already tossed out his pair of convertible pants and two T-Shirts while he was in Downingtown and substituted them for ones Laura brought from Florida.

He liked the polo shirt she bought him, so he kept that and he would at least look presentable the next time he went to Mass. He replayed the open house in his mind and thought about how well his mother looked for being 79. In fact, her birthday was on September 4th, and since she wasn't in Philly on the 4th, Paul's mother-in-law made a birthday cake for her and everybody sang her Happy Birthday. She had a smile that went from ear to ear. Paul was glad he called to wish her a Happy Birthday before they left the Fitzgerald's.

Paul wondered how many other birthdays he missed thus far, but couldn't think of any. He would miss his daughter Theresa's if he wasn't home by September 28th. Steven's was right before he left and Daniel's was on the feast of the Annunciation, March 25th. He remembered back to the day Daniel was born in Berlin, Vermont. It was a scary time because the umbilical cord was wrapped around his neck three times. But, of the three children Daniel was the only one who came home on time from the hospital with Laura. The other two kids had to stay in the hospital for several weeks.

Theresa was born while they were assigned in Naples, Italy, and she was born seven weeks early. The US Navy hospital there wasn't equipped to handle preemies, so when she was born early it gave everyone a scare. Fortunately a Navy nurse who was getting out of the Navy stayed so she could help Theresa. Her specialty in nursing school was preemies and she put together an incubator, something the hospital didn't have at the time. Added to that God incident, the Navy Chaplain, at Paul's request came up to baptize her so that she didn't have to go on the Medical Evacuation flight to Germany listed as Baby Girl Geary. So, the priest came up to baptize Theresa.

Paul remembered how when the priest was baptizing her you could see Theresa's vital signs improve on the monitors. The doctors decided they didn't need to send Theresa to Germany and they kept her at the US Navy hospital in Naples. About a year later Laura and Paul came to find out that the priest who baptized Theresa had the gift of healing.

Steven was also born six to seven weeks early when they were in Montgomery, Alabama. The base didn't feel confident that they could take care of a 33-week preemie, so they sent Laura to downtown Montgomery and The Baptist Hospital. Steven was born a few minutes before midnight on 12 June and Paul remembers the doctor asking if they wanted him to wait awhile so they could have a baby born on Friday the 13th. Paul remembers Laura saying back to the doctor, "you've got to be kidding. Let's get this over with." Steven had heard that story so much over the years, about being born in Baptist Hospital, that one day he said, "Daddy does that mean I'm a Baptist?"

All of a sudden Paul found himself flying through the air. When he realized that, he went limp as he was falling and he hit the ground hard. He laid there for a minute and tried Don's recommendation of not moving right away. First he moved his fingers, than his arms, then his legs and then lastly his neck. Everything seemed to work, so he got up. He looked back to see what sent him flying and it was just a small 2"- 3" rock sticking up out of the ground. He would had to be more careful, he thought to himself as he brushed the dirt off his legs and arms first and then his left side where he hit. While he was wiping off his shorts he noticed he tore them. Fortunately they weren't the new ones Laura brought him, but the older pair which he wore when he went up Mt. Katahdin some 79 days prior.

In that Paul tore his shorts from the waist to the crotch he figured he better change into something else the next time he stopped. When he was sure he was OK he continued on, it was 2:45. He figured he still had about four to five miles left to the Leroy A. Smith Shelter. Who was Leroy A. Smith? He thought to himself. He wondered how many of the shelters or lean-to's were named after people who had walked the trail and if anyone could answer that. It didn't matter really, but it was always amazing to him how people keep statistics on various things. Paul's mind was racing and he needed to concentrate so that he didn't fall again. He decided to say a Rosary because he was confident that would keep him safe.

What day was it? He asked himself, because that would make a difference. Of course he could say an entire Rosary which was fifteen decades. Yesterday was Monday, he thought to himself, so today is Tuesday. He checked his watch to verify it was Tuesday and when he brought his arm up to look at his Timex he noticed his arm was bleeding from the fall. He said the *Sorrowful Mysteries* and focused on the pain of it all, the scourging and crucifixion which Jesus received at the hands of the soldiers.

Paul said the "Sorrowful Mysteries" again, but this time he paid better attention to each part of the Passion of Christ. In doing so, Paul was better able to understand what Jesus went through nearly 2,000 years ago. Paul offered up the pain from his fall and when he recited the rosary he actually felt better by the time he was done. He figured it was one of those little miracles that happen all throughout the day.

There was only one other person at the Leroy A. Smith Shelter when Paul arrived at about 4:45 p.m. The guy mentioned that the two springs near the shelter were dried up, so he was on his way to another spring which was quite some walk. He asked Paul if he wanted him to fill any water bottles up and Paul politely said no, he was fine.

Paul took off his backpack and since no one was there he changed out of his ripped shorts. The fellow was gone a good half hour or so, but that gave Paul time to read the logbook which was in the shelter for people to make comments. The entries for the beginning of the summer had various entries mentioning bears spotted near the shelter. The entry for September 1st also listed one.

The other hiker got back from getting water and started cooking his dinner and he asked if Paul wanted any hot water and he accepted his offer. His lean-to mate's name was Chad and he was from Hagerstown, Maryland. He was a thru hiker who got started late, but he was still determined to finish the AT by December 31st, which is his 31st birthday.

He was an interesting guy, or at least Paul found him to be so. Chad wanted to challenge himself at something and he figured this was it. He didn't think of the idea until May and since he left his job with a generous severance package, he figured this was the time to go. He left from Springer Mountain, Georgia, on May 15th and he had averaged about 13 - 15 miles a day. His plan was when he got to the Hudson River, he would take the train into New York City and from there take public transportation to Maine and specifically, Baxter State Park, where Mt. Katahdin is. Since they close Baxter State Park on or about October 15th of every year Chad wanted to get to the top of Mt. Katahdin before the 1st of October and work his way south to the Hudson River. It sounded like a good plan, but Paul shared with him some of the challenges he would face in the White Mountains in New Hampshire.

Chad told Paul he appreciated his concern, but he was willing to face the challenges. It was difficult to reason with someone who was so committed to something and Chad was very committed to the hike.

When Chad's water came to a boil, Paul had Freeze-dried Beef stew for dinner and it was okay. However, it was no comparison to the food he had at the Fitzgerald's the previous weekend. Chad mentioned to Paul that he had to stop early for the day because he tore out a seam on his boots.

Paul asked Chad what size boot he wore and Chad said he wore a size 11, which was the same as Paul. Was this another God incident or what? Instead of asking Chad if he wanted his old boots, he just pulled them out of his backpack and told Chad he was going to throw them out the next day, so they were his for the taking. Chad said, "Are you sure?"

"Yes. However, they'll probably only last you to the Hudson River." When Paul asked Chad what he did before he found himself out of a job Chad said he was a group training specialist. Paul didn't know what that meant, so Chad explained that he was like a motivational speaker who took it one step further. Chad figured that if he could complete the hike in such grueling conditions then he could incorporate the story as part of his motivational talks. Paul told Chad he would pray for him and Chad said "Thank you. I appreciate that." After trading stories with Chad about some of the experiences he had had since he left Mt. Katahdin, Paul went to sleep at 8:55 p.m. (914 FK)

Paul slept great and he didn't see or hear any bears, but it was 5:45 a.m. when Paul heard Chad moving around the lean-to. Paul just laid there and watched as Chad packed his backpack and when it looked like he was ready to go Paul got out of his sleeping bag to wish Chad a safe trip. Chad thanked him for the boots again and shoved off at 6:15 a.m. He said he wanted to make up for the missed mileage the day before due to his boot mishap.

After Chad left, Paul got out his stove and heated up some water for oatmeal and instant coffee. When the water came to a boil he poured some of it over the oatmeal and the rest into his coffee cup. He liked the smell of the brown sugar and when he put the raisins in, it smelled even better. He looked through his pack and couldn't find the creamer, so he figured it was probably still on the Fitzgerald's kitchen counter. He drank it black, something he was trying to do since he started.

As Paul sat on the front of the lean-to with his legs hanging over the edge, he saw two deer pass within about 50 feet of the lean-to. When his titanium spork hit the side of the plate one of the deer looked up. He gazed in Paul's direction and when Paul brought the coffee cup up to his mouth, it was that movement that was enough to scare the deer away. After finishing his oatmeal and coffee he packed up and was on his way at about 7:15.

The trail followed a rocky ridge for about a mile, so Paul had to be careful. The footing was tricky, so he was glad he wasn't in a hurry or trying to keep up with another hiker. He was careful about the placement of his hiking pole tips because he didn't want to fall like he did the day before. The hike became tedious so he offered that up and said a decade of the Rosary, the *"Glorious Mysteries."* After three hours and several Rosaries he stopped for a break. He saw a boulder that looked like a good place to sit, so he went through his routine of taking off his backpack.

He took out the map and looked for overnight possibilities. He was somewhere between Delp's Trail and Little Gap, but exactly where he couldn't tell. Both the map and guidebook were a bit sketchy regarding the area. After about a 30-minute break Paul began hiking again.

Even though Paul didn't know where he was, it was pretty on top of the ridge and he was fairly sure he was on the Blue Mountain; the very same Blue Mountain Andy told him about. He could see a large city to the south and he figured it was either Bethlehem or Allentown. To the north he could see green after green and figured those were the Pocono's. After about another 30 minutes he saw a clearing to his right and it appeared to be the top of a ski area. He took off his backpack, leaned it against a tree, and went and had a closer look.

It was a ski area and he could see the top of the chairlift, so he was at the Blue Mountain Ski area. Paul thought back to when he was eating in the Greek Diner with Andy and Mary; Andy mentioned that he went skiing at Blue Mountain. Now that Paul knew where he was he believed he could make it to Lehigh Gap, which was still about five miles away.

Paul noticed after crossing the Little Gap Rd. the area about a half mile to his right was all brown. There was no vegetation and he wondered why. He stopped and without taking off his backpack pulled the map and guidebook out of the side pocket. He found Little Gap on the map and looked to the northwest. The town must have been Palmerton. He looked in his guidebook and found out that back in the 40's and 50's Palmerton had the largest Zinc mining operation in the world. He figured that the Zinc must have been responsible for everything being brown. Paul had always thought that Zinc was good; after all, he reasoned, they put it in some cough drops. Paul figured, however, that maybe they contaminated the ground water with it, or it was the process of extracting the zinc from the rock that could have made the area void of vegetation.

Paul got to PA873 at 4:55 and he took out his guidebook again to see what was in the area. Slatington, PA was about two-and-a-half miles to the south and that seemed to offer the best opportunities. He was pretty tired from the beating his knees took on the rocks. Paul was glad he was finished with Maine and New Hampshire because he wasn't so sure he would have been able to do that again. He walked along the side of the road backwards, with his right thumb sticking out.

After walking backwards about a half mile someone stopped to pick him up. The guy was headed to Walnutport, but was willing to take Paul to Slatington, about a half-a-mile further. Paul decided to splurge for a private room because he didn't want to sleep in a bunk and after Paul checked in he phoned Laura and the kids. Daniel answered and asked how dad was and then he put his mother on the phone.

Laura started by saying how wonderful the Labor Day weekend was and how generous the Fitzgerald's were. Then she said Paul should call Don Bowser when he had a chance. Don had something important to mention to Paul and even though

Laura knew what it was it would be better coming from Don's mouth. Paul could tell that even though Laura was happy he could also tell that something was wrong. Paul asked how the flight was back to Tampa and she said it was good. Then she told Paul the news that she was trying to hold back. She actually started crying on the other end of the phone, but then she got her composure and told him.

CHAPTER FOURTEEN

Escape

"What's wrong honey? Is everybody alright?"

She hesitated and said, "I lost your journal. I don't know how that was possible because it was in my carryon and I never let it out of my sight. I'm so sorry."

Paul didn't say anything right away, so Laura continued. "I've played it over and over in my mind; where my carryon was at all times and who was around it."

"Well honey," Paul said, "That's OK. I can recreate it, not everything, but most of it. My mother used to say I had the memory of an elephant because I never forget anything"

Laura finally calmed down and put Theresa and Steven on the phone. Theresa told dad about school and Steven told dad about Cub Scouts. After they hung up Paul remembered he didn't ask Laura about the next mail drop, so he called right back. When Laura got on the phone again she said the next mail drop was Port Clinton, PA. Paul said thanks and told her that he loved her so much; then he hung up the phone. He took out his map to see where Port Clinton was and it was 40 miles away.

Paul didn't think he had enough food, so he went to the supermarket to pick up some things. On the way back from the supermarket he passed a diner and decided to have dinner there. He had beef stir fry with a side salad and a piece of peach pie a la mode. He remembered as he was eating his pie that he was supposed to call Don Bowser, so he would stop at the same pay phone on the way back to his lodging.

Paul placed the call to Pittsfield, Massachusetts and Chris answered. She sounded really happy to hear Paul and he could hear her say, "Don honey, Paul is on the phone and he's calling from Pennsylvania."

Paul wondered how Chris knew he was in Pennsylvania, but figured it didn't take a rocket scientist to figure out what state he was in. After all Don spoke with Laura and she would have told him. Don got on the phone and said, "Hi Paul I spoke to Laura and it sounds like you all had a wonderful weekend. I just wanted to tell you something before we got much further into September."

"What is it Don?" Paul asked.

"Chris and I have decided to go thru RCIA and we thought you should be the second to know. My sister Donna, of course, was first."

"That's great Don, I'm happy for you guys. What was it that helped you with your decision?"

"Well, you know Chris and I have always felt a bit guilty about not being connected to any church. We've shopped around over the years, but now we know where we want to be. We really feel guilty because of our children and now that we will be grandparents we want to set a good example."

Paul said, "Did I hear you right Don? Are you and Chris going to be grandparents?

"Yes. Our second oldest is expecting in March. Anyhow, we don't want our kids to have the same halfhearted attitude as us. I think you said on the trail that you heard a quote one time that went something to the effect, 'Life is short, but eternity is forever.' Chris and I have been thinking about that almost constantly and I've actually lost a lot of sleep over it. We began exploring the possibilities and you were a big part of our decision. We are concerned for our children and our grandchildren and we don't want our laziness to be responsible for spending eternity in the wrong place. I just wish we could receive the Eucharist when we are in Rome in December. However, that will make Easter next year a very special and blessed occasion."

Paul was happy to hear about Don's and Chris' decision. They spoke for a few more minutes and Don asked Paul if he had heard anything more about the AFJROTC teaching job. Paul couldn't remember if he had told Don that he was one of the applicants whose nomination package was sent to the high school. So in case he hadn't told Don, he did. Don said he did know that, but wasn't sure if he heard it from Paul or Laura.

Then before he hung up Don remembered something else to tell Paul. He said that he stopped to see the JROTC guys and told them about their encounter over the summer. Don explained that Paul was hiking the AT, but hoped to get a JROTC teaching job in Indiana. When Don finished telling the instructors the story the colonel asked where Paul was, because he had a favor to ask of Don that might have some bearing.

Don went on to explain how every year the JROTC instructor took their seniors on a field trip and this year it is to Gettysburg, Pennsylvania. He mentioned that the chaperone, who normally went on JROTC field trips, had something come up and couldn't go, so the colonel asked Don if he was interested in filling in for the chaperone; if so, he would ask the principal if Don Bowser could go in place of the usual chaperone. When Paul asked Don when the trip was, he said "well that's the thing. It has to be before the new fiscal year and they've chosen September 21st through the 24th. We will actually be in Gettysburg on the 22nd and 23rd. Is there any possibility you'll be in that general area?"

"There's a real good possibility I'll be near there. Don I promise you this, if I'm near there I will spend some time with you guys."

"Yes, I've already run that by the colonel. However, I don't want you to rush things, so if you can't be near Gettysburg, I'll understand."

Hanging up the phone Paul was happy, even though Laura gave him the bad news regarding his journal. He would be able to recreate most of it with the help of his maps and guidebook. Despite that, the news about Don and Chris was great. It was good to hear that they were concerned for their souls and those of their families and wanted to do something about it.

Paul went back to his room and wrote all the news he had just learned in his new journal. He tried to figure out where he would be on the 22nd and 23rd of September and it looked like he would be around US30 and US30 went to Gettysburg. In fact, where US30 intersects the AT is right where Caledonia State Park is and Caledonia State Park is where Paul and Stacy had their first winter backpacking experience. It's about 15 miles from Caledonia to Gettysburg and Paul knew that section of US30 well.

Paul was tired, so he shaved and showered and then went to see where the laundry facilities were. There was no one else in the motel, so he was able to wash and dry his clothes and still get to bed by 9:30. He set his wrist alarm for 7:30 and he jotted down a few more things he thought about while he was doing his laundry. Paul said his prayers and went to sleep. (930 FK)

With the exception of having to relieve himself once, Paul slept through the night. He woke up when his wrist alarm went off and since they didn't serve any food in the lodge, he went to the same diner he had dinner the night before. Paul didn't check out of the lodge because the owners offered him a ride back to the trailhead, so he would go back to the hotel after breakfast. He ate breakfast at the diner and then picked up some things at the nearby market.

He would have loaded up on fruit, but the weather forecast, which he saw when he was at the diner, called for two hot days in a row. He settled for two bananas, some Lance Peanut butter crackers, and two homemade oatmeal cookies. He didn't know where they were homemade, but they looked good.

The owner drove Paul back to the trailhead at 9:15 and he was hiking south shortly thereafter. Paul stopped after about a mile at the George Outerbridge Shelter to take off his shirt and wet his bandana which he put under his hat. Then about a mile past the George Outerbridge Shelter Paul passed over the Pennsylvania Turnpike, though he couldn't see it. According to the sign along the AT, the turnpike tunneled through the Blue Mountain about 500 feet below where he was standing. He stopped to listen, but he couldn't hear much of anything. The hike had gotten repetitive and boring and the 935th mile wasn't as interesting as the first 100.

Paul stopped for lunch, eating his Lance peanut butter crackers and oatmeal cookies. As he was putting his backpack back on his shoulders he looked up in the sky and he could see two helicopters. He could actually hear them first, so he turned in their direction. They looked like military helicopters because of how they were painted. He recognized them as they flew overhead as U.S. Army helicopters; they were headed southwest following the ridge of the Blue Mountain. He waved, but decided they couldn't see him. He continued on, heading in the same direction as the Army Blackhawk's. Paul wondered where they were headed and whether the Army still used Ft. Indiantown Gap.

Paul thought back to the spring of 1975 when he went to Ft. Indiantown Gap because the AFROTC unit at Lehigh University challenged his AFROTC unit to a softball game. It was a fun time, even though they were beaten by Lehigh. In fact, Paul decided the highlight of his junior and senior year at Mount St. Mary's was AFROTC and he wouldn't have traded it for anything. Another memory popped into his head just then. He wasn't sure why it was that one in particular when you compared it to all the fun field trips and such, but Paul thought about the community outreach they did his junior year. It involved painting the floor in the Gettysburg food pantry. Just he and one other student from the Mount showed up and none of the Gettysburg kids volunteered, so Paul and his friend Jeff got a lot of brownie points with their AFROTC instructor. Jeff was the one and only friend from college who Paul still kept in touch with. Jeff got out of the Air Force and flew for TWA before they went under. As of Christmas of 1994 Jeff was selling real estate in the St. Louis area.

"Paul. Paul, please wait up."

Unable to finish his thought about the Gettysburg food bank and Jeff, Paul turned around to see who was calling him. He could see someone, but it took a while to recognize who it was. As the hiker got closer, he could tell it was Tom Michie. What was he doing here? Paul thought to himself.

When Tom got closer he stuck out his hand to shake Paul's hand. Paul in turn put his hand out to shake Tom's, while saying, "Tom, what are doing here?"

Tom was out of breath, so he waited before he answered Paul. Then he said, "Paul, I called Laura a couple days ago to see if she had heard from you recently. She told me all about Labor Day weekend and the fun time you all had. That was great you could all get together."

"Yeah. It was great." Paul said in reply.

"Anyhow, I told her I wanted to talk with you. So, she called last night and told me where you were. So, I got up very early this morning and started driving north. I decided to spend a couple days with you if that's OK."

"That's great Tom. I was just thinking to myself how boring this was all getting. I'd love the company. Where did you leave your car?"

Of all the things to ask, Paul wasn't sure why he asked him that. After all, Tom said he had something he wanted to talk about.

"I left the car by the trailhead."

"So Tom, what's the news you wanted to tell me?"

"Paul, I want to become a priest."

That was an amazing piece of news, but Paul didn't know how to respond. He just said, "That's great Tom!"

Paul didn't even know if that was possible, but he didn't want to burst Tom's bubble. After all, about five or six weeks earlier Tom wasn't even a practicing Catholic. Paul thought about it and asked Tom if he wanted to share his story; so he did.

"When I was at my mother's funeral I had a sense that someone was there in the funeral home. I scanned the room and besides seeing my father and sister, and all of my mother's friends, I saw Frank, Sylvia, and Kevin. They came up to me to offer their condolences. I said thanks and asked how you were doing and they said you were doing fine. Then I looked around the room because there was a commotion of some type and when I turned back to talk to Frank and the other two, they were gone."

"Did you see them again?"

"Yes. However I didn't see them again for a couple of days. After everything calmed down, you know with burying my mother, and getting to know my father again, I had this great desire to go to Mass. I hadn't been since I went with you in Hanover, New Hampshire. I went to the church near my house and besides seeing Frank and the other two, something happened after I put the host in my mouth."

"What?" Paul asked.

"Jesus spoke to me."

Tom let that sink in with Paul and when he saw Paul shake his head like he understood, he continued.

"Jesus said he welcomed me back home and He was so happy for me. Then He said 'I want you to come back into full communion with my church.' Since I didn't know what He meant, I asked Him."

"Did you ask Him right then and there?"

"No. I was too excited. So, I went to Eucharistic Adoration the next night and during Benediction he spoke to me again. So, then I asked Him."

"What did he tell you?"

"He said he wants me to be a priest."

"Did you have the chance to tell him how you felt?"

"No, though I'm positive he could tell how I felt in my heart."

"Well Tom, how do you feel?"

"I feel like my life all makes sense now; I want to strive to become a priest. Jesus told me not to be discouraged because I'll run into resistance and unbelief."

"What do you think He meant? Did He say?"

"No, He didn't, but I went to see my parish priest and I only told him I wanted to be a priest. I didn't tell him what happened and I didn't share anything else."

"What did he say?"

"He told me all the steps to the priesthood and how difficult it is. He said I need to discern whether the priestly life was for me or not and he also said I should pray on it and then if I still thought I was "called" he said he would set up a meeting with the diocesan vocation director."

"I assume you called him back. What did he say then?"

"He arranged a meeting with the vocation director and it's in one week. That's why I wanted to see you, to see what you think."

"That sounds positive, Tom. We need more priests."

"So, Paul, after talking to Laura, it sounds like you've had a lot of neat experiences. She didn't go into detail, so that was one of the other reasons I came in person. I'd love to hear about your trip and what happened after we parted ways at Dartmouth."

Paul didn't know where to begin because a lot really did happen. It would have been easier if he had his journal, but since that wasn't possible he would work his way south from Hanover, New Hampshire.

Paul described to Tom how he ran into Don Bowser and how they hit it off and then he explained what happened to Don on the trail and all about the hospital visit in Rutland.

Paul continued his travelogue with the Middlebury College students and how one of them hurt his ankle. Then Paul talked about attending the funeral in Manchester Center and the decision he made while he was there to teach AFJROTC if he was given the chance.

He continued the account of his journey by telling Tom about the terrible storm and running into Jeff and Ryan and how he stayed with them for two days in Bennington. When Paul realized he left out the part about Will helping him right after the storm, he told him that and what Will requested of him. Next he told Tom about the encounter with the Boy Scouts and all that happened, he even remembered to tell Tom about the fox that walked through camp.

Paul asked Tom if he was a Boy Scout and when he said yes, then Paul told him about the kids working on their Order of the Arrow and what they did.

"Boy," Tom said, "if their Scout leader ever found out, they could forget all about the Order of the Arrow award. Do you know if he ever found out?"

"I don't think so."

The conversation was temporarily interrupted when a north bound hiker stopped them and spoke. "It may be slow going for you guys in about another mile or so."

"Why's that." Paul asked.

"The authorities are looking for an escaped convict."

Tom asked the guy, "Do you know what happened?"

"Not everything, but apparently a guy escaped from some correctional facility near here. Some nicely dressed guys came into my camp last night and asked me for some identification. Then when they were satisfied I wasn't who they were looking for they told me what happened."

"Can you share it with us?" Paul asked.

"Yeah, I guess so. This guy escaped and killed some lady that tried to help him and they think he's using the AT in order to get away."

Paul said, "I saw some Army helicopters fly over about an hour ago; were they involved in the search for the guy?"

"I imagine so. They are pretty sure that he's in this area somewhere; be careful you might get stopped by the authorities and be very careful if you see someone in an orange jump suit."

"Thanks a lot."

Paul and Tom continued on, but neither of them could remember where Paul left off. Paul was pretty sure he left off with the scouts, so he continued from there as best he could.

"Tom instead of telling you everything, I'll just hit the highlights."

"Alright Paul, whatever you say."

"I stopped for a visit with Don Bowser and his wife, Chris. It was a nice visit and then I got started again from Dalton, Massachusetts. I had only been hiking about five or so miles when some guy had a heart attack right in front of me on the AT."

Paul went on to explain what happened with George Murray and his having to go to get help. He summarized that part of the adventure very quickly because he knew he would be coming back to Don Bowser and Judy Murray.

"And you mean Don and George were friends?"

"Yes, they were in the same hiking chapter of the Appalachian Mountain Club looking after the same section of trail. In fact, Don was supposed to go check their section of the AT together that day, but Don couldn't go because of his knee."

"That is amazing and almost unbelievable; it's just too much of a coincidence."

"Yeah, it is. I don't know if I would believe it if it had happened to somebody else."

The right shoulder strap on Paul's backpack was bothering him, so he said, "You know Tom I'd like to take a break if you don't mind."

"Sure Paul, I understand."

So, the two of them stopped at the Bake Oven Knob Shelter cut-off; they took their packs off and set them down. Then Paul and Tom each picked out a boulder to sit on. "You know Paul. I researched that thing about the Pope and St. Mary's Seminary."

"Did I have the story mostly right?" Paul asked.

"Yes. You left out some things, but the gist of the story was right. The rescue dogs were sure that someone was in the chapel and they alerted on the tabernacle like you said. I also researched your story about Claude and the miraculous medal."

"Did I get the right?" Paul asked.

"For the most part, but when you told me that story you kept saying that you weren't doing the story justice. I found a copy of the story at a church in our area with a Perpetual Adoration Chapel. In fact, it was the Adoration chapel where Jesus revealed His desire for me."

There was a quiet period in the conversation, while both Paul and Tom were thinking of something to say next. Tom asked Paul if he thought they would see Frank or any of the other companions and he thought they would. Paul asked Tom why he was asking and Tom said he had to know if Jesus had said anything to them about Tom becoming a priest.

Paul said, "Tom I don't know if they can do that. Your situation is a little bit different than mine, but they said they couldn't tell me God's plan for me. I guess it can't hurt to ask though. I believe that you need to ask God through prayer. You know Tom, I don't know what it means to be called, I'm sure it's different for each priest. However, I read somewhere that a vocation to the priesthood is a providential act. God selects some people in preference to others for the work of priestly ministry and gives them the special graces for its faithful implementation."

"I'm not sure I follow."

"In other words, if Jesus wants you to be a priest, I think it will be pretty clear."

Paul looked at his watch and said, "I think that was a long enough break, how would you like some more water."

"Yes please. Do the bottles still fill up?"

"Yes they do."

Paul and Tom started hiking again and Tom wanted Paul to continue recounting his Appalachian adventure. Tom said, "You were telling me about George Murray and getting a ride back to the trailhead from the police officer."

"Yeah. Let's see, skipping ahead a couple of days I ended up in Great Barrington, Massachusetts on a Saturday night and had to wait until Monday to get my mail drop. I called Don Bowser and he asked if he could come down for lunch, so was I ever surprised when Don, Chris, and George Murray's wife all showed up. That's when I found out that Don and George were hiking buddies."

"So, why was George Murray's wife with them?"

"That's what I was wondering, so was I ever stunned to find out that that they hadn't had the funeral yet and she asked if I would come to the funeral."

"What did you say?"

"I said yes."

"Wow. That was a nice thing for you to do."

Paul finished telling the story of George's funeral and getting to meet Don's sister and how great she was. He skipped down to getting to Kent, Connecticut, and how he found a place to stay with Tobias. He told Tom all about Tobias having a heart attack right before Mass and what he did afterwards to help out the priest and Tobias' son. Next he shared what was in Laura's dreams and how she gave him Tobias' Knights of Columbus Rosary beads as a result of her dreams.

From Kent Paul told Tom about meeting Gloria and Kevin again and how they drove Paul down to where his aunt and uncle used to live. Paul told him how God, through Kevin, let him re-live a lot of his fond childhood memories spent on Candlewood Lake. While he was telling that to Tom, Tom kept saying, "Unbelievable, that is unbelievable."

Then he told Tom about how he met Andy Fitzgerald. He shared the story of staying at the Graymoor Spirituality Center with the Franciscans and sharing a meal with students from the Franciscan University of Steubenville.

"You know Tom, one of the kids from Steubenville went to my high school in Washington DC and then I discovered that Andy went to my college Alma Mater, Mount St. Mary's."

"You guys must have had a lot to talk about, like comparing teachers and dorm life."

"Yeah. It was great," he said.

Then Paul shared the story about Andy's heat exhaustion and how he had to tell him about the Life Giving Water.

"Really, you told him about the water?" Tom asked.

"Yes because he wouldn't drink any of my water. If I hadn't shown him how my supply never ran out, he would have resisted. I guess you can become bull headed when you're dehydrated."

Then Paul gave a quick overview of the trip after Andy's recovery. He told Tom about Andy's plan to get him, Laura and the kids together for a family gathering over Labor Day weekend; it was all at the Fitzgerald's expense. That pretty much brought Tom up to date, but then Paul remembered calling Don Bowser the night before.

"Oh, there was one more thing I found out last night about Don & Chris Bowser. They have enrolled in the RCIA program at the church where George's funeral was. Plus, we may meet up in Gettysburg in about two weeks."

"Who? Don and Chris Bowser."

"No, just Don." And then he told Tom why Don & he might meet up in Gettysburg if everything worked out OK.

Tom looked over at Paul and said, "You have really had a positive influence on a lot of people on this trip. I know if it weren't for you I wouldn't have returned to the Catholic Church. Paul, can I ask you something?"

"Sure, what is it?"

"Do you think I should mention any of this in my interview process?

"Tom I don't know. Don't you think they would think you're crazy?"

"Yeah. They probably would."

"It is pretty unbelievable even to believers. Why don't you ask Jesus in prayer? After all, He did let our paths cross and He let you meet Frank and the other companions on my journey."

"Okay," Tom said.

Paul thought of something he had seen at the Grotto of Lourdes at Mount St. Mary's and he shared it with Tom. "Tom, there is a quote written on the lectern at the grotto that reads, "For those who believe in God no explanation is necessary and for those who do not believe in God, no explanation is possible."

They had hiked about three miles since their break and Tom told Paul he had really gotten out of shape since he hiked last and wondered if they could call it a day. Paul looked at the map and it showed a campsite in about another seven-tenths of a mile, so they decided to stop there for the day.

When they got to the New Tripoli Campsite cut-off they followed the blue blaze marks and the campsite was about another three-tenths of a mile from the AT. There was no one there when they arrived, so Paul and Tom picked the flattest area with the least amount of rocks to set up their tents. It was 5:45, so Paul took out his stove and fired it up. Tom took some foil wrappers out of his pack and said, "Here's dinner, I hope you don't mind. My sister showed me how to make these from her Girl Scout days."

Paul said, "Let me guess; it's a frozen chicken breast, with diced potatoes, corn, and cream of chicken soup."

"Can you read minds now?" Tom asked.

"No," Paul said. "Laura is a Girl Scout leader, and that's one of their favorite meals on Girl Scout campouts. They call them foil dinners." Since they had to use a fire for the foil dinners Paul turned off the stove and started hunting for wood. The fire pit was on the other side of the camping area from where Paul and Tom put their tents, so they didn't have to worry about smoke blowing their way.

They weren't sure how long the foil dinners would take once they got the fire started, so they just threw them in and sat down on some logs. Paul set his alarm clock to go off at 6:45 p.m.; that would give the chicken 35 minutes to cook and then they would check them to see how they were. While they were sitting on the logs watching the fire, Paul asked Tom about his sister.

Tom said his sister was a couple years younger than him and her name was Denice. He said she was married with two young boys. Her husband is away a lot because of his job, so Tom said he tries to help her out wherever he can. Tom said she's a good mother and was interested in Tom's conversion experience.

Tom told Paul that he believes that even if he doesn't get accepted into the seminary, she will probably follow his lead by coming home to the Catholic Church. Just as Tom finished telling Paul about Denice and his two nephews someone walked into camp. The guy walked right up to Paul and Tom and introduced himself.

"I'm Sheriff Johnson with the Lehigh Valley Sheriff's office and I'm looking for this man," and he showed Paul and Tom a picture of a man dressed in an Orange Jump suit. "He was on a correctional road crew and he escaped and killed a woman. We think he's using the Appalachian Trail because he knows this area and places where he can get off."

"What can we do Sheriff?" Tom asked.

"We can't force you to leave the area, but for your safety I would highly recommend it. PA309 is about two miles from here and if you hike there we can find you all a place to stay for the night."

Paul looked at his watch and there was still 10 minutes left for the chicken, so he looked over at Tom and said, "What do you think." Tom looked at the Sheriff and said, "Sheriff, how long can we take to pack up?"

"How does 15 minutes sound? I'll wait for you and douse your fire while you all pack up."

"Sheriff Johnson. Sheriff Johnson." A voice was calling.

Paul, Tom, and the sheriff looked in the direction of the new voice. Someone dressed in camouflage clothing walked into the clearing and when the sheriff recognized the guy, he said, "What's up?"

The guy in the camouflage said in reply, "They've apprehended him. We were trying to get you on the radio, but this must be a dead zone. They found him going in the other direction; he was about a half a mile past the Allentown Hiking Club Shelter on the Old Dresher road trail."

Sheriff Johnson turned towards Paul and Tom and said, "Well gentlemen, you will get to enjoy your foil dinners after all. It's a good thing I didn't make a mess of the fire pit. Thanks for your cooperation and have a good night and good hike."

The sheriff and the guy in the camouflage walked off together talking and obviously relieved that the escapee was in custody. Paul looked at his watch and the foil dinners had been in for 35 minutes. Tom found two sticks and pushed the dinners to the outside of the fire ring.

They let them sit a while so they wouldn't burn themselves when they opened them up. The one they opened was done, so they figured the other was done, too. Paul tried his foil dinner and said, "My compliments to the chef."

They sat there looking into the fire and Tom spoke first, "You know I love camping out. I wonder if I can still do this as a priest."

"You know Tom, Pope John Paul II is somewhat of an outdoorsman from what I understand. I'm sure you'll have lots of opportunities to camp."

"Well, that's good to hear."

"Have you given any thought as to whether you want to be a parish priest or in an order?"

"No. I'm ashamed to say I haven't really looked into that. I know there are various orders like the Franciscans, Dominicans, and Jesuits, but that's as far as my knowledge goes. What's the difference?"

"I'm afraid to say that my knowledge isn't much more than yours. However, I believe that they all have been given different gifts from the Holy Spirit for the good of the church. I'm most familiar with St. Francis, who when he offered himself up to God's grace he was given a radical conversion experience and from that experience he knew he was called to live the life of the Gospels; so, the Franciscan order follows St. Francis' example."

"Does that help at all Tom?"

"Not really Paul. I'm wondering what the main difference between a parish priest and someone from an order."

"Again Tom, I'm by no means an expert, but I do know that parish priests don't necessarily take the same vows as priests in an order. I know for example that parish priests don't have to take the vow of poverty like the Franciscans or Jesuits. However, they all take the vow of celibacy. You know Tom, I'm afraid the more I try to explain what I know I only confuse you more. I'm sorry."

"That's OK Paul."

Paul thought to himself a minute and said, "I would like to share a joke I heard one time about three priests who were stranded on a desert island. One priest was a Jesuit, the second was a Dominican, and the third was a Trappist. Jesuits are well known teachers and love to teach, while Dominicans pride themselves on preaching, and Trappists are best known for their solitary life spent in prayer and meditation.

One of the priests was digging in the sand and came across a lantern. When he rubbed the lantern to get the sand off a Genie popped out and said he would grant each of the priests a wish. The Jesuit went first, saying he would love to teach in one of the great Jesuit University's, so the Genie granted him his wish and "poof" he was gone to Fordham University in New York City. The Dominican said he would love to preach to thousands or millions of people and "poof" he was gone to the super bowl in Miami, Florida for the half time show. The Trappist looked around and saw that his two companions were gone and when the Genie asked what he wished for he said "I already got what I wished for."

Tom didn't laugh initially, but then when he put it all together he said, "That's a good one."

There were no other people that night at the campsite, so they figured it was because of the situation with the escaped prisoner. Paul and Tom said a Rosary together and then Paul wrote down a few things in his journal. They both went into their tents at 8:45 and went to sleep. (942 FK)

It was raining lightly when Paul woke at 5:50 a.m. He looked outside his tent as best he could because it was difficult looking out between the rain fly and the vestibule opening. He could see a deer in the clearing; it was eating bark off one of the logs that he and Tom had been sitting on the evening before. As soon as Paul zipped open the screen door to the tent and stuck his head out the deer ran away.

He walked to the edge of the clearing to relieve himself and as he was standing there he could hear the zipper on Tom's tent. He turned around when he was done his business and he could see Tom getting out of his tent. Paul told Tom he would use the small pavilion to set up his stove to heat up some water. Tom joined him at the pavilion and both decided they would eat breakfast and then use the cover of the pavilion to roll up their tents.

Paul and Tom got on the trail at about 7:00 and made the two mile trip to PA309 by 8:00. They ran into four hikers who were stopped by the police the day before when they were searching for the escaped prisoner. The south bound hikers had to camp behind a B&B along PA-309. Paul and Tom hiked with two of the guys until they reached the Allentown Hiking Club Shelter and then they parted company. The two guys told Paul and Tom how interesting it was the day before because the B&B had been set up as the command post for the search. Anyhow, Paul and Tom couldn't keep up with the pace the two hikers set, so they broke off on their own.

About a mile after the Allentown Shelter Paul and Tom crossed over the Old Dresher Road Trail which was where the police caught the prisoner the day before. They wondered why the prisoner decided on that road and after looking at their map they could see why. The Old Dresher Road Trail met up with another road which would have led the prisoner to two or three villages.

The overnight rain made it cooler, so Paul and Tom were hiking well, just not as well as the other two hikers. Paul let Tom test out the hiking poles, so that Tom could see what a difference they made. At first, Tom didn't want to try them, but then admitted the poles made it easier on his joints and lower back. Tom told Paul that he would be going as far as Port Clinton and then his sister was going to pick him up. He chose Port Clinton because that's where Laura told him Paul's next mail drop was. Their plan for the day was to try to go to The Pinnacle, which was about 10 miles from Port Clinton. Even though there weren't any campsites listed for The Pinnacle, there did look like some areas just past there where they could pitch their tents.

The hiking was boring for the next five miles and neither Paul nor Tom could think of anything to talk about. Then Tom asked Paul where he visited in Italy when he was stationed there with the Air Force, so the discussion turned to Italy. Paul explained that his job while he was in Italy was fun because he had the opportunity to visit all sorts of places.

"Did you ever get to Northern Italy," Tom asked.

Paul told Tom where he had been in Northern Italy, saying he liked the Lago di Garda area best. He told him that he and Laura stayed in Desenzano for one of his jobs and he loved it. "Our hotel was right on the lake and it was so pretty in the morning to have coffee out on the veranda watching the little fishing boats with the fishermen out for their day's catch."

"Did you ever get to Verona?" Tom asked.

"No I didn't, but I wanted to. I never took the opportunity to go, which was a real shame when you think about it, because Verona was only about 40 to 45 miles away from Desenzano. I really wanted to see the coliseum there because it is evidently the best preserved coliseum in that part of Italy."

Talking did help the trip go quicker as was true in other cases since leaving Mt. Katahdin. Paul and Tom made it to the Hawk Mountain Road by 2:15 and considered staying at the Eckville Shelter. However, that would have made the next day's hike too long; they continued on towards the Pinnacle, which was still over five miles away. They had covered 13 miles and felt pretty good, thanks to the cooler hiking temperatures.

The map showed that the Hawk Mountain Road was at 535 feet above sea level and the Pinnacle was 1,635 feet. They would have a vertical hike over 1,000 feet, which was nothing compared to the mountains in Maine and New Hampshire, nonetheless it was more difficult than either Paul or Tom anticipated. The difference was the view; it was pretty bare compared to New Hampshire. Paul and Tom both agreed that that particular section of the AT was neither pretty nor exciting.

They took a water and snack break about one mile past the Hawk Mountain Road and during their break two hikers passed by headed north. One of the two stopped to talk while the other continued on. The one who stopped to talk wanted to know where they had camped the night before, so Tom told him. The north bounder looked at his map and said, "I think that might be too far, so maybe we'll stay at the Allentown Hiking Club Shelter. Thanks, though."

Paul and Tom started hiking again and they had a pretty unremarkable hike to The Pinnacle. It was 6:15 when they found a nice even place to pitch their tents. The tents were still a bit wet from the night before, so they set them up to dry out. The view from the Pinnacle was nice; it looked down on farmland. They could see farm after farm, until they couldn't make anything out in the distance. Paul fired up his stove and got some water boiling and about the time the water came to a boil, they thought they could hear voices.

Paul turned off the stove so they could hear better and they could clearly hear people talking, so they went to check it out. About 100 yards from where they were camped they saw another tent. There were two people next to the tent and one of them was lying down on the ground and Tom recognized them as the two hikers they started out their day with near PA309. Something was definitely wrong.

Paul and Tom walked closer and could see that one of the two was lying down and the other one was kneeling over him. The one on the ground was in pain and the one kneeling kept saying, "You've got to be still, you shouldn't move."

When Paul and Tom stepped into the clearing where their tent was set up the guy who was kneeling said, "My friend has been bitten by a snake. Do either of you know what we should do?"

Paul shook his head no, but Tom said, "I have a first aid book back in my backpack and a venom extractor," and at that Tom turned around and ran back to their camp. Paul walked over and looked at the guy lying on the ground and while he didn't seem to be in pain, he looked worried.

Paul asked the guy who was kneeling, "Do you know what kind of a snake it was?"

"I'm pretty sure it was a copperhead. We were setting up our tent near those boulders over there and Jim felt a pain in his calf. He looked down and saw the snake move away very quickly in the opposite direction. It wasn't a rattlesnake, so it must have been a copperhead; the colors were what you would expect for a copperhead."

Tom ran back into the clearing and said "here it is." He was holding up what looked like a zippered pouch. Tom looked up snake bites in the index and turned to that page and then Tom read the instructions out loud and when Tom mentioned that people bitten by poisonous snakes generally had a bad taste in their mouth, Jim said very calmly, "I have that sensation and I also have involuntary muscle twitching."

Fortunately the friend of the snake bite victim did the right thing in lying him down and keeping him calm. They had to get him help, though. Tom's first aid guide said death was rare from one snake bite, but it said you had to get the poison out at which point Tom took the Sawyer venom extractor out of his first aid kit and volunteered to do that. Pete, the friend of Jim, read the directions out loud so Tom didn't make a mistake. However, it was difficult to tell if Tom was extracting poison, because all you could see when he squirted it out was blood. So, with some of the poison extracted, someone had to go for help.

Unfortunately, they were in a very remote area. The nearest road was over five miles back. The map, however, listed a private camp ground about a mile-and-a-half away. Someone had to run to the Blue Rocks Campground and see if there was a phone there to call for help. Pete volunteered to go and he took off running in the direction of the campground while Paul and Tom stayed with Jim to keep him company.

Jim was actually very calm and asked Tom why he had a snake bite venom extractor. Tom said, "You know I've had that thing in my backpack first aid kit for over two years and I was ready to remove it because I didn't think I would ever use it. However, it was a good thing I didn't take it out."

"That's for sure," Jim said.

"Where are you and Pete from?" Tom asked.

"Carlisle, Pennsylvania. It's about 15 miles south west of Harrisburg. Pete and I took a couple days off from work. We're both in the Army and stationed at Carlisle Barracks and we both were going to lose leave if we didn't use it by September 30th."

"Yeah, the old use or lose situation," Paul said. "I'm retired Air Force and I found myself in that situation several times over the years." Tom asked what they were talking about, so Jim explained how the military leave system worked.

After about 30 minutes Pete came back, huffing and puffing and out of breath. First thing he did was ask Jim how he was and then he said they might get lifted out by helicopter, an Army helicopter. Pete said when the campground owner heard that Jim, who was in the Army was bitten by a snake, he said he'd call Indiantown Gap to see if they could help.

Pete chimed in, "They said they would; they said they'd send a Blackhawk and a medic."

The plan was for Pete to go with Jim to whichever hospital they decided to take them to, so Paul helped Pete take his tent down, while Tom talked with Jim. About the time they got the tent and all of Jim's gear packed they could hear the distinct sound of a helicopter. Since the area where Jim and Pete set their tent up had a lot of trees, Pete went to a clearing to try to alert the helicopter where to land. From the time the helicopter landed it took about five minutes to load Jim on board, plus all their gear and get airborne. Paul and Tom wished them luck and Godspeed. Before Pete got on the helicopter he handed Paul one of his business cards and said that if he was ever in Carlisle to look him up.

As the helicopter flew away it all seemed so unreal. Here one minute, gone the next. When Paul and Tom were walking back to where their tents were set up, Tom could see something sparkle in one of the bushes. He walked up closer to the bush and looked closer at what sparkled. He reached down, stuck his hand under the bush and pulled out a Swiss Army knife. It must have fallen out of one of Pete's pockets. Tom handed it to Paul and said "Here, maybe when you get closer to Carlisle you can give him a call. He will surely be missing this, it looks like he's had it a while."

Neither Paul nor Tom felt like eating dinner now, so they both grabbed a granola bar and some dehydrated fruit. They were pretty tired and decided to call it a night at 8:45. Paul and Tom went into their tents and they both wrote about the day's events in their journals. (961 FK)

Both Paul and Tom slept well because it was a much cooler night than the night before and it felt good to actually zip the sleeping bag up part of the way. The thought of snakes being in the area concerned them both a bit, but they were both exhausted and didn't give it much thought. Paul had to relieve himself at first light and while he was standing there watering one of the bushes he could see Tom's flashlight go on in his tent. Then he could hear the tent zipper and he could see Tom's head poke out and he watched Tom as he checked in his boots to make sure nothing crawled in and then he put them on.

"Good morning Tom. How'd you sleep?"

"I slept very well, but I really had some weird dreams. Fortunately none of them involved snakes. How about you Paul, how did you sleep?"

"Great, I slept right thru the night. You know Tom, I was going to go back to sleep, but since you're up, maybe we should get moving."

"That sounds good to me Paul, but I'm pretty hungry."

"Yeah, I could use some oatmeal or something. I'll boil us some water."

After breakfast they packed their backpacks and were ready to go. They left at 6:55 and hoped to get to Port Clinton by 2:00 p.m. It was still nice and cool, so they quickened their pace. They were making good time and keeping their conversation to a minimum. They covered the two miles to Pulpit Rock by 7:15, but the trail was pretty flat. After Pulpit Rock they had two miles of downhill and they made it to the Windsor Furnace Shelter at 9:15. They stopped at Windsor Furnace Shelter for a water and snack break and while they were resting Paul asked Tom how his sister knew where to pick him up. Tom said he told her that they should be to the PA61 trailhead no later than 3:30. "If she's not there I'll hitch or walk to Hamburg."

"What's your sister's full name?"

"Denice Dietrich. Dietrich is her married name of course. You know Paul, we plan to find a hotel or motel in the Hamburg area and stay the night."

"What about her two kids?" Paul asked.

"Her husband is taking care of them for the weekend, so that she can do this. I'd like you to meet her and I know she'd like to meet you."

After a 15-minute break Paul and Tom continued on and by not talking they were making better time and covering more distance. In fact, they covered the three miles to the Pocahontas Spring campsite by 11:00 and they took another water break and looked at the map. They still had three miles to Port Clinton and what stood out on the map was how close together the contour lines were going down to PA61. The closer the contour lines meant the steeper the terrain.

Though they had been going downhill since Pocahontas Spring, when they got to the cliffs above Port Clinton it was reminiscent of the Daniel Webster Cliff Trail between Mitzpah Hut and Crawford Notch in the Presidential Range. Both Paul and Tom were happy they made it down the cliffs without incident and they made it to PA61 by 12:45. Getting there at 12:45 p.m. sealed the deal for Paul's staying the night with Tom and his sister because the post office was closed. He wouldn't be able to pick his mail drop until 7:30 a.m. Monday morning, the 11th of September. The good news was that Denice was there by 1:00 p.m. She said she knew her brother too well and the chances were good that he'd be there early.

Tom introduced Paul to Denice and then they headed the three miles down PA61 to Hamburg. They started looking for motels and there weren't many, so they selected the American Hotel in downtown Hamburg. It was supposedly the oldest existing building in Hamburg; it was a four story red brick building in the center of town. Tom and Denice got a room to share, while Paul got a single room right down the hall from theirs.

Paul called Laura and the kids as soon as he got to his room and filled her and the kids in on everything that happened since they talked last. He told them about Tom, the escaped prisoner, and Jim's mishap with the copperhead and when Daniel heard the part about the poisonous snake he thought that was really cool. When Laura was on the phone alone, without one of the kids listening, Paul told her what one of his theories about the missing journal. Laura told Paul she hoped his theory was right. After Paul hung up with Laura he called Pete to see how Jim was doing.

Pete picked up on the fourth ring and it was his home phone, which he'd written on the back of his business card. Pete told Paul that Jim was alright and that it was probably due to Tom's getting some of the venom out that Jim would be fine. He said he was glad to hear that Jim was doing OK and he would pass on Jim's gratitude to Tom. Pete was almost ready to hang up when Paul remembered Pete's knife.

"Hey Pete. Are you still there?"

"Yes. I'm still here."

"I almost forgot. Tom found a Swiss Army knife in some bushes. Is that either of yours?"

"Yes. Boy, I'm so glad you two found that," Pete said.

"Now I can mail it if you like, or you can come get it from me when I'm passing thru that area. It looks like the AT crosses several roads when I get close to Carlisle."

"OK Paul. How about if you call again when you get close to Carlisle? I'm sure Jim would like to thank you by treating you to dinner somewhere."

"That sounds good to me. I'll call you when I'm in the area."

Paul had time to put a load of laundry in the washing machine before he met Tom and Denice. They were all going to 4:30 Mass at St. Mary's Church in Hamburg, but Denice didn't know that yet. That was a favor Tom asked of Paul.

Tom simply told Denice that Paul needed a ride somewhere and then they would all go out for dinner afterwards. Unfortunately, Paul didn't feel appropriately dressed for Mass, but he would make do. Paul met Tom and Denice in the lobby for the short ride to St. Mary's and that's when Tom told his sister where they were headed and she didn't mind. In fact, she said, "That will be nice."

St. Mary's was an older church building, probably built back in the mid 1800's with many renovations over the years. They walked up the front steps and in through the main doors and down the aisle to the third pew. Tom and Denice were dressed okay, but Paul felt self-conscious with shorts on. Sitting in the pew behind them were the companions, Frank, Sylvia, Kevin, Will, and Gloria. It was good to see them all together and Paul felt a surge of joy come over him when he kneeled down to pray. The church was about three quarters full, so Paul had to scoot over so someone could sit next to him.

An older priest was the celebrant and he appeared to have a deep sense of caring and he reminded Paul of one of his teachers at Mount St. Mary's. During the homily he mentioned the saint whose feast day was the next day, the 9th of September. Paul had heard of Peter Claver, but didn't know anything about the Saint other than his name.

Peter Claver, as it turned out, was a Jesuit who devoted his mission in life to the African slaves in Columbia. In fact, he was so loved and respected by the African American community that they formed an equivalent of the Knights of Columbus and named it the Knights of Peter Claver. The celebrant encouraged everyone to do some research on Peter Claver so as to see another example of how to live a saintly life.

At the Sign of Peace, after shaking hands with Tom and Denice, Paul turned around and shook hands with the companions. After Mass, when everyone filed out, Tom stayed and prayed. Denice kneeled next to Tom and Paul noticed tears running down both their cheeks.

Paul let them stay a while, so he went to the exit and all the companions were standing there and when Paul walked up to Frank to shake hands Frank said, "Paul how would you and Tom like to go to dinner?"

Paul said, "I'd like that, but I need to check with Tom and his sister, but they want to spend some quiet time with the Lord, so it may be awhile."

"That's okay; we understand."

"Frank, can I ask you a question?"

"Yes Paul, by all means. What is it?"

"It's about my journal, the one I've been writing in nearly every day since I started. I gave it to Laura when I saw her last week and she can't find it."

CHAPTER FIFTEEN

With This Ring

"So what's your question, Paul?

"Do you know what happened to it, to my journal that is?"

"Yes. We took it for safe keeping."

"What do you mean safe keeping?"

"We'll give it to you when we think you're ready. I am sorry that Laura got so upset over it. We didn't mean for her to lose any sleep, but please let me interrupt so we don't drag this out any more than necessary. Let me ask you. Do you trust God?"

"Of course I do. I know I can recreate most, if not all, of what I'd written. I just feel bad for Laura."

"Be assured. Everything will turn out alright."

Tom and Denice came out of church about ten minutes later and Tom introduced Denice to Frank, Sylvia, and Kevin, but since Tom didn't know Will and Gloria Paul made those introductions. Frank invited everyone to dinner, so he picked the place and said we would meet at 6:15. The restaurant wasn't far from the hotel, so they decided to drive back to the hotel and walk. Denice asked who Frank and the others were and Tom turned towards Paul to see if Paul would answer. Paul didn't answer, so it was up to Tom to explain.

"They are some friends of Paul's that I met when we were in Hanover, New Hampshire. Frank treated us to dinner there, too."

"Yeah, I remember you telling me you had dinner there, but I was wondering how Paul knows them."

There was a bit of a pause and Tom looked back over towards Paul to see if he would help. He did, but he kept it simple by saying they were people he met along the AT and they seemed to hit it off, just some of his companions along his journey.

When Tom got to the hotel he parked the car and everyone got out. Fortunately, Denice seemed okay with Paul's answer. They would wait to see what Frank or any of the other companions had to say about how they knew each other.

On the way to the restaurant Denice spoke up. "I enjoyed going to Mass again. Besides the funeral, that was only the third or fourth time I've been to church since my first communion. I can't put it into words, but it felt right and I'm glad I went. I should probably start going again for my sons' benefit."

Denice continued, "You know I've told myself over the years that I don't have time for that. Imagine that, there are 168 hours in a week that God gives me. I should be able to devote at least one hour back to Him to give thanks."

211

Tom glanced over at Denice and he smiled. The three walked in silence until they got to the restaurant and both Frank and Sylvia were standing out front. Paul asked Frank where the others were and he said Kevin was inside getting a table and the others couldn't make it. Kevin got a table for six and it was a rectangular table with chairs. Frank said, "Paul why don't you sit there, pointing to the end of the table, and I'll sit here next to Denice to tell her about how we know each other."

Frank stood behind Denice's chair for her to sit down and everyone else took their seats. The waitress came and gave them all menus and then took drink orders, but everyone wanted water. The waitress went to get the water and then came back to take food orders. Everyone decided on one of the specials of the day, which made it easy on the kitchen staff.

After the waitress took their orders Frank asked Paul and Tom if anything interesting happened on their three-day hike together; so, Tom told them all about the exciting parts of their journey, like the escaped prisoner and then a hiker getting bitten by a poisonous snake. Of course, Frank and the other companions knew all that already, but the question had been for Denice's benefit.

Paul mentioned to everyone that he talked with Pete to see how Jim was doing and everything appeared to be OK, thanks to Tom.

"You know," said Paul, "when I was stationed in Alabama a friend was bitten by a copperhead and he didn't fare so well. Though he didn't die from the bite it was like his immune system was all messed up."

"What do you mean?" Denice asked.

"He was always getting sick. It was like his body couldn't fight off whatever he had. However, I'm sure Jim will be a different case since Tom got most of the venom out. At least that's what the emergency room guys told Pete. I'm going to try to see them when I get near Carlisle, Pennsylvania."

"Is that how you'll give Pete his knife back?" Tom asked.

"Yes," and Tom explained about the Swiss Army knife because he could tell by Denice's non-verbal expression she didn't know what he was talking about.

When dinner came Frank told Denice how they knew Paul. She just listened and didn't interrupt, but when Frank finished, then she spoke.

"You know I sensed something different about you guys and when Tom and Paul went up for communion I really wanted to go, too." Denice looked at Tom and said, "I'm glad you asked me to pick you up this weekend." Tom just nodded his head and smiled.

After dinner Frank asked Tom and Denice their plans. They looked at each other and then looked back at Frank and almost as if they were one voice they said, "We'd like to go to Mass tomorrow morning. Then we'll drive back to Lehigh Valley so we can get the other car."

Paul, Tom, and Denice said their goodbyes to the companions and walked back to the hotel. Paul forgot about his laundry, it was still in the washer, so he transferred his clothes over to the dryer. Then he went up to his room and called Laura again to tell her about Mass and the dinner afterwards and his plans for the next day. It was 10:30 by the time he got his laundry and he felt too tired to write in his journal. He set the alarm for 7:30 figuring that would give him time to eat and get ready for Mass at 10:45. Paul turned out the light and said his prayers. He fell right to sleep. (970 FK)

When the alarm went off at 7:30 Paul knocked it off the night stand trying to shut it off and he had to get out of bed in order to retrieve it. He was very happy he slept through the night without having to get up to use the bathroom.

When Paul went down to the lobby he could see Tom and Denice talking to the desk clerk, so he went over to see what they were talking about. When Paul walked up he could hear the clerk say, "Sir, all I know is that it says here that your room is paid for one night, and Mr. Geary's room is paid for two nights."

Tom looked over at Paul and Paul said, "Frank must have paid for us."

"Well I won't argue with that. That was nice of him." Turning to Paul, Tom said "Do you want to eat here or at the diner down the street?"

"It would be quicker if we ate here. I still want to shower before Mass."

"OK, we'll eat here. We've already got our stuff packed and in Denice's mini-van."

Breakfast was simple, but it hit the spot. After Paul showered they drove to St. Mary's and got there early because Denice was hoping there was a priest there, so he would hear her confession because she really wanted to receive the Eucharist. Unfortunately, there wasn't a priest there, so Paul gave her a copy of the spiritual communion prayer that she could say when he and Tom went up to receive communion. Paul looked around the church to see if he could see the companions and they were sitting towards the back.

After Mass, while Frank was standing out front, Paul and Tom stopped to thank him for dinner the night before and for taking care of their hotel bills. Frank said, "It was our pleasure. We enjoyed your company at dinner last night. So are you and your sister going to take off now?"

"Yes, we'll give Paul a ride back to the hotel and then we're going back to get my car where I left it. It was great seeing you guys again."

Paul took a nap when he got back to the hotel and it felt good just to have the day to relax. Later in the afternoon he planned to go to the Weiss Market to get some supplies for the trail for the following day. When he got up from his nap it was 5:15 and he had slept most of the day. On his way to the Weiss market he stopped at the front desk to see if someone could give him a ride to the post office in Port Clinton the next morning. The clerk seemed to think that the night clerk lived that way, so he said he would leave him a note to that effect.

He picked up some fresh fruit and some already made trail mix at the market and went back to the hotel to drop it off. Afterwards he went back to the same restaurant grille where they had eaten the night prior.

After dinner he returned to his room and wrote in his journal and made sure to write about Tom's call to the priesthood. While he was writing in his journal Frank popped into his mind and it dawned on him to call Laura and tell her that his theory was right. She was relieved when he told her that Frank had it for safe keeping, whatever that meant.

After talking to Laura and the kids Paul called the Fitzgerald's, which was something he had been negligent in doing. It sounded like Andy and Mary were doing fine, but Andy was more interested in what Paul was up to. Paul told Andy the highlights of the week and Andy said he missed the experiences, but not the drudgery and pain. When Paul told Andy about the proposed rendezvous with Don Bowser in Gettysburg, Andy said he might like to meet Don if that was OK. Andy said he would plan to take that weekend off, so Paul should give him a call when the itinerary became clearer.

Paul set the alarm for 6:00 the next morning, because the night clerk did in fact offer Paul a ride at 7:30. He figured he would use that hour-and-a-half to shave, shower, and eat breakfast. (970 FK)

Paul didn't have as good a night's sleep as the night before, probably because he took such a long nap and when the alarm went off it seemed like he had just fallen asleep; so he got up to shower and then he got his backpack ready to go. Then he went down to the lobby to see when his ride was ready to go. The clerk wanted to leave right then and there, so Paul had to skip breakfast. The ride to Port Clinton didn't take long and the night clerk was a little bit upset about something. Paul asked him if everything was alright, to which the guy said, "I don't really want to talk about it." When the night clerk pulled up in front of the post office Paul took out his wallet and gave the clerk $10, which brought a smile to his face.

He took his backpack from the backseat, thanked the driver, and went to see if the post office was open. He pulled on the door and it was still locked. He had to wait 15 minutes, so he looked at his map until the post office opened. When the postal clerk opened the door he walked in and up to the counter and asked the postal worker for his mail drop package. When the clerk handed him the box Paul said thanks and opened it right away. He was nearly out of minutes on his AT & T calling card, so the new one was very welcome. A thought came to Paul's mind.

How many minutes has he spent talking on phones since he made the first call from Monson, Maine. He didn't know, but thought that he should have kept track of that, too. There was a cardboard recycling bin near the entrance, so he put the empty box in the bin and headed out of the post office. It was 8:30 by the time Paul got back on the AT and his plan for the day was to go all the way to PA183, which was 14 miles away.

The terrain was fairly even once he made the 1,000 foot vertical ascent from PA61. The 1,000 foot ascent was in the first mile, so after that he would try to quicken his pace, while being careful at the same time. He made it to Phillip's Canyon Spring Cut-off by 10:05, so he took a water and snack break. He had figured out the mileage to US30 while he was waiting for the post office to open and it was approximately 135 miles from Port Clinton.

US 30 is where Paul hoped to meet Don Bowser or Andy Fitzgerald. That meant Paul would have to hike an average of 12 miles a day. Of course that wasn't taking into consideration the possible stop in Carlisle to see Jim and Pete. After about a 10-minute break Paul continued on. At 1:15 he arrived at the Eagle's Nest Shelter Cut-off and a sign indicated the shelter was three tenths of a mile off the AT. Paul decided he was making pretty good time because he had already gone nine miles in about five hours. He had experimented how to walk differently with his hiking poles on the rocky terrain and he felt it made a big difference. He stopped and took another water break and had some of the trail mix Laura sent. While he was sitting there on a boulder he could hear a squawking sound, so he looked up. A huge bird, which he figured was a hawk, was terrorizing a much smaller bird. Was it trying to eat it? He couldn't tell, but the small bird was making a fuss. At least he thought the sound was coming from the smaller bird.

He made it to the Black Swatara Spring cut-off at 3:35 and he was feeling the effects of the rocks on his knees. Perhaps it was the new way he was trying to use the hiking poles, so he decided to use them the way they were intended to be used. He had worked up a sweat, so he slowed down and made it to PA183 by 4:00.

Paul made his daily goal and decided to go a little bit further. According to his map and guidebook there was an old Revolutionary War Era Fort less than a mile further. When Paul got to the ruins of Fort Dietrich, he stopped to read the plaques. One of the plaques credited Colonel Benjamin Franklin for construction of the fort used in the westward expansion and defense from Indians.

He wondered who Fort Dietrich was named after, obviously someone named Dietrich, but that was Tom's sister's married name. Paul started looking for a suitable off-trail campsite to spend the night and he found a nice flat area away from the fort. As he was setting up his tent, it was apparent that other people had done the same thing because there were empty beer cans and some empty soup cans strewn about the area. He collected the 12 beer cans and three soup cans and put them in the Weiss plastic bag which he got the day before. He planned to carry the trash to the next road and place them in one of the trash cans in the trailhead parking area.

After scouting out the area Paul set up his tent and got out his stove. When he got the water boiling he poured the water into the Chicken a la King freeze-dried dinner. He took out his map while he was eating dinner to see where he would cross the next road and PA501 was about nine miles away. It was a long way to carry other people's trash. Paul decided to write in his journal, pray, and go to sleep. He went into his tent at 7:55 and was probably asleep by 8:00. (986 FK)

He woke up at about 11:45 p.m. and he thought it was morning because the light from the nearly full moon made it bright inside the tent. He unzipped the door to the tent and looked out. It was eerily quiet, so he took the opportunity to relieve his bladder and as he stood there he could hear something in the trees. He looked over towards the sound and decided it was just the breeze rustling the trees. However, there was no breeze, so he shined his flashlight towards the noise. When he shined his light he could see two green eyes. He wasn't sure what kind of animal it was and he wasn't that curious to find out, so Paul went back to his tent and zipped the door closed. He listened and he could hear sniffing and panting outside the tent and then a noise as if someone was moving the plastic trash bag with all the cans. Paul laid still and tried not to make any noise. As he lay there quietly he remembered Andy's story of when he was camping in Alaska with his son and there were bears outside their tent. After about 15 minutes he couldn't hear anything and he eventually drifted back to sleep.

Paul's wrist alarm went off at 6:15 and he listened to see if he had any visitors lurking about outside. He couldn't hear anything, so he unzipped the door and looked out. There was nothing around, so he climbed out of his tent. The plastic bag with the trash was gone, so evidently the animal carried the bag off, which included his Chicken A La King trash. Paul thought how funny that was and laughed out loud.

"What's so funny?"

Paul turned around and Will was standing there. "Oh, you startled me," Paul said, "I was laughing because some animal must have taken my trash bag."

"Yeah. I saw it. It was a coyote and it is rabid, so I chased it off."

"Thanks Will. How have you been? I was wondering why you weren't at dinner the other night."

"Gloria and I never met Tom, so that's why we weren't at dinner. We came into your life after that part of your journey with Tom. But, in answer to your question

I've been great. Every day is great. I'll hike with you for a couple of miles if you don't mind. I'm sure you don't want any run-ins with rabid animals."

"I would love the company," Paul said. "This trip is really getting tedious. If it weren't for the adventures and you and the other companions, I would give up."

"Stick with it Paul. You'll find out about the job in South Bend within a couple weeks."

"To tell you the truth, I miss my family and I feel like I've been very selfish."

"I see how it may seem that way, but remember Paul, God writes with crooked lines. It must be part of God's plan for you or I wouldn't have been sent to take care of the coyote. Besides if it weren't for you Denice wouldn't have returned to the church. You see, God is still using you as an instrument to help others. So Paul, trust in God and know that He has plans for you. "

They started hiking at 7:30 and Will carried Paul's backpack. He asked Will how his father was and Will said he didn't know, but from outward appearances he was doing OK. Will said it would be good if he got the AFJROTC job, if for no other reason than to see his father. Paul wondered how the interview process was coming along and decided he would call Janice the next time he got near a payphone. However, he didn't want to be a pest. After all, Janice said she would call Laura if she found anything out.

At 8:30 they reached the Hertlein Campsite and there were still two tents set up. They were going to take a break, but decided not to since their talking might disturb the still sleeping campers. They walked about fifty yards to a stream and found a nice spot to take a break. Paul remembered once before when he took a break that Will took off; he hoped that wasn't the case now.

It was definitely easier hiking without a backpack on his back and he could immediately notice the difference on his knees. After 10 minutes they started hiking again and almost immediately had a series of switchbacks going up to the Shikellamy overlook which gave a good look down at the Hertlein Campsite. When they made it to PA501 that's when Will said he had to go, so Paul thanked him for his help.

He looked at his watch and it was only 12:30. They had hiked nine miles in five hours. Paul didn't think they were going that fast, but without the weight of the backpack they must have been going at a good pace. Paul took out his map, while he rested near the road, to see what the next few miles had in store for him. The William Penn Shelter was only three miles away, but he would still have a lot of sunlight left, so he looked to see how far the next shelter was. Rausch Gap Shelter was 17 miles away, so he would stop at William Penn Shelter and see what strength he had left in him.

Paul continued on after a 15 to 20 minute break. The hiking wasn't difficult, but getting used to the weight of the backpack was. To the north Paul could make out the town of Pine Grove which was probably four miles as the crow flies. There were several overlooks along this section of the trail, but he wasn't curious enough to take the time to look. He crossed PA 645 at 1:45, but it wasn't even listed in his guidebook. The next two miles to the William Penn Shelter were relatively easy, but it was boring, so Paul said an entire Rosary, all 15 decades. At different places, as he prayed, he tried to interject himself into the times of Jesus. Sometimes he was successful, like when Mary walked to visit Elizabeth. He could identify with her pain as she walked the 60 or so miles. Probably the easiest place to interject his surroundings in the Rosary was when Jesus had to carry the cross on the Via Dolorosa to Mount Calvary. He imagined the pain he was feeling in his knees was like that of Jesus falling on His knee under the weight of the cross. When Paul finished the rosary he arrived at the William Penn Shelter cut-off. It was only 3:15.

Paul got out his map again to see if there were any camping possibilities in the next three to four miles. There were none listed on his map, so he decided to spend the night at William Penn Shelter. He walked the last 400 feet down a side trail to the shelter and there was no one there. Since it was a Tuesday in mid-September, he figured he'd probably have the shelter to himself, so he sat on the front ledge of the lean-to and unbuckled his backpack. It felt good not to have the extra weight on his back.

Paul unrolled his sleeping pads and took his sleeping bag out of the stuff sack and laid it out on the sleeping pads. When he pulled his sleeping bag out, something fell on the ground. That's odd he thought. He reached down to pick up what had fallen out and it was a Mallo Cup. How did that get in there? Paul thought to himself. He was sort of hungry, so he decided to have an early dinner.

He saved the Mallo Cup for dessert and hoped the chocolate wouldn't keep him awake. As he took his stove out and was ready to light it, he stopped because he could hear something out of the ordinary. Paul looked around to see what the sound was and finally figured out it was a squirrel making the noise.

He didn't know what the squirrel was doing, but the noise was unusual and something he couldn't put into words. Paul lit the stove and poured water into his aluminum pot. The water came to a boil in about four minutes and by that time he had selected an entrée. Sweet and Sour Chicken would be Paul's dinner on this 12th day of September, 1995. He tried putting in a couple pieces of mango from his trail mix to see if that made any difference and it did. It made it even sweeter.

Paul thought about the Mallo Cup while he was eating dinner and so he opened the wrapper figuring it would be stuck to the wrapper. It wasn't the two patties fell cleanly out of the brown paper holders. That was odd he thought. He wondered how the Mallo Cup got in with his sleeping bag and why it wasn't all crushed. It should have been crushed because whenever he put his sleeping bag into the stuff sack he shoved it with a lot of force. He figured that was another God incident, especially since he hadn't bought a Mallo Cup in at least two weeks.

He sat there enjoying the Mallo Cup and the quiet because the squirrel was no longer to be seen or heard. He sat at the picnic bench in front of the William Penn Shelter; the shelter was unique in that it had a loft. It could sleep a total of 16, though it must be cramped with that many he thought. Paul checked out the loft earlier while he was laying out his pads and sleeping bag because he wanted to make sure nothing was living up there. He figured the shelter was a popular party place on weekends since it was only two miles from PA645.

Fortunately there weren't any signs of partying like he witnessed the previous night. Paul wrote in his journal, and then made sure his trail mix was well secured because the squirrel would surely like it if he could get into it. Paul went to sleep afterwards. The overcast sky made the day and night about the same length and the autumnal equinox was still a week away. (999 FK)

It started raining sometime during the night after Paul relieved himself. Paul didn't set his wrist alarm, but still woke up at about 6:30 from the rain and thunder. He was glad he was in the shelter because the torrential rainfall would have soaked his tent. Since no one else was in the shelter he cooked some oatmeal and packed his backpack in the lean-to. He waited about an hour to see if the rain let up, but it didn't. It was a heavy soaking rain as evidenced by the water rushing down the hill from the shelter. Paul decided to wear his long zip-off pants because the rain made the air it a bit cool and he wore a polyester T-Shirt underneath his poncho. As he was stepping down and out of the shelter he slipped and caught his wedding band on something. It really hurt.

Once he realized what had happened he sought shelter again so that he wasn't in the rain. Paul looked to see where he snagged his ring and he caught it on one of the signs on the shelter which gave instructions to hikers. He looked at his ring finger and it was swelling. The fit of his wedding band was already tight because he put on at least 50 pounds since he got married. But now, he was afraid his finger would swell and the ring would cut off the circulation.

Paul heard someone say, "Here let me put this on it."

It was Kevin who appeared from out of nowhere and he had a tube of something. He squeezed some of the gel out of the tube onto Paul's left ring finger and the coolness felt good. Whatever it was that Kevin put on Paul's finger stopped the finger from swelling any more than it already had.

"Boy, I'm sure glad you came to my rescue. I had visions of losing my left ring finger if not worse. Thank you."

"How about if I keep you company for a while? That way you can concentrate on your balance. You probably won't be able to use both your hiking poles because of your left hand."

"Kevin, I would greatly appreciate that. Thank you so much."

Kevin put on Paul's backpack and they started hiking. The rain kept up and Paul was slipping a lot because the footing was treacherous; however, he didn't fall. At times it rained so hard he couldn't hear Kevin when he spoke and there was no place dry where Paul could get some water from one of his liter bottles without getting everything in his pack soaked. The temperature seemed to be going down instead of up and Paul started to show signs of shivering. When the rain did slow down to the point where he and Kevin could walk side by side and hold a conversation, Kevin stopped. Paul stopped, too.

"Paul. I think you should stay at the hotel in Lickdale and not on the AT tonight."

"How far is that from here?" Paul asked.

"Well, it is three miles to where the AT goes underneath Interstate 81 and then it's about a mile-and-a-half south on PA72."

He didn't want to disagree with Kevin; certainly he knew what was best for him. "OK. If you think that's best," Paul said.

The three miles to I-81 was mostly downhill. The rocks were very slick in places, so Paul was very careful to the point of being ridiculous, he walked like a man of 80 instead of someone who had turned 42 seven weeks prior. They made it to PA72 by 1:45 p.m. It had taken six hours to go the seven miles and Paul couldn't even imagine how long it would have taken without Kevin.

Kevin left Paul once he checked into the Lickdale Days Inn, which was at 2:55. The room was a pretty standard room with two full size beds, a TV, and a desk and chair. The first thing he wanted to do was get out of his wet clothes and take a hot shower. The hot water running over his neck and shoulders felt great, but his left hand was sore, especially his ring finger. He didn't want to get out of the shower, but he did after about 15 minutes. He just wore one of the bath towels around the room while he looked for his AT&T calling card and he found it in the top pouch of his backpack.

Paul called Laura's work and whoever answered said she was in a meeting, so Paul said he'd call back in about an hour. He got some nylon gym shorts out of his backpack and lay down on the bed; since he was cold he lay under the sheet and bedspread. He fell asleep and dreamed he was back in Florida watching Theresa's soccer game. She was the goalkeeper and it was down to a shootout between her team and the opponents and she was overjoyed as she stopped the last shot and her team rushed onto the field to congratulate her. Paul woke up after about two hours and he was disappointed he missed calling Laura back like he planned. He called the house and Steven answered. After Paul talked with Steven he talked with Laura.

"I waited for your call, but had to get home for the kids. What happened?"

"I'm sorry, I fell asleep."

Paul told Laura about the previous two days and especially about the day, with the heavy rain, his wedding band, and Kevin appearing out of nowhere to help out. When he finished talking Laura said she had something to pass on from Janice at AFJROTC headquarters.

One of the three who applied for the instructors' job in South Bend dropped out. Janice didn't know the specifics, but apparently he got another job. Laura said she asked Janice if she knew when the interview might be and she didn't. Janice told her that was entirely up to the school and they wouldn't rush them.

He talked with Theresa and Daniel when Laura was finished. Daniel liked school, but Theresa was a bit hesitant to say. She did say that she was looking forward to the Thanksgiving soccer tournament in Melbourne, so Paul told her about his dream. After he hung up, he went to the desk to ask about laundry facilities. The clerk told him where the washing machine and dryer were and changed a five dollar bill into 20 quarters.

The washing machine was on the same floor as Paul's room, so he put his stuff in the washing machines. Even though Paul didn't have a lot of dirty clothes, but everything got soaked with the exception of the gym shorts and a polo shirt. For some reason the rain cover didn't work as advertised. Of course, the rain was the hardest he had encountered thus far. To play it safe, he washed everything. He had to wait for the dryer to finish before he could go out for dinner and then he went to the front desk to see if the clerk could recommend a place to eat.

There weren't any nice restaurants near the hotel, but the clerk said he was off at 7:00 and he could give him a ride to a fairly nice restaurant if he wanted to wait.

Paul took him up on his offer and discovered on the way to the restaurant the clerk was in the Army National Guard, so he offered to treat the young man, whose name was Jerry, to dinner and he accepted. Jerry told Paul he went to high school nearby and when he graduated he decided to go into the Army. However, his girlfriend talked him into going into the Army National Guard with her. They were both Army medics, so he did and soon thereafter, they broke up. He was currently trying to go full-time active duty because he liked the army and said he didn't want to work in a hotel for the rest of his life.

Paul showed Jerry his left ring finger and told him what happened, that he slipped and caught his finger on a sign and another hiker came along and put some kind of gel on it. Jerry said he was very fortunate that hiker came along because he could have "thrown a clot." Paul agreed that he was very fortunate.

Jerry gave Paul a ride back to the hotel and said he might see him in the morning before he checked out. He asked Jerry what time he started work and Jerry said 11:00 a.m. to which Paul replied he hoped to be gone by then.

The pool was open until 10:00, so Paul decided to go for a swim. He went back to his room to put on some gym shorts and then back down to the pool. He was more interested in the Jacuzzi than the swimming pool, so that's where he went. However, the Jacuzzi was too hot, so Paul could only go in for 5 minutes. Then he went back to his room to shower off the chlorine and after his shower, he wrote in his journal while he watched the Weather Channel. The outlook for the next couple of days looked better; the prediction was for highs in the mid-70's and no rain. Paul didn't bother setting an alarm. (1006 FK)

A door slamming shut woke Paul up. He looked at the clock radio and it said 7:13, so he figured he would go for the complimentary breakfast and then shave and shower afterwards. He went down to the lobby and picked up a free copy of USA Today to read while he ate. It was a limited breakfast; there were just bagels, donuts, and three different kinds of cereal and coffee. Fortunately there was cream cheese and peanut butter for the bagels, so he took a coffee, two bagels and a couple containers of cream cheese and one peanut butter and went back to his room. He planned to save one of the bagels and the peanut butter for lunch.

As he sat on his bed looking through the USA Today and sipping on his coffee, he watched the Weather Channel. Just as Paul turned the TV on to the Weather Channel they were reporting the heavy rain at Pine Grove, Pennsylvania the day before. They reported having five inches of rain in two hours and showed some video of the flooding. They reported that other places in the vicinity had 7 to 9 inches. Paul finished his breakfast and then shaved and showered.

Paul heard the phone ring as he left the bathroom, so he picked up the receiver and said, "Hello". It was Jerry calling and he said he could give Paul a ride back to the trailhead if he could be ready in 20 minutes. Jerry said his manager called him to see if he could come in to work at 9:00 and Paul said that would be great, so he hung up the phone and immediately started packing.

Paul went down to the lobby after he packed; it took him about 15 minutes from the time he got the call. He checked out and went outside just in time to see Jerry pull up in a purple Plymouth Neon. After Paul wrestled his backpack into the backseat, he turned to Jerry and said, "I really appreciate this. I'm glad I didn't have to walk or hitch hike."

Jerry said in reply, "It's only about two miles, but I know how many miles you've walked so far. Maybe someday I'll do the same thing, hike the AT that is."

When they got to the trailhead he thanked Jerry and got his backpack out of the back seat. Jerry drove off and he decided to look at the map, something he should have done before he left the hotel. Paul wasn't complaining, though because he was glad to get the ride. Rausch Gap Shelter was only five miles away and the next one after that was Peters Mountain Shelter which was a total of 23 miles, which was too much for one day.

Paul planned to go to Stony Mountain which was about 15 miles and he would see how he felt. The trail was still muddy and slippery from the rain the day before, so he used his hiking poles since he could now close his left hand around the grip.

His ring finger wasn't as swollen as the day before, something he was thankful for. He hiked at as quick a pace as he could without stumbling on the rocks or the muddy trail. He was dressed in shorts and a brown cotton T-shirt. At 10:45 he made it to the Rausch Gap shelter cut-off. Paul saw no reason to go the third of a mile to the shelter just to take a break, so he sat on a boulder after he took off his backpack.

He drank some water and ate the bagel with some peanut butter. The bagel wasn't as satisfying un-toasted, but he did feel better after eating it, probably because of the protein. After 15 minutes he resumed hiking and his mind wandered to Laura and the kids. He wondered what they were going to do for the coming weekend. Then he thought about the Labor Day Weekend and how wonderful it was. His thoughts turned to whether he would get to see both Don Bowser and Andy Fitzgerald once he got near Gettysburg.

By the time he made it to Stony Mountain, he had prayed the Rosary and sang as many songs as he could remember the words to. It was 3:45 when Paul saw the old coal mines at Stony Mountain and he wasn't curious enough to explore because he still remembered the copperhead, so he looked at his map and decided there was no way he could make it to Peters Mountain Shelter, so he decided to hike a mile past PA325 and see what camping opportunities there were.

Less than a mile after crossing PA325 Paul found a good camping spot and by the looks of it other people had enjoyed it, too. There was a fire ring with logs set up around it and there was even a metal tripod over the fire pit that someone left. Paul had seen similar tripods at scouting events, which could hold a big pot suspended by a chain. Paul decided he would just use his stove because of how long it would have taken to get a fire going. There were also several flat areas for tenting, so he picked one and set up his tent.

The mountain blocked out most of the sunlight at 6:55, so he thought he should make dinner before it got any darker. He got some water boiling and selected Chicken Stew for dinner. After dinner he cleaned his pot and utensils in the stream which was close by; then he decided to have an herbal tea, so he had to start up his stove up again. While he was waiting for the water to boil a red fox walked on the outskirts of the camp. It had a big bushy tail and when Paul shouted "heah," the fox ran off and didn't look back. He wondered if foxes were nocturnal and if not why one was walking through the campsite and then he remembered the fox in Massachusetts. It was also getting dark when he saw that one.

When the water boiled he let the teabag steep a little longer than normal. It was supposedly an herbal tea that aided in sleeping and Paul wanted a good night's sleep because he hadn't slept well at the hotel. He went into his tent at 8:35 and the herbal tea worked because he fell right to sleep. (1023 FK)

Paul woke at 5:40 a.m. and he felt well rested, so he decided to skip breakfast and just have a couple granola bars while he was hiking, so he put his sleeping bag in the stuff sack, rolled up the sleeping pads, and then packed his tent. He was hiking by 6:35 and it was nice and cool, so he set a quick pace. The next 13 miles or so had a lot of ups and downs. He did the first six miles to Peters Mountain Shelter by 8:30 and was pretty proud of himself. He ate two granola bars along the way, but didn't have much water, so he stopped for a water break.

He continued on and was doing pretty good time wise, but wasn't paying attention when he was going down an embankment to cross over PA225; he stepped on a rock and the rock came lose sending him down the embankment head over heels.

He didn't move, remembering what Don did when he fell; he went limp until he came to a stop. He laid there for a minute or so and then moved his fingers and then his hand; his left wrist hurt. He cautiously took the backpack straps off and rolled over onto his knees. Using his right arm and hiking pole he tried to get up. Once he got to his feet he looked at his left wrist to see why it hurt so much.

The first thing he noticed was that his watch was gone. He looked around, but didn't see it. Nothing appeared to be wrong with his wrist, but it still hurt. Certain that nothing else was wrong with himself he decided to look for his watch. He looked around for what seemed like an hour, but was probably only 20 minutes. Finally, he gave up looking and concentrated on his wrist and after a thorough examination he determined he must have sprained it; so, even though he was upset about his watch he was thankful he hadn't broken anything. He thought back to Joe, one of his roommates at Joe Dodge Lodge, who had broken his arm in New Hampshire and he wondered how he was doing. That seemed like ages ago, but was probably only two months ago or less. Paul remembered that Joe was from Pennsylvania, but couldn't remember where in Pennsylvania without his journal.

Giving up on finding his watch he put his backpack on again and carefully started hiking again. He found himself looking at his left wrist from time to time to see what time it was. He planned to buy another watch in the next sizeable town he went through. Paul liked that watch. It was just a Timex, but it was dependable; it had an alarm and stopwatch and some other functions which he rarely used. When he caught himself looking at his left wrist again he started to laugh. He offered up a prayer of thanks that he didn't get hurt and he wondered if there was a Patron Saint for hikers. Surely there must be, there is a Patron Saint for almost every profession and disease. In his prayers of thanks, besides thanking God, he thanked his Guardian Angel. As he hiked along he thought about the beating his left side had taken on this trip. He's had Charley Horses, swollen ring finger, and a sprained left wrist.

Hiking without a watch made the journey more boring because he had no concept of time. What time was that when he fell? He couldn't remember. It was probably around noon, maybe one o'clock at the latest. He would stop at Clarks' Ferry Shelter and see how he felt and if he felt up to it he would go the additional four miles to Duncannon, Pennsylvania. Paul offered up the pain in his left wrist to Jesus, who experienced far greater pain on the cross with the metal nails which were driven through His wrists and into the wood of the cross. When he tried to imagine the pain that Jesus went through, his pain didn't seem so bad.

Paul arrived at the Clark's Ferry Shelter cut-off and was pretty exhausted, so he decided to stop for the day. The shelter was 300 feet off the AT and there was another hiker there. The other hiker had already picked out a spot in the eight person lean-to, so Paul sat on the front ledge of the lean-to and took off his backpack. It felt great to sit down and take a load off his legs.

Paul asked the lone hiker what time it was and he told him it was 5:30. The hiker introduced himself as Mike Vernley.

Paul came to find out that Mike was from Blue Ridge Summit, Pennsylvania, which was about 15 to 20 miles south of Gettysburg. Paul learned more about Mike, too. He met his wife, Georgia, when he was stationed outside London, England. Now he was with the U.S. Army and he and his family love living at Fort Ritchie. They were sorry to see Ft. Ritchie on the base closure list, but he and his family would be leaving in the spring of 1996 before the fort officially closed. Mike wasn't sure where he would be assigned to next.

Mike was also trying to use up some leave time before the end of September, or he would lose it. Paul shared two coincidences with Mike. The first was that his favorite professor and mentor from college lived in Blue Ridge Summit. The other coincidence was that Paul's AFROTC detachment from college held their Dining-In at Fort Ritchie.

Mike asked him who his professor was from Mount St. Mary's and when Paul told him Professor Edwards, Mike said, "You're kidding. It is indeed a small world."

"How do you mean?" Paul asked.

"He and his wife go to our parish, St. Rita's."

"Yes. That's right," Paul said. "He lives directly across the street from the church, so he and Mrs. Edwards don't have far to go. The professor and his wife are very devout. I don't think he teaches at the Mount any longer, so they probably go to daily Mass."

Paul went on to tell Mike some stories about Professor Edwards, because all Mike knew about Professor Edward's was that he had been a teacher at the Mount. He was sure to include the story about the trip to Madrid, his sophomore year. Paul filled him in on Professor Edwards's family and how it was that Professor Edwards was directly responsible for his going into the Air Force.

"So it's good to hear that he still lives in Blue Ridge Summit. I haven't seen him for several years, but we still exchange Christmas cards. Maybe it's worth taking a day to see him, when I get to that part of the trail. I believe Blue Ridge Summit is only two or three miles from the AT."

Mike Vernley told Paul that he hiked from Blue Ridge Summit up to Pine Grove Furnace the summer before and this summer he hiked from where he left off at Pine Grove Furnace to PA225, which is where Paul had his bad fall. Mike found it interesting what he was attempting, going the entire distance from Maine to Georgia. He asked him how his trip had gone so far.

Paul told him all about his hike from Mt. Katahdin, some 1036 miles to the north. After he recounted his Appalachian adventure Mike told him that he had always wanted to hike the Appalachian Trail in its entirety, but he had responsibilities at home. He felt he could never leave his wife and two youngsters for that period of time and Paul said leaving his family was the hardest part of his hike.

Paul told Mike that it had been a good experience so far, but if he known then what he knows now, he probably wouldn't do it again.

Paul fired up his stove to boil some water for dinner and he asked Mike if he needed any hot water. He didn't need any because he planned to get a fire started and put a can of soup in the coals. Mike mentioned that he had an extra can of Campbell's Chunky Beef if he wanted it, but he said he wanted to use up his freeze dried food because he had a mail drop to pick up the next day. This was Mike's last night out on the AT because his wife would be picking him up at noon the next day.

Paul and Mike got along well together, so they sat around the fire until about 11:00 sharing stories and telling jokes. Paul found out that Mike was originally from Wisconsin and that was where he planned to retire when he got out of the Army, which was another eight years away. However, Mike said Georgia was homesick for Norfolk, England, so there was also discussion of moving there some day after their kids were grown and gone.

At 11:15 Mike poured water over the still glowing coals and the steam and smoke rose up into the night sky. Both Paul and Mike happened to be looking up as they watched the smoke rise from the doused fire when something streaked across the sky.

"Did you see that?" Mike asked.

"Yeah, I did. It must have been a meteor entering the Earth's atmosphere. It's amazing how fast they cross the sky when they do that." "Mike," he asked, "are you any good at naming stars and constellations?"

"I can get by. That's something the Army taught us in one of our land navigation courses. How about you, are you any good at naming the stars and constellations?"

"No I'm not very good at it. My oldest brother is, though. He is amazing at that kind of stuff."

Both of them looked back at the fire and Mike said, "I think I'll call it a night." To which Paul replied, "I'm not far behind you."

Paul brushed his teeth and then relieved himself. Then with his dim flashlight he went back into the lean-to and lay down in his corner. Almost as soon as his head was in the horizontal position, he fell off to sleep. (1036 FK)

Mike's wrist alarm went off at 7:45 and Paul knew that because that's what Mike told said he set it for before they went to sleep. Mike was quick packing and he was off by 8:30. Mike started to hike and then stopped and turned around. He said, "If you do stop in Blue Ridge Summit to see your professor let me know. I may join up with you two." Then Mike handed him a business card that listed his name, phone number, and address.

Paul decided not to eat breakfast since he would be in Duncannon by 11:00, so he snacked on a granola bar along the way. When he got to the cliffs leading to Duncannon he heard someone say, "Here Paul, I thought you'd like this."

He turned around and he saw Will holding something out. It was Paul's watch minus the watch band. "I found it back where you fell," Will said, "but the watch band is broken beyond the point where it will do you any good."

So he reached out and took the watch from Will and you could see where it smashed against a rock because it had a bad gash on the watch face. The seconds were still changing every second, so Paul looked back up at Will and said "it's a Timex and as their commercial says, "It took a licking, but it's still ticking." Will had a blank look on his face and didn't seem to understand the Timex advertisement.

"Thanks Will. I think there's still another three years left on the battery, so I'm glad I didn't buy another one. I'll look for a watch band in Duncannon."

Will offered to carry his backpack down the last half mile and since it was steep with several switchbacks, Paul didn't mind at all. When they reached the bottom and were ready to cross the railroad track, they stopped and had to step back because a train was about to pass by headed south at a very fast speed; the rush of air felt good as the train passed by. Will gave him the backpack when they crossed over the Clarks' Ferry Bridge and told Paul he would see him later.

Paul thanked him again for finding his watch and carrying his backpack, but Will was out of hearing range and probably never heard him. Paul's first order of business in Duncannon was to get something to eat, followed by getting his mail drop, thirdly by calling Laura, and if he had time to buy a watchband.

He stopped for breakfast at a Truck stop/restaurant. While he drank his coffee, that the waitress assumed he wanted, he looked at the menu and decided to have three eggs, with a double order of bacon and toast. While he sat at the counter he was looking directly at the revolving dessert display and it looked too good to pass up, so he ordered two pieces of Boston Cream Pie and they were as good as they looked. After he paid for his meal he asked directions to the post office. It wasn't that far away.

When he got to the post office he pulled out his driver's license and asked for the package in his name. The postal employee verified that Paul was who he said he was and handed him the package and Paul took the package over to a counter and opened the box. The first thing Paul saw when he opened the box were pictures from the Labor Day weekend at the Fitzgerald's. The AT&T calling card went into Paul's wallet and everything else went into his backpack. He broke up the cardboard box and placed it in a container marked "recycling." Then he left the post office and went to find a payphone.

Paul called Laura's work and fortunately, this time, she was in her office. He told her about the past two days and particularly about the night before and the coincidence of Mike and how he might see Professor Edwards when he gets near Blue Ridge Summit. Paul asked her to look up the professor's phone number and he'd get from her when he called the next time. He didn't tell Laura, however, about his bad fall the day before because he didn't want her to worry more than she already was. He was after all, very clumsy and he didn't need to reinforce that.

There wasn't a store in Duncannon which had big watch bands, so Paul decided to wait. If he did visit Jim and Pete maybe they could take him to the Post Exchange and he could find one there. He would just have to resort to putting it in and take it out of his pocket whenever he wanted to check the time. It was 1:45 when he started hiking again.

On leaving Duncannon proper he noticed an Italian Restaurant, the one mentioned in his guidebook. It was called Sorrento's and they were well known for their Stromboli's, so even though he was still full from breakfast he went in and ordered a pepperoni and sausage Stromboli and asked them to wrap it very well in as much aluminum foil as possible. He planned to save it for dinner; he would warm it on the fire if he had one or he would eat it cold. When they called Paul's name he went up to get the Stromboli and the thing must have weighed two pounds at least, but maybe more.

His plan was to stay at the Cove Mountain Shelter for the night; it was four miles south of Duncannon. When he got back on the trail he noticed how different his pack felt. It was noticeably heavier, probably from the Stromboli.

It was 3:45 when Paul got to the shelter and there was no one else there. Paul figured in that it was a Friday and fairly close to a road, there was a good chance there would be a party there that night. Paul staked out his area in the shelter, following his normal routine. He laid down his sleeping pads and then his sleeping bag, like he had done many times since he began his journey nearly three months prior. He decided to start a fire in the fire pit at about 5:00. Surely, he reasoned, any other campers would welcome that sight; a campfire always seemed to help the spirits and soothe the senses.

The sense of smell, the sense of sight, and the sense of well-being, are all affected by a campfire, at least that's what he learned as an AFROTC cadet in his survival training some twenty two years prior. Paul thought of that training frequently over the years; it took place at Lake Martin, which was about 25 miles from Maxwell AFB in Alabama. What he remembered most from that experience was S.T.O.P. If you ever got into a survival situation, you should always S.T.O.P. which stands for stop, think, observe, and plan. He used that lesson many times over the years. It also worked in workplace survival situations, that is, dealing with bosses and co-workers. It helped him bite his tongue many times.

Two other hikers showed up at about 6:15 when the fire was going pretty good; Paul was just getting ready to place his foil wrapped Stromboli close to the fire to warm it up.

Paul assumed he would have college kids as his shelter mates for the night; instead it was a couple in their mid to upper 20's. They were graduate students at Penn State, which was probably about an hour and-a-half drive north from the trailhead. It was a football weekend, as they explained, and a good reason to leave town.

According to Matt, Penn State University was playing Temple University, so State College would be a mob scene for the weekend. It would have been different, they said, if either of them went there for their undergraduate degrees. Matt was getting his PhD in history and his wife was getting two master's degrees. They wanted to start a family in the spring and figured this would be one of their last camping adventures before they had kids.

Paul offered Matt and Kerry some Stromboli, but they said they didn't want to impose. However, when he un-wrapped it, they could see it was too much for any one person to eat, so they accepted his offer. As they sat there around the fire eating the Stromboli, Matt and Kerry wanted to hear about Paul's trip, so he shared most of the exciting stuff that happened since Mt. Katahdin.

When they asked Paul what was the greatest thing about the trip thus far, he couldn't put into words. Of course, he couldn't tell them about all the divine interventions he received, so he told them something along these lines. "…With one exception, all the people on the trip have been very friendly and it's restored my faith in mankind. The sights have been great, but it has been the interactions with people and events surrounding those people…"

Paul had not shared the incident about George Murray or Tobias, so he used those as a way to illustrate people's goodness.

"Paul," Kerry said, "I think those two instances show your goodness. After all Jim didn't even offer to let you stay another night in his father's house and Mrs. Murray took two days away from your backpacking trip. I think what you did was over and beyond what is generally expected of a stranger."

Paul thought about what Kerry said and he could see Matt looking at her and not necessarily agreeing with what she said.

"You know Kerry, you may be right, but by that time in my hike I realized what was really important in life. Finishing the hike wasn't as important as the journey and the experiences. I realized that helping others was more important and I got a lot more out of those experiences than bragging about having a 25-mile day, or making it through the 100-mile wilderness in four days. It felt good helping them and I've gotten so much more in return than if I hadn't helped them. It's like my mother always told us, 'It's better to give than to receive.' However, as kids you can't see that. At least I couldn't."

They were all quiet, reflecting on what Paul said and then Kerry spoke. "That's nice Paul. I'm sorry I didn't see it that way."

"That's okay, Kerry. I had a hard time three months ago believing that. Now, I know what's important in life. At least I think I know what's important in life."

Matt told Paul that while he was talking he was thinking about something that had happened at the lean-to which they were staying at, about five years prior. As Matt and Kerry told it, a couple staying in the Cove Mountain Lean-to were murdered by a hiker. They couldn't really remember the specifics, but it turned out to be a drifter from South Carolina. The lean-to had a different name back then and they weren't sure if they changed the name of the shelter because of the murder.

Anyhow, as Matt went on to explain, he was thinking of that incident when Paul was telling them how good people were. He said, "Yeah, that's like everything in life, I guess. It only takes one person to ruin things for everyone else."

They all stayed up talking until about 10:00 when they all decided to go to bed. Matt and Kerry volunteered to take care of putting out the fire so he could go to bed. (1044 FK)

Paul slept well and didn't even have to relieve his bladder during the night. However, he had a case of heartburn from the Stromboli and took some of the Gaviscon Gloria gave him in Connecticut; they were his last two.

He skipped breakfast since that Gaviscon just barely took care of the heartburn and he didn't want to risk it. Paul was planning to go all the way to US11, which was nearly 14 miles away.

He would be crossing Cumberland Valley and there would be no camping allowed for the next 23 miles. The good thing was that once he got down the Blue Mountain it was mostly flat farmland. He welcomed not having to go up and down, at least for 23 miles. Paul decided when he got to US11 he'd give Pete a call.

CHAPTER SIXTEEN

Carlisle Indians

It was a monotonous hike down the Blue Mountain and into what is referred to as the Cumberland Valley. However, the topography was one of contrasts. From one of rocks and a stark granite settings to one of farm fields and plush green pastures. His knees welcomed the mostly flat terrain; though there were some barely perceptible ups and downs in places. It was Saturday morning the 16th of September, a few days shy of 90 days from when Paul began his hike on Mt. Katahdin. Though the farm lands were green and plush, it was a little bit boring after a couple hours.

Paul took his watch out of his pocket so many times to check the time that the back of his hand was chafing. He definitely needed to get a watch band when he went to the Post Exchange on Carlisle Barracks. His knowledge of Carlisle Barracks was limited.

He knew the US Army War College was there and that most people over 40 could associate the name Carlisle to Jim Thorpe. Paul tried to remember the sequence of events in the movie about Jim Thorpe, but he couldn't even remember the name of it. Then it came to him, could it have been *Jim Thorpe, All-American*? It must have been he thought; as his memory of the movie came back he remembered it starred Burt Lancaster as Jim Thorpe.

Paul also remembered that Carlisle played some part in the Battle of Gettysburg, but he wasn't sure what part. He remembered seeing the movie *Gettysburg*, so he thought about it for a while. Finally, he remembered that, too. Jeb Stewart got into a confrontation with the Union Forces protecting Carlisle and that's why Jeb Stewart arrived in Gettysburg a day late.

Walking across the flat terrain was easier on Paul's knees and he thanked God for the reprieve. He could start to see trucks on some highway, so he stopped and looked at the map and it was I-81. As he got closer to I-81 he could hear the traffic and he wondered where everybody was headed. He wondered about the cars and trucks headed south and who was driving thru the Shenandoah Valley.

He knew I-81 went all the way north to Canada, but he couldn't remember exactly how far south it went. As he crossed over I-81 he stopped on the over pass. The 18-wheelers were numerous and he could make out a big green sign that said, "Carlisle 1 mile." That meant US11 was only about a half mile away, so he continued on.

It was 5:15 when he got to US11, so he knew he already missed Saturday evening Mass and he wondered about Catholic Churches in the area. There would surely be a chapel on Carlisle Barracks, but he decided to check out one of the churches in Carlisle if he had the chance. Of course he would need a way to get to church, but he would worry about that when the time came.

As Paul stepped out onto US11 he could see a motel about a quarter of a mile to his right, so he walked to the motel, which was a Days Inn. He took his backpack off and left it outside and went in; he asked the desk clerk if they had a room for the night and they didn't, so he asked if he could use their rest room.

After using the rest room he walked down US11 about another 100 yards to a diner he saw from the motel. Paul placed a call to Pete's phone number and someone answered on the fourth ring. It was Pete's wife and she said that Pete was out running and would be back soon, so he told her his name and that he'd call back in about 15 minutes if that was OK. When Paul mentioned his name, Sheryl, Pete's wife, said "Oh, hi Paul. Pete was saying you would be calling within a day or two. Are you in the Carlisle area?"

"Yes. I'm calling from the Middlesex diner on US11." He started to tell Sheryl where the diner was and she said she knew exactly where he was calling from. She said that either Pete or she would drive to pick him up within 30 minutes. When he asked about a good hotel in the area, she said, "We wouldn't hear of it. You'll stay with us. Besides, it's a car show weekend and you won't find a hotel room in the Carlisle area."

When the first motel said they didn't have any rooms, he just assumed it was because there was a big transportation company next door and they rented all their rooms to truckers. Paul wasn't familiar with the Carlisle car show, but he would find out later that Carlisle Car Show weekends are well known to car enthusiasts from across the country. You had to make motel reservations months in advance.

After he hung up the phone he went into the diner to see if he could get a root beer float. He left his backpack in the entry way next to some arcade games and went and sat at the counter. When the waitress asked what he wanted he said he wanted a root beer float and the bill because he was in a hurry. After he savored the root beer float he paid and went back outside the diner to wait for his ride and while he was waiting for Pete or Pete's wife to pick him up he surveyed the topography of the area. It looked like he was in a plain surrounded by mountains to the north and hills to the south and he got out the map to see if his observations were right.

The mountains to the north ran from southwest to northeast and the hills to the south did the same. As he looked at the map it looked as if the mountains formed a funnel. They must make for some windy weather patterns, he thought to himself.

After Paul put the map back into his pack he saw a car drive up and he recognized the driver. It was Pete. Pete got out and helped Paul with his backpack, putting it in the backseat of the Ford Taurus. There was a child's car seat in back with a child of about three or four. Paul got in the Ford Taurus and turned towards Pete and asked, "What's your son's name?"

"That's Peter Jr."

Paul turned around and said "hi" to Pete Jr. and Pete Jr. didn't say anything in response; he just sucked on his pacifier all the harder.

Pete pulled out onto US11 and headed south, passing several hotels and truck stops. When they got to Carlisle Barracks they passed through the security checkpoint and onto the post. Pete's house was small and it looked older than some of the others.

On the way to the Post Pete shared with Paul that Carlisle Barracks had survived the latest round of base closures, so the Army he explained, would be tearing the houses down and putting up new ones eventually.

"We're moving next summer, so we don't have to worry about it," he said.

When they pulled up to Pete's duplex he parked in the street because his wife was cleaning lawn chairs in their driveway. Paul walked up to Sheryl and introduced himself; as he was shaking her hand he could hear the screen door open and when he looked in the direction of the noise he saw a familiar face. It was Jim and a young woman. The woman was Jim's wife.

Jim and his wife, Maria, came over to say hi to Paul and as Jim introduced him to Maria he told her that this was one of the guys who helped him out when he was bitten by the snake. Maria gave Paul a hug and said, "Thank you so much for helping him."

After Paul settled into the guest room he shaved and showered and then he got dressed and joined the two couples outside. Pete fired up the gas grille and asked Paul how he liked his steak grilled. "Medium," he replied. Jim walked to the cooler and opened it and asked if he wanted a beer and Paul said, "Yes, please."

Paul handed Pete his knife when he sat down in one of the lawn chairs and Pete said, "You know, I would have felt really bad if I lost this thing. I've had it since I was about 15 years old and they don't make this particular one anymore. It's the sentimental value of it more than the cost. I got it from my Uncle. The thing is, I don't know when I would have realized it was missing because of all the urgency of getting Jim out of there. So, frankly, when you called me I didn't know I had dropped it."

"Yeah, I know what you mean. The sentimentality of certain things put more value on it than money."

It was a nice evening. The steak was great and the baked potato was superb. However, even better than the meal was being able to share in the camaraderie of being on active duty once again. Pete, Sheryl, Jim, and Maria reminded him of the good times he and Laura had had over the years with their military friends and he wondered if they would ever form those kinds of bonds again in civilian life. He missed the military lifestyle already.

During dinner Paul asked about the chapel and if anyone happened to know when Catholic services were the next morning. Both couples were Protestants, but Jim mentioned that his next door neighbor was Catholic, but Jim said they went to the Catholic Church downtown, however, and asked if he wanted him to call his friend. Paul said he'd appreciate that, so Jim got up to use the phone. While Jim was away the conversation turned to Tom and how he was.

Paul shared the story of how they met in New Hampshire and then again in Pennsylvania about a week ago. They found that very interesting and coincidental. Sheryl reflected on Jim's snake bite and how if Paul and Tom had never met in New Hampshire, things could have turned out differently for Jim. "It's miraculous," as Sheryl put it.

Jim came back out and said his neighbors were going to 8:00 a.m. Mass downtown and offered to give him a ride. Neil and Colleen, Jim's neighbors, said they would pick Paul up at 7:35 the next morning, or if that was too early they said Catholic Mass on the Post was at 9:00. Paul said he'd like to go to Mass downtown, so that he could get a feel for the surrounding community, so Jim called his neighbor back to say Paul would love to go with them and that he would be ready at 7:35.

After Jim and Maria left, Paul used the phone to call Laura. He meant to call earlier, so that he could talk with the kids, but the time had gotten away from him. He told her about the past two days and how nice it was to be with Pete and Sheryl. Then he told Laura he'd be sure to call on Sunday at a reasonable hour. After he hung up, he said goodnight to Pete and Sheryl and asked if he could borrow an alarm clock, but Pete said they didn't have an extra one. Pete did say, however, that he always got up at 6:30 on Sunday mornings and he would be sure to wake him. Paul wrote in his journal, said his prayers, and went to sleep. (1059 FK)

St. Patrick's was an older church and it traced its history back to the mid-1800s and Mother Katharine Drexel played some part in the building of the current church building. Paul didn't know much about Katharine Drexel other than she established an order of nuns to work with Indians and African Americans. The stain glass windows were pretty, but the pews weren't comfortable for a six-footer. Paul liked the church community and felt it was a place where he could be happy. On the way to St. Patrick's, which was less than two miles from Carlisle Barracks Neil and Colleen explained to him how St. Patrick's actually had three churches.

There was the one downtown, where Paul went with Neil and Colleen and that was referred to as the Shrine Church. There was also one south of town and that's where the school was. The third church, which was just a chapel, was only open between Memorial Day and Labor Day and it was located in a State Forest well south of town. After Mass they returned to Carlisle Barracks and Paul asked Neil if they could drop him off at the PX. Neil didn't think the PX was open yet, but they swung by to check. Like Neil thought, it wasn't open, so they returned to Pete's house.

Pete and Sheryl were still at the Protestant service at the Post chapel, but they left the front door unlocked. Paul let himself in and he used the phone. Unfortunately, Laura and the kids weren't home, so he left a message. Next, Paul called Don and Chris's number. Don answered and sounded happy. "Hey, guess what Paul?"

"What."

"We got our tickets yesterday for the Rome trip and also found out that our son will be able to join us for a couple days while we're in Rome. He had to trade some shifts and promise some favors with some friends, but he said it was worth it."

"That's great Don. Are we still on for next weekend?"

"Yes. Where are you now?"

"I'm in Carlisle, Pennsylvania, which is about 35 miles from Gettysburg as the crow flies. However, it's about 60 plus miles to US30 by way of the AT. Do you think if I get to US30 I can get a ride?"

"Sure Paul. Let me know when you get to US30."

"Where will you be staying in Gettysburg?"

"I don't have that information at home, but I think it's the Ramada Inn and Conference Center."

After he hung up he decided to walk to the PX. Just as Paul was ready to head out the door Pete, Sheryl, and Pete Jr. came home. They asked how he was doing and whether he needed to do any laundry. Paul said he'd like to do some laundry, but he was going to walk to the PX. By the time he got to the PX they were open and to his delight they had a watch band that fit his Timex. He bought the watch band, another

AT&T phone card and some snacks for the next couple of days. On his way back to Pete and Sheryl's it started to rain and he didn't have any raingear. He was soaked by the time he got to Pete's house.

That afternoon Paul did his laundry and watched some pro-football with Pete. Sheryl and Pete Jr. had prior commitments, so Pete and Paul ate some frozen pizza and drank a couple beers. Pete like Paul, didn't really get in to football, so he flipped from game to game, focusing more on the plays than the players. When Sheryl got home at 5:15 she had a couple roast chicken's which she picked up at the GIANT food store. Paul offered to help, but Sheryl told him to sit and enjoy himself, so he took the opportunity to call Laura and the kids and this time they were home. In that he talked with Laura the night before he just talked with the kids. Theresa talked about soccer, Daniel talked about Cub Scouts and Steven talked about his teacher.

After the call to Florida he packed his backpack before he went to bed, but checked the weather first. The forecast for the next two days called for heavy rain. He went to bed at 9:30 when Pete and Sheryl did. Pete said he would drive him back to the trailhead at 7:15 the next morning.

Paul slept well, but woke up at 5:15 when a clap of thunder rattled the house. He got up to shower and noticed that Pete was already up and fixing breakfast.

"Quite the storm we're having. It's too bad you have to hike in it."

"Yes, but I must continue because I'm meeting someone in three days."

"How do you like your eggs Paul?"

"Over easy."

They had a nice breakfast and Paul was glad he was able to use the bathroom before they left for the trailhead. Coffee always had a way of stimulating his digestive system and this morning was no exception. Just as they were ready to go out the door Sheryl came out with Pete Jr. and she said goodbye and Paul thanked her for her hospitality.

They left the house at 7:10 and the rain was still coming down in buckets and it was raining so hard the windshield wipers could barely keep up. When they got to the trailhead Paul thanked Pete for everything, but Pete asked him if he wanted to reconsider hiking in such heavy rain and wait another day. Paul said that was a very gracious offer, but he felt like he had imposed too much already.

Paul decided to hike without any raingear, preferring to keep it dry until he needed it. He slung the backpack onto his right knee and hoisted his backpack onto his shoulders. He started hiking at 7:20 and he was happy to have his watch back on his wrist; it made it so much easier to tell time. He just wondered if it would be OK with all the rain, it says on the back that it's water resistant, not water proof. He wondered if the gash affected anything, but he shrugged it off and continued on.

Paul looked at his map before he left Pete's house because he knew he wouldn't be able to look at it in the pouring rain. He hoped to make it to the Alec Kennedy Shelter which was about 12 miles from where he got back on the AT. The hiking was slow going because the rain had turned the farmland into a swamp. Whereas he didn't think the hiking poles would help, they helped significantly. When his feet got stuck in the mud he was able to lean on one of the poles to get unstuck. He crossed over the Pennsylvania Turnpike and looked down at the cars and they didn't seem to be as affected by the rain as he was. However, their windshield wipers were working with a fury.

About an hour after crossing over the turnpike he stopped to take a break. According to the road sign he was on Trindle Rd. In the shelter of a school bus stop he took out the map of the AT and he found Trindle Rd. on the map and it was also listed as PA641. He wasn't so sure he could make the Alec Kennedy Shelter, but there were no places along the next six or so miles where he was allowed to camp legally. He considered hitching a ride back into Carlisle and staying at a hotel because he didn't want to inconvenience Pete and Sheryl. After a snack and a lot of water Paul put his backpack back on and crossed PA641.

The fields on the south side of the road were just as bad as the north side and it sounded like Paul was pulling suction cups off of something when he would try to get unstuck. Paul couldn't remember the last time he had experienced something like this, so he figured it had to have been when he was a kid and didn't have the sense to come in out of the rain.

Paul got to the next road and unfortunately there was no bus stop to offer protection from the rain, so he continued on. It was 11:45 and he felt like he wasn't making any headway. About 30 minutes later the rain just stopped. He could still see clouds to the southwest, but he was in the clear for now. The trail seemed to have more rock in it then where he had been hiking, so he switched the hiking poles to his left hand because his right hand was getting a blister. He walked along not paying much attention to where he was stepping and the next thing he knew his feet slipped out from underneath him and he was airborne. He braced for hitting the ground which came a split second later. When he landed he was lying in a big mud puddle and he didn't like the way it felt. His right arm hurt almost immediately. He knew he should have laid there awhile before getting up, but he was in mud five or six inches deep. He struggled to get up, but he couldn't because of his backpack. He unhooked the waist belt with his left hand because his right arm hurt when he tried to use it.

After Paul got the backpack off he still struggled to get up, but couldn't. Instinctively he used his right hand and that sent a sharp pain through his body. He lied there in the mud for what seemed like ages, but was probably only a minute. Then he could hear someone say, "Are you okay young fella?"

Paul looked up, but could only see someone from the knees down. He heard the voice say again, "Are you okay?"

"I can't get up because my right arm hurts," he said.

Paul could see the legs move closer and someone stoop down. The stranger gripped him under his left arm pit to help him get up. After two tries he was able to stand and see who was helping him. They were about the same height, but the man was a good ten years older than him.

"Thank you for helping me," Paul said.

"That's quite alright. My name is Lee Brown and you are?" Lee put out his right hand to shake Paul's, but when Paul put out his right hand to shake Lee's, it hurt. Shaking Lee's hand awkwardly with his left hand Paul said, "My name is Paul and unfortunately I've done something to my right arm."

"Let me see."

Lee carefully looked at Paul's arm. First he took a bandana out of his back pocket to wipe some of the mud off and when he got to the point where he could see Paul's skin he said, "Well, there aren't any bones sticking out. Do you think you can make it another quarter mile?"

"Not with my backpack on."

"Don't worry about that, I'll carry it for you. My car is parked near the trailhead."

Lee picked up his backpack and put it on his back, getting mud all over him as he did. Lee walked a few paces ahead of him to make sure Paul didn't trip on anything else. They made it to PA174 in about 10 minutes and Lee took off Paul's backpack and rested it against the brown Appalachian Trail sign and said, "You wait here. I'm going to get my car; I should be back in less than five minutes." Paul watched Lee as he walked quickly down PA174 towards Boiling Springs. Lee turned right at the first street and within a minute he could see a car turn left out of the side street where Lee had turned in.

As Lee passed back by Paul, he made a signal with his hand indicating he would do a U-Turn. Lee drove down to someone's driveway and pulled in and backed out again onto PA174. Lee's Subaru Forrester pulled up and onto the shoulder where Paul was waiting. Lee got out of the car, but noticed he was sticking out a little into the street, so he got back in and repositioned the car, so it wouldn't get hit by a passing car.

As Lee got out of his car he said, "Let me get that backpack for you; I'll put it in the back. You sit in the front passenger's seat." Paul opened the car door and got in while Lee put the backpack in the rear. Once Lee got in he said, "What do you want to do? Do you want to go get it X-Rayed somewhere?"

Paul thought about it for a minute and said, "Do you know if Carlisle Barracks has a hospital?"

"They have a clinic and I know for a fact they can take X-Rays. Do you want to go there? Are you active duty?"

"I just retired from the Air Force about three months ago.

"Well, we can go see if they can help you out then. I don't think they'll turn you away."

"If it's not too much trouble; I'm just sorry to make such a mess in your car."

"Don't worry about it. It can't be helped and besides it's only dirt."

Lee pulled out onto PA174 and headed into Boiling Springs, turning right after the Boiling Springs Tavern. From there it was less than six miles to Carlisle Barracks. During the six-mile drive to the Barracks Paul found out that Lee was a retired Army officer living in Boiling Springs. He and his wife purchased a property and were going to open a Bed & Breakfast sometime in the near future. Their remodeling was in its final stages. Paul shared with Lee that since he retired from the Air Force he's been hiking the Appalachian Trail, from Maine to Georgia. Paul added a caveat, that his trip might be finished now, but Lee told him that it might just be a bad sprain. They drove thru a different gate then before and the clinic was visible almost immediately.

Paul thanked Lee for his help, but Lee said he'd stay and see how things turned out. In that it was a Monday the clinic wasn't crowded and they took him almost right away to be X-Rayed. He kept apologizing for getting dirt all over the place. Paul considered calling Pete, but decided to wait for the X-Ray results. The doctor read the X-Ray within 15 minutes and the prognosis was a fractured right radial. "As fractures go," the doctor said, "it's not a bad break, but you'll need to get a cast and then go through a couple weeks of therapy."

When he mentioned to the doctor that he was hiking the Appalachian Trail, the doctor frowned and said, "You'll want to curtail your hiking for at least two weeks, maybe longer if there is nerve damage that we can't see on the X-Ray."

The doctor had one of the nurses get Paul enough Tylenol 3 for two days and asked if he could come back in two days when the swelling went down. Not knowing whether he could stay with Pete and Sheryl, he hesitated and asked the doctor if there were billeting quarters on the post. When the doctor said there was, then he said he could be back on Wednesday.

Paul went out to tell Lee what was going on and he asked Lee whether he could impose one more time, for a ride to billeting. Lee said he would do that, but he said he had a better idea. "Why don't you come stay with my wife and I. We could use this as a learning experience for when we open our B&B next year."

"Are you sure I won't cause any problems?"

"No. We would be delighted to have you and I'm sort of curious about your trip and I'd like to hear about any B&B's you've stayed in along the way from Maine. After all, we need to do some research about hikers since the Appalachian Trail goes directly through our town now. We just need to run by the commissary before we go back to Boiling Springs." On the way to the commissary Lee remembered it was Monday and they were closed, so they returned to Boiling Springs, by way of the GIANT grocery store.

While Lee went into the GIANT Paul stayed in the car and he thanked God for Lee showing up when he did. He wondered what would happen to someone if they broke a bone on some remote part of the AT. When Lee got back in the car he gave Paul a windshield tour of Carlisle before heading back to Boling Springs. Lee's house was right across the street from a lake and it was called the Children's Lake, but he never found out why it was called that.

Lee must have alerted his wife that he was bringing someone home, because she wasn't at all surprised when they walked through the back door. The Brown's house was lovely and it smelled good inside. Kitty, Lee's wife, was baking some banana bread for a meeting they were going to that night. Lee introduced Paul to Kitty and told her about his unfortunate accident and why he was staying with them for a couple days. The news didn't seem to faze Kitty at all because she was very gracious and took it all in stride.

Paul apologized for the mess he was making and said he'd clean it up, however, Kitty said not to worry about it. She said his job was to take care of his arm for the next couple of days.

The Brown's gave him a choice of two rooms to sleep in, so Paul took the bed without a footboard. Kitty then showed him where the bathroom was and said, "Now don't hurt yourself and don't be too proud to ask for help. I've had a broken right arm before and know what a pain it can be."

Paul thanked Kitty and he said he would like to shower and call his wife to let her know what happened. Showering with a broken right arm was hard, harder than when he fractured his left arm in college. However, it felt good to let the hot water run over his neck and shoulders. Paul soaped as well as he could with his left hand and then shampooed his hair. When he was sure he had all the soap and shampoo off he shut off the shower. Fortunately there was a grip he could hold onto with his left hand when he stepped in and out of the tub/shower. However, drying off with a towel was rather tricky, but he got it done.

Next, he wanted to call Laura to let her know what happened.

Lee showed him which phone to use if he wanted some privacy, which he did. Paul called their number in Brandon, Florida and Daniel picked up. "Hi Daddy, how are you?'

"I've been better Dan. Can you put mommy on the phone and I'll talk to you all after I talk with her?" Dan put the phone down and Paul could hear him calling for Laura, "Mommy. Daddy's on the phone and he wants to talk to you." Then he could hear Laura pick up the phone and say "What's wrong?"

"I had a bad fallen today and fractured my right radial."

"That's awful, what happened?"

"It was raining really hard this morning and when it stopped I let my guard down a little and I slipped and fell. I was stuck in a big plop of mud and couldn't get up, so I took my backpack off and that helped somewhat, but I still couldn't get up. By the grace of God some guy happened along and he helped me get to the clinic on Carlisle Barracks. The doctor wants me to come back in two days to make sure he didn't miss anything."

Paul then told Laura how he's staying in Boiling Springs, Pennsylvania with the guy who helped him on the trail. After he told Laura what he planned to do for the next two days he asked her if she heard anything from AFJROTC Headquarters and Laura said, "As a matter of fact, there was a message on our answering machine from Janice, she wants one of us to call her back. Maybe you can do that tomorrow."

"She didn't give any indication of what was up?"

"No. She said just to call by Wednesday."

After Paul made his call to Laura he called Don Bowser to let him know that their weekend rendezvous might not happen and why. He told Don that after he saw the doctor again on Wednesday he would know better.

The Brown's invited Paul down for a simple dinner and Kitty even cut his dinner into bite sized portions, so that he wouldn't have to worry about cutting anything. Lee and Kitty wanted to hear about his trip, so he told them everything, with the exception of the providential happenings; he tried to be pretty clear about the three or four B&B's he stayed in along the way. When he got up to the present, at the point when he broke his arm, Kitty said, "Wow. That's quite a story you have there."

Paul found out in the course of their conversations that he and Kitty had something in common. They were both born in Connecticut. However, the difference was that he lived there until he was only one and Kitty lived there until she met Lee. Lee was from Massachusetts, so he was familiar with Bard College when he got to that part of his adventure.

The way the Brown's ended up in Boiling Springs was that during Lee's Army career he was stationed at Carlisle Barracks and he and Kitty liked the area so much they decided to stay after they retired from the Army. Instead of being just 10 years older than Paul he was 15 years older. In fact, he mentioned that he was eligible to draw Social Security.

After dessert and decaf coffee Paul said he wanted to turn in, so Lee went up to make sure there were no tripping hazards. He had a restless sleep and it was restless for two reasons, the first being his broken arm. He could never sleep on his back, so it was difficult to find a comfortable sleeping position. Whenever he rolled to his right side the pain woke him up. The second reason Paul couldn't sleep was because he wondered what news Janice had for him at AFJROTC Headquarters. Was the high school in South Bend no longer hiring? Was he out of contention for the job? When Paul looked at the clock radio it was 1:45 a.m. and since he couldn't sleep he said the *Sorrowful Mysteries* of the Most Holy Rosary. In the second decade where Jesus was scourged, Paul offered up the pain in his arm. In the fifth decade, at *The Crucifixion*, Paul thought of how much Jesus' arms must have ached when He hung on the cross. The Rosary calmed his mind and his pains seemed bearable. He fell off to sleep. (1066 FK)

Paul woke to the smell of bacon. He glanced over at the clock radio and it read 9:13. He felt refreshed as he lay there. He figured he had a good six hours of sleep, but maybe seven. He swung his legs over the side of the bed and used his left arm to sit up. He put on some gym shorts, but left the same T-shirt on. It hurt too much to lift his arm and besides, he was trying to be good about not moving it. He walked downstairs and into the kitchen. Kitty looked up as Paul walked in and asked "can I fix you a couple eggs?'

"Yes please. Over easy."

Lee came in as he was finishing up breakfast and said he was going into Carlisle and asked if Paul wanted to go. He said he would like to, but had to make an important phone call to Montgomery, Alabama.

Once Paul got on the phone with Janice he found out why she called. She mentioned that the high school in South Bend was ready to set up an interview and that Paul was the only one in contention. Janice said the other guy dropped out because he got a job with Fed Ex. "Really? So does that mean I get the job?"

"You still need to go for an interview because they can still decide whether they want you or not. Remember Major Geary, you turned down that school in Virginia."

"What if they don't want me?"

"Then we'll have to start all over; we advertise it again, get candidates, and then set up interviews."

"Has this ever happened before Janice?"

"Yes. It has happened, but I think it's looking pretty good for you. The school has to weigh whether they want to go without an officer position for another 3 - 4 months or take you."

Feeling somewhat relieved, Paul shared with Janice how he had an unfortunate hiking accident the day before and had to stop hiking anyhow. She said she was sorry to hear about his accident and asked him if he wanted her to set up the interview a couple weeks out. He said that would be great because right now he couldn't even salute. Paul said he'd probably return to the Tampa area within a week, but that Janice should still call Laura if there were any further developments with the South Bend position. He thanked Janice for her help and said he'd keep in touch.

After Paul hung up he called Laura to let her know what was up. They did a lot of "what ifs" and a plan for each one, such as when he should return to Tampa. He wanted to see Don Bowser over the weekend and then he should probably go to DC to see his mother and brother before catching a plane back to Tampa. Laura would check into places where he could do physical therapy when he got back and she would start to check out flight information to South Bend, Indiana.

Paul went to look for Lee when he was done with his phone calls and he found him in the kitchen having a cup of coffee. As Lee was drinking his last sip he told him that Kitty would do his laundry if he wanted to go get it, so he went up to his room to get it. As he opened the backpack the first thing he noticed was his Nalgene water bottle. He had a blue one and a green one, but the blue one was the only one visible because the green one was underneath something.

The blue one, however, was only a third full. He looked for the green one and it was empty. Paul drank the remainder of the water in the blue Nalgene bottle and put it back in his pack and he waited about two minutes and got it out again. It was empty, with the exception of less than a mouthful of water. Well, that settled that. He always wondered when the water bottles would no longer refill miraculously and the answer appeared to be when he had finished his trip.

He took both Nalgene bottles out and set them on the dresser. Then he got all his dirty clothes and put them in one of the plastic bags he had. Kitty had already retrieved his pants and socks from the bathroom, the ones he was wearing when he fell in the mud. He carried the plastic bag down to the kitchen and Lee said, "You can just leave that there," pointing to the corner. "OK, let me show you the town."

Lee gave Paul a good tour of Boiling Springs, starting with the Children's Lake. "You see right there where the water is bubbling out of the lake? That's how the town got its name. The water comes out of the artesian wells at 53 degrees and when the lake freezes in the winter it gives the appearance the water is boiling."

From the Children's Lake Lee took Paul up to the Allenberry Playhouse and Resort. Lee explained how the place put on some great shows and there were various places to eat and stay overnight.

Lee said, "The place kind of reminds me of that movie *Holiday Inn*, the one with Bing Crosby and Fred Astaire. Did you see that movie Paul?"

"Yeah. It's one of my favorite Christmas movies."

"Anyhow, we're very fortunate to have the theater and resort here in town. Do you like to fish?"

"Only at Red Lobster."

Paul looked over at Lee to see if he got it and when he noticed Lee smile he added, "No. I've never been much of a fisherman. Why do you ask?"

"Boiling Springs is well known for the trout fishing on the Yellow Breeches Creek. Fly fisherman from all over the world know about the Yellow Breeches."

From the Yellow Breeches Lee drove over to Carlisle Barracks and Lee showed Paul some of the things of historical interest on Carlisle Barracks like the Indian Graveyard. Then they went to the commissary.

The Browns were having dinner guests and said Paul was invited. They were having friends over from the Boiling Springs Civic Association for dinner and then holding their monthly meeting. While Paul was in the commissary he saw a familiar face. He waved and his acquaintance hand signaled for him to meet him outside. Paul excused himself from Lee, saying he would meet him outside after he finished his shopping.

CHAPTER SEVENTEEN

Gettysburg

Paul walked outside the commissary and looked for Frank and he was standing off to the right near the MWR office; he was with Kevin. He walked up to them both and asked how they were and Frank spoke for both of them saying "We're doing very well, but our time with you is coming to an end. We'd all like to get together for dinner tonight at the Boiling Springs Tavern. Does 5:30 work for you?" Paul thought about it and figured that Frank already would have known that he didn't have to go to the Brown's dinner, so he said "That works for me. Should I make reservations?"

Frank smiled and said, "I've already done that. We'll see you at 5:30 tonight." Then they both shook his left hand and turned to walk away. He watched as they walked down the sidewalk towards the PX parking lot and as he was watching them he heard someone say, "Hi Paul, what happened to you?"

He turned towards the voice and saw Jim walking towards him. Jim looked sharp in his Class "A" uniform and Paul was caught off guard and said in reply, "It's a long story, so I'll give you the abbreviated version." So, he explained to Jim how after Pete dropped him off the day before it was in a drenching rain, but he decided to continue anyhow. He told Jim that when he got near Boiling Springs on the AT he fell and fractured his right arm. Then Paul explained how Lee happened along shortly thereafter and brought him to the Carlisle Barracks clinic. He said he had a follow-up appointment with the doctor tomorrow and then he would probably be heading back to Florida. He couldn't remember if he had ever shared with Jim that he was trying to get an AFJROTC assignment, but he didn't mention it since it looked as if Jim was in a hurry.

He asked Jim why he was in his Class "A's" and Jim said he was on his way to an awards ceremony and he had to pick up some things for the reception afterwards. As they were shaking hands goodbye Lee came out of the commissary and saw them there and Lee came over to where they were talking and Paul introduced the two.

He told Lee that Jim was someone he met on the AT about two weeks earlier, but he decided not to tell Lee the whole story since Jim was on a mission. Instead, he would wait to tell Lee about Jim and Pete on their way back to Boiling Springs.

Jim said as a final note that if Paul needed anything to give him a call, writing down his phone number on an index card he took from his left breast pocket.

As Paul and Lee rode back to Boiling Springs Paul told Lee about his dinner plans that evening. Lee asked if it was dinner with Jim and he said no and explained how he ran into someone else he met while he was on the AT. Lee remarked at what a small world it was and Paul agreed. There was some kind of security exercise going on when they tried to leave the Post, so Paul used that opportunity to tell Lee about Jim and the copperhead.

It was 1:55 when they got back to the Brown's s house and it smelled wonderful when they walked in. The smell, as it turned out, was what Kitty was cooking for dinner that evening for the Boiling Springs Civic Association. Paul said he'd like to take a nap, so he went up to his room, set the alarm clock for 4:15, took a Tylenol 3, and lay down on the bed.

Paul was surprised when the alarm went off at 4:15. He struggled to turn it off and in doing so jarred his right arm, which sent a piercing pain throughout his body. He got up to use the rest room and then went back to his room to get dressed. Kitty had washed and folded his clothes, so he picked the nicest ones he had for a special dinner.

You could see the Boiling Springs Tavern from Lee and Kitty's house, but he still left at 5:10, leaving himself a little extra time to do some investigative work. Paul asked Kitty what time their meeting would be over, so that he wouldn't intrude, and Kitty said she wanted him to meet the Civic Association committee. However, in answer to his question, she said, "Our meetings usually go till 9:00 or so."

It was a pleasant walk along the lake to the Tavern and it took less than five minutes. Paul didn't see Frank or any of the other companions, so he walked up to the hostess and said he was meeting a party for a 5:30 dinner and he said the reservation could be under Geary, but he didn't know for sure. The girl looked at the reservation book and said, "Yes, Mr. Geary a party of six. Would you like to be seated now or wait for your guests?"

"I'll wait, but could you tell me something please?"

"Yes Mr. Geary. What is it?"

"Do you know when the reservation was made?"

The hostess looked down at the reservation book and then back up at Paul. "It says the reservation was made on September 5th."

"Thank you." Paul said in reply.

Paul went to sit down in the foyer to wait for Frank and the others. His investigative worked proved what he suspected, that it had been known for some time that his hike would end here. After all, the water bottles no longer refilled by themselves and there were probably other signs that pointed to the end of his hike, but he wasn't able to decide what those were, yet. At 5:25 p.m. the door opened and Frank, Kevin, Gloria, Will, and Sylvia walked through, so he got up to greet them. The hostess showed them all to their table and told them who their waiter would be for the evening.

The waiter, whose name was Roger, took their drink orders and since everyone was just going to have water, that's what Paul had as well. Paul looked at the menu while he was waiting in the foyer for his companions and he looked for something he didn't have to cut. Though the Mediterranean Scallops on rice looked great Paul thought it would be too hard to manage with his left hand. He figured the rice would be flying in every direction, including his lap, so he decided to order the Pecan encrusted chicken breast and would ask one of his companions to cut it for him if he couldn't manage.

When Roger came to take their order everyone ordered something different off the menu. It was Gloria, who was sitting to Paul's left, who ordered the

Mediterranean Scallops. He ordered the Pecan Chicken and the waiter mentioned that that was a good choice for your first time to the tavern. Once Roger took everyone's order Paul proposed a toast; they all lifted up their water glasses and Paul said, "To my companions, the seen and unseen travel companions on my Appalachian Journey. I will miss you guys; I will think of you often and try to live up to your expectations. Thank God for sending you all to me." Everyone responded, "Praise God in all His goodness."

Gloria set her glass down and said, "Paul I didn't get to know you as well as the others, but I'm glad God gave me this opportunity. I wish you the best." After Gloria spoke, each companion said a few words of thanks and encouragement. Frank was the last to speak and he said, "Paul. We join in your thanks to God. His plan is perfect, but few can see that or accept that like you. You will have certain doubts about all of this, especially in trying times, but know that God is with you always."

And looking directly at Paul he asked, "Do you know now what God's plan is for you?"

"It's not that clear to me, but I sense that God wants me to live my life in such a way that it will draw others to Him, so they can know His love for them and all mankind, in both seen and unseen ways. I pray that I don't let Him down and that He will continue to love and support me whenever I fall short of His expectations."

Neither Frank nor any of the other companions indicated whether Paul's response was right. Maybe there wasn't a right answer. The closest Paul got to a non-verbal reaction was from Will. He squeezed his lips together like when someone put Chap Stick on their lips, making sure they spread it evenly.

The waiter brought out the salads and then the main courses. Paul didn't need help cutting his chicken because it was fork tender and like Roger said, it was a good choice. The conversation turned to some of the more humorous things the companions witnessed on their journey with Paul. Will had the winning story and it had to do with Paul's reaction to the morning after the storm when Paul realized that other hikers could see Will, too. They all laughed at that. Then Paul talked about what a great relief it was to know that God was as close as a prayer.

It was a great dinner and as always Frank paid. They all went outside after dinner to say their goodbyes and Paul asked whether he would ever see them again and Sylvia answered, "You never know." As Paul hugged each companion he felt tears in his eyes and he got all choked up. He felt like he was losing a good friend, or in this case friends. He watched as the companions from his journey walked up PA174 towards the Post Office. That reminded him he had another mail drop somewhere, but couldn't remember where. He'd be sure to ask Laura tomorrow after he got the doctors prognosis on his arm.

As Paul walked up the steps to the Brown's their guests were just leaving, so he sat out on the front porch so as not to interrupt anything. Kitty saw Paul sitting there and asked how his dinner at the Tavern was and he said it was terrific. "Yeah, we're fortunate to have the Tavern in such a small town. Would you like to come in for some coffee and a piece of cake?"

He declined Kitty's kind offer, but instead he went to bed. Lee said he would take Paul to the clinic at 9:45 the next morning, so Paul went up to his room and also used the bathroom. It was impossible to write with his right hand, so he gave up trying to update his journal. It was then he realized he never asked Frank about his missing journal. He was sure that someday it would just appear out of nowhere. Paul said his prayers, thanking God for His help and for his seen and unseen companions on his journey. He went to sleep at 10:35. (1066)

Paul slept better the second night after his accident, which was surprising since he had such a long nap. He got up once during the night to relieve his bladder and had an accident in the bathroom because he wasn't as good an aim with his left hand as he was with his right. He had to use about a quarter of a roll of paper towels to cleanup his mess, so at 7:15 Paul went to the bathroom to retrieve the plastic bag with the urine soaked paper towels and went downstairs to the kitchen. No one was there, so he went outside to the big trash can and threw the bag in it. When he came back into the kitchen Kitty walked in and said she heard the door, so she came to see who it was and Paul explained what he had to do and Kitty said, "That's alright. I'll give the commode a good cleaning today."

Lee and Paul left for Carlisle Barracks at 9:00 and it only took 15 minutes to get to the gate. They got to the clinic 15 minutes before his appointment and they took him back right away. First, the technician took the half cast off his right arm and when she noticed it was a bit wet said, "Major Geary did you put a plastic bag over your arm when you showered?"

"Yes, but some water still got in."

Paul's arm was re X-rayed, but they left the half cast off until after the doctor took a look at his arm. When the doctor looked at his arm he was satisfied that his original diagnosis was correct.

"How is the pain?" The doctor asked.

Paul thought about it for a second and then said, "It only hurts when I move it, so it actually isn't bad if I keep the elbow close to my body."

"Well, Major Geary, have you decided to end your hike?"

"Yes. It was nice while it lasted, but I may have a job lined up. I won't know if I get the job until I interview for it, so it's a good thing I've got a support network to help."

The doctor frowned at Paul's remark, so he wasn't sure if the doctor understood his comment or not. What he meant was that he had people like Lee and Kitty looking out for him in Pennsylvania, but more importantly God and Laura looking out for him everywhere else.

After they left the clinic they drove back to Boiling Springs because Paul needed to make some phone calls to see what was next for him. He called Laura to tell her what the doctor said and to tell her what he wanted to do next. Laura's answer to one of Paul's questions helped shape his plan.

It turns out that Laura picked Blue Ridge Summit, Pennsylvania as Paul's next mail drop; Laura didn't choose Blue Ridge Summit because he was low on supplies or anything, but because she knew that was where Professor Edwards lived. She figured it would be a nice visit for Paul and his favorite college professor.

His second phone call was to Andy Fitzgerald in Downingtown to tell him he was ending his Appalachian adventure because he broke his arm. Andy had said previously that he would like to rendezvous in Gettysburg so that he could see him and meet Don Bowser. Paul hoped Andy might offer to pick him up in Boiling Springs and drive him to Gettysburg, which was only about 30 miles away.

He was delighted to find out that Andy would pick him up the next morning and take him to Blue Ridge Summit to see Professor Edward's and to pick up his mail drop. Then they'd go to Gettysburg and meet up with Don and the JROTC students.

To make matters even better, Andy offered to drive him down to Washington DC, which was about 75 miles south of Gettysburg. Paul didn't have to ask Andy to do any of that for him, but he was happy when Andy insisted on it.

After he got off the phone he sat and reflected on how great God is and he could see that all of the events that happened on the trip were gifts from God, even the broken arm. Paul saw that each trial along the way was an opportunity for virtue and he prayed that he didn't let anyone down. Paul could see that all the people he had met along the way were people who he was drawn to because they shared something in common. They were all brothers and sisters in Christ and they were all proud of that fact.

At 12:15 Paul called Don Bowser because he knew that was Don's lunch time. He told Don that everything was on track for Gettysburg and that, in fact, his friend Andy Fitzgerald would be picking him up and bringing him down. He also shared with Don that Andy wanted to meet him and Don was delighted and said, "That's great. I'd love to meet him, too. He sounds like a good friend."

Paul got off the phone and went downstairs to tell the Brown's his future plans and to invite them for dinner that evening at the Tavern. Paul knew they wouldn't accept money for all they had done for him, so he'd treat them to dinner; he figured it was the least he could do.

He spent the rest of the afternoon getting ready for dinner and for his departure the next day. At least that was his intention, but he laid down on the bed at about 3:30 and fell asleep. A tapping on Paul's door at 5:00 p.m. awakened Paul out of a deep sleep. He was upset with himself for wasting away the afternoon, but he rationalized that he probably needed it.

Dinner reservations were for 6:00, so he had an hour to get ready. He tried to shave left handed and he wasn't very successful. Unfortunately, he didn't have a styptic pencil, so he had to resort to the old toilet paper trick. When he walked down stairs to meet Kitty and Lee, Kitty reached up to Paul's right temple area and took off a piece of toilet paper saying, "you missed one."

The trio left for the Tavern at 5:45, walking alongside the Children's Lake. He felt confident enough to get the Mediterranean Scallops and Lee had the same as Paul, but Kitty had one of the salmon and spinach specials, which looked terrific. The dinner conversation bounced around from Carlisle Barracks and the Allenberry Playhouse and resort, to God's providential hand in everything. Paul never asked Lee why it was he was out walking on Monday and came to find him face down in a mud. Lee said he couldn't explain it, but he just had this feeling come over him that he needed to hike that section of the trail because he was responsible for it.

Lee added that he volunteered with for the Appalachian Trail Conservancy and that was his section of trail. So, like George Murray and Don Bowser who were responsible for a certain section of the trail, Lee had a section of the AT and that's why he discovered Paul face down in the mud two days before.

God works in mysterious ways, Paul thought to himself.

Paul, Lee, and Kitty walked back to their house at about 8:05 and Paul finished the packing which he still had left. He asked if Lee wanted his Svea stove and gas bottle and Lee said he could find a use for it. Paul wondered if that was OK. Lee, after all, was part of God's plan for his Appalachian journey. Paul said his prayers, adding a decade for Don's and Andy's safe travel for the next couple of days and when he turned out the light on the night stand he saw it was 10:10. (1066 FK)

Paul tossed and turned all night and finally at about 2:30 a.m. Paul took his last Tylenol 3, figuring that would help him sleep. He did fall asleep shortly thereafter and was awakened at 8:30 by the smell of bacon.

Paul put on some gym shorts and a shirt which he had bought at the PX the day before. It was a button up shirt, so that he could put it on easier over his half cast. Paul went downstairs at about 9:00 and Lee and Kitty were both sitting at the kitchen table reading the newspaper. Lee looked up when he walked into the room and said, "Good morning Paul. What time are you expecting your friend to show up?"

Paul sat down at the table and said, "He should be here sometime after 10:30." Both Lee and Kitty thanked Paul for dinner the night before and mentioned how his stay there had been a good dry run for when they start their B &B. Paul asked when that would be and Kitty said probably that next summer, the summer of 1996. She mentioned they were spending Christmas in Germany and they didn't need any worries or concerns while they were getting ready for that trip.

The doorbell rang at 10:20 and it was Andy. When Kitty answered the door, she said, "You must be here to pick up Paul. Come on in I'm Kitty." Paul heard the doorbell ring, but he was in the bathroom. The Tylenol 3 helped Paul sleep, but Paul remembered that one of the effects of the codeine was that it can cause constipation. Paul sat on the toilet for another five minutes and realized he wouldn't be able to go, so he struggled to get up with his one good arm and flushed the toilet. He went back to his room and made sure he had everything.

Fortunately, Lee had already carried his stuff downstairs and it was already in Andy's car. When he walked downstairs he could hear Andy and Kitty talking and Andy was saying, "Well, Mary and I will have to come and spend a weekend here when you open. You know we've stayed at Allenberry before. They have some wonderful shows and now that I know we can stay here that's all the more reason to come back."

When Paul walked into the sitting room Andy stood up and came to shake Paul's hand, but realized he would have to shake with his left hand. "Paul, it's good to see you again. It's hard to believe it's been less than three weeks. It must seem like an eternity to you." He shook Andy's hand and then turned around to thank Kitty and Lee.

"Lee, you were a God send on Monday and you both still are. I'll keep in touch once life gets back to normal. I can't thank you all enough for all you have done for me."

Kitty gave Paul a hug and Lee shook Paul's hand and when they went outside Paul tripped over something on the porch and Lee said laughing, "Don't break your other arm."

It was roughly 11:00 a.m. when Paul and Andy started their drive to Blue Ridge Summit. Andy decided on the route before they left and it was a pretty drive. It took about an hour and fifteen minutes because it was mostly secondary roads going through a couple state parks. Andy mentioned he spent some time there as a teenager and so the road was vaguely familiar to him.

On reaching Blue Ridge Summit they stopped first at the Blue Ridge Summit post office and then stopped at a nearby restaurant and they both had cheeseburgers and French fries. Thinking back to the day Andy had heat exhaustion he asked the waiter if they could make them both Jamocha shakes. The waiter said that wasn't on the menu, but he would do his best. Paul's meeting with Professor Edwards was arranged for 2:45 and since the Professor was such a stickler for punctuality, Paul made sure they were there on time.

As Paul an Andy drove into Professor Edwards's driveway he could see Mrs. Edwards out on the porch reading. Paul remembered Mrs. Edwards as very nice and demure, a true lady in every sense of the word. Paul introduced Andy to Mrs. Edwards and she called her husband. When Professor Edwards came out onto the porch he said, "JP, aren't you a sight. What happened, battling windmills were you?"

So, Paul explained to the Edwards what happened to his arm, but he gave them the abbreviated version.

It was nice to visit with Professor Edwards. Paul told him how his family was doing and shared certain bits and pieces of his Appalachian journey. The professor in turn told them about what each of his three sons were doing. Paul saw Professor Edwards look at his watch after about and two hours and fifteen minutes and he asked, "JP do you and Andy have any dinner plans?"

Paul looked at Andy and Andy nodded his head yes. "Andy wants to eat at ééGeneral Pickett's Buffet in Gettysburg. Are you familiar with it?"

"Yes. I've eaten there a couple times. The ambiance is much better than the food, but you only live once."

They said their goodbyes and started driving to Gettysburg, which was about 15 - 20 miles to the north east. As they were driving Andy asked a question, "Paul why does the professor call you JP?"

"It goes back to the first time I had him in class. He called me Joseph in class and I didn't respond. He didn't know I went by my middle name because he went by the student roster. So, he called me JP and it caught on and he was the only one that ever called me JP and he still does."

Also as they were driving towards Gettysburg Andy said, "Oh, I just made a connection to something the professor said when we got there."

"What's that?" Paul asked.

"He said, have you been fighting windmills or something to that effect. I get the Don Quixote connection now."

"Yeah. We had to read that, but fortunately we read it in English. Did you ever read Don Quixote?"

"No, I never did," Andy replied.

"You know, I remember Professor Edwards saying we should read it 10 years after we read it the first time to see if it made any difference. I did read it about 10 years later and he was right, I did understand it better.

As they turned north they past what used to be called Charnita, which was a ski area. It changed its name to Ski Liberty at some point in time, but Paul couldn't remember. He did share with Andy how he learned to fly while he was at the Mount and he learned to fly at the airport which was directly behind the ski area. Paul mentioned how scary it was if you had to land towards the east, coming down the back side of the mountain.

"Fortunately, I only ever had to do that twice. However, someone crashed the year after I graduated, but I don't know how many people died," he added.

Andy made a hotel reservation at the Ramada, which was owned by Sheraton when Paul went to the Mount. The Ramada was where Don thought the colonel said the JROTC group was staying, which wasn't the case. Andy carried Paul's backpack up to the room in addition to his own bags; it took him two trips. Once Andy had everything in he asked Paul if he wanted to look at the National Park Service Visitors' Center and then have an early dinner at General Pickett's Buffet. It wasn't a long drive to the visitors' center and they were there in less than 10 minutes and after spending some time there they went to General Pickett's Buffet which was across the street from the Visitor's Center.

General Pickett's Buffet got its name for its close proximity to where Pickett's Charge occurred. The food was good and plentiful, but Andy had to cut several of Paul's selections, particularly the ribs. The thing they liked best about the restaurant was that in the foyer there was memorabilia from when they filmed the movie *Gettysburg*. There were numerous pictures hanging in the entryway signed by the various actors and they all thanked General Pickett's Buffet for supporting them during the filming of the movie.

Very full, they both drove back to the hotel and the hotel had a nice area around the indoor pool where they could sit and enjoy a beer; it was nice just to sit and relax for a change. Paul phoned Don after they got back up to their room and said they would meet them the next day at their hotel, which was about five miles from the Ramada on US30.

They both slept well, probably because they had a full day the day prior. Andy decided he wanted to go the Mount and then to the Saint Elizabeth Ann Seton Shrine, which was only about a mile-and-a-half from the Mount. Paul mentioned that he had never been to the Seton Shrine. Andy told Paul the Seton shrine was where St. Joseph's College was when they went to school at the Mount. Then when St. Joseph's closed and Mount St. Mary's became co-ed, the basilica was the logical place to be the final resting place for Elizabeth Ann Seton's remains.

In September 1975, Pope Paul VI declared Elizabeth Ann Seton a Saint and the Sisters of Charity, the nuns who ran St. Joseph's, decided to lay St. Elizabeth Ann Seton's bones to rest in the basilica. Driving down Route 15 and crossing into Maryland, Andy changed his mind and thought they should visit the Seton Shrine first since Paul had never been before and then they'd go by their Alma Mater.

When Paul and Andy entered the basilica a docent gave them a tour of the basilica pointing out various things in the life of Elizabeth Ann Seton. Paul was surprised to find out that there was a connection between the Sisters of Charity and Sister Catherine Labouré. It was Catherine Labouré, who Mary, the Mother of God, gave instructions for casting the Miraculous Medal. He also learned that St. Vincent de Paul had a connection with the Sisters of Charity. In fact, it was St. Vincent de Paul who helped a nun start the order of the Sisters of Charity.

As they were getting ready to leave the basilica Paul looked up at the three mosaics above the pipe organ. He asked the docent who the mosaics were of and she said the three mosaics were of King David, Pope Gregory, and Pope Pius X, all of whom had something to do with sacred music. The docent shared the following…"We all know that David wrote the psalms, however, most people don't know that it was Pope Gregory who incorporated the chant into the Mass, and that Pius X felt that sacred music should be put more fully into the liturgy of the Mass."

After thanking the tour guide they drove the short two miles to Mount St. Mary's, with the first stop being the Grotto of Our Lady of Lourdes.

As they left the church Andy remarked that it was too bad that the Catholic Church gets such bad press. Granted he added that some of it is warranted, but he said he gets upset that you never hear about all the good things the Catholic Church has done over the years. "They have started hospitals, universities, and charitable organizations. They feed the hungry, clothe the naked, and provide shelter to the homeless all around the world. And what do they ask for in return, but to love your neighbor as yourself."

In that Paul and Andy had been to the grotto three weeks prior, over Labor Day weekend, they made it a short visit, by lighting some candles for their families and then they went to look around the campus. One of Andy's classmates taught there, so they went to visit him and he gave them a tour.

Andy's classmate taught in the business department and he showed them all the new stuff since they had been students there some 20-25 years before and they ate in the student dining hall, which surprised both of them with how good the food was. Both Paul and Andy mentioned that they frequently had to eat peanut butter and jelly when they were students there because the food was so marginal.

They got back on US15 north towards Gettysburg at 2:30 and if Don Bowser's estimate was right, then the JROTC group would get to the Gettysburg area between 4:30 – 5:00. Paul mentioned to Don the night before that General Pickett's Buffet might be a good place to eat, so Don said he would recommend that to the JROTC instructor. Paul hoped they could rendezvous there, since it was very convenient to the Ramada. They got back to their room close to 3:00 and both decided to take a nap.

At 4:15 the phone rang and it caught both Paul and Andy napping. A dazed Andy answered the phone and it was Don calling to say they would meet at General Pickett's Buffet at 6:00 p.m. Paul decided to shower before going to dinner, so he asked Andy to help him put the plastic bag over his right shoulder and tape it. With the bag secure, he climbed into the shower very carefully. It felt good to stand there letting the water hit his neck; when Paul felt confident he had all the shampoo out of his hair he turned off the shower.

Paul carefully stepped over the tub and out onto the towel mat to dry off and then he carefully pulled the tape off the plastic bag, but the tape was so soaked it tore the bag. He got frustrated and just tore the bag off his arm sending water everywhere around the bathroom, including onto his dry underwear. He decided not to shave because his growth didn't look that bad, and he did have a good excuse after all.

They were ready to go at 5:45, so they left for General Pickett's Buffet. When they pulled into the parking lot there was a white GMC Savannah Van with Massachusetts license plates and people were still inside.

Paul couldn't see Don in the van, so he and Andy went into the restaurant. Don was in the process of requesting a couple tables when they walked up. Paul tapped Don on his shoulder and when he turned around and saw Paul he smiled and tried to shake his hand. Realizing he couldn't use his right hand Don offered him his left hand. After awkwardly shaking hands Don mentioned that he got separate tables, one for the adults and two for the students.

Paul introduced Andy to Don and then Don went back outside to get the JROTC instructor and his cadets. They stayed in the foyer looking at the *Gettysburg* pictures when the JROTC colonel and cadets filed into General Pickett's Buffet and Don introduced them all. After they were seated Paul and Don had an opportunity to catch up on things. He brought the photos that Laura sent from Labor Day weekend, so that Don could put faces to the names of the people Paul always talked about.

He also told Don what his plans were; he would go to Washington DC the day after tomorrow and then spend time with his mother and older brother. Then he then planned to go back to Tampa and wait for his interview in South Bend, Indiana. Paul asked Phil, the JROTC instructor, about what he could expect in the interview for the JROTC instructors' job and Phil gave him some helpful suggestions based on his limited teaching experience.

Phil had only been teaching JROTC for three years, but as he told Paul and Andy, "I've loved every minute of it and I'm busier now than when I was on active duty." Phil said the first year was most difficult because he was so use to people doing what he told them to do in the military. He said it was much different with students. He realized after the first year that they really didn't care about how much he knew until they knew how much he cared. Once they knew how much he cared then it made all the difference in their relationships.

The four adults were having a good time, but the cadets were getting antsy. So, the senior cadet asked if they could all go upstairs to the gift shop to look around. Phil said yes and said they should be ready to leave in 20 minutes.

While the kids were gone Andy asked Don about when Paul and he met in Vermont and Don shared the story, particularly the part about George Murray. When Don Bowser finished talking Phil said, "I didn't know all that. No wonder you guys wanted to get together again. That's an amazing story." And turning towards Paul, Phil asked, "Are you going to be able to give this all up? I mean, are you upset it had to end this way, with a broken arm and all?"

"Maybe in ten or fifteen years when I'm not physically able to do it; but, I'm not unhappy it ended this way. I want to get back to my wife and family, and after all, I accomplished my goal."

"Wasn't your goal to hike the AT?" Phil asked.

Paul thought about it for a few seconds looking at Don and Andy, and then turning back towards Phil he said, "I thought that was my goal when I started. However, the point of the journey became the journey itself. In other words, I wanted to know God's plan for me and I'm pretty sure I know that now."

Phil looked towards Don and then back at Paul and said, "Would you mind sharing that with us?"

"I want to share my story with others. You see there are other things that happened on my journey that I haven't shared with either Don or Andy and frankly, I haven't figured out how to do that yet. You see, all the events of life are gifts from God, but not everybody can see that. You see, our joy is made complete in the companions God gives us. Let me illustrate by telling you about when Jim was bitten by the snake.

Now most people could only see that as something bad, but it let Tom Michie see why it was he carried that snake bite kit with him for over two years. It was so he could help another person. Now that's just one of many examples that happened along the way."

"Well, what good was there in your breaking your arm?" Phil asked.

"First, it brought Lee and Kitty Brown into my life and I was actually able to give them some pointers in starting their B&B. You see I stayed in several B&B's while on my journey, so I could tell them about the things the other hosts did. Secondly, and more importantly, I knew it was time to stop hiking and get back to my family. And I'm sure there are other things that I haven't considered."

The senior JROTC cadet came in looking for Phil and Phil looked at his watch and said. "Oops, those 20 minutes went by fast." Turning towards Don, Phil said, "Are you ready to go back to the hotel?"

Everyone got up to leave and when they got to the parking lot Don asked what Paul and Andy's plans were for the next day. Andy said, "We can spend most of tomorrow with all of you; now I'm not a tour guide, but I can tell you everything I know about the battlefield."

Andy asked Don how their hotel was and he said, "It's great. The kids want to go swimming when we get back, but I think I'll relax."

After some discussion Phil decided he would take the kids back to the hotel and Don would spend some more time with Paul and Andy and then Andy would drive Don back to his hotel afterwards.

So, Andy, Paul, and Don went to a micro-brewery in Gettysburg and tried a couple of their beers while they talked about Don and Chris' trip to Rome in December. Don told him their itinerary for their Italian holiday and it sounded so good that both he and Andy said they wished they could go. "I can give you guys the name of my travel agent if you'd like. Chris and I would love to have you come along."

Paul looked at Don and said, "I don't think that would be possible for me if I get the new job, but thanks for the offer my friend."

"How about you Andy, would you and Mary like to go?" Don asked. "Now I don't know you that well, but from what Paul told me about you and your wife, it could be a great experience."

"I'm truly honored that you would even ask us; however, we're going to Vermont on a ski vacation with our kids and grandkids."

"I'm not much of a skier, but Mary and the kids love it. I'll probably sit in the lodge and be the dedicated chauffer and such."

After the micro-brewery they drove Don back to his hotel on US30 and then they returned to the Ramada. There was a good sense of well-being in the car, so neither of them spoke and aside from nearly hitting a deer on Business 15 the two basked in the solitude. Paul was thinking about the next day and getting to see his mother and older brother. He didn't mention his broken arm to his mom when he told her he would be visiting because she was a champion worrier. He just said the Appalachian Trail was not too far from Washington DC and he would stop to see her. However, he did share the news with his brother.

Andy was thinking about Don's offer and how nice it was of him to ask him and Mary to go to Italy and Andy said Don was everything Paul said he was. Andy pulled into the Ramada parking lot and was fortunate to find a parking space which would make it easier to load their stuff the next day.

Paul was tired, so he went to bed after brushing his teeth. This was the fourth or fifth day since Paul fractured his arm and his teeth just didn't feel clean and he looked forward to using his electric toothbrush again when he got home to Brandon. Andy set the alarm for 7:00 and then he went to sleep.

They both slept well that night and they both felt great the next day, which was Saturday, the 23rd of September. They ate breakfast in the hotel's restaurant, packed, and then checked out. They met Don, Phil, and the kids at Longstreet Tower, which was Andy's recommendation. The cadets were well behaved and Paul only hoped that if he got the AFJROTC Instructors' job he would have the same kind of kids.

Andy impressed everybody with his tour and, in fact, when they were on Little Roundtop some other people were listening to what Andy was saying. Evidently they thought he was one of the paid tour guides because he was so knowledgeable.

They all ended up at the visitor's center at 2:15 and Phil told the cadets they could go inside while he said goodbye to Mr. Geary and Mr. Fitzgerald. The cadets all shook hands with both Paul and Andy and thanked them for the tour and for recommending General Pickett's Buffet.

After the kids went into the Visitors' Center Phil came and shook Paul's hand and told him he wished him luck in getting the job. Then he thanked Andy and went inside with the cadets. Don shook Paul's hand and then said, "This is from Chris," as he gave Paul a hug. Then Don shook Andy's hand and also thanked him for being their tour guide.

It was 2:30 by the time Paul and Andy started driving towards Washington DC on US15 south. They planned to eat in Thurmont, Maryland, so that they wouldn't have to find a place to eat in Frederick, which would be more congested. They passed by Mount St. Mary's and it looked more beautiful than the day before because the sun was shining down on the mountain. The huge statue of the Blessed Mother, which stood high over the grotto entrance, glistened as the sun shone down.

Thurmont was seven miles past the Mount and besides having a Roy Rodgers where Andy always stopped when he was in the vicinity; it was the home to Camp David, the Presidential Retreat. They both remembered Monsignor Kline's story of the seminarian who snuck out and went down to Thurmont only to see Winston Churchill playing pinball in a truck stop. In their minds, they both wondered if Monsignor Kline was still alive.

After the stop at Roy Rodgers, Paul and Andy continued their journey towards Washington DC and Andy asked Paul about something he had said the night before to Phil. "Paul, you said other things happened on the trip that you hadn't shared with Don or me. Are they as miraculous as the water bottles?"

Paul thought how best to answer and said, "Yes, but more so."

"Well you've got my curiosity aroused. When will you be able to share them with us?"

"I don't know. I need to discuss it with Laura first. She knows everything that happened because she read my journal at your house. I need to discern what God's plan was for me in sharing everything."

"Can you share anything with me?"

"I will tell you this. I wrote down everything in a journal and I was pretty good about keeping it current. I think you saw me do that several nights before we went to sleep. I filled almost the entire composition book, except for two pages, and let Laura read it at your house three weekends ago. I had to start a new one because there were only those two pages.

Anyhow, Laura took the composition book with her back to Florida and it disappeared. She never let it out of her sight, but it disappeared. She played over and over again in her mind what she did when she left the Lehigh Valley airport and she couldn't explain it. She was really upset with herself, but I found out why it was missing and you'll have to believe me that it was miraculous to say the least."

"Well Paul when you discern what you are going to do, please keep me in mind. I'd love to know everything. Remember this though, I read somewhere that the evil one will cause you to doubt if things really happened. Undoubtedly, someone will criticize whatever you say and then you will doubt yourself and whether things really happened or not. Look at the water bottles. There is no natural way to explain how that could happen, but I witnessed it and from what you tell me Tom did, too."

He looked over at Andy and nodded his head to show that he understood what Andy had just said. They drove in silence for about the next 30 minutes and he was trying to think of something he could share with Andy, but nothing came to mind. Andy also was wondering what other miraculous things happened that Paul didn't feel comfortable sharing. He tried to remember back to what happened during their weeklong hike together, but nothing stuck out.

The 495 Beltway traffic was as bad as Paul remembered it from years prior, but they made it to his mom's house by 4:40. Fortunately, all the traffic was going the opposite direction and everyone was headed out of the city for the suburbs. Paul took Andy the route he would always take when he came home from college. They got off at the Connecticut Ave. exit heading south towards Washington DC and then turning left whenever they could cut thru to Brookville Rd.

Quincy St. was off Brookville Road and it was Paul's childhood home and where his mother still lived. Quincy St. was less than one mile from Chevy Chase Circle by taking Brookville Rd. Paul reflected out loud to Andy what a great place it was to grow up back in the 50's and 60's. He told Andy of how he walked to the Circle to catch the DC transit to anywhere downtown. Now of course, Washington DC had the Metro.

Paul liked his visits home, but didn't like contending with the traffic, especially outside the Beltway. Inside the Beltway it didn't seem so bad, but maybe that was just in his mind; perhaps "Out of Towner's" thought it was worse inside the Beltway.

They caught a break in the traffic going out of town, so Paul told Andy to turn left onto Bradley Lane and Quincy St. was just one block away when they got to Brookville Rd. Paul's mother's Ford Taurus was in the driveway as was his brother Bill's. That was good, Paul thought, he wouldn't have to make a special trip over to his brother. He could see his mother standing in the living room and looking outside, she started waving when he got out of the car. Bill and Maura came out to welcome them both and Paul introduced Andy to Bill and Maura and as they were walking up to his mother's house Paul asked Bill, "Did you tell her about my arm?"

"Yes. About 15 minutes before you drove up and as we suspected she got nervous and started worrying out loud. When she saw you get out of the car she said, 'well, he looks OK.' "

Paul's mom was standing at the door to greet Paul and his guest as they came in. She wasn't sure how to hug Paul because of his cast, so she just kissed him on his cheek when he bent over to hug her with his one good arm. Since his mom saw Paul three weeks prior at the open house, Paul didn't have to tell them about the entire trip. However, they did want to hear about the previous three weeks and particularly how he fractured his arm.

Dinner was superb. Paul's mother made Paul's favorite casserole and Maura made his favorite salad dressing. They were all so full from the dinner no one could make room for the Boston cream pie, that is, until breakfast the next morning. It was a nice homecoming.

Mass at Blessed Sacrament was at 10:20 the next morning and Andy drove. Andy commented on Mass afterwards and on the music in particular and Paul's mom shared with Andy that Paul, his two brothers, and his father all sang in the choir together at one time or another. She said occasionally the music director would do the same Kyrie Eleison from the boys' childhood and she said if she shut her eyes she could see and hear all four of them up on the altar.

After Mass they drove to brunch at Bill and Maura's and then took a trip to Arlington National Cemetery to visit Paul's father's gravesite. Andy had only been to Arlington National Cemetery once and that was when he chaperoned one of his kids' school trips to Washington DC.

Paul took Andy to see the Changing of the Guard and Lee's Mansion, while his mother waited in the shade by her husbands' grave. She sat on a folding chair that Bill put in Andy's trunk, since she wouldn't be able to do much walking. After Arlington they drove to see the monuments; Andy remarked at how much better it was without forty 8th graders in tow. After seeing the monuments they drove back to Chevy Chase, Maryland, to Paul's mother's house.

Bill and Maura were there preparing dinner, the one Paul's mother had frozen and it was his second favorite casserole. His mother had taken the Crab and Shrimp supreme out of the freezer the night before so it would be thawed out. It was as good, if not better, than the hot chicken salad the night before.

Andy went back to Downingtown, Pennsylvania after dinner because he wanted to be sure he still had some daylight when drove over the Conowengo Dam on Route 1. Paul thanked Andy for all he had done for him and his family and they both agreed to keep in touch and Andy left at 7:15 and thought he'd be home by 9:00 p.m. and Paul's mother said, "Please call us when you get home or I'll worry all night."

Paul called Laura after Bill & Maura left and Laura answered the phone. She said the kids wanted to talk with grandma after Paul hung up, just in case he forgot to put her on the phone. He said he was able to find a reasonable flight for Tuesday that would get him into Tampa at 7:25 p.m.

He also told Laura about his time in Gettysburg with Don and Andy and how he hoped that if he got the AFJROTC job he would be as good with the kids as Phil and Don were. After Paul spoke with Theresa, Dan, and Steven he put his mother on the phone, so she could talk with her grandchildren.

Paul stayed up talking to his mother until well after midnight. They talked about his backpacking trip and all the marvelous encounters he had had. Thinking about what Andy had said about having doubts with what he experienced he shared almost everything with his mom. When he told her about the companions she said, "That's amazing; you've been blessed to see such things." When he got to the part about his fracturing his arm she said, "It makes so much sense now."

"What makes so much sense?" he asked.

"Everything does. Why you got passed over for promotion and got out of the Air Force, why you had these encounters, and even why you had your accident when you did. It is all part of God's plan for you."

Paul was glad that his mother approved, but he still didn't understand why everything happened as it did. Most kids growing up had difficulty talking to their parents, but he never did. Maybe, he thought, that was part of God's plan, too. He always realized that she had a great outlook on life, with the exception of being a champion worrier. He remembered back to when he was in Italy and nearly had a car accident that was his fault. In that incident he took his eyes off the road to talk to someone in the backseat and drove into oncoming traffic. Miraculously the car jumped back into the lane he was supposed to be in. When he prayed that night and thanked God for not letting him crash, he sensed in his heart that God was saying back to him, "Your mother suffered enough when your father died; I couldn't take you in a car crash, too."

Paul went to bed and he was fortunate to go right to sleep. He slept until 8:15 a.m. and what awakened him was someone ringing the doorbell. He could hear his mother get out of bed and start saying, "I'm coming, hold on." She made it downstairs and opened the door.

It was Stacy, Paul's longtime hiking buddy. Paul could hear him say, "Hi Mrs. Geary, I heard Paul was in town and thought I'd stop by to see him. I'm just in town for a meeting and have to go back to Portland on Wednesday." His mom invited Stacy in and called Paul, "Paul, Stacy is here."

He put on some gym shorts and went downstairs and Stacy and his mom were in the kitchen area. He walked in and Stacy said, "Paul, what happened?" He told him what was obvious, that he broke his arm from falling. Over the course of the next hour-and-a-half he shared the highlights of his trip. Stacy was particularly curious about where they had snow shooed in New Hampshire and he was glad to hear that the AT looked pretty much the same from Crawford Notch to Ethan Allen Pond as it did back in December of 1977 when they more or less tried to snowshoe it some 18 years before.

Stacy, as it turned out, was just on a quick visit to see his mom and to see a client. Stacy did something in computers or computer software that Paul couldn't quite understand and Stacy said his meeting with the client was for the next day. Paul asked where his client was and when Stacy said Old City Alexandria, Paul asked what time the meeting was. When Stacy told him it was a lunch meeting he asked Stacy if he could drop him off at Washington National on his way to Alexandria.

Stacy said, "I can do that, but that will get you there very early for your flight." He said that was OK because he would read a book to pass the time.

Stacy said goodbye to Paul and to Paul's mother and then left at 10:00. He spent the rest of his Monday looking through closets and drawers because his mother wanted to downsize. Some things brought back special memories from his childhood and those things he put in a separate pile for his brothers to go through. The rest of the stuff he tossed in the trash. Some of the things required two arms to look at and for those his mother held them up.

Bill, Maura, and their daughter Kerry came over for dinner at 6:45 p.m. and Maura brought everything. Kerry had been away at friends for the weekend, so it was nice to see her. They all had fun just sitting around the table and reminiscing about the past. Maura told the story about one of the first times they all met. It was for a Washington Senator's baseball game, back when Washington DC had a professional baseball team. The funny thing was that they each remembered that night a different way.

Bill remembered sitting two or three rows behind the dugout, while Maura remembered what she wore, and Paul remembered eating three hot dogs and two bags of peanuts. No one could remember who won. When they tried to remember the year, they narrowed it down to 1968, just a couple years before Washington DC lost the team to Texas and it became known as the Texas Rangers.

Paul called Laura, but forgot that the boys had scouts, so he left a message. Theresa called about 20 minutes later when they returned from scouts and they all got to talk. Bill, Maura, and Kerry were still there, so they talked first since Kerry had school the next morning and it was already 8:30. When Steven got on the phone he mentioned that his Cub Scout Den got the award that evening for being the sharpest looking Den. By the time Laura got on the phone there really wasn't much to say, but he remembered Stacy's visit that morning and told her that Stacy would be driving him to the airport.

Before Laura got off the phone she remembered that the school in South Bend called and wanted to know if he could interview on the 23rd of October, so she told them yes, but that she would see Paul the next day and would ask him for sure. The principal, Mr. Leach, said that was fine.

Paul and his mother went to bed earlier then the night before, but not by much. He felt bad that he hadn't kept up on his prayers, particularly the Rosary. It helped him relax. Anyhow, he thanked God for his family and friends and for all those whose path he had crossed on his Appalachian journey. He wondered if Don's Gettysburg trip went well and whether he took the day off to recuperate. He also wondered if Tom had discerned his calling and whether Jim had any side effects from the snake bite. He pondered those things and others and then fell off to sleep during the *Joyful Mysteries*.

After breakfast he took a shower without the half cast on, so that he wouldn't have to use a plastic bag. As long as he locked his elbow close to his side it didn't hurt. It had been a week and a day since he fractured it and the doctor said he could begin his own physical therapy after one week. The shower felt good and it was nice not having to worry about water getting in the plastic bag. He figured he would go another day without a shave. He wondered when he could shave again with his right arm.

The doorbell rang at about 10:30 and it was Stacy. So, after Stacy said hi to Paul's mom and he carried Paul's stuff out to the car, which Stacy borrowed from his mother. Paul decided not to bring his backpack back to Florida. Instead, he took one of his mother's old suitcases to put his stuff in and he left his hiking boots and most of his other apparel. He threw out all his underwear, except for what he was wearing. He could get the backpack at some other time, possibly if they visit at Christmas. With suitcase in trunk and all the goodbyes said, Paul and Stacy drove to the airport.

Paul always felt safe driving with Stacy. He was exact about every move he made and always knew a quarter of a mile before he was going to do something. If Stacy made a mistake and didn't make a turn when he was supposed to he would calmly say, "Well I can fix this" and then go on for a block or two and make the correction.

The traffic was light, so they got to Washington National at 11:15. He said thanks to Stacy after he got the suitcase out of the trunk and then Stacy drove off. Paul checked in for his flight and then went to get a cup of coffee and a doughnut for consumption while he read the USA Today. When Delta boarded his flight he was happy no one sat next to him because he had a window seat and could rest his arm on the arm rest between his seat and the middle seat.

The plane to Tampa was running about 15 minutes late, but he figured they would make that time up. When the pilot announced that they were getting ready for landing at Tampa International Airport, Paul was excited. He figured Laura would have all three kids with her. Even though he had seen them all less than a month prior, they wouldn't want to miss Dad's arrival.

CHAPTER EIGHTEEN

Journey Home

"Hi daddy, we're over here."

Paul could see all four of his family waving when he came thru the gate. When he rushed up to them he forgot he couldn't use his right arm and when he tried to put it out his arms to hug them all, a pain went through his body. It was great to see them all even though it had only been over three weeks since Labor Day weekend. It felt like at least two months. Paul was happy to be home again. Laura and the kids all looked great with their bronzed color skin. On the way to the luggage turnstile he stopped to call his mother to tell her he made it to Tampa and that the flights were good. If he hadn't called her she would have worried until they got home in 45 minutes or more if they stopped for dinner, which they did.

It had been so long since Paul had seafood, they stopped at Paul's favorite seafood restaurant in Brandon. The seafood pasta at Shell's tasted as good as ever and Paul wondered if they had anything comparable in South Bend, Indiana. Paul was making a mess eating left handed, but he didn't care because he had his support network. Laura asked Paul how his mother was and he said, "She's doing well, but her knees are giving her problems. I hope she moves into that military retirement facility in Chevy Chase. The one floor living would suit her and she wouldn't have to worry about keeping up the house."

"What will happen to her house?" Daniel asked.

"She'll have to sell it," Laura said. "Daddy's right, the house is too big for grandmother. It will be a big adjustment, but grandma can handle it."

"Will she be able to take all her stuff," Theresa asked.

"She'll be able to take enough to fill three rooms," Paul responded.

After reassuring the kids that moving into Knollwood would be a good move for grandmother they left the restaurant and they were home in less than 10 minutes. The kids all showed Paul one of the projects they were working on for school and then went to bed. Then, Laura took off Paul's half cast to look at his arm. She decided he could probably go without the cast based on the doctor's last instructions. It felt good without the cast, but it was still awkward to sleep. Paul worried that Laura would roll over on his arm or bump it, so he had difficulty sleeping. He wished they had a king-size bed, but maybe for their next bed, he thought.

In that the kids had to leave for school before 7:30 Paul was up at 7:15. Laura had put in for a day off, which she surely deserved and after the kids were off, it was just Paul and Laura. Paul shaved left handed, but tried to switch the razor to his right hand to see how that worked, but he couldn't get it up to his face even if he bent over. Laura walked in and saw him struggling, so she finished shaving him. Then after he showered they spent the next two hours snuggling.

At 2:00, which was 1:00 Alabama time, he called Janice at AFJROTC to tell her he was back home. Janice said she heard the principal called to schedule the interview for the 23rd of October and hoped that was far enough away for him to do his physical therapy. Paul thanked Janice for all her help and said that if he got the job in South Bend he would stop by Air Force JROTC headquarters on his drive north. She said she was just doing her job, but it would be nice to see him again.

Paul spent the next week doing physical therapy and the pain was so bad the physical therapist figured there was something else wrong besides his radial. The therapist strongly urged Paul too see an orthopedic doctor, which he did and the orthopedic doctor diagnosed a problem with his ulnar nerve. The surgeon said Paul had two choices. One involved surgery, but wasn't a guarantee he would get 100% use of his arm, and of course the surgery could cause a whole range of other problems. The second choice involved incorporating something called the Ulnar Glide into his physical therapy. The doctor told him he might not ever get 100% use of his right arm, but it would be close.

He decided he'd go with the second option that didn't require surgery. So, for the next two weeks until he went for the interview in South Bend, he went for physical therapy three times a week. He could work on the Ulnar Glide anytime on his own. The kids got a laugh whenever he did the Ulnar Glide at home because they said he looked like Ronald McDonald doing his wave.

Paul used his free time trying to reconstruct the two AFJROTC interviews he had had before. Neither one was the same, but he figured it couldn't hurt to type everything down as he remembered the interviews. Typing was easier than writing because he could rest his right arm on the desk, whereas if he wrote he had to hold his arm up. Printing out the list of questions which he remembered, he compared both interviews. Paul thought he did much better at the school in Virginia than the one in Florida. The school in Virginia was a new unit, but the one in Florida was a well-established unit. Their questions weren't similar in any way except for the question, "Why do you think you'd be good at this job?" He pondered that, but it wasn't easy to answer in a sentence. He hoped that whoever did the interview in South Bend would settle for a long answer because he planned to tell a story in order to illustrate why he would be a good teacher and mentor to high-school-age kids.

As the date for the interview drew closer he gained most of the mobility in his right arm. At least he could salute, which was something he couldn't do three weeks prior. He did have difficulty buttoning his top button and tying his tie, so to get around the tie problem he decided to wear a clip-on to the interview. The button problem he would get around by asking someone to do it for him.

Paul's flight out of Tampa took him to Chicago for a connecting flight to South Bend, Indiana and his interview was on the 23rd of October, but he got to South Bend on the 21st, so he could check out South Bend. Unfortunately, it was a Notre Dame Football weekend, so all the rooms in South Bend were booked. He had to look elsewhere for a hotel room.

Benton Harbor, Michigan was about 15 -18 miles north of South Bend and that's where he found a room. So, instead of spending two days in South Bend, he was actually limited to one day of looking around. Paul got up on Sunday morning and headed back down to South Bend because there were rooms available in South Bend for Sunday night. The hotel in Benton Harbor was OK, but just OK. On the way to Benton Harbor the evening before he noticed a Catholic Church on the main road connecting South Bend to Michigan. As he passed by the church Sunday morning he noticed people were entering the church, so he found a parking space and went into the church.

It was called Christ the King Catholic Church and it was sort of a sterile architectural style. However, when he entered the church he felt a feeling that he had felt a handful of times before. He felt like he wanted to be a part of that community and thought the Geary family would be happy there. The priest, who was called Father Steve, gave a great homily and the music was uplifting.

There was a baptism during Mass and Paul liked the way Father Steve invited all the children to come and stand around the baptismal font. The baptismal font was in the shape of a large crucifix with running water. One level of the crucifix was higher than the other, so the water flowed from one level to the other like a waterfall. At the sign of peace Paul looked around for the companions, something he had gotten used to. He hadn't seen them since the dinner in Pennsylvania and he missed them, but knew they were there in spirit.

Paul stopped to talk with Father Steve, who was standing outside the entrance, after Mass. Father Steve said he didn't recognize him and asked if he was new to the parish. Paul told him why he was there and said he hoped to be part of his parish someday. Father Steve wished Paul good luck and said he would pray for him. He felt uplifted as he walked across the parking lot to his rental car and before he got into the car he looked back at the church and said a prayer in his mind.

Paul checked out the Days Inn which was about two blocks away and they had lots of vacant rooms. The room ended up being cheaper than the one he had the night before and it was definitely much cleaner. After checking out the room he decided to go find the high school where he had the interview the next morning. Washington High School was about eight miles from the Days Inn and only three or four miles from the airport. Paul looked first at the outside of the school and then the surrounding area. The high school seemed to be in good shape. It was clean and well cared for, as were all the homes nearby. After he checked out the area around the high school he decided to go to look around the University of Notre Dame.

He wanted to visit the Grotto at Notre Dame and when he found it he was surprised at how much smaller it was than the one at the Mount. The Grotto at Mount St. Mary's took up a chunk of the 1,400 acres a top their property, but the one at Notre Dame was just tucked in between the two lakes and the Cathedral. Fortunately, it still had a feeling of peacefulness. The Grotto re-creates the one at Lourdes, France, but on a minuscule scale. There were no candles left to light, so he just said a prayer to the Blessed Mother and asked for her intercession in getting the job at Washington High School if it was God's will. After sitting there for twenty minutes Paul walked around the campus.

Paul had visited the campus when he was 15, so he still remembered where certain things were. He went to find the log chapel which was built back in the early 1800's. In addition to all the other reasons the chapel was important; it was where his neighbor was married back in the 1920's. Mr. Culhane, his neighbor, used to tell him stories about when he was a student at Notre Dame and he liked the story about Knute Rockne being his chemistry teacher. He walked around to look at the football stadium, where Notre Dame beat the University of Southern California the day before. One of the gates was open, so Paul went in to look at the field. It seemed small compared to other college football fields, but on leaving the stadium there was a sign that said they were going to add another 30,000 seats after the next football season.

After walking around the campus for the better part of two hours Paul stopped at a restaurant close to the hotel. After dinner he went back to his room and placed a call to Laura and the kids. He told her about the church he went to and then how nice Washington High School looked, at least on the outside. She wished Paul good luck on the interview the next morning and said she would see him at the airport at 9:15 p.m.

Paul spent the next 30 minutes getting his uniform in order. First he put his rank on the shoulders and then he put his ribbons on. Then he put his name tag on and lastly he used the hotel iron in order to iron his shirt. He didn't enjoy ironing because he could never do as good job his wife. It always amazed him how he and Laura could use the same iron and same ironing board, but when Laura ironed his shirts they always looked as if they were done at the dry cleaners. Satisfied that everything looked alright, he hung everything back in the closet and put his Corfam shoes under the chair which was next to the TV. He set the clock radio for 6:15 and his watch alarm for 6:20 just in case he slept through the first alarm. It was 10:15 when Paul's head hit the pillow and after saying his prayers he fell off to sleep.

When the alarm went off at 6:15 Paul jumped out of bed; he turned off the clock radio and then his alarm watch so he didn't wake up any neighbors if he had any on either side. Then he shaved and showered, but he put civilian clothes on to go eat breakfast. He'd change into his uniform after he ate.

The Days Inn offered a continental breakfast and it was pretty good. After breakfast Paul returned to his room and changed into his uniform, leaving the tie for later. Then he went to check out of the hotel. Since his flight was at 2:00 in the afternoon he would have to change somewhere during the course of the day before he caught his flight. The last thing Paul did at the hotel was to ask the desk clerk if she could button his top button. She looked at him funny, so he explained why he couldn't do it and showed her how he couldn't get his arm all the way up.

The interview was for 8:30, so Paul allowed 45 minutes to get to the school. He figured he would rather get there early and sit in the parking lot, then to be late. He walked up to the front of the school at 8:20 and pulled on the door. It was locked, so he went to the door closest the school and read on the note. It said to ring the bell in order to gain entry. So he rang the bell and a voice on the other end said, "Yes. Can I help you?"

"This is Major Geary and I have an 8:30 appointment with the principal."

"OK Major. Pull the door when you hear the buzzer."

He did as instructed and went to the main office. He met the person whose voice he heard on the speaker and it was the principal's secretary and she went by Miss Pat. She was lovely and the first thing she said was, "So Major, which church do you plan to join? We could use some men's voices in our choir."

It turned out that Miss Pat had read Paul's resume and under the "other hobbies" area he had listed that he sang in his church choir. Since the principal's secretary could carry a lot of weight, Paul didn't want to shoot himself in the foot, so he just said, "I haven't decided yet because it depends on where we live. Where do you sing Miss Pat?"

Miss Pat told Paul where she sang and for the next 15 minutes he talked to Miss Pat since the principal was running late. Mr. Leach came into the outer office at 8:45 and introduced himself to Paul. The principal stood about 5'9" and he was sharp looking. He apologized for being late, but said it was unavoidable. He invited him into his office and told him to have a seat at the table. Mr. Leach was the only person in on the interview, which was unlike both the other schools where he interviewed. There were four or five people in on the Virginia interview and three for the Florida interview. He felt comfortable with Mr. Leach's questions, but he felt as if Mr. Leach was just going thru the motions.

After Mr. Leach interviewed Paul he gave him a tour of the school, ending up at the AFJROTC room. The Chief Master Sergeant called the room to attention when the principal entered and the kids snapped to attention. Mr. Leach introduced him to the Chief and to the cadets.

Chief Master Sergeant Thomas was sharp. He was about 5'11" and he too, was trim. You could tell the cadets liked the Chief by their interaction. Paul felt that somehow he had run into the Chief in the Air Force, but he couldn't remember when or where. He hoped that if he did know the chief from somewhere that it had been a positive encounter.

Mr. Leach left Paul with the Chief and asked if one of the cadets could escort Major Geary back to the office when he was done visiting the unit. Paul talked with the Chief for about 45 minutes and then one of the cadets took him to the front office. Before he left, the Chief asked, "Major if you are offered the job when can you start?"

That caught him completely off guard, so he thought about it and said, "Do you have a calendar I could look at?" They walked into the Chief's office and Paul looked down at the calendar. He flipped the calendar to November and said, "I should be able to be here around Thanksgiving, but preferably the week after that."

Paul went back to the office to see Mr. Leach again, but he was busy; so, he talked with Miss Pat again until the principal returned. When the principal returned he said, "Major I'd like you to go downtown to see Mr. Eleff. He's the Director of Human Resources. He'll have some papers for you to sign if we offer you the position."

He was confused by the principal's choice of words. "If we offer you the job." Were they looking at other people? Was he not happy with the way the interview went? These were all thoughts that went through his mind as he drove downtown to the South Bend Community School Corporation office building.

Mr. Eleff was expecting him and Paul found him to be very nice. It turned out his wife was one of the guidance counselors at Washington HS, so he talked to Paul about the various people that worked there. Then he had him fill out some rather standard stuff, like how his name should read on paychecks and such. He asked Mr. Eleff if there was some place he could change because he had a 2:00 flight and it was already noon. Mr. Eleff said he could use his office to change because he was actually headed to lunch with his wife.

Paul went out to the car to get his stuff to change into and came back to get dressed in Mr. Eleff's office. It only took 15 minutes to get to the airport, so he had an hour and twenty minute wait. He grabbed a bite to eat at the bar, which was the only eating establishment in the airport. Paul's plane took off five minutes early and they got into O'Hare on time. Paul got something more substantial to eat in Chicago; he had a Roast Beef sandwich and potato chips. His flight to Tampa left on time and the flight to Tampa arrived ten minutes ahead of schedule. All in all the 23rd of October, 1995 had been a great day. Paul thought the interview went well and everyone who he met at Washington High School treated him well, particularly Miss Pat.

Laura and the kids were all waiting at the gate when he walked through the door from the jet-way. After they got Paul's suitcases they headed back to Brandon.

Laura asked Paul how the interview went and he told her everything. Theresa wanted to know if he visited Notre Dame while he was there and he told her he had. He mentioned too, that he went into the football stadium, but didn't tell her he was disappointed. Steven asked if they do move to South Bend if they would take Heidi. No one knew where that concern came from, so Paul told them that Heidi was considered part of the family and of course she would be going.

They patiently waited two weeks and when they didn't hear anything they thought Paul didn't get the teaching job. However, on the 9th of November CMSgt Thomas called. He wanted to be sure Paul would take the position if offered. Paul said, "of course I'll take it." About ten minutes after the Chief hung up Mr. Leach called and said they wanted to offer him the position. He wanted to know how much time he would need to get himself and his family there and Paul said 30 days should be good.

Laura was at work, so Paul called to tell her they were moving to South Bend. She was very happy and was delighted she could hand in her resignation. She would give them her two-week notice the next day. Dinner that night was nice because they celebrated by going to Shell's and Paul called his mother to tell her the good news when they got home from Shell's. Since South Bend was closer to Washington DC than Tampa was, his mother was thrilled.

Laura handed in her resignation the next day and they weren't surprised. Laura had told them about the possibility of her leaving, but they said they were sorry to see her leave. In that Paul was typing better, he decided to reconstruct his Appalachian Journey, so he went to AAA for state maps of Maine, New Hampshire, Vermont, Massachusetts, Connecticut, New York, New Jersey and Pennsylvania. It was more difficult finding AT maps, but he did his best. He realized he could have called his mother to get the trail maps out of his backpack, but he didn't want to inconvenience her.

Paul tried as best he could to reconstruct his journey, but some details were hard to remember. After all, he thought to himself, that's why he kept a journal, but he tried not to dwell on that fact since Laura still felt really bad about it. Looking at the maps and a guidebook helped bring back certain events, but he wasn't sure he did some things justice. He worked on reconstructing his journal for two hours every day, in addition to going to physical therapy.

The therapy became more painful with little to show for it. Some days they worked his arm to the point where he couldn't lift it when he got home, so he stopped going to physical therapy on the 17th of November. His typing seemed to improve by Monday the 20th of November, but then he had to get ready for their last Thanksgiving in Florida.

Paul decided he would drive to Indiana ahead of the family to look for a place to live and a place for the kids to go to school because that way the kids could finish out the semester in Brandon. His plan was to leave on the 7th of December and drive to Montgomery, Alabama, to see the folks at AFJROTC headquarters and Will's dad, like he promised. Then he would continue on to Indiana, which he figured he could do in one day. He would find a house to live in, a school for the kids to attend, and start teaching. Then he would fly back for Christmas, pack out of their house, and drive the whole family to South Bend. Things fell into place one by one.

Paul arranged for the packers to show up on the 26th & 27th of December. Then they would start driving the afternoon of the 27th and take two days to get to South Bend. They would meet the movers at their house in South Bend on the 29th if they had a house and if not the stuff would go into storage until they found a house.

The Geary family spent their last Thanksgiving in Florida the way they spent the previous two years. Theresa's traveling soccer team took part in a soccer tournament in Melbourne, Florida, which was about a two-hour drive away. The team always got a block of rooms in a hotel and all the families stayed there, but Paul decided he would rather take his chance that they could get a space available room on Patrick AFB, which was five miles away from the soccer fields. They had been successful the previous two years and they were also as lucky to get a space available bungalow their last Thanksgiving in Florida. Although Paul didn't particularly care for the beach, he did enjoy Cocoa Beach. He wasn't sure why that was, but maybe it had to do with his watching too much *I Dream of Jeannie* as a youth.

Paul continued spending two hours a day reconstructing the AT journey. He frequently got upset with himself because of his tying skills or lack thereof. Some days he would barely squeak out a page because of all his typos. Paul's enthusiasm for reconstructing his journey waned the closer he got to his departure for South Bend.

On the 7th of December 1995, 54 years after the day that would live in infamy, Paul headed north on I-75. He took I-75 to I-10 and cut across the panhandle of Florida and picked up Route 230 which took him to Montgomery, Alabama. He arrived at 3:45 p.m. and was able to get space available billeting on base. Paul then went to AFJROTC Headquarters and met the director, Mr. John Andrews.

John hadn't changed much in the eight years since Paul saw him last; perhaps he was a little grayer, but still the gentlemen. Janice came in to the office while Paul and John were talking and she gave him a package of material which she thought might help. The meeting was short because the end of the business day was 5:00 and Paul didn't want to keep them because he didn't want to start out with any hard feelings.

Paul called Les, Will's father, from his room in the Visiting Officers' Quarters, to see if he wanted to meet for dinner. Les said he wanted to meet him, but he would have to cancel his evening plans, which he did. Les gave him directions to where he lived, so Paul put on some other slacks and a polo shirt and left the VOQ at 5:45. It took him about 30 minutes to get to the east side of town because the traffic was much worse than he remembered it eight years prior. When Les opened the door Paul couldn't believe how much he resembled his son. Les invited him into his house and they talked for a solid hour before either of them thought about their stomachs. They continued their conversation over dinner at the Golden Corral which was less than a mile from Les' house.

Les told Paul how much he appreciated what he had done for him and told Paul how he was turning his life around. "Since my son would have been a teacher, I will do that for him since I never gave him the chance." He told Les that the thanks belonged to God and not him. Then Paul told Les he would be back down to Montgomery that next summer for certification and he'd check in on him if he wanted him to.

Les said in response, "I would greatly appreciate that. When are you going to leave for Indiana?"

"Tomorrow morning. I hope to get on I-65 by 8:00 and if I can do that I can probably make it all the way to South Bend. Paul said good bye to Les and when he put his hand out to shake Les's hand, Les gave him a bear hug. When he got back to his room on base he decided to write about the meeting with Les as an addendum to his Appalachian journey. It was 10:45 by the time Paul got to bed.

When the alarm went off at 7:00 he felt like he didn't have a restful sleep. He kept thinking about some of the things Les shared with him at dinner, so he left the VOQ at 7:25 to go get a bite to eat before he started his drive to Indiana. When he went outside the temperature was much cooler then the day before so, instead of wearing shorts he put on wind pants over the shorts and went to a nearby restaurant called the Wheel. He ordered a breakfast sandwich to go and ate most of it before he got back to the VOQ. He didn't make his 8:00 departure because the breakfast sandwich didn't agree with his stomach, but he was on his way by 10:45 and the good thing about leaving later was that the traffic wasn't bad going up I-65. He made it to Birmingham in less than two hours.

When Paul crossed over into Kentucky it started raining and by the time he made Louisville the rain had turned to sleet. The sky was darker than it should have been for 3:45, but that was due to the cloud cover. As he crossed over the Ohio River a big truck which was in the center lane tried to move into Paul's lane and nearly pushed him off the bridge. Paul leaned on his horn and flashed his lights and the driver moved back to the center lane. His heart was beating so fast that he thought he could hear it. As the truck pulled away he read what was written on side of the truck. It read, "Bates Casket Company. Batesville, Indiana." Wow, how weird was that? He thought to himself.

By the time Paul made it 10 miles into Indiana the sleet had turned to wet snow, so when Paul noticed the truckers were pulling off, he did as well. He was glad he got new tires for the Camry before leaving Brandon, but decided the truckers knew the road conditions better than he did.

His trip to South Bend the next day was just as eventful, everything from a minus 35 degree wind chill temperature to frozen wiper fluid and near zero visibility. He was happy his brother Dave gave him his Christmas present early; it was a winter jacket by Columbia.

The Geary family spent four-and-a-half years in South Bend and they enjoyed every minute of it. Paul loved working with the Chief and all the other teachers at Washington HS. They were first-class teachers who were all concerned for the safety of their students and dedicated to giving them the best education possible. When Paul had the opportunity to move to Pottstown, Pennsylvania he took the job. Pottstown was less than 25 miles from where Laura's parents lived and only two hours from Paul's mom. Paul took everything he learned at Washington HS and just hoped he could be as successful in Pottstown.

The students at Pottstown HS were no different than the students in Indiana. He liked Pottstown and seemed to have an easier time adjusting to the new environment. He and his new NCOIC worked well together and they both made a big difference in the students' lives. In the spring of 2009, however, Paul had a life changing experience, brain surgery.

He made an attempt to return to teaching, but it was obvious he wasn't the same after the surgery. Paul retired from teaching that December and he and Laura decided to take their second chance at life and move west by about two hours because it was expensive living in the suburbs of Philadelphia. It may have been God's plan all along, at least that's what Paul believed, but they ended up in Boiling Springs, Pennsylvania, which was where he broke his arm some 15 years earlier. It's where his Appalachian journey came to an end, or so he thought.

In July of 2010 something showed up in the mail he didn't expect. He was cutting the lawn when he saw the mail carrier put the mail in the mailbox, so he stopped cutting the grass and walked over to the mailbox and opened the door. In with the bill's and the junk mail was a manila envelope. It had Paul's name on it and in the return address section it read simply, Frank, Boiling Springs Tavern. Paul opened the envelope and it was his journal from his hike, the one that Laura thought she lost. Instead of mowing the lawn he went inside to read through it. Laura was away, but Paul was so excited he couldn't wait; he read it without her.

Paul gave up on reconstructing his hike back in the spring of 1996 because he got so involved with work, plus their new computer wouldn't read what he had written on their Apple Computer. In addition to all that, Paul started to doubt if some of that stuff really happened. It's funny, because all of a sudden he remembered driving to Washington DC 15 years earlier and Andy Fitzgerald saying that the longer Paul waited to do something the more he would doubt himself and not get it done. He continued flipping through the journal and it was almost as if it were yesterday. He flipped through all the pages and when he got to the last page there was a handwritten note which said, "Paul and Laura please be our guests at the Tavern at 6:30." Paul couldn't believe it.

When Laura came home at 4:45 Paul told her the great news; the lost journal arrived in the mail. Plus they would be going to dinner at the Boiling Springs Tavern at 6:30. Laura was just as happy as Paul and they both sat down and flipped thru the journal. As they got to certain people and events one of them would say, "I wonder how it's going for him or her."

Paul did his best to keep track with certain people from his Appalachian journey. Tom Michie got "the calling" and he became a priest, a Jesuit. He was somewhere in South America, but they've lost touch. Tom did send a Christmas card one year and he reflected back on the hike and how Paul was God's instrument of redemption for him. Tom also said Denice returned to the church as did her husband and two children and Denice became very active in their parish in Towson. She was expecting their fourth child as of that Christmas card.

Don and Chris did go to Rome with Donna and they both entered the Catholic Church at the Easter Vigil in 1996. They all kept in touch for a while, but Don passed away unexpectedly in 2004. He could have retired, but he loved teaching. His administrators realized Don was too valuable to let him go, so as long as he was willing to stay they pretty much let him teach what he wanted, but without all the bureaucratic nonsense. Chris wrote Paul on Don's passing to see if he could come to the funeral, but unfortunately Paul was on a weeklong field training exercise with his students. She did write about six months after Don's death to say the high school and the JROTC unit, in particular, paid him a nice tribute for his years of "making a difference" in the lives of his students. Chris became very active in her parish in Pittsfield and was a member of the Legion of Mary, along with Judy Murray.

The great thing about teaching in Pottstown was that Paul and Laura became best of friends with Andy and Mary and, in fact, they also decided to live in Downingtown, which is also where Laura's older brother lived. Andy got him to become a member of the Knights of Columbus and it was everything he said it was. Andy never pressured Paul in regards to writing a book or anything, but he did occasionally ask about the journal.

Professor Edwards moved out to California to be near one of his sons, but Paul lost track of him. Professor Edwards does, however, live on in Paul's memories of the Mount and whenever he thinks of that great trip to Madrid during his sophomore year in college. Mount St. Mary's is less than 45 miles away now, so Paul visits there often.

Laura and Paul left for Boiling Springs Tavern at 6:15 and got there at 6:25. Nothing in Boiling Springs was far away and Paul liked that. He would frequently see Lee and Kitty and they did open a B&B. As they walked up to the host Paul said they were meeting someone. "They're with me," Paul heard someone say. When Paul turned around he saw Frank, Sylvia, Kevin, Will, and Gloria, his Appalachian Companions. They hadn't changed at all; they all looked the same. Paul gave every one of them a bear hug and then he said, "I've missed you guys." Tears started to flow from his eyes and when Laura saw that Paul couldn't speak because he was so choked up she stepped in and said, "Hi everybody. I've heard so much about you over the years and now I'm so pleased to get to meet you in person." Laura gave everyone a hug as well, but unlike Paul she kept her composure.

"Shall we sit down?" Frank asked.

They all went to sit down at a round table, the same round table where they had last seen each other 15 years prior.

Paul started asking questions first, "Frank, why did you choose to return the journal today?"

"That was God's plan Paul. It always was. I just couldn't tell you when it would be."

"What should I do with it?" He asked.

"Paul, God hopes you feel inspired to write your story."

"You mean about the companions on my journey?"

"Yes, but not just that. He wants you to write about His love for you and for everyone who freely chooses to follow His will. Your Appalachian Journey is a starting point. It has led you to greater things, though you may not have given it any thought. Tell your whole story about God's love for you and all the graces you've received from Him and are available to all who ask in Jesus' name. Of course, it has to be in line with God's will."

Paul looked at all his companions sitting around the table and they were looking back at him. Sylvia turned to talk to Laura, but he couldn't hear the conversation. They were sitting to his right and he couldn't hear. Unfortunately, he lost most of the hearing in his right ear, probably due to the surgery or the drugs he had to take for a year afterwards. Paul was just so thankful he could hear well in his left ear and he thanked God for that every day.

"You know I've thought of you guys a lot. I still look around at the Sign of Peace, hoping you all are there."

"Paul, we are there, in spirit," Gloria responded. "Whenever we pray together as a community in the Body of Christ, we're there along with your earthly father and all the other faithful departed."

Paul, Laura, and the Appalachian Companions finished dinner at 8:45 and walked outside to the parking lot together. When it came to saying their goodbyes, Laura said hers first, thinking he would want some time alone with his companions. She went and got in the car and waited for him because she knew he would get emotional. Paul seemed to appreciate life more since his surgery and would often get teary eyed at saying goodbyes.

Laura watched as he gave each of them a hug and she noticed that they all seemed to be telling him something. After saying his goodbyes Paul got in the car with Laura for the short drive home. When he pulled out of the Tavern parking lot onto PA174 he looked left to see if any cars were coming and where the companions were some 30 seconds earlier they were nowhere to be seen. They were unseen.

On the way home Laura said Paul needed to tell his story now that he had his journal back, but Paul said he wasn't sure people would find it interesting.

Laura disagreed and said "You have to tell your story because you've been so blessed. Your companions need a voice for themselves and others like them. You are their witness and by writing about it you can help save souls; you can help save the souls of the mothers who have aborted their babies and those who are considering it. God willing, by your witness, you will help others to see what's necessary for the salvation of their souls."

Paul looked over at Laura to see if she was finished talking, but she looked at him and took his hand that was resting on the console between their seats and said, "I firmly believe Jesus helped you through this past year because he wants you to tell your story."

Paul didn't say anything in response to what Laura said, but he knew she was right. He just didn't know how to go about it.

When they got home he realized the lawnmower was still where he left it between the sidewalk and the street. He went to put the lawnmower away while Laura wheeled the trash can out to the curb. As Paul swept the grass clippings from the sidewalk he reflected on what each of the companions told him in parting.

Frank thanked him for his prayers some 26 years ago, because that's what made the difference; he still had a chance at life. Sylvia said she was glad that her father and grandfather asked for forgiveness because that's what made her visible to others. Kevin's and Gloria's parting words were about how much Paul's humor helped along the way. Lastly, Will said he was so happy that his earthly father lived and made the life that he couldn't have.

After the broom was put away and the recycling bins carried out to the street, Paul put the garage door down and went into the house.

He went into the den and opened his journal; he turned the desk top computer on and opened a new document. He flipped through the journal and tried to decide what he would say. The numbers 20 and 16 came to mind. What was 20 and 16?

He looked up from his desk and turned to look at the bookshelves that lined the walls and he saw his New American Bible next to a picture of Pope John Paul II. Could 20 and 16 refer to bible verses? He walked over and took the bible from the shelf and started with the New Testament. Paul opened to Matthew 20:16 and it read... "Thus, the last will be first, and the first will be last." Paul smiled to himself and said, "Thank you Lord." Then he began to type.

Springer Mtn., Georgia - 2160.2 miles. That's what the sign reads on top of Mt. Katahdin, in Maine. It's a long way to hike and it was something Paul Geary always wanted to do, but never had the time to try it before the summer of 1995. However, the summer of 1995 presented Paul with a new set of circumstances. He was without a job and had plenty of time on his hands. Paul wasn't sure what his life had in store for him, so he asked his wife and kids if he could take six months off in order to decide what was in their future...

GLOSSARY OF TERMS

Absolution	- Remission/forgiveness of sin.
AFJROTC	- Air Force Junior Reserve Officer Training Corps is a high school version of college ROTC, but with an emphasis on citizenship rather than training for active duty Air Force.
AFROTC	- Air Force Reserve Officer Training Corps is a two through four-year course of study in a civilian college or university which may lead to an officer's commission in the USAF.
AMC	- Appalachian Mountain Club, which is headquartered in Harpers Ferry West Virginia, has the overarching responsibility for the Appalachian Trail.
AT	- Appalachian Trail runs more than two thousand miles from Maine to Georgia or vice versa.
Blaze	- A 2" x 6" vertical paint mark on a tree or other permanent landmark to mark the trail. The AT uses white paint while other trails along the way use various other colors. A double blaze mark indicates a change of direction is about to happen.
Blondie	- A chocolate chip cookie-like brownie, sometimes with pecan pieces and coconut.
BVM	- Blessed Virgin Mary is from the Latin, Beata Virgo Maria, and refers to the Virgin birth of Jesus Christ by Mary.
Class "A"	- Military Dress Uniform
CMSgt	- Chief Master Sergeant is an E-9, the highest non-commissioned officer, in the USAF
CROO	- Name given to the AMC staffs who work in the huts in the White Mountains of New Hampshire during the summer .
Knights of Columbus	- The world's largest Catholic fraternal service organization dedicated to providing charitable services and promoting Catholic education on a wide-range of issues.
Lourdes	- Town in the south of France where Mary, the mother of Jesus, appeared to a French girl named Bernadette Soubirous, in February of 1858 and where many miraculous cures have taken place ever since.

Miraculous Medal	- In a Marian apparition, which is a supernatural appearance by the Blessed Virgin Mary, Mary asked a young French nun by the name of Sister Catherine Labouré to introduce the medal to the French people for obtaining special graces from God. The devotion spread widely around the world.
Mountie	- Nickname of students attending Mount St. Mary's University in Emmitsburg, MD
MWR	- Morale, Welfare, & Recreation
PX	- Post Exchange is the name of the retail store on Army installations.
Rosary	- A scripturally based prayer which is a sequence of prayers whose center is Jesus Christ and it focuses on the events of His life and that of His mother's. The prayers that make up the rosary are listed on the next page.
VBS	- Vacation Bible School
VOQ	- Visiting Officers Quarters

The following are some of the prayers that comprise a Rosary:

The Apostle's Creed

I believe in God, the Father Almighty, Creator of heaven and earth; and in Jesus Christ, His only son, our Lord, who was conceived by the Holy Spirit, born of the Virgin Mary, suffered under Pontius Pilate, was crucified, died and was buried. He descended into hell; the third day He rose again from the dead; He ascended into heaven, and is seated at the right hand of God, the Father Almighty; from thence He shall come to judge the living and the dead. I believe in the Holy Spirit, the holy catholic church, the communion of saints, the forgiveness of sins, the resurrection of the body, and life everlasting. Amen.

Our Father

Our Father, who art in heaven, hallowed be Thy name; Thy kingdom come, Thy will be done on earth as it is in heaven. Give us this day our daily bread, and forgive us our trespasses, as we forgive those who trespass against us, and lead us not into temptation, but deliver us from evil. Amen.

Hail Mary

Hail Mary, full of grace, the Lord is with thee. Blessed art though among women, and blessed is the fruit of thy womb, Jesus. Holy Mary, mother of God, pray for us sinners, now and at the hour of our death. Amen.

Glory Be

Glory be to the Father, and to the son, and to the Holy Spirit, as it was in the beginning, is now and ever shall be, world without end. Amen.

Fatima Prayer/Decade Prayer (Optional)

O my Jesus, forgive us our sins, save us from the fires of hell, lead all souls to Heaven, especially those most in need of Your mercy.

Hail, Holy Queen

Hail, Holy Queen, Mother of Mercy, our life, our sweetness and our hope. To thee do we cry, poor banished children of Eve; to thee do we send up our sighs, mourning and weeping in this valley of tears. Turn then, most gracious advocate, thine eyes of mercy toward us, and after this our exile, show unto us the blessed fruit of thy womb, Jesus. O clement, O loving, O sweet Virgin Mary! Pray for us, O Holy Mother of God that we may be made worthy of the promises of Christ.

Some places to look on-line for prayers and devotions: www.catholic.org/prayers; www.Rosary-center.org; www.catholicity.com

Appalachian Trail Maps

Appalachian Trail

National Scenic Trail/Maine to Georgia
National Park Service/U.S. Department of the Interior

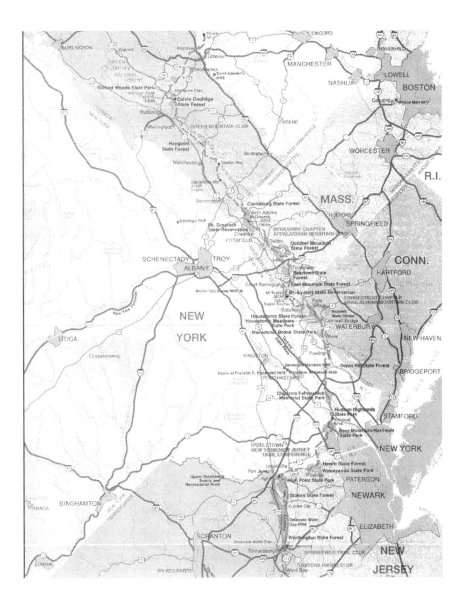

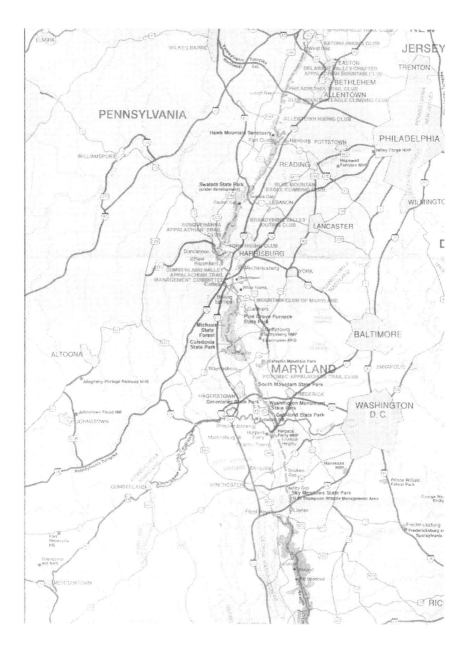

CPSIA information can be obtained at www.ICGtesting.com
Printed in the USA
BVOW07s1226040913

330042BV00001BA/55/P

9 781600 478840